As One

Telling Stories for Inclusive Worship

As One

Telling Stories for Inclusive Worship

Marlene Ch. Marak

Christian World Imprints

First Published in 2019 by

Christian World Imprints
Christian Publishing & Books from India
C-3, Shop No. 14, Ground Floor
Wazirpur Industrial Area, **Delhi-110052**
cwidelhi2017@gmail.com
www.ChristianWorldImprints.com
Phone: +91 11 41526079

ISBN: 978-93-5148-381-6 (HB)
ISBN: 978-93-5148-382-3 (PB)

Printed in India.

My parents
Swanson W. Momin & Margaret Ch. Marak

CONTENTS

PREFACE

Humans will die without stories. Coherence, which is central to identity construction, is impossible without stories because we create our selves through the stories we tell. We are the stories we tell. By "stories we tell" I mean the stories we tell *about us* as well as the stories *around us*. We exist in and through our stories. Stories not only give sense and meaning to the experiences of our life, but they enable us to build a hospitable world to live in. In theological language, we may say that our stories are intertwined with God's story. The biblical story of salvation has no redeeming efficacy until it comes into contact with the stories of our lives.

As One is a search for identity. In this book, I propose connecting storytelling in the sacred spaces of worship as a step towards acknowledging and celebrating women's presence and identity in worship. The underlying premise of this work is that storytelling can be an ideological tool to challenge gender segregation and contribute towards overcoming gender and other discriminatory boundaries. To achieve my objective, I employ a "narrative communication" method that integrates feminist perspective with aspects of narrative theory and Christian communication theory, to look at the significance of storytelling as a medium for developing inclusive worship.

I speak especially from and for the context of the tribal Baptist Christians in North East India. Churches in this part of the world are influenced by patriarchal traditions both from local cultures and inherited from early missionaries. Symptoms of gender apartheid in worship are seen in the use of sexist language, discriminatory biblical theology, androcentric language about divinity, and sexist hymns and songs. The appropriate response to counter gender apartheid is the creation of inclusive community. The theological rationale for pushing the agenda of an inclusive community comes from God's call to all to worship as equals, to share communion, and to live in community. The cause of building inclusive community is also served by recovering the practice of the Lord's Supper as a common meal shared by the community and re-envisioning baptism as initiation into a new reality where the old prejudices and distinctions have no meaning. Here, I also explore ways by which women can tell their stories in worship. We have to overcome our storylessness by using the scripts of our lives as our sacred story. Our stories can be woven into our prayers, sermons, and rituals. We can also read the stories of the Bible as women and re-imagine biblical narratives to challenge traditional perceptions. Our stories invite our hearers to experience our story, to view things from our perspective, so that we and our hearers do not remain strangers but enter into a relationship of friendship and communion.

ACKNOWLEDGMENTS

I gratefully acknowledge my indebtedness to all those who helped me complete my PhD thesis which forms the basis of this book. First of all, I thank Rev. Dr Gwen Ince, my Research Supervisor, for helping me unravel stories and discover the depth of their significance. I am fortunate she was with me to guide and mentor me through my long journey, encouraging me and sharing my burden. I am also much indebted to Christine Sorensen for her kind assistance and valuable advice. This work benefited from comments by the examiners, Rev. Dr Elizabeth Joyce Smith of the Anglican Diocese of Perth and Rev. Dr Janet Wootton of Congregational Federation/University of Winchester, and my gratitude to them knows no bounds.

My sincere thanks go to the University of Divinity (previously known as MCD University of Divinity) for providing me the opportunity to pursue my research. I would also like to thank the United Faculty of Theology, my Recognised Teaching Institution under the University of Divinity, for its unfailing support as well as its exacting academic standards, which helped me develop my ability to think critically.

For financial assistance, I am thankful to the University of Divinity for making the International Postgraduate Research Scholarship available to me, without which I would not have been able to accomplish this project. I have also been financially supported for the duration of my studies by a Leadership Development Grant from the American Baptist International Ministries, Valley Forge, USA, in partnership with the Council of Baptist Churches in North East India (CBCNEI), and so I express my thanks and gratitude to Rev. Benjamin Chan and all the staff at ABC-USA and Rev. Dr Ngul Khan Pau and the staff at CBCNEI. My research was also undertaken with generous financial assistance from the Uniting Church Theological College (UCTC) and I thank Rev. Professor Randall Prior and all the Faculty at UCTC for their much-needed support throughout the years of my research.

I express my gratitude to Rev. Professor Mark Lindsay, the then Director of Research, University of Divinity for his support throughout the course of my study. Many thanks are also due to Professor Peter Sherlock, the Vice-Chancellor of University of Divinity, who in his previous capacity as Research-Coordinator during my study was always available whenever I needed help. I am thankful to Stephen Connelly, the Chief Librarian, and all the staff of the Dalton-McCaughey Library for assisting me enthusiastically. I also thank the authorities and staff of the Baillieu Library of Melbourne University for the superb research resources they provided to me.

I am very grateful to Rev. Dr John Smith and the Congregation of Mark the Evangelist and the Hotham Mission for providing me and my family with a home, for involving us in the life of the Congregation and giving us a community to belong to. I am also deeply beholden to the Centre for Theology and Ministry (CTM) and its staff for work opportunities and for counting me as their own.

My appreciation and heartfelt thanks go to the following institutions, churches, communities, and individuals without whom I would not have been able to do my research (in no particular order): Rev. Chris Turner and the members of Ivanhoe Baptist Church, Ivanhoe, Melbourne; Rev Saw True Chain and Ahsah Mee and the members of Myanmar Christian Church; The Naga community in Melbourne; Rev. Dr Ian and Karin Parsons; Dr Visier and Pari Sanyü; Rev. Kiliona Mafaufau and family; Michael Spaull and family; Rev. Jillian Stewart; Rev. Meewon Yang; Biju and Susha George; Dr Madhu (MD) and Alka.

There are also those who were far away but have been supportive: The community of Eastern Theological College, Jorhat, Assam; Tura Baptist Church, Tura, Maghalaya; Shillong Baptist Church, Shillong, Meghalaya; Town Baptist Church, Dimapur, Nagaland; Jorhat Baptist Church, Jorhat, Assam; Khuzama Baptist Church, Khuzama, Nagaland; Rev. Dr Ezamo and Lireni Murry; Rev. Dr Lima Jamir and Rev. Dr Narola Imchen; Kezhalezo Angami; and Abenla Ao.

I am grateful to my family members in various villages, towns, and cities for their unstinting support. I thank my husband Zhodi Angami for being the source of my inspiration and for providing invaluable insights and suggestions. His thoughts and ideas are scattered throughout these pages. And I thank my daughter, Mima Tejoé Marak, just for being.

Mitela ("thank you") to everyone who has been with me on this journey.

1

INTRODUCTION

Preliminary Remarks

If I am asked to define myself or my people, I would say that we are *golpo*[1] people, storytellers, people who tell stories and stories about stories. Tribal people of North East India are storytelling people. While storytelling is a universal characteristic of cultures across the globe, it is appropriate that I should state why stories are important for the tribes in my region. We not only love stories, but identify ourselves and our tribes through the great stories we share.[2] Perhaps the importance we place on stories has something to do with the fact that before mid-nineteenth century, we had no written script and relied on oral stories passed from generation to generation to keep the memory of the tribe.

---

1. *Golpo* means "story" in A·chikku (Garo) language.

2. For example the Angami (including the Mao, Memi, Rengma, and Chakhesang tribes), Sema (Sumi), and Lotha (Kyong) regard themselves as belonging to the same group because they share a common story that traces their origin to Khezhakenoma. These tribes, so the story says, were the sons of Koza of Khezhakenoma. Koza had a stone that miraculously doubled the paddy (rice still in the husk) when paddy was spread upon it. The sons used to take turns to spread their paddy on the stone, but one day their mother saw them quarrelling heatedly over whose turn it was to use the stone. Fearing bloodshed, she broke egg on the stone, covered it with bush-wood, laid faggots about it, and set it on fire. The stone broke with a thunderous sound and its spirit went up to heaven in a cloud of smoke. The three sons went separate ways and became the ancestors of the Angami, Lotha, and Sema tribes. J. P. Mills, *The Rengma Nagas* (London: Macmillan, 1937), 4ff.

Except for Assamese and Manipuri, written text started in the region only with the publication of the Bible during early- and mid-19th century, after the arrival of the Christian missionaries. The first known Christian missionary to North East India was Krishna Chandra Pal, William Carey's first convert. He was sent by William Carey from the English Baptist Mission at Serampore in 1813. Chandra Pal is said to have worked for eight months at the Khasi foothills below Cherrapunjee and converted four sepoys, an Assamese, and two Khasis.[3] Around that same time, William Carey implemented a colossal scheme to translate the Bible into all the languages of India.

Assamese, Khasi, and Manipuri languages came to be included in Carey's plan. For the Assamese Bible, Carey employed a pundit to translate the Bible. Thus according to one source, the Assamese New Testament was completed in 1819 and the translation of the whole Bible was finished in 1833.[4] According to another source, the first Assamese Bible was translated by Atmaram Sarma from Kaliabor in Nowgong District and printed in 1813 and that the second edition appeared in 1833.[5] A recent inquiry supports 1813 as the year of the publication of the first Assamese Bible by Serampore press. It further adds that the translation was made with the help of Hemchandra Goswami and Bholanath Baruah.[6] Unfortunately the first Assamese translation was not helpful. The pundit or pundits who made the translation used Sanskrit words extensively and misinterpreted theological terms using categories of Hindu religion that very few could comprehend. Better translations were made available through the efforts of Baptist missionaries. In 1836, the Baptist Foreign Mission Society of the United States sent Nathan Brown to Sadiya, in Assam. Within a year, Brown mastered the Assamese language and was able to preach in Assamese. Soon he had portions

3. Andrew May, "The Promise of a Book: Missionaries and Native Evangelists in North-East India," in *Missionaries, Indigenous Peoples and Cultural Exchange*, ed. Patricia Grimshaw and Andrew May (Eastbourne: Sussex Academic Press, 2010), 88.

4. Victor Hugo Sword, *Baptists in Assam: A Century of Missionary Service 1836-1936* (Guwahati: Spectrum Publications, 1992), 34-35.

5. Pona Mahanta, *Western Influence on Modern Assamese Drama: From 1857 to the Present Time* (Delhi: K. M. Mittal, 1985), 32. Mahanta's source is a Maheswar Neog, *Asamiyā Sāhityar Ruparekhā* ([Gauhati, 1962?]), 231.

6. Eva Hazarika, "'ধৰ্ম পুস্তক'ৰ অনুসন্ধান প্ৰকাশ [Inquiry of Publication of Religious Book]," *The Dainik Janambhumi*, Jorhat, September 29, 2012. Based on the evidences, my conclusion is that the Assamese New Testament was first published in 1813 and the whole Bible came out in 1833.

of the New Testament translated into Assamese and printed.[7] Nathan Brown and his colleague O. T. Cutter started the first Assamese journal, *Orunodoi* (meaning "sunrise"), "a monthly paper, devoted to Religion, Science and General Intelligence," in 1846 from Sibsagar, and this had a great impact on Assamese language and literature.[8]

The first translation of the Gospels into Khasi language was also done through the initiative of Carey. According to a source, a portion of the Gospel of Matthew was circulated in 1817, and the 500 copies of the New Testament translation in Khasi was said to have been printed in 1824.[9] According to another report, the first translation of the Khasi New Testament was printed in 1831.[10] Back then, the medium of education was in Bengali and so the earliest Khasi New Testament was translated and printed in Bengali script.

When the first missionary to be in residence in the Khasi hills, an Anglo-Indian named Alexander Burgh Lish, came to the Khasi Hills in 1832 from Serampore, he continued to use the Bengali script to revise the translation of portions of Matthew's Gospel. He also wrote some books on Khasi vocabulary and grammar.[11]

However, the credit for formulating and standardizing of Khasi language is given to Thomas Jones. He came from the newly-formed Welsh Missionary Society to Sohra (Cherrapunjee) on 22 June 1841. Within eight months he picked up the Khasi language. Very soon after, he recorded the Khasi language in Roman script. He was adept as a translator. In 1842, he produced the Khasi book, *Ca Citab Nyngoong*

---

7. Robert F. Cramer, "Foreign Mission Society," in *Baptist Advance: The Achievements of the Baptists of North America for a Century and a Half*, ed. Davis Collier Wooley, et al. (Nashville, TN: Broadman Press, 1964), 77; F. S. Downs, *The Mighty Works of God: A Brief History of the Council of Baptist Churches in North East India: The Mission Period 1836-1950* (Guwahati: Christian Literature Centre, 1969), 20.

8. Mahanta, *Western Influence on Modern Assamese Drama*, 33-34, 41f.

9. May, "The Promise of a Book," in *Missionaries, Indigenous Peoples and Cultural Exchange*, ed. Grimshaw and May, 88; Frederick S. Downs, *History of Christianity in India*, vol. 5, Pt. 5: *North East India in the Nineteenth and Twentieth Centuries*, CHAI History of Christianity in India (Bangalore: The Church History Association of India, 1992), 66.

10. P. K. Bandyopadhyay, "The Coming of the Alphabet: A Study on the Scripts of Some North-Eastern Languages," in *Linguistic Situation in North-East India*, ed. Mrinal Miri (Shillong: North-East India Council for Social Science Research, 1982), 71.

11. May, "The Promise of a Book," in *Missionaries, Indigenous Peoples and Cultural Exchange*, ed. Grimshaw and May, 90.

Ban Hicai Pule Ci Ctin Cassi (The Khasi First Reader) and a translation of the Welsh Catechism called *Ca Cot Ticir*. In 1843, he translated and published *Ka Kitab Nongialam* (Christian Instructor), and *Ka Gospel U Mathi* (a part of the Gospel of Matthew). The complete Gospel of Matthew was published in 1846.[12]

Since the Bengali alphabet was abandoned, Thomas Jones who Romanized the Khasi language has come to be regarded as the father of the Khasi alphabet and literature. Likewise, among the various Naga tribes, the Garos, the Mizos, and other communities, the missionaries were responsible for standardizing tribal languages using Roman script.

The absence of written tradition among the tribals until the modern era meant that from time immemorial tribals had depended on oral storytelling to communicate their history. Stories also were the substance from which religious beliefs were drawn and social norms constituted. Many in my generation grew up listening to stories of migration, and myths and legends from our grandparents. This did not change after written script was introduced. We still love to sit by the kitchen fire and exchange stories. Mothers still carry their babies on their backs, tied with a piece of cloth, and sing their stories while they work in the field.

Side by side with traditional ways of transmitting folklore, modern day children, like children elsewhere, recite nursery rhymes and read picture books. It does not matter where we are born, for we all get acquainted with narratives from early childhood. Children's narratives are simple in form but they provide a means of comprehending the world we are born into. As we grow older, we learn to tell narratives of our own. Thus narratives provide a method of learning and a way of telling what we have learned. It is a human cognition mode helping us to learn about the world and about ourselves as well. And as our knowledge base increases, we acquire the skill to understand different characters and characterization, and intricate plots and sub-plots in narrative. Then we are able to appreciate lengthy plays, complicated dramas, and convoluted novels.

12. D. Ben Rees, "Jones, Thomas (1810-1849)," in *Vehicles of Grace and Hope: Welsh Missionaries in India 1800-1970*, ed. D. Ben Rees ([Pasadena, CA?]: William Carey Library, 2002), 100-103; B. L. Nongbri, "Christianity, Khasi Language and Literature: An Historical Analysis of the Interaction of Christianity with Traditional Culture," in *Christianity and Change in Northeast India*, ed. T. B. Subba, Joseph Puthenpurakal, and Shaji Joseph Puykunnel (New Delhi: Concept Publishing, 2009), 177-93, see esp. 178.

Narrative is thus a pervasive presence in the individual's life and the life of the community. It is as natural to human nature as the act of thinking and communicating. In fact, in thinking we think narratively, and in communicating we communicate narratively. The link between narrative and communication is neither new nor surprising. Several decades back, Gregory Gizelis[13] explored rhetorical aspects of narrative communication in folklore. And critics such as Walter Fisher[14] and Didier Coste[15] studied narrative theory in the context of communication. Fisher claimed that all human communication may be viewed from the perspective of narrative. Likewise, Coste looked at narratology as a theory of communication. Nevertheless the relation between narrative and communication is an uneasy one as narrative has not been fully accepted into the study of communication.[16] Yet the fact remains that narrative is not merely a form of communication but every communication has narrative embedded in it. If narrative is the basic cognitive means by which humans perceive the world, it stands to reason that the transfer of data in communication must have narrative structure in order to be decoded by the receiver of communication.

Based on this tentative but undeniable connection between narrative and communication, I propose a "narrative communication" approach, a combination of narrative and communication theories, as the method of analysis for this project. Gender communication that shares feminist epistemology has a place in communication studies.[17] This is a stepping stone towards my own feminist form of narrative communication.

I use the word "feminist" and its cognates with a few qualifications. Feminist theory is essentially a product of white middle-class, European and American women. This implies that at its core the feminist approach is based on the perspectives and concerns of women whose experiences are very different from those of women in Asia and Africa. Thus using

13. Gregory Gizelis, *Narrative Rhetorical Devices of Persuasion: Folklore Communication in a Greek-American Community* (Athens: National Centre of Social Research, 1974).

14. Walter R. Fisher, *Human Communication as a Narration: Toward a Philosophy of Reason, Value, and Action* (Columbia, SC: University of South Carolina Press, 1987).

15. Didier Coste, *Narrative as Communication*, Theory and History of Literature 64 (Minneapolis, MN: University of Minnesota Press, 1989).

16. Katherine Miller, *Communication Theories: Perspectives, Processes, and Contexts* (New York: McGraw Hill, 2005), 92.

17. Charlotte Kroløkke and Anne Scott Sørensen, *Gender Communication Theories & Analysis: From Silence to Performance* (Thousand Oaks: Sage Publications, 2006).

the story of the Syrophoenician woman in Matthew 15-21-28, Musa W. Dube argues that because of their gender, race, and class privilege, not only white men but white women too fail to expose the power relations in the text. [18] To be politically correct I should be using an alternative description. "Tribal women's perspective" comes to mind. However the "feminist" appellation also has global relevance. In a broader sense, feminism can refer to the consciousness of oppression, invisibility, dehumanization, and domination under unjust structures, regardless of race, culture, class, or geographical location. It is in this sense that I use the term feminist and its cognates.

More than the obvious connection between narrative and communication, I propose a narrative theory that is bound to the ideal of communication, especially the purpose of communication to create communion and community. This theory will be the yardstick by means of which to measure the integrity of gender relations.

A number of studies on narrative practice have shown that cross-disciplinary approaches to narrative analysis can be viable research methods. The range of narratological applications spans a wide field of diverse disciplines, from the study of stained glass through a narrative lens,[19] to sociological narrative analysis,[20] and from the application of narrative in education,[21] to narratological reading of biblical texts.[22] Thus the groundwork has been laid for me to incorporate methods from diverse disciplines to comment upon the content and practice of worship. This work will add a tribal women's perspective to "women's ways of worship." It will apply an eclectic method under the rubric of "narrative communication" with a feminist perspective, in order to evaluate the content and practice of worship and evolve forms of

18. Musa W. Dube, *Postcolonial Feminist Interpretation of the Bible* (St. Louis, MO: Chalice Press, 2000), 157-96; Cf. Ellen T. Armour, *Deconstruction, Feminist Theology, and the Problem of Difference: Subverting the Race/Gender Divide* (Chicago: University of Chicago Press, 1999).

19. Wolfgang Kemp, *The Narratives of Gothic Stained Glass*, trans. Caroline Dobson Saltzwedel (Cambridge: Cambridge University Press, 1997). Originally published in German as *Sermo Corporeus* (Munich: Schirmer/Mosel Verlag, 1987).

20. Jaber F. Gubrium and James A. Holstein, *Analyzing Narrative Reality* (Los Angeles: Sage Publications, 2009).

21. Carol Witherell and Nel Noddings, eds., *Stories Lives Tell: Narrative and Dialogue in Education* (New York: Columbia University, 1991).

22. Mieke Bal, *Lethal Love: Feminist Literary Readings of Biblical Love Stories* (Bloomington: Indiana University Press, 1987).

worship that build community, bring inclusiveness to fruition, and reconcile gender differences especially in the context of tribal churches in North East India.

The Research Problem

During my early youth, when I lived in Tura, my home town, community worship was a central component of my life. I attended church every Tuesday, Thursday, Friday, and Sunday. On Tuesdays we had women fellowship. Thursdays were for Bible Study and prayer meeting. On Fridays we had worship service for the Baptist Youth Fellowship. There were two worship services on Sundays; one in morning and another in the evening. Each time I attended church, I walked down forty odd steps of stones, meandering down from my house, across a stream to a paved road, and then climbed up to the church, which stands on a hillock. It took me some twenty minutes to reach church. By the time I sat down in the church I would be somewhat out of breath but refreshed by the walk. On Sundays there would be approximately 1000 members worshipping together. My world felt fine. I was at peace with my church.

The church has grown bigger since then. But the way of worship is still the same. The services are conducted in my native language. The hymns we sing are translated from English. Being a Baptist church, there is no set liturgy. The order of service follows a regular pattern, though not always in the same order—announcements, call to worship, opening hymn, invocation, special songs, responsive reading, offering and offertory prayer, scripture reading, sermon, closing hymn, and benediction or closing prayer.

Had I not gone on to study theology, I might not have noticed anything wrong with the way we worship. But in 1991 I answered a call to join the Christian ministry and got enrolled in the Bachelor of Divinity degree course at Eastern Theological College, Jorhat, Assam. During my training I undertook the study of social and cultural theories along with biblical, historical, theological, and Christian ministry principles and issues, which are normative to theological education in India. Among all areas of study, I found feminist theology to be one of the most provocative. Initially, I really could not understand what all the hue and cry of feminism was about. I had the impression that feminists must be a bunch of disgruntled women who were twisting the interpretation of the Bible to support their views. I did not know then that what I regarded as normative biblical interpretations were in fact based on structures of domination such as patriarchalism and imperialism. But soon I realized that my cultural and religious upbringing was keeping me from understanding the insidious nature of patriarchal culture and the complicities of power, domination, and gender in Scriptural texts and in society.[23]

In my defence, I came from a community where females are comparatively in a better situation than their counterparts in other societies. My community, the Garo aka "A·chik", is a matrilineal tribe.[24] My cultural milieu is far more egalitarian than those cultures in which feminist theories,[25] or the womanist approach,[26] or mujerista and Latin

---

23. The pyramidal structure of domination has appropriately been named as "kyriocentrism" and "kyriarchy." From the root word *kyrios*, we have "kyriocentrism," a term used by Luise Schottroff to define "society's orientation in terms of the class of ruling men." Luise Schottroff, *Lydia's Impatient Sisters: A Feminist Social History of Early Christianity*, trans. Barbara and Martin Rumscheidt (Louisville, KY: Westminster John Knox Press, 1995), 34, 231 n115. From the same Greek word, Elisabeth Schüssler Fiorenza coined "kyriarchy" to express the multiplicative intersecting structures of domination, recognizes that it is not only the patriarchal system but also the intersection of differences in race, class, caste, gender, ethnicity, and other structures of domination such as colonialism and imperialism that are the source of inequality between men and women and between those who are at the centre and those who are at the margins of society. Elisabeth Schüssler Fiorenza, *Wisdom Ways: Introducing Feminist Biblical Interpretation* (Maryknoll, NY: Orbis Books, 2001), 118-24.

24. In a matrilineal system family lineage is traced through the mother. Children take their mother's surname (clan title) and not their father's. In addition to the name, it is not the son but the daughter, usually the youngest daughter, who inherits the family property. The youngest daughter never leaves the house even after getting married; her husband leaves his mother's house and joins her household. Thus the family life is organized around the mother's house.

25. Feminist discourse is for the most part a white North American women's movement, but its critical principles have influenced the development of women's consciousness worldwide. Sally Noland MacNichol and Mary Elizabeth Walsh, "Feminist Theology and Spirituality: An Annotated Bibliography," *Women Studies Quarterly* 21 (1993): 177-96.

26. On Womanist consciousness: Emilie M. Townes, *Womanist Justice, Womanist Hope* (Atlanta, GA: Scholars Press, 1993); James Cone and Gayraud S. Wilmore, eds., *Black Theology: A Documentary History, vol. 2, 1980-1992* (Maryknoll, NY: Orbis, 1993), 257-351; Diana L. Hayes, *Hagar's Daughter: Womanist Ways of Being in the World* (New York: Paulist Press, 1995).

American[27] discourses sprang up. However, once the problem was identified and named, I became increasingly aware of the ubiquitous presence of patriarchal influence even in my matrilineal society.

The other main ethnic groups in my state of Meghalaya are the Khasis and the Jaintias. While the A·chik people are predominantly Baptist, the Khasi and Jaintia groups are Presbyterian. Patriarchy is blatantly evident in the Khasi-Jaintia Presbyterian Synod of the Presbyterian Church of India, which has been averse to the inclusion of women as elders and pastors. The use of masculine terms such as *Rangbah Balang* (Executive member of the church) and *U Tymmen Basan* (Elder of the church) in the Presbyterian Church of the Khasi and Jaintia Hills has not helped the cause of gender equality.[28] According to a report (2018), at least one woman has been elected as *Rangbah Balang* of a congregation. But there is no woman serving as *U Tymmen Basan*, or Elder, which is the more important post.[29] While men with theological degrees are given pastoral positions, women with theological degrees are appointed as counsellors and other "assistant" posts.

A similar situation is prevailing in the Mizoram Presbyterian Synod. To put it in perspective, according to a 2011 report, the Mizoram

---

27. On Mujerista and Latina contexts for theologizing: Ada María Isasi-Díaz, "Toward an Understanding of Feminismo Hispano in the U.S.A.," in *Women's Consciousness, Women's Conscience: A Reader in Feminist Ethics*, ed. Barbara Hilkert Andolsen, Christine E. Gudorf, and Mary D. Pellauer (Minneapolis, MN: Winston Press, 1985), 51-61; idem, "*Mujeristas*: A Name of Our Own," in *The Future of Liberation Theology: Essays in Honor of Gustavo Gutiérrez*, ed. Marc H. Ellis and Otto Maduro (Maryknoll, NY: Orbis Books, 1989), 410-19; Elsa Tamez, *Against Machismo* (Oak Park, IL: Meyer Stone Books, 1987).

28. Gertrude Lamare, "Presbyterian Church Patriarchy," Raiot, September 22, 2015, http://raiot.in/presbyterian-church-patriarchy/ (accessed September 14, 2018); Wandahilin Kharlukhi, "The Significance of the Feminist Interpretation of the 'Image of God' for Women's Liberation in the Khasi Society" (MTh Thesis, United Theological College, Bangalore, 1999). Wandahilin Kharlukhi is one of the first two women to study theology from the Khasi-Jaintia Presbyterian Synod, the other one being Ladbasuk Lyngdoh. Both studied BD at Eastern Theological College and MTh at United Theological College. From my discussions with Wandahilin during our study at UTC, I gathered that her research is based on the question how and why there is a Patriarchal Church in a matrilineal society.

29. I learned this from a Khasi student, Nangsanbor Wahlang, when he was doing his MTh studies at Eastern Theological College.

Presbyterian Synod has 465 ordained pastors and 5,018 ordained elders, of which not a single solitary one is a female pastor or church elder.[30]

The rigid patriarchal structures of the Khasi-Jaintia Presbyterian Synod and the Mizoram Presbyterian Synod helped me to understand the presence of patriarchy in the Church. In turn, it made me conscious of more subtle forms of male domination in my own church. Patriarchy was, and is, more subtle in the Baptist churches.

Outwardly, the Baptist churches in North East India are more progressive than the Presbyterian Church of India in terms of the role of women in the church. Women preach, teach, become pastors, serve as deacons, and in fact have far more activities to do in the church than men. It is only when we dig deeper that the insidious tentacles of patriarchy become apparent. And on closer study, we find that the number of women in ministry is negligible.

Women in Ministry under CBCNEI Churches

The CBCNEI is the largest Christian body in North East India, predominant in Nagaland, the Garo Hills of Meghalaya, the hills of Manipur, and sections of Assam. The Catholic Church is the second largest group, found scattered throughout the region. The Presbyterian Church of India (PCI) is a very close third, established in the Khai-Jaintia hills of Meghalaya, northern Mizoram, the Cachar district of Assam, and parts of the hills of Manipur. In 1990, according to a report, 43 percent of Christians in the region belonged to CBCNEI, 26 percent to the Catholic Church, and 23 percent to PCI.[31]

The disparity between men and women in ministry is evident in the number of women in ministry under the Council of Baptist Churches in North East India (CBCNEI). The CBCNEI comprises six Conventions (based on States) and four associate members directly affiliated to CBCNEI. The six conventions of CBCNEI are: Assam Baptist Convention (ABC), having 6 associations, 746 churches, and 35,169 baptised members; Arunachal Baptist Church Council (ABCC),

---

30. Mary Vanlalthanpuii, "The Changing Roles of Churchwomen in Mizoram (1904-1994): A Study of Mizoram Presbyterian Church Synod," *IOSR Journal Of Humanities And Social Science (IOSR-JHSS)*, 19/10, Ver. VII (October 2014): 5.

31. Downs, *History of Christianity in India*, 69 n15. Cf. Lalsangkima Pachuau, "Church-Mission Dynamics in Northeast India," *International Bulletin of Missionary Research* 27/4 (October 2003): 154-61, esp. 155.

having 19 associations, 1,027 churches, and 92,284 baptised members; A·chik Baptist Dal·gipa Krima also known as Garo Baptist Convention (ABDK or GBC), having 13 associations, 1 Centre, 2750 churches, and 2,83,923 baptised members; Karbi Anglong Baptist Convention (KABC), having 13 associations, 315 churches, and 31,746 baptised members; Manipur Baptist Convention (MBC), having 29 associations, 1,303 churches, and 1,96,217 baptised members; and Nagaland Baptist Church Council (NBCC), having 20 associations, 4 associate members, 1585 churches, and 5,86,593 baptised members. The associate members are: Evangelical Church of Maraland (ECM), having 91 churches and 42,588 baptised members; Mising Baptist Kebang (MBK), having 115 churches and 4,300 baptised members; Shillong Baptist Church (SBC), having 184 baptised members; and Zomi Baptist Church (ZBC, no data available). Thus as of 2017, there are 100 associations under the six conventions and four associate members. Under these associations and associate members, there are altogether 7,935 local churches with a total of more than 1,273,004 baptised members.[32] It should be kept in mind that the actual number of people attending church is much higher than the number of baptised members because children and unbaptized members have not been counted.

There are two conventions under CBCNEI which has no woman pastor or ordained minister—the KABC and ABCC.[33]

ABC has given ordination to one woman in its Annual General Meeting of 2017, in which two men were also ordained.

MBC has three ordained women ministers.[34] There would have been four but the first one to be ordained, Nemneikim Vaiphei of the Kuki Baptist Convention, left the Baptist fold and joined the Methodist Church. She is presently serving as its Executive Secretary in Manipur. It is worth noting that one of the associations under MBC has a woman as

32. The primary information came from A. K. Lama, the then General Secretary of CBCNEI, through his PA, Meera Areng, on 27 September 2012. Since then, the statistics have been updated. See Appendix A: "CBCNEI at a Glance—2017" for details.

33. See Appendix B: "Women in Ministry Under CBCNEI" for a list of ordained women and women working as pastors and associate pastors in the churches of CBCNEI.

34. Tingneilhing Kipgen, Women Secretary, MBC, message to the author on July 22, 2018. Cf. Tingneichong G. Kipgen, *Women's Role in the 20th Century Manipur: A Historical Study* (Delhi: Kalpaz Publications, 2010), 114.

its Executive Secretary—the Thangal Naga Baptist Association headed by Apila Thangal.

NBCC has 509 ordained ministers of which eight are women. Seven of them are from the Ao Baptist Arogo Mundang (ABAM), one of the associations under NBCC. One is from Chakhesang Baptist Church Council (CBCC; another association of the NBCC). It is worth noting here that unmarried women who are ordained under ABAM are given ordination with the understanding that they will never marry. In a recent case, Awala Longkumer's ordination was revoked by ABAM because she got married.

NBCC has four women pastors and one associate pastor—two pastors under the Chakhesang Baptist Church Council (CBCC), one pastor under the Angami Baptist Church Council (ABCC), one pastor under the Chang Baptist Lashoung Thangyen (CBLT), and one associate pastor under Sumi Baptist Convention (SBC).[35] There are some churches that have women working under the designation "associate pastors." But this is a misleading nomenclature because these so-called associate pastors are actually secretaries of women's fellowships or youth fellowships.[36]

An important point for understanding the situation of women ordination in North East India is that of the actual participation of ordained women in the ministries of local congregations. In Nagaland, for instance, Except for Senangshila Benjamin, none of the ordained women appears to have served or serve as ministers in local congregations. Senangshila served as a licensed pastor at Süngratsü Baptist Church,

35. In 2012, there appears to have been two women pastors and one associate pastor among the NBCC churches. Cf. Narola Imchen, "Women's Issues in the Ministry," in *Women in Ministry: Practical Issues and Challenges*, ed. Narola Imchen (Jorhat, Assam: Women Study Centre, 2012), 34-35, 38. There have been some changes since then. For instance, when Narola wrote, a woman named Talijungla Longkumer was the pastor of Jorhat Ao Baptist Church, Jorhat. She moved with her family to Mokokchung and the Jorhat Ao Baptst Church now has a male pastor.

36. Women, youth, and children departments are important ministries of the churches. But there is a fundamental problem in assigning women "associate pastors" (most of the time) to these departments. The root of the problem is that churches and societies regard these wings as of less consequence. For instance, many tribal communities have a single word to refer to women and children, e.g. *tetsürtanur* in Ao and *nhiechu-thenu* in Angami. Such words are used in a dismissive manner to indicate that these groups are less important than men. The same attitude applies to the youth who are often regarded as immature, and youth worship service is seen as a form of keeping them happy.

Mokokchung, for about 4-5 years. According to information received from friends who come from her village, Senangshila eventually stopped working as a pastor due to very strong negative response to her ministry from a congregation predisposed to patriarchal views.

Under GBC, there are eight women ordained ministers, sixteen full-time women pastors, and many women associate pastors.[37] One difference that the GBC has from other conventions of the region is that its churches are organised as "mother churches" and "sister churches." A mother church takes care of several sister churches under it. Once a sister church has a strong congregation and qualified leaders, including one who is theologically trained and ready to take up the role of pastor, the sister church may seek separation from its mother church and establish itself as a full-fledged church, a mother church.

Among the CBCNEI Conventions, the GBC has the most desirable record in terms of the participation of women in ministry. The high number of women pastors under GBC is because there is comparatively lesser opposition to women's leadership in the churches under GBC. In the year 1993, during the occasion of its celebration of 125 years of Christianity in the Garo Hills, the GBC decided that by 2015 all member churches under it would appoint fulltime pastors who have bachelor's degree in theology as their minimum qualification. Consequently, churches have sent men and women to study theology and have employed them as pastors. The churches are not concerned whether the pastor is male or female so long as the person is theologically qualified. In fact, when I was working as the Women Secretary of Tura Baptist Church, I found out that some churches have men serving as Women Secretaries. This was not because the members of those churches looked down on women but because they wanted someone who is literate to lead the department and to represent their church at the association and convention levels. I do not mean to imply that women in ministry under GBC do not face discrimination because of their gender. The point I wish to make is that women under GBC are comparatively better off than their counterparts in other conventions under CBCNEI.

Besides having a good number of pastors, associate pastors, and ordained ministers, the GBC also has a woman working as the head of one of its Krimas. Sangeeta Arengh is the Executive Secretary of Puksora Centre. In the past, Exwilline A. Marak has served as the executive head

37. In 2012, there were twenty-two associate pastors. Rettiar G. Momin, former General Secretary, GBC, Tura, email message to author October 11, 2012.

of Krima VII, and Piljelota A. Sangma served as the executive head of Krima I. Piljelota A. Sangma passed away while in office.

This brief survey shows that ordination within the CBCNEI is confined to a few associations. Six of the associations have ordained women but the other 98 associations show no inclination to ordain women and some have expressed their strong opposition to the ordination of women.[38]

A clarification about the difference between pastors and ordained ministers in the Baptist churches of North East India is necessary. Pastorship in Baptist churches is not an ordained office. In fact, in many places the pastors are not theologically trained. In some remote villages, pastors are uneducated cultivators who work in their fields throughout the weekdays and take care of worship on Sundays. This indicates that the selection of pastors is not based on theological training or level of education.

The existence of only a negligible number of women pastors in the Baptist churches speaks of the reluctance of the people to have women as leaders and pastors in the churches. As congregationally ordered churches, Baptists regard every church as an autonomous institution with the right to call whomever they wish to the pulpit ministry. This means that if people wished they could have women pastors. However, with regard to ordination, Baptist churches of the region function more like hierarchical churches in that, unlike the selection of pastors, the decision for ordination is made by the associations; local congregations are not free to ordain women or men.

Furthermore, most of the activities women engage in are for fundraising and cooking for church meetings. Women who have theological degrees are not called to take up positions as pastors or assistant pastors; they are mostly employed as Sunday School teachers, mission school teachers, women secretaries in the local church, and hostel wardens. The most striking instance of the imbalance of power in church administration is seen in the virtual absence of women leaders at the association, convention, and council levels of the Baptist churches.

38. Outside the Baptist churches of North East India, the Lutheran Church has one ordained woman and there is none in the Presbyterian Church of India.

Women in Ministry in Baptist Churches Outside CBCNEI

There are several Baptist groups in North East India that are not associated with the CBCNEI:

1) Baptist Church of Mizoram, Serkawn, Lunglei, Mizoram

2) Evangelical Baptist Convention, New Lamka, Churachandpur, Manipur

3) Lairam Jesus Christ Baptist Church/Lairam Isua Krista Baptist Kohhran, Lawngtlai, Mizoram

4) Lower Assam Baptist Union, Alamganj, Kokrajhar, Assam

5) North Bank Baptist Christian Association, Sonitpur, Assam

6) Tripura Baptist Christian Union, Arundhitinagar, Tripura

The identity of different Baptist groups of North East India have been determined by the works of different foreign missions. The CBCNEI family is connected to the missionary work American Baptists (American Baptist Missionary Union/American Baptist Foreign Mission Society; known today as American Baptist International Ministries). The Baptist Church of Mizoram is linked to Baptist mission from England (Baptist Missionary Society; known today as Baptist Missionary Society, World Mission). The Evangelical Baptist Convention of the Paite tribe in Manipur, Mizoram, and Assam trace its origins to a Presbyterian missionary named Watkins R. Roberts. The Lairam Jesus Christ Baptist Church grew from the work of the missionaries of Baptist Missionary Society of England. The Lower Assam Baptist Union has links with the American, Australian, and New Zealand Baptist missions. The North Bank Christian Association is linked to Australian Baptist Mission and the Baptist General Conference of America. The Tripura Baptist Christian Union has 13 associations. It arose from the missionary work of Mizo Christians and the New Zealand Baptist Missionary Society.

The Lairam Jesus Christ Baptist Church has four women ordained as lifetime church elders in their local churches: 1) Upa Ngunchiangi of Lungzarhtum, Upa Lalduhawmi of Diltlang, Upa Nukimi of Archhuang, and Upa Sangi of Sangau.[39]

39. T. Vanlaltlani, *Mizo Hmeichhiate Kawngzawh* (Aizawl: Mizoram Publication Board, 2005), 89; referred in T. Vanlaltlani, "History of Mizo Women and Future Hope," in *No More Sorrow in God's Garden of Justice: Tribal Women Doing Theology*, Women Study Series 4, ed. Limatula Longkumer (Jorhat, Assam: Women Study Department, Eastern Theological College, 2007), 102.

Besides that, the only Baptist group to have ordained a woman is the Baptist Church of Mizoram (BCM).[40]

On March 11, 2012, the BCM ordained R. L. Hnuni, who was then the Principal of the BCM sponsored theological college called the Academy of Integrated Studies, Aizawl, Mizoram. The decision was made with great difficulty. A proposal to ordain her was passed in 2011 by the Pastoral Committee but turned down by the Executive Community of the Assembly of BCM, which is its highest decision-making body. The Executive Committee reversed the decision in 2012, paving the way for the first woman to be ordained in Mizoram.[41] According to information received, Hnuni's ordination is a "second class" ordination; she was ordained on the condition that she will not seek to become a minister/pastor of a local congregation.

Discrimination against Women

While interacting with students in the theological college where I have taught for twenty years, I have collected, over the years, a few of the reasons why churches in North East India think women should not be allowed into ordained ministry.

1) Some say it is because of culture. They concede there is nothing in the Bible that says women shouldn't be ordained but it is against culture. Tribal culture, they say, is against women leading men. (My response to them: If you take culture as more important than the teachings of Christ, you are implying that you do not think much of the teachings

---

40. From its inception, the Baptist Church of Mizoram had a close affinity with the Presbyterian Synod of Mizoram. It is unlike other Baptist bodies of North East India in the sense that it follows a centralized form of government like the Presbyterian Synod of Mizoram.

41. The Times of India, "First Woman Priest for Mizoram," *The Times of India*, March 11, 2012, https://timesofindia.indiatimes.com/city/guwahati/First-woman-priest-for-Mizoram/articleshow/12224006.cms (accessed July 23, 2018); DNA: Daily News and Analysis, "Woman to be Ordained, but Not Made Priest in Patriarchal Mizoram," *DNA: Daily News and Analysis*, Feb. 20, 2012, http://www.dnaindia.com/india/report-woman-to-be-ordained-but-not-made-priest-in-patriarchal-mizoram-1652578 (accessed September 3, 2018). The BCM is known to have ordained women church elders from 1952. According to a report, there are 18 women ordained as church elders in the BCM. The Evangelical Church of Maraland, which shares close affinity with BCM, also ordains women as church elders but not for pastoral ministry. T. Vanlaltlani, "History of Mizo Women and Future Hope," in *No More Sorrow in God's Garden of Justice*, ed. Longkumer, 102.

of Christ. As a matter of fact, female priests and women performing "priestly" roles are not unusual in tribal societies. For instance, in Khasi society, the youngest daughter of the family functions as priestess of the house, including funeral ceremonies.[42] And when a Khasi priest, called *Lyngdoh*, offers sacrifices, he must have the assistance of a female priestess known as *Ka Lyngdoh*[43]).

2) Others say the Bible does not allow women's ordination. They say in Judaism only the Levite *men* were priests. And in the New Testament too, all the twelve disciples are men. Women played supporting roles and not leading roles. (My response: So how are you going to turn tribal men into Jews? How are they going to become Levites? Remember, in the Old Testament priesthood was only for those selected from the tribe of Levi. Remember, also, that all the twelve disciples were not just men but Jewish men).

3) It will be bad if a woman conducts the Lord's Supper when she is menstruating or when she is pregnant. Women of childbearing age are often denied entry to priesthood because of fear that they may become pregnant and give birth. Traditional culture and interpretations of the Old Testament are used to support the denial of ordination to women. (My response to them: These are signs of fertility and creation of new life and should be seen in the light of God's work and manifestation as Creator. If God the Creator is worshipped, why do we think so little of pregnant women who are partners with God in creating new life?).[44]

---

42. Hamlet Bareh, *The History and Culture of the Khasi People* (Calcutta: n.p.), 330, 332; Valentina Pakyntein, "Gender Preference in Khasi Society: An Evaluation of Tradition, Change and Continuity," *Indian Anthropologist* 30/1-2 (June-December 2000): 27-35.

43. Darilyn Syiem, "Women and Sacred Medicines among the Khasis in the Highlands of Northeast India," in *Women and Indigenous Religions*, Women and Religion in the World, edited by Sylvia Marcos (Santa Barbara, CA: Praeger, 2010), 117.

44. Esther Mombo reports of an African woman priest called Ndonga who was rested because she gave birth to a baby. According to Mombo, researches have shown that in some African cultures women served as priests but that their roles were curtailed after the advent of Christianity. She says, "In the light of this, African women, both lay and ordained, have embraced culture critically, appropriating and reviving some cultural practices and values that are life-giving and affirming. At the same time they have challenged those practices and values that are not life-affirming, as in the case of Ndonga and her parish." Esther Mombo, "The Ordination of Women in Africa: An Historical Perspective," in *Women and Ordination in the Christian Churches: International Perspectives*, ed. Ian Jones, Kirsty Thorpe, and Janet Wootton (London: T & T Clark, 2008), 134-35.

4) Women cannot perform baptisms because they are physically weaker than men. The majority of the Christians of the region are Baptists who practise baptism by immersion. This view holds that women are not strong enough to hold and lift up those being baptised. (My response to them: Physical strength cannot be a criterion for serving God. Furthermore, this excuse is lame because some women are stronger than some men and churches have often ordained men who are old and infirm).

5) Women cannot go out after dark because it is unsafe, whereas it is often necessary to visit church members at night. (My response to them: This apparent concern for the safety of women is nothing but yet another excuse employed to deny leadership to women. Thank you for thinking about our safety, but instead of confining women to the house after dark, effort should be placed on making the society a safe place for women, children, and all vulnerable members of the society).

6) Women have their own department, the Women's Department, in the churches where they are given the freedom to do as they like. Men do not have Men's Department. Why are women so greedy? Why do they want to involve in the main church as well? (My response to them: Why should any freedom be *given* to women by men? Who gave men the authority? Freedom is a birthright. Will men to happy if the situation is reversed and men run their Men's Departments while women run the churches?).

The issues raised against women's ordination in North East India serve as a pointer to the context of this study. As will become self-evident in this study, the Baptist churches of North East India are dealing with issues that the Western churches faced during the 1960s and 70s. This necessitates a study approach that has to keep shifting between postmodern discussions and issues from a conservative perspective that Western readers might consider passé. The fact is that things which women in Western societies take for granted are unavailable to women in this region. Yet every attempt is made to challenge the Baptist churches in the region and others too to take big strides on issues of gender equality and community formation.

I believe that there are yet many other places around the world where women are being discriminated against in similar ways. The context may be different and the issues may be different, but all kinds of excuses are used for excluding women. These excuses range from theological expostulations to doctrinal statements to cultural/traditional practices. History informs us that almost every single "privilege" women enjoy today had to be fought for by women in the past. Whether it is the right to vote, or the right to equal pay, or the right to sit in Board rooms, or the right to play certain sports, women had to argue, initiate mass movements, and go to legal courts to get it. It has not been different with the Church. Women had to struggle to be included in the ministry of the Church whether it is to be part of decision-making, or to preach and teach, or to be ordained as priests.

Interweaving my cultural narrative with feminist narratives enabled me to appreciate the distinctiveness of my own community while at the same time it armed me to identify and offer critique of those aspects of my societal tradition that demean women. For instance, I understood matriliny was not the equivalent of egalitarianism.[45] Traditionally, women were regarded as the "jewel of the tribe" and "the lotus of the village pond,"[46] but they were also regarded as weak, useless, and without wisdom. Their property was regulated by their male relatives and they were expected to find fulfilment in serving the men. I understood that the name of the Supreme Being of my tribe is really *Tatara Rabuga*, a male sounding word with female attributes.[47] When Christianity came, this Creator God was forsaken and replaced by a name of Bengali and Sanskrit origin "Ishwar," which is transliterated "Isol" to suit the native tongue. Like many other Asian societies, my native language does not have masculine and feminine pronouns; the same pronoun is used for both males and females. The use of distinctive pronouns in English, from which the A·chik Bible and songs are translated, and the practice of addressing God as "Father" have become causes of a spiritual fissure in the community.

The spiritual rift is evident within the Christian community throughout the world. It is evident in the gender divide seen in the Church across geographical locations and denominational affiliations. Gender discrimination is a worldwide reality. Perhaps its presence is

45. Marlene Marak, "Matriliny and the Status of Women in the A·chik Society," in *No More Sorrow in God's Garden of Justice: Tribal Women Doing Theology*, Women Study Series 4, ed. Limatula Longkumer (Jorhat, Assam: Women Study Department, Eastern Theological College, 2007), 81-92.

46. Referring to A·chik women. Gabrielle Bertrand, *Secret Lands Where Women Reign* (London: Robert Hale Limited, 1958), 63-64.

47. Marlene Marak, "Tatara Rabuga: The Supreme Being of the A·chik People," in *Tribal Christian Theology: Methods and Sources for Constructing a Relevant Theology for the Indigenous People of North East India*, ed. Razouselie Lasetso and Yangkahao Vashum (Jorhat, Assam: Programme Coordination, 2007), 210-19.

felt more so in some places than in others, yet it appears to be always there. Except for some scattered pockets of women in a few nations, the vast majority of women continue to play second fiddle to their male counterparts both in the church and in society.[48] Ideally, the Church is the melting-pot of races, cultures, and genders. It is meant to be a community cutting across racial, cultural, and gender barriers (Gal 3:28). It is meant to practise communion, where the members literally and figuratively share in a loaf and drink from a cup. It is meant to communicate a message of salvation, of liberation from oppression and prejudice. However, when we look at the practice of the churches, the artificial gender wall remains sturdy as ever.

The issues facing women have been dealt with extensively in feminist literature. I do not intend to regurgitate what has already been stated and established in the immense body of feminist writings available today. However, I do intend to revisit some of the issues that are relevant to the discussion of my research, take the findings of those works and apply them to the context of worship.

Why Worship?

Worship is the heart of theology. The rites and rituals, the liturgy, the hymns and psalms, the prayers, the readings, the sermon, the icons, the architecture, the lights, the stained glass, everything about worship is littered with theological statements. The way I see it, worship is the arena of the litmus test of Christian theology and practice. It is on the crucible of church worship that our theological positions will be tested and tried, accepted and abandoned, as the case may be.

Worship is the space where one would expect to find the best of humanity because this is when our mind and spirits are directed towards God. One would expect that in the sacred space of worship human desire

48. Caroline Sweetman, ed., *Gender in the 21st Century*, Oxfam Focus on Gender (Oxford: Oxfam, 2000); Jacqueline Scott, Rosemary Crompton, and Clare Lyonette, eds., *Gender Inequalities in the 21st Century: New Barriers and Continuing Constraints* (Cheltenham: Edward Elgar Publishing, 2010); Manuela Barreto, Michelle K. Ryan, and Michael T. Schmitt, eds., *The Glass Ceiling in the 21st Century: Understanding Barriers to Gender Equality, Psychology of Women* (Washington, DC: American Psychological Association, 2009); Catherine Wessinger, ed., *Religious Institutions and Women's Leadership: New Roles Inside the Mainstream* (Columbia, SC: University of South Carolina, 1996); Cheryl A. Kirk-Duggan and Karen Jo Torjesen, eds., *Women and Christianity*, Women and Religion in the World (Santa Barbara, CA: ABC-CLIO, 2010).

for control and for dominating each other will cease. One would expect but not find. Worship has been corrupted by patriarchal practices of past generations and perpetuated by the present patriarchal generation.

The language of worship is androcentric—in hymns and psalms, and in prayers and sermons. It is peppered with male images. God is depicted in many ways as a male God by the use of male metaphors such as King, Lord, Shepherd. Ministers of the Church are linked to notions of exclusive male priesthood. The heroes most celebrated are male heroes who save the nation, win wars, are called by God, and who provide leadership. The ultimate prize for faithfulness is to be made "sons" of God. Most of the time, it appears as though women are incidental. Some say these are only metaphors pointing towards higher and greater truths. But metaphors are powerful things. They leave lasting impressions on the human psyche. The full implications of the impact upon both women and men who are buffeted continuously with notions of male superiority have been underplayed if not ignored entirely.

For women who are aware that women do not figure in the language of the liturgy, worship is an uncomfortable experience. Women have to pause at every metaphor, or phrase, or hymn to consider whether they are being counted. As Nancy A. Hardesty notes, women have been subconsciously translating in their heads for years.

> Every time we have heard the words man or men, we have mentally calculated whether or not we are included.
>
> For example, during the announcements at church we hear, "Men of the church are invited to a prayer breakfast next Saturday morning." Women rather quickly figure out that they are not invited. On the other hand, we hear the minister declare, "Rise up, O men of God, renew your commitment to God." This time women are not sure whether or not they are invited. Is this a Father's Day sermon? Or is the minister simply paraphrasing the hymn? And does the hymn include women?[49]

And that is just the tip of the iceberg. The metaphors about a male God, the male categories and images give the impression that men are superior to women. This impression is further strengthened by the presence of clergy that is comprised solely of males. Surely the perennial input of male language and imagery into the women members of the congregation is detrimental to their spiritual health and sense of self-worth.

---

49. Nancy A. Hardesty, *Inclusive Language in the Church* (Atlanta, GA: John Knox Press, 1987), 1.

The "malespeak" of the Church—language that is symbolically or metaphorically male, words and phrases that are male-oriented—effectively excludes women from the spiritual and religious experience. Malespeak keeps women from spiritual experience. What it does is to ignore women's spirituality and create a community where the sharing of power is unequal and unjust. Male-oriented language stands in the way of authentic communication that is necessary for a community of open commensality. As a result of distorted communication and denial of women's narrative, churches continue to pander to the outrageous concept that salvation of women is somehow dependent on male intervention. Barring women from ordained ministry is indicative of a theological position that women's salvation has to be brokered by males. The chauvinistic attitude arises from the nature of the "Saviour" who was incarnated as a male. Feminist theologians argue that the maleness of Christ is not theologically significant.[50] Of course, the idea that Jesus was incarnated as a male is based on misplaced priority. The point of the New Testament is that God became incarnate. God could have become incarnate as a female, for sex was not the priority of incarnation.[51]

An artistic presentation of Jesus Christ was made by Renée Cox who posed as Christ standing naked among twelve brown and black disciples to portray the Last Supper in a five-panel photographic montage called *Yo Mama's Last Supper* (1996).[52] This was exhibited at the Brooklyn Museum of Art in February-April 2001. In *Yo Mama's Last Supper*, Cox is naked while the twelve men are all clothed thereby heightening her nakedness and sex. The eyes of the men are averted and their bodies turned away from her, as though they were conspiring against her. This generated a controversy.[53] Cox was not only a black woman but she was revising traditional narrative about Jesus. Although the media focused on

50. However, this does not mean that Christ should be presented as an androgynous being. Cf. Eleanor McLaughlin, "Feminist Christologies: Re-Dressing the Tradition," in *Reconstructing the Christ Symbol: Essays in Feminist Christology*, ed. Maryanne Stevens (New York: Paulist Press, 1993), 118-49.

51. Joan Gibson, "Could Christ Have Been Born a Woman? A Medieval Debate," *Journal of Feminist Studies in Religion* 8/1 (1992): 65-82.

52. A helpful source, from which I have expanded, for the following discussion is Julie Clague, "Symbolism and the Power of Art: Female Representations of Christ Crucified," in *Bodies in Question: Gender, Religion, Text*, ed. Darlene Bird and Yvonne Sherwood (Aldershot: Ashgate Publishing House, 2005), 31-45.

53. Nicole R. Fleetwood, *Troubling Vision: Performance, Visuality, and Blackness* (Chicago: The University of Chicago Press, 2011), 106ff.

the nakedness of Cox/Christ, we can be sure that the opposition to Cox was not because she depicted Christ as naked. Christ has been depicted naked in many Renaissance paintings.[54] The reason for the "scandal" was because people could not imagine Christ as female, far less a black female. Another significant work is that of Serge Bramly and Bettina Rheims' *I.N.R.I.* This is retelling of the story of Jesus. It has a series of photographic tableaux of the life of Jesus in modern settings. Jesus is represented by people of different ages and races, and includes a young woman as Christ crucified.[55] This work evoked a scandal. Some other important Christa images include *Christa* by Edwina Sandys, *Crucified Woman* by Almuth Lutkenhaus-Lackey, *Crucifixion, Shoalhaven* by Arthur Boyd, *Christine on the Cross* by James M. Murphy, and *Bosnian Christa* by Margaret Argyle.[56]

The negative response to these works show the bias of patriarchal cultures in which Jesus can be safely depicted as Black, Chinese, Indian, or any other ethnic identity but not as female. The Christological doctrine of the maleness of Christ asserts that the ethnic identity of Jesus is incidental but that his sex is an ontological necessity. Thus, according to this lopsided doctrine, which goes back to Thomas Aquinas and is also found in Augustine, only the male can represent the fullness of human nature.[57] Marcella Althaus-Reid rightly comprehended that the female body, its sensuality regarded as indecent and offensive, is viewed to be

---

54. Leo Steinberg, *The Sexuality of Christ in Renaissance Art and in Modern Oblivion* (Chicago: University of Chicago Press, 1983).

55. Serge Bramly and Bettina Rheims, *I.N.R.I.* (New York: Monacelli Press, 1999).

56. A discussion of these Christa images is found in Clague, "Symbolism and the Power of Art," in *Bodies in Question*, ed. Bird and Sherwood, 31-45. Also of relevance idem, "The Christa: Symbolizing My Humanity and My Pain," *Feminist Theology* 14/1 (September 2005): 83-108; idem, "Divine Transgressions: The Female Christ-Form in Art," *Critical Quarterly* 47/3 (Autumn 2005): 47-63.

57. Aquinas, *Summa Theologica*, Part I, Q.92, 1 and 2; Q.99,2; Part 3, Supplement, Q.39, 1; Augustine, *De Trinitate* 7,7,10. Referred to in Rosemary Radford Ruether, *To Change the World: Christology and Cultural Criticism* (New York: Crossroad, 1988), 45; cf. idem, *Sexism and God-Talk: Toward a Feminist Theology* (Boston, MA: Beacon Press, 1983), chap. 5. A more positive assessment of Augustine is found in Genevieve Llyod, "Augustine and Aquinas," in *Feminist Theology: A Reader*, edited by Ann Loades (Louisville, KY: Westminster John Knox Press, 1990), 90-98.

contradictory to the divinity of Christ.[58] We can be certain the antidote for a male Christ is a female Christ—Christa.[59]

Most of the traditions of the churches have come from a dominant hegemony, consciously or unconsciously practised by the male members of the community, that causes women of the community to be nothing more than passive receivers. It is no surprise that women continue to experience themselves as aliens in a male Church. They have no language to tell their stories. They are victims of deception, imprisoned in gilded cages—some fancier than others, but that is about it. Thus worship has become a tool for driving a wedge between women and men, splitting them apart, and creating a spiritual fissure in the community of faith.

The Need for Storytelling in Worship

It is within the context of patriarchal impunity, particularly as seen in worship, that I will explore the possibilities of transformation that can be brought about through narrative communication. An underlying premise of this endeavour is that in order for gender reconciliation to take place, women need to have an oppositional/alternative discourse or counter hegemony in response to the existing structure of male hegemony. This is where storytelling comes in. We ought to seek avenues for women to tell their stories in worship. Women need spaces in worship to voice vague feelings, uncertainties, apprehensions, passions, dreams, and other experiences which would remain untold if not for the device of narratives. Incorporating narratives of women's experiences into worship could lead to fuller communication and heal female-male relationships.

Storytelling is straightforward. Anyone can tell stories. However, not all stories (noun) are good stories and neither are all acts of storytelling (verb) psychologically or socially helpful. Some stories instigate violence and mayhem, some stories endorse racism, some are sexist, and some are depraved. And people can tell stories to conceal facts, to intimidate others, to confuse people, to create enmity, and many other evil things. Obviously,

58. Marcella Althaus-Reid, *Indecent Theology: Theological Perversions in Sex, Gender and Politics* (London: Routledge, 2000). Also of relevance Lisa Isherwood and Mark D. Jordan, eds., *Dancing Theology in Fetish Boots: Essays in Honour of Marcella Althaus-Reid* (London: SCM Press, 2010).

59. Rita Nakashima Brock challenges the patriarchal and heroic images of Christ and proposes Christology based on the imagery of Christa/Community. Rita Nakashima Brock, *Journeys by Heart: A Christology of Erotic Power* (New York: Crossroad, 1988).

storytelling that can be applied for inclusiveness in worship needs to be guided by principles that are wholesome, by harnessing the positive potential of storytelling. I propose that the underpinning principle of storytelling for reconciliation be that of narrative communication. This is an interdisciplinary approach combining narrative theory and communication studies.

Ways and Means of Storytelling

Storytelling is usually understood as the oral narration of events. Indeed oral medium of storytelling is the basic form of narrative communication. However, storytelling is not confined to narration by word of mouth. From ancient times, people used images scratched and painted on cave walls and pottery to tell stories. Recent studies have shown that Stone Age cave painters used animation techniques similar to modern cartoon to create the illusion of movement and make the still images come to life.[60] As the flickering light of torches passed over the images, the onlookers would have felt like they were seeing live action; such as wild beasts charging across the cave walls or pouncing on prey.

Over the centuries people have used songs, riddles, poetry, quilting, painting, and other crafts to narrate their lives.[61] Storytellers, by whatever names they may be called, appear to be indispensable in every culture across the world to keep the community glued together, to respond to political and social changes. Bards of Celtic lands,[62] wandering minstrels, troubadours, trouveres, minnesingers, meistersingers, and jongleurs of

60. Bruce Bower, "Stone Age Art Gets Animated: Ancient Cave Paintings Depict Moving Animals," *Science News* 181/13 (June 30, 2012), 12, http://www.sciencenews.org/view/generic/ id/341206/description/Stone_Age_art_gets_animated (accessed July 22, 2018).

61. Albert Bates, *The Singer of Tales*, 2nd ed., Harvard Studies in Comparative Literature 24 (Cambridge, MA: Harvard University Press, 2003); Anne Pellowski, *The World of Storytelling: A Practical Guide to the Origins, Development, and Applications of Storytelling*, expanded and rev. ed. (New York: H. W. Wilson, 1990); Rob Parkinson, *Transforming Tales: How Stories Can Change People* (London: Jessica Kingsley Publishers, 2009), 143 ff.

62. K. W. Nicholls, *Gaelic and Gaelicized Ireland in the Middle Ages*, 2nd ed. (Dublin: Lilliput Press, 2003); Thomas McKean, "A Gaelic Songmaker's Response to an English-speaking Nation," *Oral Tradition* 7/1 (1992): 3-27, http://journal.oraltradition.org/files/articles/7i/4_mckean.pdf (accessed July 22, 2018); Sioned Davies, "Storytelling in Medieval Wales," *Oral Tradition* 7/2 (1992):231-57, http://journal.oraltradition.org/files/articles/7ii/4_davies.pdf (accessed July 22, 2018).

medieval Europe,[63] skalds of Scandinavia,[64] Griots and griottes (praise singers) of Western Africa,[65] ashiks of Turkey and elsewhere,[66] rawi qissas (narrator of legends/long poems) of Arabic culture,[67] Indian kathakars,[68] and others have used songs, poetry, music, and dance to tell stories. Women were part of the bardic traditions.[69] Kathak is performed by both women and men. Both griot (men) and griottes (women) function in Africa.

Tribal people have their own storytellers. Because tribal culture is very diverse, it is not possible to identify tribal storytellers with a name or designation. In some places, the storyteller is the priest. In other places, it is the oldest man or woman in the village. But very often it is the ordinary people. While there is a strong oral tradition of storytelling in the region, people have also employed music, dance, and song to

---

63. Helen L. Kaufmann, *The Little History of Music* (New York: Grosset & Dunlap, 1949); Jack Lindsay, *The Troubadours and their World of the Twelfth and Thirteenth Centuries* (London: Frederick Müller, 1976).

64. Ingrid De Geer, "Music," in *The Cambridge History of Scandinavia*, vol. 1, *Prehistory to 1520*, Cambridge History of Scandinavia 1, ed. Knut Helle (Cambridge: Cambridge University Press, 2003), 550-56; Birgit Sawyer and P. H. Sawyer, *Medieval Scandinavia: From Conversion to Reformation, Circa 800-1500*, Nordic Series 17 (Minneapolis, MN: University of Minnesota Press, 1993), 24-26.

65. Thomas A. Hale, *Griots and Griottes: Masters of Words and Music* (Bloomington, IN: Indiana University Press, 1998); Jan Jansen, *The Griot's Craft: An Essay on Oral Tradition and Diplomacy*, Forschungen zu Sprachen und Kulturen Afrikas 8 (Münster: Lit, 2000); Barbara G. Hoffman, *Griots at War: Conflict, Conciliation, and Caster in Mande* (Bloomington, IN: Indiana University Press, 2000).

66. Yildiray Erdener, *The Song Contest of Turkish Minstrels: Improvised Poetry Sung to Traditional Music*, Milman Parry Studies in Oral Tradition (New York: Garland Publishing, 1995).

67. Rob Parkinson, "Talking to the Rawi: An Encounter with a Traditional Teller of Tales in a Moroccan Market Place," (1999), http://www.imaginaryjourneys.co.uk/word_files/talkingtothe rawi.pdf (accessed July 22, 2018).

68. Sunil Sehgal, *Encyclopaedia of Hinduism (H-Q)*, vol. 3 (New Delhi: Sarup & Sons, 1999), 734-40.

69. Anne L. Klinck and Ann Marie Rasmussen, eds. *Medieval Woman's Song: Cross-Cultural Approaches* (Philadelphia, PA: University of Pennsylvania Press, 2002); Anne L. Klinck, ed., *An Anthology of Ancient and Medieval Women's Song* (New York: Palgrave Macmillan, 2004).

communicate traditional values and ancient stories.[70] Tribal songs range from songs of sorrow and lament to those of love and romance, from lullabies to martial songs, from verses and proverbs to nationalism and patriotism, and from short personal accounts to mythic epics. Singing, accompanied by music and dance, was a major means of communication in the tribal societies. As it was noted earlier, written tradition in the region is fairly new. Thus one could say that tribal songs (and crafts too) are the history book, the science text, and the theological discourse of tribal people. I am interested in looking for ways in which women can tap the potential of this ancient means of knowledge and communication and use the traditional women's songs as well as sing new songs of the soul to tell our stories.

Another medium of telling stories is the craft of quilting. The earliest quilting techniques date back to ancient Egypt. An ivory carving of thirty-fifth century BCE depicts a pharaoh draped in a quilted garment. Evidence of ancient appliqué dating back to 1900 BCE was found in the tomb of Princess Isimkheb. Ornamental quilts were produced in China during the Zhou dynasty around 770-221 BCE. A quilted carpet believed to have been made during 100 BCE was found in the tomb of a Scythian chieftain near Mongolia.[71] Every quilt, whether ancient or modern, tells a story or stories.[72]

During the 1800s, when slavery was prevalent in the United States, an informal organization known as the "underground railroad" helped slaves escape to the North and to Canada. The underground railroad was neither an underground tunnel nor a railroad but a network of safe houses, secret routes, transport, and network of sympathetic people to assist runaway slaves. During this time, women quilted to raise funds for the abolition of slavery. For this purpose they reworked and renamed existing patchwork patterns to fit the purpose of their quilting. A pattern

---

70. Cf. Soumen Sen, "Folk-Songs of the North-Eastern Hills: An Introduction," *Indian Literature* 30/4 (1987): 11-16; Abhik Gupta, comp., "Mizo (Hmar), Ao-Naga, Zo, Khasi and Darlong Folk-Songs," *Indian Literature* 30/4 (1987): 17-34; R. N. Mosahary, "Boro Folk-Songs: A Few Examples with their Contents," in *Essays on North-East India*, ed. Milton S. Sangma (Shillong: Deptt. of History, North-Eastern Hill University, 1994), 124-46.

71. Spike Gillespie, *Quilts around the World: The Story of Quilting from Alabama to Zimbabwe* (Minneapolis: Voyageur Press, 2010), 11.

72. For a discussion of quilts as texts see Judy Elsley, *Quilts as Text(iles): The Semiotics of Quilting*, Berkeley Insights in Linguistics and Semiotics 16 (New York: Peter Lang, 1996).

that was originally known as *Jobs Tears* was renamed the *Slave Chain*. Another pattern formerly known as *Jacob's Ladder* came to be called *The Underground Railroad* and also as *Wagon Tracks* or the *Trail of the Covered Wagon*.[73]

A quilt that tells a story is known as a story quilt. Harriet Powers, an African-American woman who was born as a slave in Athens, Georgia, in 1837, created extraordinary quilts using traditional appliqué techniques. Her quilts are records of Bible stories and events in her life. Harriet Powers probably made many quilts during her life, but only two of them, the *Bible Quilt 1886* and the *Pictorial Quilt 1898*, are known have survived.[74]

Then there is the story about an eleven-year-old slave girl named Clara who worked as a seamstress and who used scraps of fabric to stitch the escape route of the "underground railroad" into her quilt. Her secret map sewn in a quilt showed the slaves the path to freedom. Clara's story is based on true events in the history of black Americans.[75]

There is the heartwarming story of a homemade quilt that preserved the memories of Patricia Palocco's immigrant Russian family. Patricia Palocco tells the story of her own family. Her great grandmother, Anna, immigrated to America in the early twentieth century, when she was a young girl. Anna's mother decided to make a quilt to help her family remember home. And so, using a bundle of old clothes, Anna's dress and her babushka (traditional Russian headscarf worn by women), Uncle Vladimir's shirt, Aunt Havalah's nightdress, and an apron of Aunt Natasha, Anna's mother made the "keeping quilt." For about a hundred years the quilt was passed down from mother to daughter. Five successive

---

73. Elaine Hedges, "Quilts and Women's Culture," in *In Her Own Image: Women Working in the Arts*, ed. Elaine Hedges and Ingrid Wendt (New York, NY: The Feminist Press, 1980), 16-17; Glenna Matthews, " 'Little Women' Who Helped Make This Great War," in *Why the Civil War Came*, ed. Gabor S. Boritt (Oxford: Oxford University Press, 1996) 43.

74. Mary E. Lyons, *Stitching Stars: The Story Quilts of Harriet Powers* (New York: Scribner's, 1993); Gladys-Marie Fry, *Stitched from the Soul: Slave Quilts from the Ante-Bellum South* (New York: Dutton, 1990). A discussion of these story quilts is found in Susan Meeske, "Quilt Me a Story," in *Ways of Knowing: Literature and the Intellectual Life of Children*, ed. Kay E. Vandergrift (Lanham, MD: Scarecrow Press, 1996), 31-50, https://1yearofquilts.weebly.com/uploads/3/6/0/0/3600737/quilt_me_a_story_by_susan_meeke.pdf (accessed July 22, 2018).

75. Deborah Hopkinson, *Sweet Clara and the Freedom Quilt* (New York: Knopf, 1993).

generations were connected by the "keeping quilt" which served as the tablecloth during the Sabbat and on birthdays, the chuppah in weddings (wedding canopy), wrapper for newborn babies, and leg-warmer for Anna in her old age. The "keeping quilt" is now at the Mazza Museum in Findley, Ohio.[76]

Yet another is the story of Miss Anderson, an elementary schoolteacher of the 1950s. When the books and supplies in the classrooms and library were destroyed by a flood caused by burst pipes, she decides to make a quilt from the handkerchiefs her students had given her and sell it in order to buy replacements books and supplies.[77]

Although both men and women engage in quilting, women seem to have a greater hand in quilting stories than men.[78] This is partly because traditionally the activities of weaving, quilting, embroidery, and needlework have been recognized as women's domestic activity in many cultures. Women snatched the small, often hemmed in, spaces to give vent to their creativity. They used the texture, colour, shape, and patterns of quilts to communicate their stories visually.

In the late 20th and 21st centuries, women have turned to quilt and other artistic productions to tell their stories and communicate their hopes and aspirations. For instance, in 1990 The Clothesline Project was started in Cape Cod, Massachusetts. In this programme, women victims of violence or abuse designed T-shirts and hung them on a clothesline to raise awareness of violence against women.[79] A similar project was also initiated by the Baptist Union of Great Britain. Another programme is that of the Manchester Mosaic. The Manchester Mosaic is a patchwork

---

76. Patricia Polacco, *The Keeping Quilt* (New York: Simon, 1988).

77. Carol Crane, *The Handkerchief Quilt* (Ann Arbor, MI: Sleeping Bear Press, 2010).

78. Rozsika Parker, *The Subversive Stitch: Embroidery and the Making of the Feminine* (London: Women's Press, 1984); Linda Otto Lipsett, *Remember Me: Women and Their Friendship Quilts* (San Francisco: Quilt Digest Press, 1985); Pat Ferrero, Elaine Hedges, and Julie Silber, *Hearts and Hands: The Influence of Women and Quilts on American Society* (San Francisco: Quilt Digest Press, 1987); Patricia J. Cooper and Norma Bradley Allen, *The Quilters: Women and Domestic Art – An Oral History* (New York: Doubleday, 1989); Elizabeth Wayland Barber, *Women's Work: The First 20,000 Years – Women, Cloth, and Society in Early Times* (New York: W. W. Norton, 1994); Marla R. Miller, *The Needle's Eye: Women and Work in the Age of Revolution* (Amherst, MA: University of Massachusetts Press, 2006).

79. The website of The Clothesline Project is http://www.theclotheslineproject.org/.

wall-hanging made by survivors of domestic violence and each panel tells the personal story of a woman who has suffered abuse or violence.[80] In 2004, an international network of women's organizations called the World March of Women constructed a global "solidarity quilt," in line with a global charter for humanity, to represent their vision of a new world of equality, peace, freedom, solidarity, and justice.[81]

Now patch quilting is relatively unknown in North East India. Although there are some textile works that are close to quilting, the textile work of the region is dominated by the art of weaving. The question I have is whether tribal women can make use of weaving to tell their stories and deal with contemporary issues like women elsewhere have used the quilt as a means of expression.

In terms of world history, the development of weaving technology goes back to Upper Palaeolithic period. Impressions of woven textiles, baskets, and nets on fragments of fired and unfired clay were recovered from Dolní Věstonice and Pavlov in Upper Palaeolithic Moravia, Czech Republic. This earliest archaeological evidence of textile technology comes from the period between ca. 29,000 and 24,000 BCE.[82] The bone Venus figurine from Lespugue, in France, and a statuette discovered at Gagarino, in Russia, both believed to be Gravettian (ca. 20,000 BCE), are seen wearing "string skirts."[83] The earliest evidence of a complete garment, a linen shirt, was found in a first dynasty (ca. 3000 BCE) Egyptian tomb at Tarkhan, in Egypt.[84] In the ancient world, weaving was closely associated with the Goddesses. The Goddesses wove and wore garments

80. Women's Co-ordinating Group, Churches Together in England, *What is This Place?* 55, https://www.cte.org.uk/Publisher/File.aspx?ID=138037 (accessed July 23, 2018).

81. Catherine Eschle and Bice Maiguashca, *Making Feminist Sense of the Global Justice Movement* (Lanham, MD: Rowman & Littlefield Publishers, 2010), 132.

82. O. Soffer, J. M. Adovasio, and D. C. Hyland, "The 'Venus' Figurines: Textiles, Basketry, Gender, and Status in the Upper Paleolithic," *Current Anthropology* 41/4 (August-October 2000), 511-37, https://www.researchgate.net/publication/235979951_The_Venus_Figurines_Textiles_Basketry_Gender_and_Status_in_the_Upper_Paleolithic (accessed July 23, 2018).

83. E. J. W. Barber, *Prehistoric Textiles: The Development of Cloth in the Neolithic and Bronze Ages with Special Reference to the Aegean* (Princeton, NJ: Princeton University Press, 1991), 255-57; idem, *Women's Work: The First 20,000 Years*, 56.

84. Barber, *Prehistoric Textiles*, 146-47.

and encouraged women to weave. Isis is said to have introduced the craft to the community.[85]

In the modern world, manual weaving has become very rare. The craft has been swept aside by mechanical textile industry. But weaving survives in North East India where it is an indispensable aspect of the socio-economic and cultural life of the tribal peoples. It is estimated that there are approximately 1.3 million handlooms and 1.4 million weavers in North East India.[86] In this region, women are responsible for the production of woven cloth, which differs from the rest of India where males play the major role in weaving.[87] In most tribal cultures it is taboo for men to take part in spinning and weaving. Thus it is women who have both preserved and continued tribal heritage by weaving their stories into every work and weft. Their designs, and the stories they tell, have become deeply rooted in tribal consciousness. By their weaving activity, women have become the custodians of tribal cultures.

North East India is composed of eight states: Arunachal Pradesh, Assam, Manipur, Meghalaya, Mizoram, Nagaland, Sikkim, and Tripura.[88] There are over 300 language groups, mostly tribal communities, in the region. Each tribe has its own weaving tradition and distinctive patterns. They are too numerous to be identified and listed here.[89]

Weaving is done not only for producing clothes to keep the body warm or for decency but they have social and religious significance. Tribal stories and legends about weaving make it clear that weaving is rooted in religious belief—because it is an art given by God or Gods. In Meitei tradition of Manipur, it is said that weaving is an imitation of the process of creation. During the sacred dance of creation, Maiba and Maibi, the male and female messengers of God, depicts creation by simulating the

---

85. Hilda Ellis Davidson, *Roles of the Northern Goddess* (London: Routledge, 1998), 91-99.

86. Paritosh Chandra Dutta and Ram Krishna Mandal, *Globalisation, Growth and Inequality in North East India: Economic Disparity* (Delhi: Kalpaz Publications, 2011), 42. This estimate did not include the state of Sikkim as it is a late inclusion to the region.

87. Ch. Victoria Devi, "Exploring the Lives of Manipur's Women Weavers," *Indian Journal of Gender Studies* 19/1 (February 2012): 31-55.

88. A good introductory book to North East India with photographs, though excluding Sikkim: Aglaja Stirn and Peter Van Ham, *The Seven Sisters of India: Tribal Worlds between Tibet and Burma* (Munich: Prestel, 2001).

89. See Appendix C: "Woven Creations of North East India" for a concise list of woven garments produced in the region.

sound of spinning and weaving. The dance of cosmic creation and the art of textile weaving are believed to have been taught by Leismbi, the God of handicrafts.[90]

According to an Adi-Ashing folktale of Arunachal Pradesh, the spider went to Doinyi-Polo where Doinyi-Irni, the daughter of the Sun and the Moon, dwelt. The spider secretly watched Doinyi-Irni weaving cloth and learnt the technique. She stole the loom and ran away. Thereafter, she taught other spiders and human beings the art of weaving.[91]

The Mishmi tribe of Arunachal Pradesh tell of a time when people went naked, for they did not know how to weave cloth. Then the God Matai taught the art of weaving to a girl named Hambrumai. This girl wove wonderful designs. Sitting by the river side, she observed the waves and ripples made by water. She wove ripples on cloth. Laying down in the forest and looking up at trees in the forest, she saw the interlacing patterns of their branches, and she wove them on cloth. Thus she wove the patterns of nature on cloth, be it ripples of water, tree branches, bamboo leaves, ferns, or flowers. When she put on her woven cloth, she looked like she was wearing nature. One day, Hairum, the porcupine, saw Hambrumai's cloth and he was tempted by its richness. He came to her cave to steal it. The cave entrance was small and as Hairum tried to force his way in, he dislodged a rock. The rock fell by the riverside and crushed Hambrumai to death. The rock also broke her loom and some of the broken pieces fell into the river and were carried by it from the hills down to the plains. Wherever people found a piece of her loom, they learnt to weave. Her designs turned into butterflies and those patterns can still be seen on their wings. After she died, the Gods Bronmai and Mollo, who had themselves learnt the skill of weaving from Hambrumai, made the sword of her loom into a diamond pattern. This is why the Mishmis have many diamond patterns on their cloth.[92]

Weaving is also connected to tribal social customs. Tribal dress protocol is largely based upon the symbolic significance of the woven

90. Indianetzone.com, Manipur, https://textiles.indianetzone.com/1/manipur.htm (accessed June 19:2019). For more on traditional weaving of Manipur, see Amita Pandya and Joymati Thoudam, "Handloom Weaving, the Traditional Craft of Manipur," *Indian Journal of Traditional Knowledge* 9/4 (October 2010): 651-55.

91. Sujata Miri, *A Book of Paintings – On Themes from the Hills of Northeast India* (New Delhi: Mittal Publications, 2005), 27.

92. Verrier Elwin, *The Art of Northeast Frontier of India* (Shillong: Northeast Frontier Agency, 1959), 24-25.

clothes. In the past, different clothes were designated for different people and different purposes. Some could be worn only by priests, some were meant only for those who have given feast of merit, and some were for great warriors (such as those who have been successful headhunters). Every piece of cloth is designated for a specific purpose—to be worn for ceremonial occasions, for dancing, for courting, for marriage, or for ordinary use.

For instance, a shawl called *Meyni* was originally meant to be used only by the Konyak king, who is called *Ang*, and by the elders.[93] In modern days, with the introduction of democracy and the waning of *Ang* system, these norms are no longer strictly followed. At the same time, people still respect the Angs and their children are called princes and princesses.[94] Among the Meiteis of Manipur, the long coat called *Saijounba* was prepared for the most trusted courtiers of the king. Another cloth called *Namthang-khut-hut* was to be used only by women of the royal family. In Mizoram and Manipur, the *Thangsuo Puon* of the Hmars and the *Thangou Puon* of the Paiteis are to be worn only by those who have killed their enemies in war or tribal feud. For the Tangkhul Nagas of Manipur, the shawl denoting a headhunter's status as called *Thang-gang*.[95] Similar shawls originally meant for headhunters and those who have given feasts of merit are also found among other tribes.

Although tribals have long given up headhunting and their social life and composition have changed greatly, some of the traditional distinctions remain. The shawl of headhunters and rich people of the olden days are worn today by those who have high standing in society and those who have distinguished themselves by high level of education, wealth, and good reputation. Some of these practices need to be critically evaluated as classism is inappropriate in the modern world.

Among the Thai Phakes of Assam, girls who have not attained puberty wear a long white cloth called *Fafek*. Those who have attained

93. Indira Gandhi National Centre for the Arts (IGNCA), "Textiles of Nagaland," http://ignca.gov.in/divisionss/janapada-sampada/northeastern-regional-centre/textiles-of-nagaland/ (accessed June 19, 2019).

94. Cf. S. Eunice, "The Status of Konyak Women Under Ang System," in *No More Sorrow in God's Garden of Justice: Tribal Women Doing Theology*, Women Study Series 4, ed. Limatula Longkumer (Jorhat, Assam: Women Study Department, Eastern Theological College, 2007), 75-80.

95. Indira Gandhi National Centre for the Arts (IGNCA), "Textiles of Manipur," http://ignca.gov.in/divisionss/janapada-sampada/northeastern-regional-centre/textiles-of-manipur/ (acccessed June 19, 2019).

puberty wear a stripped cloth called *Fa Nangwait*. However, those who have unmarried elder sisters will not wear *Fa Nangwait* even after reaching puberty in order to show that she is not prepared for marriage.[96] According to the customary practice of some tribes, the younger siblings are not ready for marriage till their older brothers or sisters are married.

There are stories associated with the designs and patterns of tribal woven gear. A Chinese fence design representing the multi-coloured Jana flower is found on the Hrusso bags of Arunachal Pradesh. According to Hrusso lore, there was a great Tibetan king who had the power to talk to the Sun. He had a huge palace that could accommodate the Sun. This king was born every day with the rising of the Sun, and he went down every day with its setting. At some point, the king left the earth and the Jana flower is said to have emerged in his place. The Sherdukpens of Arunachal Pradesh also have many stories associated with their designs. One is of a girl who falls in love with a snake, who was actually a handsome youth in disguise. When she was weaving, the snake coiled himself on her lap. She copied the markings on his form and produced a very exquisite piece of cloth.[97]

In literary studies, weaving is seen as analogous to storytelling. The process of weaving is comparable to the spoken word, whereas the woven cloth is similar to the written text.[98] Now the overview of weaving in tribal cultures of North East India is meant to show not only that there are rich traditions of weaving in the region, replete with symbolic meanings, but also that this tradition can be tapped as a resource for telling the stories of women. How may weaving be enacted in worship? What stories should we retell? What new stories should we weave?

The purpose of storytelling in worship is to recover women's voices that have been silenced by centuries of living in a world created by men and communicating like men. As Tani E. Barlow states, "Civilization is a tissue of ideological forms obscuring and justifying domination, and men's

---

96. Indira Gandhi National Centre for the Arts (IGNCA), "Textiles of Assam," http://ignca.gov.in/divisionss/janapada-sampada/northeastern-regional-centre/textiles-of-assam/ (accessed June 20, 2019).

97. Indira Gandhi National Centre for the Arts (IGNCA), "Textiles of Arunachal Pradesh," http://ignca.gov.in/divisionss/janapada-sampada/northeastern-regional-centre/textiles-of-arunachal-pradesh/ (accessed June 20, 2019).

98. Kathryn Sullivan Kruger, *Weaving the Word: The Metaphorics of Weaving and Female Textual Production* (Selinsgrove, PA: Susquehanna University Press, 2001).

domination of women is the origin of this system."[99] The Church has been complicit in the oppression of women and has also actively silenced and subjugated women. Storytelling aimed at recovering women's voices involves the "language" by which women may communicate.[100] By this I do not mean to suggest that men's and women's brain are different as assumed by some people like the author of *Men are from Mars, Women are from Venus*.[101] The difference we observe between men and women are nothing more than gender roles that we have been socialised to adopt as acceptable for our gender although they are harmful and oppressive for women. What I mean by "women's language" is the use of women's symbolic universe derived from their experiences. "Recovery" connotes the fact that women's voices were silenced but not eliminated, for throughout the ages women have used the spaces in their mundane activities to express their deepest self. Therefore, recovering women's voice entails not only written or spoken words but unspoken thoughts and unclear feelings. It requires the telling of traditional stories from women's perspective, the reading and telling of stories found in women's songs, poetry, and arts and crafts, and recounting the experiences of women. In the context of worship, it means the application of these forms in the liturgical space of the service of worship. Yet, recovery of women voice is not the only goal. There is a need to progress, to create new memories and enact new rituals, in order to broaden the scope of worship and make it truly a foundation for truthful communication, authentic communion, and community without bias.

Research Method and Structure

The use of story and storytelling as a methodology of research is seen in the propaedeutic theory of storytelling of John Navone and Thomas Cooper,[102] in the study of narrative and religious experience by the

99. Tani E. Barlow, *The Question of Women in Chinese Feminism* (Durham: Duke University Press, 2004), 315.

100. For feminist views on "language," "speech," and "silence," Deborah Cameron, ed., *The Feminist Critique of Language: A Reader*, 2nd ed. (London: Routledge, 1998).

101. John Gray, *Men are from Mars, Women are from Venus: A Practical Guide for Improving Communication and Getting What You Want in Your Relationships* (New York, NY: HarperCollins, 1992).

102. John Navone and Thomas Cooper. *Tellers of the Word* (New York: Le Jacq Publishing, 1981).

authors of *After Eden*,[103] in various expressions of story theology,[104] and in emerging African narrative theology.[105] Thus there is a wealth of resources available for me to base my work on. The novelty of my research is the eclectic method that I adopt, combining narrative and Christian communication theories. It also stands out as a work that addresses a specific context—Baptist churches among the tribal societies of North East India. I draw insights from feminist analysis and women's perspectives from various cultures to support my position.

In the second chapter, I define the method of research. To state it briefly, the method is "narrative communication." The terms "narrative" and "communication" are interrelated. In fact, putting them together appears to be superfluous. Narrative is communication and communication is narrative. However, in this research, I narrow the scope of narrative down to story and storytelling and limit communication to its definition as communion and community. Thus "narrative communication" as the term is applied in the research is *storytelling that activates communication, creates community, and establishes communion*. At every instance of storytelling, the questions asked over and over is, "Does this story, and its telling, create community? Does it advance communion?" We want stories that improve communication, sustain communion, and build up the community. Storytelling has to be applied to build community consciousness. That aspect becomes most evident in the function of stories to foster community and communion between diverse groups.

In the third chapter, I highlight the discrimination against women in the present day practices of worship. The preponderance of androcentric and sexist language, the literal interpretation of the Bible in order to silence and subjugate women, and the constructions of the divine as male all point to a structure that has institutionalised discrimination against women, a kind of apartheid in the Church. Some of the

103. Mary Stewart Van Leeuwen, et al., *After Eden: Facing the Challenge of Gender Reconciliation* (Grand Rapids, MI: William B. Eerdmans, 1993), esp. chap. 7.

104. C. S. Song, *The Believing Heart: An Invitation to Story Theology* (Minneapolis, MN: Fortress Press, 1999); John Dominic Crossan, *The Dark Interval: Towards a Theology of Story* (Sonoma, CA: Polridge Press, 1988); Terrence W. Tilley, *Story Theology* (Wilmington, DE: Michael Glazier, 1985).

105. Joseph Healey and Donald Sybertz, *Towards an African Narrative Theology*, Faith and Culture Series (Maryknoll, NY: Orbis Books, 1996).

patriarchal practices arise from tribal culture but others are a heritage from the West.

In chapter four, I expound on the notion of community as koinonia. Trinitarian koinonia, in particular, offers a magnificent model for modelling the community as people who are diverse yet united just like the mystical union of the Godhead. I also look at the tribal experience of spiritual renewal to underline the implication of the presence of the Holy Spirit in the community. During revivals, brought about by the Holy Spirit, women were prominent in the Christian movement. Viewed from that perspective, equality in the life and ministry of the Church is a testimony to the dynamism of the presence of the Holy Spirit.

In the fifth chapter, I explore the notion of Church as an inclusive community of believers. Tribal communitarian life provides a positive frame of reference by which the Church as an inclusive community may be conceptualized. Additionally, I study the Lord's Supper and baptism in order to bring out their significance for evolving inclusive community.

In chapter six, I attempt to develop models of worship based on storytelling. Such models must be based on an understanding that human stories are valid stories for narration in the sacred space of worship. When human stories are told, worship becomes a moment for crossing boundaries. Storytelling opens up the lines of communication between diverse people. The church becomes a place where there is respect and love for one another. The stranger becomes a friend. Rituals, which are empty without human stories are revitalized. Freed from the shackles of words that oppress and demean, hymns and songs fulfil their potential.

Women (and men) become co-authors with God when they weave their stories together with God's stories. When human stories and divine narratives meet, we create new possibilities for relating with God and with one another. Storytelling models require that we weave human stories into our prayers, sermons, rituals, and other aspects of worship and liturgy. It also would involve retelling biblical narratives from new perspectives that recover women's memory. Tribal communities can also add their own ways of storytelling, using signs and symbols that are meaningful to their culture and history.

This book is a search for the soul of worship, for worship beyond sexual differentiation. Its purpose is not to replace the male hegemony with a female hegemony. The purpose is to bring balance and equilibrium by allowing the language-less and voice-less to speak and enter into dialogue with the ones who have these. The final theological rationale is simple—worship in spirit and in truth (John 4:23) is when it is an experience of the community, when women and men worship God as one. Authentic worship will come about when our stories embrace the story of God who recognizes no gender boundaries.

2

THE METHOD

NARRATIVE COMMUNICATION AND COMMUNITY FORMATION

Communication Theory and Narrative Approach

The words "narrative" and "communication" are interrelated. Narratives are essentially communication and most aspects of communication can be categorized as narratives. An explication of a narrative communication method is pyramidal—starting from broad definitions and gradually whittling down to more focussed articulation of narrative communication theories.

What is Communication?

Communication is one of those human activities that everyone recognises but few can define satisfactorily. The diversity and complexity of communication is evident in the range of human activities that come within its purview. It encompasses those means of communication such as radio, television, movies, newspapers, web blogs, and the telephone. It includes expressions through music, art, dance, and drama. And it embraces human activities such as conversations between people, lectures, online chats and games, SMS exchanges, and social rituals such as handshakes, smiles and frowns, waving good-bye, and kneeling for prayers. It is no surprise therefore that there is no scholarly consensus about the definition of communication. In this study we will simply give a general definition of communication from which we will move forward to a Christian understanding of communication.

Gregory J. Shepherd notes that the earliest known use of the word "communication" is in 1382 to refer to the conveying of material things such as letters. From 1690, the word came to mean the exchange of ideas. A postmodern conception of communication, according to Shepherd, has to be based on its premodern understanding:

> The word [communication] arose from the Latin *munia*, meaning gifts or services. Gifts, of course are not conveyed, but conferred; services are not relayed, but rendered. Communication, then, might be understood in this premechanistic sense as an activity of mutual giving and servicing. (The prefix, "co-" implies mutuality; the suffix, "-tion" denotes an act or process.) Importantly, both voluntarism, or self-sense, and obligation, or other-directedness are implied in this conception. After all, a gift must be freely conferred for it to be a gift; there is no sense to be had from a notion of non-voluntary giving. I cannot steal from you and call it a gift. At the same time, services, to count as services, must be rendered unto others.[1]

In further explication of the word, Shepherd says,

> Communication is *the simultaneous experience of self and other*.... Communication is the experience of transcending one's (current) self, overcoming one's (current) self, to become more than what one was through connection with another.[2]

Thus the word communication implies a form of interrelatedness, a sharing of ideas and exchange of services or resources. Dictionaries give its meaning as "imparting," "conveying," "exchanging of ideas," "knowledge," by means of speech, writing or signs. Scholars have been unable to establish a single definition. In fact, the general view is that multiple definitions are necessary because it means different things in different contexts.

Many attempts at definitions of communication are based on a linear concept of the communication process in which communication is considered as a delivery process where the sender delivers his/her

1. Gregory J. Shepherd, "Community as the Interpersonal Accomplishment of Communication," in *Communication and Community*, ed. Gregory J. Shepherd and Eric W. Rothenbuhler (Mahwah, NJ: Lawrence Erlbaum, 2001), 30.

2. Gregory J. Shepherd, "Communication as Transcendence," in *Communication as ... : Perspectives on Theory*, ed. Gregory J. Shepherd, Jeffrey St. John, and Ted Striphas (Thousand Oaks, CA: Sage Publications, 2006), 22. See also Shepherd, "Community as the Interpersonal Accomplishment of Communication," in *Communication and Community*, ed. Shepherd and Rothenbuhler, 32.

messages to a receiver. In fact, however, communication must be seen in a more dialogical way as an ongoing process in human society. It requires people to engage or be involved in some kind of activity or conversation in language common to both the communicator and the reader or the audience which is targeted.[3]

Robert S. Fortner defines communication as "a dynamic, symbolic process by which people in dialogue construct the meanings and share the emotions through which they understand value, and live in society, and by which they both behave and justify their behavior."[4] Significantly, Denis McQuail says that "communication presupposes an appropriate mutual co-orientation and a measure of understanding. It also necessitates some sharing of time and experience for we live in the same social and physical world..."[5] He also says that communication implies change and that it can be both the cause and effect of changes in social structure, which is the ordered relationship between the actors.[6]

Christian Communication

By and large, a faith based theoretical approach towards communication has not been expounded fully. Christian communicators depend heavily on theories developed from non-theistic perspectives. Some attempts have been made towards the study and practice of communication from a Christian perspective such as communication for evangelism,[7]

3. erin daina underwood and Lawrence R. Frey categorise the two general conceptual perspectives of communication scholars towards the study of community as: (a) the transmission perspective (linear-flow, instrumental, or information-exchange perspective); and (b) the constitutive perspective (ritual, cultural, or meaning based perspective). erin daina underwood and Lawrence R. Frey, "Communication and Community: Clarifying the Connection Across the Communication Community," in *Communication Yearbook 31* (New York, NY: International Communication Association/Lawrence Erlbaum, 2008), 370-419. eBook Taylor & Francis e-Library, 2009, 377-80.

4. Robert S. Fortner, *Communication, Media, and Identity* (Lanham: Rowman and Littlefield Publishers, 2007), 18.

5. Denis McQuail, *Communication*, Aspects of Modern Sociology, Social Processes. 2nd ed. (London and New York: Longman, 1984), 3.

6. McQuail, *Communication*, 12.

7. John Holdsworth, *Communication and the Gospel* (London: Darton, Longman and Todd, 2003).

communication ethics,[8] and cross cultural evangelism.[9] These efforts provide essential substance for constructing a Christian theory of communication.

A theistic view of communication is founded on an understanding of God's self-revelation through creation. Further, the creation of humans in God's image signifies that human beings are communicators, because they are the likeness of a communicating God. To flesh out some of those themes and related issues, it is necessary to look at the basic tenets of feminist interpretation of the creation narratives.

Generally, feminist interpretations of the Gen 1-3 narrative have focused on elements that have been missed or neglected in traditional interpretations. Some base their analysis on the findings of Source Critics who aver that Gen 1-3 has two differing accounts of creation. According to this view, Gen 1:1-2:4a comes from the Priestly (P) source and Gen 2:4b-3:24 arises from the Yahwist (J) source. The P document is the latest source, originating from the fifth and sixth centuries BCE, whereas the J document is the earliest, dating back to the tenth century BCE. Based on the fact that the tradition behind Gen 2:4b-3:24 is older than Gen 1:1-2:4a, Helen Schüngel-Straumann says:

> This historical placing of the origin of both sources means that all traditional arguments which are based on a chronological sequence of Genesis 1 and 2-3 are rendered worthless. Nobody can possibly regard the so-called story of the Fall or the Garden as a further explanation of Genesis 1, as has been the case in the past.[10]

For Schottroff too, making a distinction between the two creation narratives is seen as a significant move for feminist interpretation. She believes that in the creation story in Gen 1 men and women were created

8. Clifford G. Christians et al., *Media Ethics: Cases and Moral Reasoning*, 7th ed. (New York: Allyn & Bacon, 2004).

9. David J. Hasselgrave, *Communicating Christ Cross-Culturally: An Introduction to Missionary Communication* (Grand Rapids, MI: Zondervan Publishing House, 1978).

10. Helen Schüngel-Straumann, "On the Creation of Man and Woman in Genesis 1-3: The History and Reception of the Texts Reconsidered," in *A Feminist Companion to Genesis*, ed. Athalya Brenner (Sheffield: Sheffield Academic Press, 1997), 54. However, the Documentary Hypothesis has its critics. See Ilana Pardes, *Countertraditions in the Bible: A Feminist Approach* (Cambridge, MA: Harvard University Press, 1992), 3-4. There is also a basic problem to regarding one text as being less sexist that the other—it does not do away with the problem of having to deal with the sexist text.

equally in the image of God but wrong ideas were inferred from it in its history of interpretation. Even Paul interpreted it wrongly. According to Schottroff, the misinterpretation arises from a conflation of two creation narratives and a biased exegesis of the Fall.[11]

Much attention is also given to the development of *ha 'adam*. Feminist scholars argue that in Gen 1 to 2:22, it is wrong to translate *ha 'adam* as a male man or as a proper name. Although it can also be understood singularly, the use of the definite article *ha* with *'adam* appears to denote a collective noun. This is further supported by the plural "let them have dominion" in Gen 1:26.[12]

Many feminist scholars are interested in the second creation narrative, which itself has two distinct parts (Gen 2:4b-25 and Gen 3). In her discussion of Gen 2-3, Phyllis Trible argues convincingly that since *ha'adam* is a generic term, it is not man that was created in Gen 2:7 but an "earth creature."[13] Others have similarly resorted to alternative words based on rhetorical and literary analysis of the text. Mary Phil Korsak translates *adam* by "groundling."[14] Early on E. A. Speiser pointed to the play on words in the designation *adam* and wrote: "The closest approach in English to the juxtaposition of the Hebrew nouns before us might be 'earthling: earth.'"[15] However, Korsak rejects "earthling" and explains: "'Earthling' would have been a happy solution but 'earth' was needed for *'ares* and, if one plays this vocabulary game, one English word can only correspond to one Hebrew word, not two."[16] Mieke Bal sees *adam* as

11. Luise Schottroff, "The Creation Narrative: Genesis 1:1-2.4a," in *A Feminist Companion to Genesis*, ed. Athalya Brenner (Sheffield: Sheffield Academic Press, 1997), 36.

12. Leonard J. Swidler, *Biblical Affirmations of Woman* (Philadelphia, PA: The Westminster Press, 1979), 75-76. Against *ha'adam* as a generic term see Susan S. Lanser, "(Feminist) Criticism in the Garden: Inferring Genesis 2-3," *Semeia* 41 (1988): 67-84.

13. Phyllis Trible, *God and the Rhetoric of Sexuality*, Overtures to Biblical Theology (Philadelphia: Fortress Press, 1978), 75ff.

14. Mary Phil Korsak, *At The Start... Genesis Made New: A Translation of the Hebrew Text* (Louvain: Leuvense Schrijversaktie, 1992), 3.

15. E. A. Speiser, *Genesis*, The Anchor Bible (Garden City, NY: Doubleday, 1964), 16.

16. Mary Phil Korsak, "Genesis: A New Look," in *A Feminist Companion to Genesis*, ed. Athalya Brenner (Sheffield: Sheffield Academic Press, 1997), 48. Korsak also notes that André Chouraqui uses *glébeux* and *glèbe* for *'adam*.

a "character-to-be," "the unfinished state" of an earth creature who she calls clod.[17]

In an early work, Phyllis Trible argued that it should be interpreted as androgynous. Later she modified that interpretation because "androgyny assumes sexuality, whereas the earth creature is sexually undifferentiated."[18] She points to the play on words in *'adam* (earth creature) and *ha'adama* (the earth): "While uniting creature and soil, it also separates them. *'Adam* is not yet; *ha 'adama* already is."[19] She concludes about *ha 'adam*:

> ...with the definite article *ha-* preceding the common noun *'adam*, This work of art is neither a particular person nor the typical person but rather the creature from the earth (*ha 'adama*)—the earth creature. The very words that differentiate creature from soil indicate similarity. Thus, through the pleasure of language Yahweh God makes distinctions that result not in opposition but in harmony. A punned separation articulates unity.[20]

According to Trible, sexuality is created only in Gen 2:22-23 when God performs surgery on Adam.

> Only after surgery does this creature, for the first time, identify itself as male. Utilizing a pun on the Hebrew word for woman, *'issa*, the earth creature refers to itself by the specific term for man as male, *'is*.[21]

---

17. Mieke Bal, "Sexuality, Sin, and Sorrow: The Emergence of the Female Character," in *Women, Gender, Religion: A Reader*, ed. Elizabeth A. Castelli and Rosamond C. Rodman (New York, NY: PALGRAVE, 2001), 157. Originally published as idem, "Sexuality, Sin and Sorrow: The Emergence of the Female Character (A Reading of Genesis 1-3)," *Poetics Today* 6 (1985): 21-42, and also appears in idem, "Sexuality, Sin, and Sorrow: The Emergence of the Female Character," in *Lethal Love*, 104-30.

18. Trible, *God and the Rhetoric of Sexuality*, 141 n17.

19. Trible, *God and the Rhetoric of Sexuality*, 77.

20. Trible, *God and the Rhetoric of Sexuality*, 80.

21. Trible, *God and the Rhetoric of Sexuality*, 98. So Swidler, *Biblical Affirmations of Woman*, 77. Contra Helen Schüngel-Straumann, "Genesis 1-11: The Primordial History," in *Feminist Biblical Interpretation: A Compendium of Critical Commentary on the Books of the Bible and Related Literature*, ed. Luise Schottroff and Marie-Theres Wacker (Grand Rapids, MI: Wm B. Eerdmans, 2012), 11. Schüngel-Straumann believes that gender differentiation occurs at the centre of Gen 1:27.

Trible argues against the interpretation that because the woman is taken from the earth creature, it implies the subordination of women by men.[22] When *ha 'adam* is taken from *ha 'adama* it did not mean that *ha 'adam* was subordinate to the earth. Similarly, when *'issa* is taken from *'is* it does not mean derivation or subordination but differentiation. Trible also asserts the verb "call" does not mean naming; the man is not establishing dominion over the woman by naming her.

> *'Issa* itself is not a name; it is a common noun, not a proper noun. It designates gender; it does not specify person. Moreover, this word appears in the story before the earth creature "calls" it: the narrator reports that "Yahweh God built the rib which he took from the earth creature into a woman [*'issa*] (2:22).[23]

Mieke Bal echoes the same approach at this point:

> Of both words *'is* and *'issa*, which in this text indicate sexually differentiated being, *'issa*, woman, appears first. It is *'issa* who changes the meaning of *ha 'adam* from earth-being into earth-man. In this semiotic sense, the woman was first formed, then the man (*contra* "Paul").[24]

The naming of the woman takes place in Gen 3:20. Trible sees this as the consequence of the breakdown of equality between male and female.

> It chillingly echoes the vocabulary of domination over the animals.... Now, in effect, the man reduces the woman to the status of an animal by calling her a name. The act itself faults the man for corrupting one flesh of equality, for asserting power over the woman, and for violating the companion corresponding to him. Ironically, he names her *Eve*, a Hebrew word that resembles in sound the word *life*, even as he robs her life in its created fullness.[25]

---

22. The point also is that the woman was not created out of the man as is usually assumed. For instance Gerda Lerner says (*The Creation of Patriarchy* [Oxford: Oxford University Press, 1986], 181): "The creation of Woman out of Man's body is here taken to impose a very special interpretation upon this event —woman was created as part of man, therefore Man must cleave to her, choosing her above all other kinship relationships, and they shall be one flesh." Lerner's argument fails when it is understood that prior to the creation of sexuality in Gen 2:22-23, *ha 'adam* referred to the undifferentiated "earth creature."

23. Trible, *God and the Rhetoric of Sexuality*, 99-102, quote is from 100. On the contrary, others think that the passage is about naming and domination. E.g. Lerner, *Creation of Patriarchy*, 181-82.

24. Bal, "Sexuality, Sin, and Sorrow: The Emergence of the Female Character," in *Women, Gender, Religion: A Reader*, ed. Castelli and Rodman, 159.

25. Trible, *God and the Rhetoric of Sexuality*, 133.

According to Bal:

> The word *ha 'adam* had been used by the narrator as self-evident; the serpent was only indicated by its generic name; *'is* and *'issa* were nouns used for sexual differentiation. Eve, *hawwa*, a name that means, as her mate says, "the mother of all living," is solemnly applied to *'issa* in view of her sexual and social role. The name is, like many biblical names, motivated and hence descriptive. The man, in giving her this particular name, determines the character further: Eve is imprisoned in motherhood. There is no more question of the sexual attraction celebrated in 2:23-24.[26]

Korsak translates Gen 3:20 thus:

> The groundling called his woman's name Life (Eve)
> for she is the mother of all that lives[27]

In a midrash of Gen 2-3, Korsak renders this section thus:

> The Groundling gave the woman a name
> 'Life-Giver'[28]

Feminist discussion of Gen 1-3 is deeply fragmented.[29] Trible's views have been challenged.[30] As Beauvoir says, "each argument suggests its opposite."[31] And Bal talks about "the relative arbitrariness of all readings."[32] Anyway, my purpose in this section is not to present all the views but simply to highlight some of the ways in which feminist scholars have sought to reinterpret biblical text, especially the creation narratives.

The theology behind the creation narratives lies at the core of gender relations, and that is a basic issue for this research. But the

---

26. Bal, "Sexuality, Sin, and Sorrow," in *Women, Gender, Religion: A Reader*, ed. Castelli and Rodman , 170.

27. Korsak, *At The Start*, 11.

28. Mary Phil Korsak, "...et Genetrix," in *Genesis: A Feminist Companion to the Bible (Second Series)*, ed. Athalya Brenner (Sheffield: Sheffield Academic Press, 1998), 26.

29. A helpful discussion of various scholars is found in Alice Ogden Bellis, *Helpmates, Harlots, and Heroes: Women's Stories in the Hebrew Bible*, 2nd ed. (Louisville, KY: Westminster John Knox Press, 2007), 37-56.

30. E.g. John J. Collins, *The Bible after Babel: Historical Criticism in a Postmodern Age* (Grand Rapids, MI: Wm B. Eerdmans, 2005), 86-96. Pardes (*Countertraditions in the Bible*, 24) says, "In Trible's hands the Bible almost turns into a feminist manifesto, where every detail suspiciously ends up supporting woman's liberation."

31. Simone de Beauvoir, *The Second Sex* (New York: Vintage Books, 1953), xxxix.

32. Bal, *Lethal Love*, 1.

immediate reason for the discussion above is because a theistic theory of communication arises from God's self-revelation in creation. Christian communication is grounded on the biblical theology of God as a creator who communicates and creates community. Matthias Scharer and Bernd Jochen Hilberath refer to God as a communicative being:

> It is not, in the first place, God's self-revelation in history that shows God to be the communicative being; this is already manifested by God's self-revelation as creator.[33]

God is a communicator. In the accounts of creation in Genesis 1 and 2, God is said to have created the heavens and the earth, and all living things that dwell therein. And Gen 1:27 states that God created humankind/earth creature/groundling/clod in God's image.[34] The issue of creation of humankind in the *imago Dei* has been a topic of serious theological debate and extensive studies that are impossible to even begin to summarise here.[35] The basic premise of *imago Dei* is that in certain ways human beings correspond to God. That correspondence is seen in human ability to be "creators" like God. In the Genesis account God brings all the birds and animals to the human to see what it would call them (Gen 2:19-20).[36] Then the human contributes to the creation activity of God by using the power of speech/communication to name to creatures. Gerda Lerner says that life is created by divine word, divine breath, "but human naming gives meaning and order."[37] Earlier God

---

33. Matthias Scharer and Bernd Jochen Hilberath, *The Practice of Communicative Theology: An Introduction to a New Theological Culture* (New York, NY: Crossroad Publishing, 2008), 65.

34. These are words that feminist scholars use for *ha 'adam*; discussed above.

35. There is a wide variety of perspectives on *Imago Dei*: Stanley J. Grenz, *The Social Goal and the Relational Self: A Trinitarian Theology of the Imago Dei* (Louisville, KY: Westminster John Knox Press, 2001); Susan Windley-Daoust, *The Redeemed Image of God: Embodied Relations to the Unknown Divine* (Lanham, MD: University Press of America, 2002); J. Richard Middleton, *The Liberating Image: The* Imago Dei *in Genesis 1* (Grand Rapids, MI: Brazos Press, 2005); J. P. Moreland, *The Recalcitrant* Imago Dei*: Human Persons and the Failure of Naturalism* (London: SCM Press, 2009); Dominic Robinson, *Understanding the* "Imago Dei"*: The Thought of Barth, von Balthasar and Moltmann* (Surrey: Ashgate, 2011).

36. Till the point of differentiation that takes place at Gen 2:23, *adam* is the earth creature or groundling. Korsak (*At the Start*, 3-7) uses the neuter "it" to refer to the groundling, and I think she is correct to do so because until sexual differentiation is made *adam* is neither male nor female.

37. Lerner, *Creation of Patriarchy*, 181.

had used the power of speech to call forth the creation into existence. Now the human imitates God and employs the power of word to give it shape and identity.

According to the Hebrew Scriptures, God continued to communicate with human beings through the prophets and the written word. It is not without reason that the Jews call themselves "the people of the Book." Jewish self-understanding, their religious and cultural identity, have been constructed over thousands of years around the Torah and other Jewish Scriptures.[38] Hebrews 1:1-2 gives a succinct summary of God's communication over the ages: "Long ago God spoke to our ancestors in many and various ways by the prophets, but in these last days God has spoken to us by a Son…."[39] In other words, God communicated through the prophets and eventually chose to communicate through the son, Jesus Christ. The full implication of the phrase "God has spoken to us by a son" comes to the fore when we connect speech with creation. God's speaking to us through a son is beautifully expressed in the Prologue of John's Gospel (John 1:1-18).

Besides the concept of an ever communicating God and the power of speech/word, a theory of Christian communication must include an interpretation of the purpose of communicating in the light of the creation accounts, and the implications of the Fall of humanity,[40] the significance of the life, death, and resurrection of Jesus Christ, and the presence of the Holy Spirit as an agent of communication between God and humanity.

Calling attention to the current state of affairs in Christian communication studies, Fortner insists that communication theory informed by Christianity would be based on the theological assumption that God created human beings. Since the ability to communicate is an intrinsic characteristic of the human condition, one ought to assume that God must have a purpose in creating humankind with the ability

38. Jeffrey Rubin-Dorsky and Shelley Fisher Fishkin, *People of the Book: Thirty Scholars Reflect on their Jewish Identity* (Madison, WI: The University of Wisconsin Press, 1996); Moshe Halbertal, *People of the Book: Canon, Meaning, and Authority* (Cambridge, MA: Harvard University Press, 1997). Some Baptists and some other protestant denominations also regard themselves of "people of the Book."

39. Unless indicated otherwise, all Bible quotations are from the New Revised Standard Version (NRSV).

40. The designation of "the Fall" for Gen 3 has been challenged as the text itself does not have the word "fall" or "sin." Carol Meyers, *Discovering Eve: Ancient Israelite Women in Context* (New York: Oxford University Press, 1988), 76-77.

to communicate. Taking his theological clue from the Genesis accounts of creation, Fortner maintains,

> As with other aspects of God's creation, communication, too (or God's expectations of it), must have been "good." God's creation of this aspect of human-ness was meant for good: for relationships, to demonstrate compassion, to mete out justice, to share knowledge, to achieve peace, and thus to assist others (care for one's neighbour), to spread the message of God's love—and salvation—to the world, and so on.[41]

Based on Fortner's line of reasoning, a key question for a Christian theory of communication is: What is God's design for communication? Or, with what expectations did God provide the ability to communicate to humankind? By looking back at the creation account, and interpreting communication through it, it is possible to understand communication as establishing relationship between God and humans, between humans and other humans, and with the wider creation.

Next, a Christian theory of communication must be informed by the theological assumptions found in the biblical account of the Fall. The narrative of the Fall is in itself a powerful narrative. Without a doubt, this narrative, which is foundational for both Christian and Jewish faiths, has a lot to answer for. It has been used over the centuries to put a leash on women's freedom and keep them submissive to men. The dynamics of religious narrative that have such a devastating impact on a whole section of humanity need to be scrutinized minutely. But the focus at this point is on extracting theological insights from the narrative of the Fall in order to evince a Christian theory of communication.

Appreciating the fact that the Fall story is a narrative that is retrospectively describing how life is, the story is to be read as an account with profound theological connotations. The simplest and most direct way of speaking about the ramifications of the Fall in terms of communication theory is to say that the original purpose of communication was subverted in the Fall. On this matter, Fortner says that a "communication dysfunction" occurred in the Garden.[42] The serpent used communication as a means of deception and when God came seeking Adam, inviting him and Eve to admit their mistake, and get back into relationship, they refused to do so.

Following the Eden episode, God, desiring communion, commonness and community with creation, kept up the effort to bring humans

41. Fortner, *Communication, Media, and Identity*, chap 2 and especially 36.
42. Fortner, *Communication, Media, and Identity*, 36.

into relationship with their Creator and with each other, and in time sent God's son to communicate with creation in a "fully human" form (John 1:14 cf. Heb 1:1-2). God's expectations for communication have not been realised because they too have been affected by the Fall. Consequently, although human life revolves around communication activities, we fail to communicate more often than we realise and we use communication to hurt, mislead, manipulate, subjugate, and violate. The task of Christian communication, then, is to continue God's effort to build relationship, creating and nurturing faith despite rejection and despite the propensity for failure.

A Christian paradigm for continuing to struggle for healthier, fuller, and balanced communication is found in the life and ministry, and death and resurrection of Jesus Christ. Among many aspects of the life and teaching of Jesus, his proclamation of the Nazareth Manifesto (Luke 4:16-18) is noteworthy. Communication models that emulate the ethics of Christ's ministerial declaration focus on restoring relationship to those who have been relegated to the fringes of society, giving voice to those who have been silenced, and bringing back the beauty of sight to those who face the tyranny of censorship. Furthermore, Christ's kenosis, manifested through ministering to all, especially to the poor and downtrodden of society such as women, children, lepers, and sinners, is a basis for Christian communication from the grassroots.

Christian communicators, as followers of Christ, have to act in love and strive towards liberation of all humanity. Throughout the narratives of his life and ministry Jesus consistently appears as the liberator to those enslaved by religion, political force, societal constraint, racial discrimination, gender distinction, economic status, and physical or psychological disability. The Church is charged to perform similar ministry in the world as the embodiment and communicator of freedom. For Dietrich Bonhoeffer Christ and the Church are inseparable. The Church is usually regarded as the community of Jesus, but for Bonhoeffer the Church is "Christ existing as community."[43] The Church can accomplish its purpose of continuing and embodying Christ by establishing

43. "Christ is the corporate person of the Christian community of faith.... The community of faith is God's final revelation as 'Christ existing as community,' ordained for the end of the world until the return of Christ." Dietrich Bonhoeffer, *Act and Being: Transcendental Philosophy and Ontology in Systematic Theology*, Deitrich Bonhoeffer Works 2, trans. H. Martin Rumscheidt (Minneapolis, MN: Fortress Press, 2009), 111-12.

commonness and solidarity in place of divisions and bridging the gulf between the rich and poor.

To help the Church achieve that task, the presence and power of the Holy Spirit has been given. This means that the Christian communicator is never alone in fulfilling the purpose of communication. The Holy Spirit, the Advocate, is there to erase the confusion of Babel and usher in clarity and understanding of a Pentecost, which is essentially the restoration of broken communication.[44] Significantly, just as the Spirit "blows where it wills" (John 3:8), likewise the flow of communication cannot be artificially contrived by human intelligence alone. There will always be mysterious elements in any communication process, because the Holy Spirit is the agent of communication between God and humanity. The primary task of the Holy Spirit, the Advocate, is to teach us *everything* (John 14:26) and guide us into *all* the truth (John 16:13). This objective is not achieved through a single act but continues over time in human history. So while we may not know the entire truth of God's purpose, we may be certain that our powerful ally, the Spirit, is leading us in the right direction so long as we hear and respond to the blowing of the Spirit.

Communication is a gift of God to humanity. To be truly human is to be in communication with others and with God. It is an abrogation of the image of God in humans when communication is denied or manipulated to maintain systems of oppression and injustice. Appropriately, the Church has to distance itself from the hierarchical structures and powers and reconnect with the poor and marginalised. Thus, the Good News to the poor proceeds from a reconciliation that establishes the dignity of all peoples, nations, groups, communities and cultures. The versatile and pluriform characteristic of God's creation demonstrates that communication must support and develop diverse cultures and ways of life while still enabling communication between them. We could say then, communication is initiated by God to serve a divine purpose.

Biblical accounts make it clear that God is not an individualistic God dwelling in isolation. God exists in community as three Persons in One.[45] We, who are created in the image of God, are by our very nature, meant to live in community. Furthermore, God is constantly communicating with

44. World Association for Christian Communication, *Statements on Communication by World Association for Christian Communication*, rev. ed. (London: WACC, 1995), 5.

45. Russ Parker, *Healing Wounded History: Reconciling Peoples and Healing Places* (London: Darton, Longman and Todd Ltd, 2001), 157.

the creation in order to live in koinonia, in community, with creation. To live in community and to communicate mean essentially the same thing.

The statement on communication issued by the World Association for Christian Communication (WACC) defines Christian communication as liberative and creating community.

> We cannot communicate with people whom we regard as "inferior," whose basic worth as humans we do not respect.... Genuine communication presupposes the recognition that all human beings are of equal worth. The more explicit equality becomes in human interaction, the more easily communication occurs.[46]

Therefore the Christian task in communication is the promotion of human dignity, reconciliation, and establishing community.

What Is a Narrative?

Within the broad spectrum of communication theory and practice, a fully-fledged discipline on its own, is the study of narrative. Obviously, we have placed narrative within the context of communication because we would like to see how narrative fulfils the purpose (God's expectations) of communication. We turn now to this specific dimension of the communication phenomenon.

Very simply the meaning of the word narrative is a spoken or written presentation of events.

> Our encounter with reality produces a meaningful and understandable flow of experience. What we experience is a consequence of the action of our organizing schemes on the components of our involvement with the world. Narrative is the fundamental scheme for linking individual human actions and events into interrelated aspects of an understandable composite.[47]

Generally speaking, scholars conform to this or similar definitions of narrative and contend that narratives are characterised by a sequence of events that take place in time, whereas non-narratives are single frames

46. WACC, *Statements on Communication*, 8.

47. Donald E. Polkinghorne, *Narrative Knowing and the Human Sciences* (Albany, NY: State University of New York, 1988), 13. Further see Rick Altman, *A Theory of Narrative* (New York: Columbia University Press, 2008), 1-27; Brian Richardson, *Narrative Dynamics: Essays on Time, Plot, Closure, and Frames* (Columbus: Ohio State University, 2002).

in time without any sequence, such as pictures.[48] Most narrative theorists require two or more events for there to be a narrative. Some of them insist that those events must be causally related. Against this overwhelming opinion of the majority, H. Porter Abbott voices the view of a few who regard a single event as sufficient grounds for a narrative when he says, "narrative is *the representation of an event or a series of events*."[49] Whatever the case may be, a definition that has parameters, though generally accepted, inhibits the possible spectacular range of meanings. Roland Barthes, writing in 1966, gave a comprehensive definition of narrative:

> The narratives of the world are numberless. Narrative is first and foremost a prodigious variety of genres, themselves distributed amongst different substances—as though any material were fit to receive man's [sic] stories. Able to be carried by articulated language, spoken or written, fixed or moving images, gestures, and the ordered mixture of all these substances; narrative is present in myth, legend, fable, tale, novella, epic, history, tragedy, drama, comedy, mime, painting (think of Carpaccio's *Saint Ursula*), stained-glass windows, cinema, comics, news items, conversation. Moreover, under this almost infinite diversity of forms, narrative is present in every age, in every place, in every society; it begins with the very history of mankind [sic] and there nowhere is nor has been a people without narrative. All classes, all human groups, have their narratives, enjoyment of which is very often shared by men [sic] with different even opposing, cultural backgrounds. Caring nothing for the division between good and bad literature, narrative is international, transhistorical, transcultural: it is simply there, like life itself.[50]

The same passage from Barthes is cited by Abbott in his definition of narrative. Yet surprisingly, taking his cue from literature on psychology, he contends that narrative capability in humans begins when they are three or four years old when they learn to follow a noun with a verb.[51]

It is not clear what Abbott would say about the communication that passes between a newborn infant and her mother. What is to be said of the infant's narrative expressed in her bawling, her smiles, and her gurgling? They could mean "I am hungry," "I am wet and very uncomfortable," "Pick

---

48. Arthur Asa Berger, *Narratives: in Popular Culture, Media and Everyday Life* (London: Sage Publications, 1997), 4-7.

49. H. Porter Abbott, *The Cambridge Introduction to Narrative* (Cambridge: Cambridge University Press, 2002), 12. Emphasis in the original.

50. Roland Barthes, "Introduction to the Structural Analysis of Narratives" in *A Barthes Reader*, ed. Susan Sontag (New York: Hill and Wang, 1982), 251-52.

51. Abbott, *Cambridge Introduction to Narrative*, 2. Contra Belinda Buckley, *Children's Communication Skills: From Birth to Five Years* (London: Routledge, 2003).

me up,""Your heart-beat is soothing," or any number of things. Having said that, Abbott's definition is significant in that it includes fixed and silent objects as communicating events of narrative. Following his lead, we can therefore incorporate non-sequential paintings and photographs, and hoardings and posters within the ambit of narratives.

The saying, "a picture speaks a thousand words" is not drivel. On June 1972, Huỳnh Công Út (Nick Út) took a photograph that compelled Americans to take notice of the horrors of the Vietnam War. It showed a nine year old Vietnamese girl, her clothes seared from her body by a napalm bomb, screaming and running down a road. In the background is her burning village murky with black smoke.[52] On June 5, 1989, several photographers captured images of a lone man facing down a column of tanks on the Changan Avenue to the south of Tiananmen Square. The unknown protestor became known as the "Tank Man." One photo of the Tank Man taken by Jeff Widener and smuggled out of China became the symbol of democratic resistance to the tyranny of the government of China.[53] In March 1993, Kevin Carter took a photo of a severely emaciated little Sudanese girl, head slumped to the ground, crawling to a food centre. A vulture stands on the ground nearby as though waiting for her to die so it can devour her flesh. This photograph brought the tragedy of civil war, drought, and famine in Africa to the world's attention.[54] One frame of an incident, caught in a split second, and printed in newspapers or flashed on TV could tell a story more convincingly and evoke emotions with greater intensity than a book of a thousand pages.

Furthermore, considering the fact that our understanding of the "other" will always be limited, it is necessary to keep the definition broad and open, particularly to the marginalized because it is the marginal narrative

---

52. Denise Chong, *The Girl in the Picture: The Story of Kim Phuc, the Photograph, and the Vietnam War* (New York: Viking, 2000).

53. Joseph Cummins, *The World's Bloodiest History: Massacre, Genocide, and the Scars they Left on Civilization* (Beverly, MA: Fair Winds Press, 2010), 269; Simon Sebag Montefiore, *One Hundred and One World Heroes: Great Men and Women for an Unheroic Age* (London: Quercus, 2007), 316.

54. John Taylor, *Body Horror: Photojournalism, Catastrophe and War* (Manchester: Manchester University Press, 1998), 135. Barbie Zelizer, *About to Die: How News Images Move the Public* (Oxford: Oxford University Press, 2010), 166-70. Many more references to photos of war, disaster, grief, tragedy, and murder are found in these works. Further see Robert Hariman and John Louis Lucaites, *No Caption Needed: Iconic Photographs, Public Culture, and Liberal Democracy* (Chicago: The University of Chicago Press, 2007).

that remains the strangest. The images we see and the text we read and hear, whether in sequence or not, are received and interpreted upon the grid of our culture, experience, and moral and religious sense. It stands to reason then that those of us who have not experienced blindness will not know how the blind-from-birth perceive colours. The fact that we do not know how the blind communicate is not reason enough to assume that there is no narrative of the blind with regard to colour as a phenomenon or geometric distance. One must assume that wherever communication is taking place, in any form, there is narrative to be found.

Finally, narrative breeds narrative. In other words, we are able to use our imagination to create narratives around narratives, instinctively employing previous "stories" we have experienced to interpret present data. Our world of meaning is derived from our social matrix, arising out of commonly accepted signs, in language, gestures, or even attitudes. Valentin N. Vološinov/Mikhail M. Bakhtin's analysis, in 1926, of a word, "well," exchanged between two people is a good illustration of how utterance is saturated in social dynamics, that is, in shared experiences and extraverbal contexts.

> Two people are sitting in a room. They are both silent. Then one of them says, "Well!" [tak! an expletive in Russian, meaning "so" or "well"] the other does not respond.
>
> For us, as outsiders, this entire "conversation" is utterly incomprehensible. Taken in isolation, the utterance "Well!" is empty and unintelligible....
>
> What is it we lack, then? We lack the "extraverbal context" that made the word *well* a meaningful locution for the listener. This *extraverbal context* of the utterance is comprised of three factors: (1) the *common spatial purview* of the interlocutors (the unity of the visible—in this case, the room, a window, and so on), (2) *the interlocutors' common knowledge and understanding of the situation*, and (3) *their common evaluation* of that situation.
>
> At the time the colloquy took place, both interlocutors *looked up* at the window and *saw* that it had begun to snow; *both knew* that it was already May and that it was high time for spring to come; finally, *both* were *sick and tired* of the protracted winter—*they were both looking forward* to spring and *both were bitterly disappointed* by the late snowfall. On this "jointly seen" (snowflakes outside the window), "jointly known" (the time of the year—May), and "unanimously evaluated" (winter wearied of, spring looked forward to)—on all this the utterance *directly depends*, all this is seized in its actual, living import—is its very sustenance. And yet all this remains without verbal specification or articulation. The snowflakes remain outside the window; the date, on the page

of a calendar; the evaluation, in the psyche of the speaker; and nevertheless, all this is assumed in the word *well*.[55]

Taking our clue from this particular parable, we can say that narrative is often bound to specific social locations, to the multitude of languages which Bakhtin calls "heteroglossia."[56] A consequence of this understanding is that narrative cannot and should not be pinned down to compartments and categories, not even to narrative genres, but should be regarded as influenced by the shifting terrain of our social environment.

Narrative Theory

The beginning of narrative theory is traced to the works of Aristotle who in his *Poetics*, written about 330 BCE, discussed Greek poetry of his time, including a discussion on tragedy which is also a form of poetry. His analysis of the elements of tragedy—plot, character, thought and diction, mimesis and diegesis—continues to be relevant for narrative analysis today.[57] Other landmarks in the study of narrative theory are Vladimir Propp's *Morphology of the Folktale*, which isolated the components of Russian folktales thereby revealing the structure of narratives,[58] Seymour Chatman's *Story and Discourse*, which synthesized previous major studies on narratology and expounded a communication model of narrative analysis,[59] and Mieke Bal's *Narratology: Introduction to the Theory of*

55. V. N. Vološinov, "Discourse in Life and Discourse in Art (Concerning Sociological Poetics)," in *Freudianism: A Critical Sketch*, trans. I. R. Titunik and ed. with Neal H. Bruss (Bloomington and Indianapolis: Indiana University Press, 1987), 99. Some believe that the books attributed to Vološinov (and Pavel N. Medvedev) are believed by some to have been written by Bakhtin himself, hence I use both names. All emphases are in the original.

56. M. A. R. Habib, *Modern Literary Criticism and Theory: A History* (Malden, MA; Oxford, 2008), 22.

57. David Depew and John Durham Peters, "Community and Communication: The Conceptual Background," in *Communication and Community*, ed. Gregory J. Shepherd and Eric W. Rothenbuhler (Mahwah, NJ: Lawrence Erlbaum, 2001), 3-21.

58. Vladimir Propp, *Morphology of the Folktale*, 2nd ed., trans. Laurence Scott (Austin, TX: University of Texas Press, 1968).

59. Seymour Chatman, *Story and Discourse: Narrative Structure in Fiction and Film* (Ithaca, NY: Cornell University Press, 1978).

Narratives, which identified three layers found in narratives: stories, texts, and fabulas.[60]

A relatively new development in the study of narratives is the relation of narratives to ideology and culture. Feminist scholars examine the place of feminist narrative within a patriarchal culture[61] and Christian feminist writers seek to read the "silences" in the biblical canon and call attention to its patriarchal origins.[62] Kwok Pui-lan proposes oral hermeneutics for Asian women, insisting that those societies in Asia and Africa that have oral culture need to interpret the Bible orally.[63] However, "orality" should not be limited to oral communication but may also be "narrative text." Furthermore, text that is valid for women ought to be differentiated from the traditional text that defined women as peripheral to history. Feminist scholarship is critical of the fact that social scientific knowledge and communication studies are traditionally based on men's experiences that legitimize and perpetuate the secondary status of women. In order to include women's narrative, feminist scholars posit a redefinition of texts, events, and ideas. Thus they search for women's experiences of life in non-traditional texts such as "diaries, letters, and gossip of ordinary women."[64]

Importance of Narratives

Humans are compulsive storytellers, *homo narrans*, ceaselessly narrating. The most basic and among the earliest remembered experiences of communication we have in life is narratives. Most children grow up listening to lullabies, moving on to songs and nursery rhymes, advancing to fairy tales and comics, and then to movies, theatre, novels and other stories.

---

60. Mieke Bal, *Narratology: Introduction to the Theory of Narratives*, trans. C. van Boheemen (Toronto: University of Toronto Press, 1985).

61. For instance, Rachel Blau DuPlessis, *Writing beyond the Ending: Narrative Strategies of Twentieth-Century Women Writers* (Bloomington: Indiana University Press, 1985).

62. Elisabeth Schüssler Fiorenza, *In Memory of Her: A Feminist Theological Reconstruction of Christian Origins* (London: SCM Press, 1983).

63. Kwok Pui-lan, *Discovering the Bible in the Non Biblical World* (Maryknoll: Orbis Books, 1995).

64. Kathryn Cirksena and Lisa Cuklanz, "Male is to Female As ___ Is to ___: A Guided Tour of Five Feminist Frameworks for Communication Studies," in *Women Making Meaning: New Feminist Directions in Communication*, ed. Lana F. Rakow (New York & London: Routledge, 1992), 38-40.

In the traditional societies of the indigenous tribes of North East India, most children do not have experiences of listening to bedtime stories as that is not part of their culture. Their experience of storytelling is different. Tribal people do sing traditional lullabies to children to put them to sleep. And in the modern tribal society children learn English nursery rhymes and read fairy tales when they start attending school.

In traditional tribal communities, the storytellers are usually the older folks telling stories by the fireside or beneath the trees to the younger generation. It is around the kitchen fire at night that stories are often told not just to entertain the children but to transmit their understanding of the meaning of life. As a tradition, stories of their myths, legendary heroes, creation and migration are passed down by word of mouth from generation to generation. Stories are also told or sung in the formal, ritual setting of their feasts, festivals and ceremonies. Village institutions, such as the bachelors' dormitory, are often considered to be the main place where the village elders tell stories of war and valour, legends and myths, to the younger generations. These storytelling settings show that among the indigenous tribes of North East India, storytelling is usually not directed to the individual but to the ears of the community. What is most apparent is that storytelling is a universal experience across cultures and geographical distances. Since narratives pervade human life so extensively, we ought to consider our lives as woven on an endless chain of narratives, in a complex tapestry, one linked to the other, impacting our lives, affecting the choices we make, and determining how we relate to others.

The words "narrative," "narration," and "to narrate," etc. are derived from the Latin words *gnarus* ("having knowledge or experience of"), *narrare* ("relate," "tell," "tell about"), and *narratus* ("narrative," story"), and goes back to proto-Indo-European root *gno* ("knowledge"). The Greek word γνώριμος ("knowable," "known") has the same root. This etymological explanation captures the two sides of narrative: knowing and telling. In other words, narrative is a mechanism for getting knowledge as well as conveying it. When we talk of the study of narrative, we are talking about the study of the ways humans experience and understand the world and how they express that knowledge to others. So stories describe human knowledge regarding experience and action, and stories also help us to make sense of experience and to make meaning in our lives.[65] Telling of experience as a story helps to form or shape our identity and helps us to know who we are.

The narrative form of communication is the primary way through which humans organise their experiences into temporally meaningful episodes.[66] Thus we can see that narrative as a form of communication is important because it furnishes or provides us with both a method for learning about the world, people, and events and a way to tell others about what we hear and learn.

Narrative Communication and Community Formation

There can be no doubt that there is an explicit connection between communication and community. Communication makes relationship possible and relationship builds up community. If communication creates community, we may also deduce that the loss of community is, in some ways, related to a loss of communication or misuse of communication.

Community, Communion, and Communication

Human beings are social beings and live with others in a society or a community. The words "community," "communion," and "communication" share the same etymological root. They all derive from the Latin word *communis* (*com*, "together," "common," *munis*, "bound," "under obligation").[67] *Communitas* is the noun form of the adjective *communis*. *Communitas* and *communis* carry a sense of what is "common." "Common" (Greek κοινός) is what "belongs to more than one, to many or to everyone." "*Munis*" of *communis* is itself derived from *munia* or *munus* ("gift," "service,"

65. Elizabeth McIsaac Bruce, "Narrative Inquiry: A Spiritual and Liberating Approach to Research," *Religious Education* 103/3 (May-June 2008): 323.

66. Even more specifically on communication as storytelling see Eric E. Peterson and Kristin M. Langellier, "Communication as Storytelling," in *Communication as ... : Perspectives on Theory*, ed., Gregory J. Shepherd, Jeffrey St. John, and Ted Striphas (Thousand Oaks, CA: Sage Publications, 2006), 123-31.

67. Cezar M. Ornatowski, "Rhetoric and the (Re)Constitution of Collective Identity: The Example of Poland," in *Bending Opinion: Essays on Persuasion in the Public Domain, Rhetoric in Society*, ed. Ton Van Haaften et al. (Leiden: Leiden University Press, 2011), 302.

"obligation," "office," "duty," implying reciprocity).[68] The etymological meanings convey a sense of reciprocal human relationship. In simple words, community is "sharing things in common," communication is "making common," and communion is "common undertaking" or "common task."

Scholars have noted the close relationship between communication and community. For instance, Shepherd notes:

> Community arises from the same Latin root of *munia*, where the reciprocal giving and mutual service that takes place in communication works to make a common people, or *communis*, a community which is bound together through gifts and service. It is important here to note that commonality is given in this premodern equation. *Munia* (or communication) to the common group is required so that a community can be made and maintained.[69]

Communication, for Shepherd, is an interpersonal experience. Likewise, community is viewed through an interpersonal lens.

> In all experiences of communication we give our selves. We render, each to the other, our uniqueness, our differences, our individuality (all of which is a product of earlier communication experiences). In so doing, we express our obligation to each other, and partake of one another; each is taken into the other and made a part of the other (hence another associated word, *communion*).... To say that communication is interpersonal is to say that when communication occurs, something communal is made. It is something of self and other, but not self and other. It is something synergistic. It is community.[70]

Shepherd's explanation clearly establishes the link between communication and community. Their connection with the concept of communion is also evident.

Sometimes community is defined as human relationship based on shared possessions, attributes, values, purpose, or symbol. It is used to refer to people living in close relationship in a specific locality, or a body of people unified by common profession or religion, or having

---

68. Cf. Roberto Esposito, *Communitas: The Origin and Destiny of Community*, Cultural Memory in the Present, trans. Timothy Campbell (Stanford, CA: Stanford University Press, 2010), 3-4.

69. Shepherd, "Community as the Interpersonal Accomplishment of Communication," in *Communication and Community*, Shepherd and Rothenbuhler, 30.

70. Shepherd, "Community as the Interpersonal Accomplishment of Communication," in *Communication and Community*, Shepherd and Rothenbuhler, 31-32.

similar interests and beliefs, and extending mutual support to one another. However, the etymological derivations shift the focus from narrow local movements to a synergic process that continues to expand and move outward to incorporate more and more in the process as communication, community, and communion increase.

Community must no longer be restricted to a locality or to a group of like-minded people but extended to diverse peoples, regions, and religions. Living in a community does not mean that everyone in the community would have the same moral and ethical values, tastes, interests, social position, economic status, class, race, sex, or religious faith. Rather, living in community means taking into account the other two words that share the same root with "community"; "communication" and "communion."

Martin Buber pinpoints the spontaneous nature of community:

> Community is the being no longer side by side (and, one might add, above and below) but *with* one another of a multitude of persons. And this multitude, though it moves towards one goal, yet experiences everywhere a turning to, a dynamic facing of, the others, a flowing from I to Thou. Community is where community happens.[71]

Living in community signifies living in communication and communion despite diversities and differences in race, class, gender, culture, or faith. It means the acceptance of others, who are different, as equals and as partners and collaborators in all situations. To be in communion in community means, to use the analogy of the Eucharist, to be able to say "peace be with you" to the other and to drink from the same cup and eat of the same bread. And to be in communication in community means to be able to talk, to dialogue, to express, to accept, to understand, to listen and to exchange ideas and possessions. In other words, it is to make meaning together fully understanding that for a given situation different individuals would perceive and react to the situation differently.

> Perhaps communication becomes the perpetual opening of possibilities, and recognition of its value serves as a precondition for witnessing diverse cultural narratives. Communication, not self assertion, makes community possible. For an essential element of a mature community resides in the rich complexity of its relationships. Contradictions and mystery, order and negation, at once feed the development of human communities and host the elements that permit

71. Martin Buber, *Between Man and Man*, trans. Ronald Gregor Smith (London: Fontana Library, 1961), 51.

> private and collective distortions. Our work is not in the denial of acceptance of a universal narrative or a monoculture but in the protection of our continued discussion of truth and experience of collective life.[72]

The quest for community is not a quest for uniformity or toleration: it is the fulfilment of individual and social needs through living in communion and in communication despite human contrariness and imperfection.

Communication Creates Community

With the advancement of modernity and communication technology there has been a parallel increase in individualism and desire for privacy and people live in isolation from other people. Evidently, the modern means of communication have created a global village but a global village with concrete dividing walls between people, segregating them, and keeping them "excommunicated," i.e. out of communication. This is contrary to the purpose of genuine communication. The objective of communication is to create community and stimulate community spirit. Clearly, genuine communication would mean enabling meaningful structural changes to take place in society to break the status quo.

Christian communication needs to lead the way beyond the divided churches, above the walls of denominations and aim for ecumenical communication. The Church is a community and the central task of this community is to proclaim God's kingdom which is characterised by equality, justice, love and peace. The way towards achieving this is by making communication accessible, multiform, and liberating.

> Therefore, one aim of our work is the breaking down of all kinds of barriers which prevent the development of communities with rights and justice for all—particularly such barriers as race, sex, class, nation, power and wealth. Genuine communication cannot take place in a climate of division, alienation, isolation and barriers which disturb, prevent or distort social interaction.
>
> True communication is facilitated when people join together regardless of race, colour or religious conviction, and where there is acceptance of and commitment to one another.[73]

---

72. W. Marc Porter and Isaac E. Catt, "The Narcissistic Reflection of Communicative Power: Delusions of Progress against Organizational Discrimination," in *Narrative and Social Control: Critical Perspectives*, Sage Annual Reviews of Communication Research 21, ed. Dennis K. Mumby (London: Sage Publications, 1993), 183.

73. WACC, *Statements on Communication*, 6-7.

Christian faith and community formation are inter-related because Christians are called to live in community. The Church is a community and it is also a means of communication. Addressing the First International Congress for the Community of the Faithful in May 1986, Pope John Paul spoke about transformation of the parish (church) into community. He said:

> The parish is not principally a structure; a territory, a building. The parish is first of all a community of the faithful. That, in fact, is how it is defined by the new Code of Canon Law. That is the task of the parish today: to be a community, to rediscover itself as a community. One is not a Christian by oneself. To be a Christian means to believe and to live one's faith together with others, to be a Church, to be a community.[74]

A classic description of a Christian community is found in the New Testament. The writer of the Acts of the Apostles presents a short description of the group life of the Christian converts in Jerusalem in Acts 2:44-47.

> All who believed were together and had all things in common, and they would sell their possession and goods and distribute the proceeds to all, as any had need. Day by day as they spent much time together in the temple, they broke bread at home and ate their food with glad and generous hearts, praising God and having the goodwill of all the people. And day by day the Lord added to their number those who were being saved.

The early Christians survived as community because of sharing their experiences through spoken word, written word i.e. epistles, the eloquent speech of the apostles and the quality of love exhibited within the community. The community also survived because of the vision of love, the love that God has for them and the love they could share with the world. They had not attained the perfection or achieved the full potential of a world community founded on the love of God, yet they knew it was there and that it was not an implausible idea. They got a glimpse of what that love could do for humanity and strove for it. This spirit of sharing, narrating, hoping, loving, caring, and believing that the world can become one community in the early Church provides the impetus for community formation today. As people belonging to the community of Jesus, Christians should profess the Kingdom of God, where love, trust,

---

74. Mary E. Britt, *In Search of New Wine-Skins: An Exploration of Models of Christian Community*, Pastoral Investigation of Contemporary Trends, National Catholic Research Council (Melbourne: Collins Dove, 1988), 15.

justice and peace reign. In a way they are like conditions that promote the Kingdom of God.

Paul's use of the "body" metaphor for the Christian community is particularly relevant. The Christians at Corinth were told, "Just as the body is one and has many members, and all the members of the body, though many, are one body, so it is with Christ…" (1 Cor 12:12-31). Differences are a natural thing in the community and we should not be surprised by it because the community consists of individuals. Rather than allowing the differences to break up the community, the variety and diversity should be celebrated as complementary parts of a body. One member cannot say to another, "I have no need of you." The way to live in community with our differences is by understanding that "If one member suffers, all suffer together with it; if one member is honoured, all rejoice together with it" (12:26).

We shape the community and in turn we are shaped by the community. Whether our community fosters love, trust, justice, peace and equality depends on how we shape our community collectively, how we communicate and commune with one another. The society or community exists as a body of knowledge shared in varying degrees by members of the society influencing each other.

The fact that communication creates community also means that it promotes the expression of diverse cultures and not simply that of the powerful nations or groups. When the structures of communication are set up in such a way that the cultures of the minority and the powerless are rejected as though certain cultures have less value than others, when it aims to fulfil the individual and social needs of a few and not of all, it infringes the human rights of those people and cultures on the margins. But by far the most devastating misuse of communication for power and control is that of the patriarchal discourse that spans all cultures all over the world. Women are unable to experience true community and communion not only because they are regarded as inferior but more so because their stories have been suppressed.

Patriarchal Discourse and Women's Narratives

Humans take communication for granted. After all, every human is able to communicate, except for those who have some disability that curtails their ability to communicate. Computers, mobile phones, tablets, and other gadgets, linked by the internet to Facebook, WhatsApp, QQ, WeChat,

Tumblr, Instagram, Twitter, Skype, Viber, LINE, Snapchat, Pinterest, LinkedIn, Myspace, StumbleUpon, YouTube, Vine, flickr, and a host of evolving social media, microblogging platforms, and social networks have revolutionised communication. As soon as you hear about one app or site, another one, claiming to be snazzier and better, pops up. So we assume all is well with our communication. In fact, many claim that communication was never better than it is now. Sadly, this is not the fact. What goes for communication is in fact a vehicle or medium developed by men to serve the purpose of keeping the balance of power in society skewed in favour of men. As discussed earlier, the word "communication" implies an egalitarian existence for it is concerned with sharing or making things common. The problem with communication is because of the dominance of patriarchal discourse in the society, which subtly silences women's communication. Patriarchal discourse impairs, stifles, and suppresses the unique experiences of women. The prevalence of patriarchal discourse points to an imbalance of power in society. Mary Ellen Brown says,

> Patriarchal discourse is impersonal, objective, scientific, rational and logical, and it leaves these values unquestioned and thus naturalized. Patriarchal discourse also naturalizes the power of men to dominate society's ways of thinking, communicating and experiencing; thus it attempts to exclude other modes of experience. Patriarchal discourse is a discourse of power, but disguises the fact through its claims to be based on universal truths rather than truths constructed by itself in the interest of those in power. It claims to be asocial and apolitical.[75]

No wonder the position of women in the society is that of subordinate, oppressed, excluded, silenced, muted or sidelined. Brown continues to say, "patriarchal views devalue personal experiences and knowledges and pretend that women and the challenges they offer to institutionalized knowledges do not really exist."[76]

Michael Presnell identifies the problem: "As in other areas of communication research, it is important that we do not assume that

---

75. Mary Ellen Brown, "Soap Opera and Women's Culture: Politics and the Popular," in *Doing Research on Women's Communication: Perspectives on Theory and Method*, ed. Kathryn Carter and Carole Spitzack (Norwood, NJ: Ablex Publishing Corporation, 1989), 162.

76. Brown, "Soap Opera and Women's Culture," in *Doing Research on Women's Communication*, ed. Carter and Spitzack, 165.

women and men perform and interpret narratives the same way."[77] To a large extent, social-scientific knowledge is still based on men's experiences of the world, with no regard for women's experiences. Therefore, men's experiences and their worldview become the norm in theorising human behaviour and tautologically re-establishing the secondary and inferior status of women.[78] Often stories or narratives by women are considered as gossip and so they are trivialised, ignored or become invisible even to researchers and therefore get excluded as part of human history.[79]

Feminist scholars see that women have been excluded "formally (legally)" or "informally (ideologically)" in areas of public life, education, employment and religious practice. Therefore they find it is necessary to redefine "legitimate" texts, "significant" events and "important" ideas. In doing this, the feminists turn to less public forms of communication such as diaries, letters, or gossip of ordinary women, rather than looking at public speeches, published philosophical treatises or state documents—the records of heads of state or "great thinkers." Thus we find that feminist scholarship has to dwell on the non-traditional texts and ways for analysing women studies and empowering women.[80] Turning to non-traditional texts implies removing the restrictions placed on the meaning of story. For a long time, story only meant those "once upon a time" tales of a male-dominant world. Now those boundaries must be realigned to include songs and tunes, images and imaginations, and expressions and impressions. The possibilities are limitless.

Existing communication theories have not engaged sufficiently with the worldview of women. So it is pertinent for women to find a relevant theory and method for themselves in order to communicate and come out of their state of being silenced or muted by "patriarchal discourse, social constraints or historical methodology."[81] It is to the advantage of women that communication as a discipline is known for its openness to critical

---

77. Michael Presnell, "Narrative Gender Differences: Orality and Literacy," in *Doing Research on Women's Communication: Perspectives on Theory and Method*, ed. Kathryn Carter and Carole Spitzack (Norwood, NJ: Ablex Publishing Corporation, 1989), 118-119.

78. Cirksena and Cuklanz, "Male is to Female As ____ Is to _____," in *Women Making Meaning*, ed. Rakow, 38.

79. Presnell, "Narrative Gender Differences: Orality and Literacy," in *Doing Research on Women's Communication*, ed. Carter and Spitzack, 121.

80. Cirksena and Cuklanz, "Male is to Female As ____ Is to _____," in *Women Making Meaning*, ed. Rakow, 39.

81. Brown, "Soap Opera and Women's Culture," 171.

debate or argument. The continuing discussions on what communication studies should encompass open the way for women's communication to be a significant factor in this field.

Women's perspective on communication brings us back to stories and storytelling. All human beings need stories to survive. Stories are a reality of human experience and action. John Westerhoff says, "Stories provide us with both a memory linking us meaningfully to the past and a vision calling us to a purposeful future."[82] If there were no stories, humans would be living in an unreal and incomprehensible world. Since stories communicate life and fabricate the society, without stories there would not be community. Thus we find that stories are the principles and foundation to human existence and an insight into the spiritual life of humans. For a Christian, it is even more important to tell stories because the existence of the community comprises common memory and a common vision that come through shared stories.

Narrative communication is promising as a form that would allow women to speak for themselves, telling stories of their experiences. Our task is to engage with existing communication or narrative theories and construct relevant methods that would serve the purpose of enabling women to find their voice, as well as all who are silenced such as the gay and lesbian, the refugee and the dispossessed, and the marginalised, because everyone ought to have a voice "in a world of human discourse."[83]

When women tell stories to each other, they identify with each other. They may tell their stories through song, poem, dance, or prayer. Each one of these is story or an attempt to tell story; a story becomes complete only when it is understood by others. It is not only storytellers but ordinary people who tell stories. People make stories and those stories make people who they are. The telling of a story is a powerful act because it is an articulation of who "you" are and what your place is in the community or what place your community has in the world of communities. Your stories define who you are because you become known to others through your stories. Women have not been able to tell their stories, and when they did tell stories, those stories were not understood because the images and signs of language had been created

---

82. John H. Westerhoff, *Living the Faith Community* (New York: Seabury Classics, 2004), 26.

83. Kathryn Carter and Carole Spitzack, eds., *Doing Research on Women's Communication: Perspectives on Theory and Method* (Norwood, NJ: Ablex Publishing Corporation, 1989), 11-12.

and determined by men. Therefore, women need to create space to make their own signs and symbols, their narrative world, their tapestry of stories. In other words, women will experience community through *their* narrative.

Reinforcing Cohesion and Loyalty in the Community

Will feminist discourse create a new set of meanings that cannot be understood by others? Are men and women reading the Bible differently? Why has the Christian story of the gospel been so divisive? Is the Christian story one story or layers of stories? What happens when members of a community tell and share their stories? These questions and many more arise when we dig deeper into storytelling, storymaking, and community formation. We cannot deal with all the issues that arise but we may be able to provide some general directions by exploring the possible effects of authentic narrative communication.

Stories Give Identity and Promote Unity in Community

A classic example of the use of storytelling in community is found in the biblical story of Israel. Their identity and unity was imbedded in their sharing of common stories. Their stories tell of their descent from great patriarchs such as Abraham, Isaac, and Jacob, of their liberation from slavery in Egypt, of Exile as a consequence of breaking the covenant they made with God, and of a future messiah who would fulfil God's promises to them. They had a tradition of re-telling the stories and passing them on from generation to generation (such as at Passover) so that every new generation shared the experiences and the expectations of their ancestors. This practice not only preserved their identity as a distinctive people but also engendered their social and religious values and political consciousness.

Other peoples and nations across cultures and continents have their own stories too, such as stories of common descent, historic struggle, or shared experiences, which enabled them to preserve their identity and kept generations loyal to the common cause. A group of people in a certain place may undergo a common experience such as a struggle for freedom (against slavery, colonialism, refugee struggle), which becomes their story and thereby the cause of their common identity. In due course of time, in the telling and re-telling of that story they develop common signs and symbols, independent of the story. These may be gestures such as greeting with handshake, kissing and hugging, *namaste* (Indian practice of pressing the palms together with the fingers pointing up; *sempah* in Indonesia, *sampeah* in Cambodia and *wai* in Thailand),[84] *pranama* (Indian/Hindu practice of bowing and touching the feet of an elder or teacher—*charanasparsha*), *salaam* (Malaysian custom of using both hands to clasp the hands of the other and then placing right palm on the heart to symbolize greeting from the heart),[85] *adab* (bowing and raising the right hand towards the face), *kowtow* (from Cantonese *kau tau*—the East Asian practice of giving respect by bowing so low that the head touches the ground), *hongi* (Maori greeting in which two people press their noses together; *honi* in Hawaii), *kunik* (Inuit greeting by pressing nose against the cheek or forehead and breathing in; similar to the practice of pressing cheeks together and inhaling in the traditional greeting of the Polynesian island country, Tuvalu), *mano* (Filipino practice of bowing and touching the back of the hand of an elder with one's forehead), spitting upon another,[86] or sticking out the tongue.[87] These may also develop in relation to the foundational story, such as national icons (national flag, anthem). Thus members of a community are able to communicate more easily with one another rather than with strangers.

People will remain strangers and isolated individuals unless bound by a common story or series of stories. They will be without identity because identity is gained only in relationship. I cannot be known except in relationship and in comparison with others in a community. According to linguist Charlotte Linde, our identity is "a narrative, a life story that is cast in terms of cultural system of coherence and that is constantly

---

84. A.K. Krishna Nambiar, *Namaste: Its Philosophy and Significance in Indian Culture* (Delhi: Spiritual India Publishing House, 1979).

85. Elizabeth Devine and Nancy L. Braganti, *The Traveller's Guide to Asian Customs and Manners* (New York: St. Martin's Griffin, 1998).

86. An old and less common form of blessing among the Maasai community in Africa, used for greeting and bidding farewell, is spitting in the face or on the hair, bestowed by the older on the younger. This honour is received with a bow with hands raised in front of the chest. Gillies Turle, *The Art of the Maasai: 300 Newly Discovered Objects and Works of Art* (New York: Knopf, 1992), 43.

87. Sticking out the tongue is a traditional Tibetan greeting still practiced in some villages of Tibet. Tsepon Wangchuk Deden Shakabpa, *One Hundred Thousand Moons: An Advanced Political History of Tibet*, vol. 1, trans. Derek F. Maher (Leiden: Brill, 2010), 164. Apparently, this was meant to show that they are not the reincarnation of a cruel king of the ninth century who had a black tongue.

and interactively reconstructed in the telling."[88] We live in a narrative world, a world created by and in our stories. So the story is a part of us and we are part of the story.[89] When people have a common story, they can interact with each other almost effortlessly because they belong together in the same story and have many things in common; they speak the same "language," they abide by a common norm of social conduct and niceties, they are guided by the same moral compass. In very simple terms, someone from Australia will relate more easily with other Australians, and displaced people will relate better with people in similar circumstances. And this is because they share the same story, which arises out of their experiences.

Stories Can Be the Cause of Discord and Division

Communities have many stories, but very often they have a core story or great story that stands as the signifier of the community, as its cultural basis, or as representing its historical roots. The community regards their core story with strong passion and emotional fervour. Many regard it as the most sacred heritage they have. If the core story of a community is interpreted in a different way other than the commonly accepted interpretation, it is met with fiery resistance and can lead to unmitigated hostility.

> The power of stories to shape the identity of communities is seen in the emotional (and at times physical) violence that greets those who challenge the community's common interpretation of its foundational story.[90]

Patriotism often stems from the core story of a people or nation. Unfortunately, so does fanaticism. The difference between the two is that patriotism has room for allowing for the stories of others to co-exist whereas fanaticism considers that there can be only one story in the world. Over the ages, we have seen the same story elicit laudable patriotism (though not always) as well as despicable forms of fanaticism. In a sense, one can never be certain of the consequences of the telling of a story. It is a volatile situation we find ourselves in; we cannot not tell stories, and

88. Charlotte Linde, *Life Stories: The Creation of Coherence* (New York, NY: Oxford University Press, 1993). The summary of Linde's notion is from Etienne Wenger, *Communities of Practice: Learning, Meaning and Identity* (Cambridge: Cambridge University of Press, 1998), 282.

89. Crossan, *The Dark Interval*, x.

90. Navone and Cooper, *Tellers of the Word*, 248.

we have to tell them knowing full well that there is every chance of our stories being misunderstood.

In fact, it is too simplistic to think that storytelling will result only in strengthening the community. Myra Mendible, while talking about the role of storytelling in reclaiming the silenced voices of the Cuban exiles and her father's storytelling to connect her, his Americanized *cubanita*, to her roots, states:

> Given the primacy of storytelling in the formation of national identity, it is not surprising that competing groups tinker with the past to fashion more positive, self-serving stories based on history but creatively embellished by memory.... This fusion of public and private history articulates aspects of Cuban exile group identity and contains the seeds for both discord and solidarity. It is a richly textured and polyvalent voice indeed that speaks to us through these collective memories, a chorus of conflicting stories that deny us the comfort of tidy, official History.[91]

It is unavoidable in storytelling that the stories should be imaginatively modified by some agenda or an exigency. Narrative hybridity then leads to discord or division within the community.

Take the story of Jesus. Be it among the Christians at Corinth during the time of Paul or in the Church today, there are always issues for the followers of Jesus to fall out over. Christian communities are founded on the one story of Jesus. Yet people who hear the story understand the meaning of the story in different ways. So the community has been beset by schisms and divisions from very early on and it continues to splinter into numerous denominations and sectarian groups. And the debate continues in churches and among theologians—who Jesus is, how he is related to the Father and the Holy Spirit, whether the human Jesus or the resurrected Christ is more important, what should be the place of the various traditions that the churches accrued in the span of their life, and so on. Consequently, the community has become a casualty of the story that brought it into existence.

The breakdown of community demonstrates that in this case communication has fallen short of its divine purpose. Authentic communication must seek to retell the story of Jesus in such a way that reconciliation takes place instead of divisions. The purpose of

---

91. Myra Mendible, "Imagining Cuba: Storytelling and the Politics of Exile," in *Telling Stories to Change the World: Global Voices on the Power of Narrative to Build Community and Make Social Justice Claims*, ed. Rickie Solinger, Madeline Fox, and Kayhan Irani (New York: Routledge, 2008), 243.

communication, as we have discussed earlier, is to create commonality, communion, and community. Division is the antithesis of communication. I am aware that overcoming divisions and factions is a colossal task that is not easily achieved. But we have to believe there is power in the story of Jesus.

I should point out that there is a huge difference between "diversity/difference" and "division." Difference and diversity are not necessarily the cause of division. Unity in the community cannot be achieved by rooting out diversity and obliterating differences. Unity is not to be confused with uniformity. Difference and diversity cause division only when they are viewed as defects. When they are taken as positive qualities, and we embrace their multidimensionality, diversity and difference enrich community.[92]

Dialogue between churches and honest theological pursuit are bridging the divide between churches and Christian communities.[93] For instance, Protestant churches have by and large assumed in the past that tradition has no important role to play in the life of the Church whereas the Catholic Church gave authority to tradition as being on a par with Scripture. In recent times, Protestant scholars have become more amenable towards Church tradition because God's work and revelation is revealed in the history of the Church. As James Dunn states:

> Having reflected on the debate [of Scripture versus Tradition] off and on for most of my academic career, a conviction has steadily grown and developed within my thinking that a positive way forward out of any such impasse is to perceive scripture and the NT in particular as 'living tradition'.... To reconfigure the older debate into the single phrase, 'living tradition', is intended to be equally

---

92. Paul Avis, "Rethinking Ecumenical Theology," in *Paths to Unity: Explorations in Ecumenical Method*, ed. Paul Avis (London: Church House Publishing, 2004), 93ff.; Peter Fisher, "Symphonic Discord: The Place of Diversity in Unity Statements," in *Paths to Unity: Explorations in Ecumenical Method*, ed. Paul Avis (London: Church House Publishing, 2004), 13-28.

93. Yves Congar, *Dialogue between Christians: Catholic Contributions to Ecumenism*, trans. Philip Loretz (London: G. Chapman, 1966); Harding Meyer and Lukas Vischer, eds., *Growth in Agreement: Reports and Agreed Statements of Ecumenical Conversations on a World Level*, Faith and Order Paper 108 (Geneva: WCC, 1984); Jeffrey Gros, Harding Meyer, and William G. Rusch, eds., *Growth in Agreement II: Reports and Agreed Statements of Ecumenical Conversations on a World Level, 1982–1998*, Faith and Order Paper 187 (Geneva: WCC, 2000).

> affirmative of the points of lasting value on both sides [Protestant/Catholic] of the debate and equally critical of others.[94]

Conversely, Catholic scholars are challenging uncritical allegiance to the authority of the Church and its traditions.[95] Thus, at least in certain areas, the gap between Protestant and the Catholic (and Orthodox) churches is getting narrower and there is greater awareness of community that transcends denominational boundaries. The Church can take the process ahead by insisting less and less on absolutes, "rights" and "wrongs," and emphasizing more the kind of unconditional love that we find in families, in parents' love for their children and children's love and regard for their parents. In the movement towards greater ecumenism, the community is creating a new story arising from greater awareness the other's views. Yet the old story is right at the centre of the new story.

Stories are Transformative

We can envision the possibility of change in the Christian community and in the world because stories are a potent force for change. When we understand our identity through our story, we are discovering something new about ourselves. Maybe that perception of who we are was already there, but we become more acutely aware of it. When we communicate with others in a community through the sharing of a common story, we can learn new ways of relating with others. Therefore, stories give us a colloquial means by which to manage our lives and in the process they keep on transforming us.

According to Hoffman, stories are "powerful and delicate instruments, shaping our identity and defining our meanings. They are transmuters, carrying us into those mysterious depths of life that we cannot master but where we must learn to cope and entering into them be transformed."[96] He thinks of narrative as "a form of thinking and speaking especially suited to realities that we cannot control conceptually, that we cannot capture with our words and images." He adds that "narratives offer us

94. James D. G. Dunn, "Living Tradition," in *What is it that the Scripture Says? Essays in Biblical Interpretation, Translation and Reception in Honour of Henry Wansbrough OSB*, ed. Philip McCosker (London: T & T Clark, 2006), 276.

95. William V. D'Antonio, et al., *American Catholic Laity in a Changing Church* (Kansas City, MO: Sheed and Ward, 1989).

96. John C. Hoffman, *Faith-Full Stories: The Narrative Road to Religion* (Toronto: The United Church Publishing House, 1994), 11.

(directly or by implication) a way to think about the world. Whatever the intention of the storyteller, their tales invite us to experience things from a particular perspective, to worship certain gods, to adopt certain heroes, to accept certain values."[97]

Stories enable us to bring closer that which is distant, understand what is mysterious, and express what cannot be defined. The parables of Jesus are such stories that demand the listener's participation and invite transformation.[98] To read/listen to a parable of Jesus is to be transformed by a vision of the kingdom in the temporal world. In other words, a story is an invitation to immerse oneself into the story and relive it once more and thereby get to know the experience within (or behind) the story.

The Great Commission of Jesus Christ (Matt 28:19-20) is a call to be apprehended in his name. The traditional interpretation is that it means "to convert" people and make them Christian. However, as I see it, conversion is not about changing religion or lifestyle but the transformation of the person and the society. To become a disciple means to follow Jesus in his tumultuous journey across the rough country and to be baptized means to experience with Jesus, collectively as a community of faith, his death and resurrection (Rom 6:4). All stories ultimately end in persuasion, but the story of Jesus invites a total conversion. It offers to all who receive it a transformation that involves being recreated by the power of God's Spirit.

Stories Bring Reconciliation

Since communities consist of people of various age groups, diverse levels of education, different genders, and distinct personalities, it is natural that there should be differences of opinion and differing views within the community. These differences can sometimes fester and grow until they become irreconcilable barriers between people or explode into violent confrontations. Stories are a means of keeping the peace or reconciling differences in traditional communities. In such instances, stories serve as human communication bringing balance to the human society.

In the traditional Garo community, a story is told of how ancient patriarchs averted fratricidal war. It happened that Bonepa set his field on fire to prepare it for cultivation and accidentally killed his neighbour's

97. Hoffman, *Faith-Full Stories*, 36.

98. According to Crossan, parables are meant to change not reassure us. Crossan, *The Dark Interval*, 39.

son Nambok Me·a Namsang Pante who was in the field. When Bonepa and his neighbour Misipa were on the verge of killing each other, three celestial beings appeared and settled their conflict by telling them to take the bones of Nambok Me·a Namsang Pante and place them like posts to mark the boundary of their fields. A new plant called the *mendu* grew from his bones and they stood to demarcate the boundary of the fields.[99]

During a time when there was no standard of measurement for land, when boundaries were set by landmarks such as stones and trees, the most common cause of discord would have been boundary disputes. At this time, this story "authorized" the use of *mendu* plants as the socially acceptable, and thus legally binding, means of demarcating land boundaries. I presume that this story must have helped settle or avoid innumerable disputes. And today, this particular story continues to remind the people of a number of things: (1) often disputes are set off by unintentional accidents; (2) often humans fail to look at the bigger picture, beyond their immediate concerns; (3) often dialogue becomes impossible when the disputants try to shout over the top of each other; (4) often the intervention of a peacemaker, be it celestial beings or humans, is needed to prod people towards a peaceful solution; (5) wars, or personal battles with others, are always wrong and (6) often some form of restitution is necessary to satisfy the wronged party even if the wrong act was not intentional. In the story, restitution is made by the heavenly beings who bring back the dead son to life, albeit in the form of a plant.

Such solutions do not really happen in real life, but the principles offered by the story for reconciliation are noteworthy. The lessons of the story gain even greater import when people remember that it comes from a time when killing their enemy was a good thing to do. Human stories like this, drawn from the community's past experiences and memories handed down from past generations, together with various rituals symbolically affirming the cessation of animosity, are powerful means of reconciliation in the community.

However, such instances of stories of reconciliation deal with the issue of conflict within the community at the overt level. The covert component deserves some attention too. It is at the silent, unseen, submerged, and unacknowledged levels of interpretation of narratives that the most brutal and appalling subjugation of segments of the community takes place.

99. Full story in Appendix D: "The *Mendu* Plant as a Boundary Marker."

Distressingly, this form of domination is so insidious that the victims are unaware that they are being victimized.

What is even more alarming is that the foundational narratives of communities are not spared from being interpreted in such a way as to benefit some members to the detriment of other members. Patriarchal discourse, discussed earlier, is a pervasive negative influence on narratives across cultures. The foundational Jewish-Christian story of the Garden of Eden event was interpreted as proof that women were weak, of inferior intellect, lustful, not made in God's image, and the cause of the Fall. Irenaeus (second century) argued: "Having become disobedient, she [Eve] was made the cause of death, both to herself and to the entire race" (*Against Heresies* 3.22). Tertullian (second century) claimed: "You [Eve] are the devil's gateway...you are the first deserter of the divine law. You are she who persuaded him whom the devil was not valiant enough to attack. You destroyed so easily God's image, man" (*On the Apparel of Women* 1.1).[100] Rabbi Johanan gave a sexual twist to the interpretation narrative. According to the Babylonian Talmud, he said: "When the serpent copulated with Eve, he infused her with lust" (*Yeb.* 103b).

The sexist interpretation of Eve became the excuse for branding all women as weak and not fit to be in ordained ministry. Thus down the centuries the collective fate of women in the Christian world was sealed by the patriarchal/sexist interpretation of the biblical narrative.[101] Feminist interpretation of the creation narratives have shown that the foundational narrative can be interpreted through an inclusive lens. The move towards greater egalitarianism in Church and society in the present time is largely influenced by feminist ideology. However, among the Christians in North East India, sexist interpretations of the creation narrative continue to have an appeal. Their narrative is flawed by sexism and patriarchal perspective, yet it wields tremendous power to determine and shape human relations, and should not be underestimated.

Unless those myths created by sexist interpretations to silence women are torn down and discredited, the dissonance within the Church and society will go on. The power of myths is not so easily broken because

100. Cf. Alvin J. Schmidt, *Veiled and Silenced: How Culture Shaped Sexist Theology* (Macon, GA: Mercer University Press, 1989), 43-44; Swidler, *Biblical Affirmations of Woman*, 81-82. Similar sentiments were expressed by many more including Ambrose (fourth century), Epiphanius (fourth century) and John Damascene (eighth century).

101. Mary Daly, *The Church and the Second Sex* (New York: Harper & Row, 1968), chap. 2.

they are powerful narratives in themselves, having stood the test of time, being believed and cherished by many. Something of equal magnitude and influence must be created to challenge the supremacy of oppressive myths. The way to achieve this is by means of counter narratives.[102]

With regard to the Christian community, the Church has been listening to the patriarchal version of the biblical story for a long time. In recent years we have been introduced to other versions such as feminist interpretation, African perspectives, and Asian readings. These are "counter narratives" or narratives that argue against metanarratives. The clash between traditional patriarchal narratives and counter narratives can be the cause of some confusion. One cannot simply tear down the interpretive structures built over centuries and supplant them with new ones without causing tremendous upheavals. And there are questions that we cannot afford to ignore: Are patriarchal interpretations narratives of lies? Can we be certain that the counter narrative will be absolutely correct, perfectly fulfilling the purpose of the narrative, and hence, narratives of truth? Is there only one truth in a narrative or layers of truth? Is truth always relative to the interpreter?

Take the example of the account of the Fall. The history of biblical interpretation has been rather confused about who sinned in the Garden of Eden. New Testament writers are ambiguous about the issue. In 1 Tim 2:13-14, it is stated that Adam was not deceived, Eve was the transgressor.[103] But in 1 Cor 15:22, the cause of sin is laid on Adam: "For as all die in Adam, so all will be made alive in Christ."[104] In 1 Tim 2:13-14, Eve is the transgressor, Adam is exonerated. But in 1 Cor 15:22, where *adam* is used as a generic word and not as a proper name, both Adam and Eve were the transgressors. Of course, because of the English translation, many readers tend to think that Adam in 1 Cor 15:22 is a proper noun and assume that Paul is talking about the man Adam. The creation narrative was not written to allocate blame. It was possibly intended as an aetiological narrative, told to explain why things are the way they are in the world. The creation story could be a narrative around which we can continually weave our own stories of pain, suffering, joy,

102. Healey and Sybertz, *Towards an African Narrative Theology*, 205.

103. The text of Genesis does not support the New Testament and Christian tradition of assigning blame to the woman (Eve). Jean M. Higgins, "The Myth of Eve: The Temptress," *Journal of the American Academy of Religion* 44 (1976): 639-47.

104. Van Leeuwen, et al., eds., *After Eden*, 214 n74.

hopes, mistakes, and betrayal and find our redemption in the very act of telling them.

At first sight, the phrase "counter narrative" connotes a sense of hostility and acrimony towards the existing narrative it has to stand up against. This need not be the case. If narratives become no more than a matter of claiming the truth in order to promote certain ideologies, it will mean a loss of focus on the purpose of storytelling, which is to create commonality in community and bring reconciliation. Counter narrative, therefore, is not about truth claims; although it has to try to be as truthful as possible. The test of a great narrative is its malleability and openness to new insights, acknowledging that we are closest to the truth not when there is only one voice but when there are numerous voices of crowds and masses of people saying different things and seeing things differently. Insights from a feminist perspective may challenge existing interpretations but if they advance the cause of inclusiveness and reconciliation, we can be certain that this counter narrative is desirable.

In retelling the stories of creation in Genesis, feminists have stressed the egalitarian dimensions of their interpretation. The understanding of *ha 'adam* as a generic term to denote the earth creature rather than a male person is significant. The *imago Dei* is present in the wholeness and unity of humanity. Almost all, if not all, feminists insist that the status given to women in the Creation narratives is not that of a subordinate "helper" but an equal partner. In her analysis of "Eros contaminated" Trible notes that in the encounter with serpent, the woman was the spokesperson for the couple and that the man was also present: "The story is careful to specify that the man is with her (*'immah*), just as it earlier included him by the use of plural verb forms in the dialogue."[105] The man cannot be excused as being an unwitting partaker of the forbidden fruit. Feminists insist that supporting the superiority of one gender against the other is not being truthful to the biblical witness. Reading biblical narrative through an inclusive lens enables the reader/listener to come out of the rut of blame game that has dogged the interpretation of the text for ages. One realizes, too, that the potential of the sacred narrative to give fresh revelation to shape our relationship with God, with each other, and with ourselves, can never be exhausted.

When we allow many voices to tell their stories, and particularly if those voices come from the margins, from those sections of society

105. Trible, *God and the Rhetoric of Sexuality*, 113.

whose voices had been silenced such as women, children, and the poor, we create a narrative world which will heal old wounds and bring about reconciliation between estranged members. Telling stories is a powerful means for creating new relationship between victims and perpetrators of violence.

In South Africa, a "confessional discourse" was used by the Truth and Reconciliation Commission (TRC) to construct a new national narrative and thereby a new South African identity. It included testimony, in which the victims of violence repeated their narratives of abuses, and confessions of perpetrators who expressed their sorrow and sought forgiveness.[106] The catharsis experienced in the telling of their stories was meant to facilitate a movement towards reconciliation and provide hope for a new identity.[107]

Of course the effectiveness of the TRC itself is debatable. It had its share of weaknesses. For instance, such a mechanism is susceptible to the possibility that those who were guilty of gross criminal activities could downplay their role and seek amnesty, for the Commission was empowered to grant amnesty. For some victims, the TRC opened memories they would rather forget. Another criticism is that it favoured the perpetrators of abuse because reconciliation was not based on justice (punishment for crime).[108] Nevertheless, the TRC was an unconventional approach to conflict resolution that based its process on truth-telling and on the persuasive power of storytelling.[109]

---

106. Susan VanZanten Gallagher, "Reconciliation and Hope: Confessional Narratives in South Africa," in *The Gift of Story: Narrating Hope in a Postmodern World*, ed. Emily Griesinger and Mark Eaton (Waco, TX: Baylor University Press, 2006), 207-21.

107. "On a more general level the aim [of TRC] was to establish a South African identity. People were lost in their proper identities because before there was a black and a white identity where everyone found themselves. The hearings, the forgiveness and the reconciliation facilitated a united identity." Daniela Kröner, *The Truth and reconciliation Commission in South Africa – A Learner's Diary, Seminar Paper* (Norderstedt: GRIN, 2006), 3.

108. Richard A. Wilson, *The Politics of Truth and Reconciliation in South Africa: Legitimizing the Post-Apartheid State* (Cambridge: Cambridge University Press, 2001); Audrey R. Chapman and Hugo van der Merwe, eds., *Truth and Reconciliation in South Africa: Did the TRC Deliver?* (Philadelphia, PA: University of Pennsylvania Press, 2008); Annelies Verdoolaege, *Reconciliation Discourse: The Case of the Truth and Reconciliation Commission*, Discourse Approaches to Politics, Society and Culture 27 (Amsterdam: John Benjamins, 2008).

109. Cf. Megan Shore, *Religion and Conflict Resolution: Christianity and South Africa's Truth and Reconciliation Commission* (Surrey: Ashgate, 2009).

Stories Build Inclusive Community

As mentioned earlier, the text of narrative is not necessarily confined to printed stories that have a sequence of events following set patterns. Limiting narratives to those formats that conform to traditional structures is to reject other means of narrative communication that do not come within the purview of the littérateurs. Ironically, narratives would be out of the reach of lay people whose lives the stories tell. I have been saying, therefore, that the boundaries of narrative must be expanded to include marginal narratives. So I am saying, in effect, that the text of our narrative is found in every thought and act at every time and place in our life. The laughter lines on a man's face may tell us of a man who finds happiness despite the adversities of life; the deep furrows on a woman's brow may tell us of a woman whose life has not been easy in any way; a teenager with his head shaved and arms tattooed may tell us of a lonely boy craving attention; and an amputee on a wheelchair may tell us of a girl of indomitable spirit. The slump of shoulders, the grimace of pain, or the twinkle in someone's eyes, are stories. These stories may become nothing more than pauses, erased pages, or meaningless scribbles unless they are recognized and acknowledged as stories.

An individual story remains mute unless it is told by the individual in one form or another, such as through music, dance, craft, painting, poem, drama, biography, diary, or any media, to an audience that recognizes and appreciates the story.[110] Thus essentially, the telling of a story needs two players, one to tell and the other to listen. The "telling" could be done by a narrator or an instrument like a painting along with the active collaboration of a "listener" who responds to the "story" by mimetically experiencing the story and transforming it with his or her own data of meaning. There can be no narrative to begin with without such reciprocal cooperation between the teller and the listener. Thus by their very nature, stories require communicators to develop close ties.

Human beings are social animals and must live in relationship. Our notion of the self is fleshed out only within the framework of our

---

110. An interesting and thought provoking analysis of the use of journals and diaries is found in Joanne E. Cooper, "Telling Our Own Stories: The Reading and Writing of Journals or Diaries," in *Stories Lives Tell: Narrative and Dialogue in Education*, ed. Carol Witherell and Nel Noddings (New York: Columbia University, 1991), 96-112.

relationship with others.[111] In other words, to be human, we must be able to tell our own story as well as hear others' stories because stories let us know how we exist and how we know things. Reiterating the notion that storytelling is inbred in the human psyche, Navone and Cooper assert that, "Story is constitutive of consciousness; it is definitive of what a human being is."[112] Likewise, others have stated that individuals recapitulate and reinterpret their lives through storytelling[113] and that communities are born out of shared stories.[114] Thus stories are intrinsic to the identity of the individual and the collective community. To be rendered incapable of telling our own story is to be deprived of humanhood. Thus for William Bausch, "A person without a story is a person with amnesia. A country without its story has ceased to exist. A humanity without its story has lost its soul."[115]

Stories, then, build bridges between humans. They are our umbilical cord to the universal human family. They connect us with others who share similar histories and, more significantly, with those whose experiences are so different from our own that we won't have understood them at all without the medium of story to help us imagine what we have not seen or felt in person. Stories have the potency to reach across cultural and linguistic barriers and enter into human life. The influence of the story is synonymous with the unraveling power of metaphor. Cynthia Ozick writes:

> Through metaphor, the past has the capacity to imagine us, and we it.... Those who have no pain can imagine those who suffer. Those at the center can imagine what it is to be outside. The strong can imagine what it is to be weak.

---

111. For instance, Martin Buber contends that humans are at all times engaged with others in a dialogical "I-Thou" or a monological "I-It" mode of consciousness. Martin Buber, *I and Thou*, trans. Ronald G. Smith (New York: Scribner's, 1968). This notion is echoed in various fields of study including feminist research. For example Carol Gilligan et al., eds., *Mapping the Moral Domain: A Contribution of Women's Thinking to Psychological Theory and Education* (Cambridge, MA: Harvard University Press, 1988).

112. Navone and Cooper, *Tellers of the Word*, 36. Similarly, Jerome Bruner maintains that storytelling is intrinsic to human thought. Jerome Bruner, *Actual Minds: Possible Worlds* (Cambridge, MA: Harvard University Press, 1986), 16ff.

113. Catherine Kohler Riessman, *Narrative Analysis*. Quantitative Research Methods Series 30 (Newbury Park, CA: Sage Publications, 1993), vi.

114. Tilley, *Story Theology*, xv.

115. William J. Bausch, *Storytelling: Imagination and Faith* (Mystic, CT: Twenty-Third Publications, 1984), 33.

> Illuminated lives can imagine the borders of stellar fire. We strangers can imagine the familiar hearts of strangers.[116]

Thus stories enable us to recognize the other and respond with understanding to their situation, they build up our perception of affinity with one another, they buttress our sense of interconnectedness, and they bring us closer towards the ideal of an inclusive community because they draw the edges of society in towards the centre and draw the centre out towards the edges.

At the edges of exclusive communities are the marginalized and their marginal narratives. They stand at the periphery of the community, with little or no power, no say in decision-making, and having little or no participation in community events. Often they are abused and discriminated against with social, political, religious, and legal sanction. They have hardly any means of preserving their human integrity because their voices are effectively silenced. Such a community is not a community but a pretense of community. Unfortunately, some level of marginalization exists in every community. Recognizing the authority of marginal narratives has significant implications for building an inclusive community. It implies displacing metanarratives (comprehensive interpretations of truth and reality) and focusing instead on the text and sub-text of human stories. Openness to narratives that had been previously silenced or thwarted will be a giant leap towards building a community that is truly inclusive. Instances of the formation of communities and communities within a community are fairly common. When women, who have been silenced, tell their individual stories and listen to the stories of their sisters, they empathize with one another and form a community based on the common bond they feel. Within that community, each one is drawn towards those whose views or experiences are similar and they seek out each other and create their own community within the community. Thus a plethora of communities of women exist. There are communities of single women, married women, mothers, mothers with autistic kids, single mothers, widows, widows of war, working women, homemakers, lesbians, black women, indigenous women, women with cancer, women

---

116. Cynthia Ozick, "The Moral Necessity of Metaphor: Rooting History in a Figure of Speech," *Harper's* 272 (May 1986): 65. Cited in Carol Witherell and Nel Noddings, "Prologue: An Invitation to our Readers," in *Stories Lives Tell: Narrative and Dialogue in Education*, ed. Carol Witherell and Nel Noddings (New York: Columbia University, 1991), 4.

who support cancer research, unemployed women, career women, and so on.

The presence of many groups within a community may not be a sign of division within the community but of inclusiveness. It is people's understanding of inclusiveness that is often flawed. Inclusiveness is not about being similar or having no differences but respect of differences. In order to help resolve conflict in the context of turbulent race relations in South Florida, Deryl G. Hunt developed the "The Ellison Executive Mentoring Inclusive Community Building Model" (The Ellison Model). This model recognized that cultural differences based on ethnicity, race, gender, age, class, education and other factors can cause conflict and emphasized the need for people of various cultures to work together. Hunt identified values that lead to "discommunity"—diversity (different), disrespect, dishonour, disunity, fear—and values that lead to unity and "community"—respect, honour, trust—where diversity still exists but not as diversity in terms of being "different" but as "variety."[117] A truly inclusive community follows an inclusion paradigm in which diversity is celebrated and there are many voices telling many stories.

It is noteworthy that the Kingdom envisaged in the parables of Jesus, those powerful stories invoking our involvement and response, is a Kingdom of inclusion. According to Bausch, the parable stories of Jesus: (1) uncover our competitiveness and envy, and invite us to brotherhood and sisterhood instead; (2) uncover our wrong centring, and invite us to a right centring; and (3) uncover our need to hoard and to exclude, and invite us to share and include.[118] Parable-stories uncover our prejudices and at the same time invite us to further inclusiveness.

The stranger is to be included as well. Jesus' parable of the Good Samaritan equalized love for the stranger with love of neighbour (Luke 10:25-37). Jesus himself is the ultimate stranger in the gospels. He was homeless, having no place to lay his head (Matt 8:20; Luke 9:58).[119] He was dependent on the hospitality of others, particularly his women disciples, for his sustenance (Luke 8:1-3; Mark 15:40-41 par). He had to use a borrowed room and table to exemplify the fellowship of the Kingdom (Matt 26:17-19 par). After his crucifixion and death, his body

117. Claire Michèle Rice and Deryl G. Hunt, "The Ellison Unitary Model in Conflict Resolution Training," *Peace and Conflict Studies* 11/2 (Fall 2004): 35-54.

118. Bausch, *Storytelling: Imagination and Faith*, 117-28.

119. Cf. David A. Fiensy, *Jesus the Galilean: Soundings in a First Century Life* (Piscataway, NJ: Gorgias Press, 2007), 122.

was taken and buried by a stranger, Joseph of Arimathea, who, until then, was unknown (Mark 15:42-47 par). The early Christians continued this ethic of Jesus, of welcoming strangers into the midst of the community (Rom 12:13; Heb 12:1-2). In a context of diversity, experiencing a stranger intruding into our life and experiencing being the stranger, like seeing the landscape through the eyes of the other, is important.

> Perhaps it is the stranger who teaches us how to treat strangers. The ability to appreciate otherness in individuals and communities is a way of redeeming the stranger and of redeeming the world. It is not up to humankind alone to bring redemption, but redemption will not come until we make way for it through doing our share in perfecting the world. Is it not perhaps the stranger who calls us to account and who shows us the way?[120]

Becoming familiar with the stranger—experiencing being the stranger and having the stranger intrude into our life—involves a dialogical relationship. In a similar vein, Maurice Freedman's idea of the "community of otherness" conceptualizes a community that keeps its focus on the self, the other, and the community.[121] In a "community of otherness" conflict is not a bad thing because it provides the impetus for growth of the community. However, here too, the context of diversity also necessitates dialogue. Plurality of discourses, languages, and social, economic and political backgrounds within the community make it susceptible to disintegration unless the community engages in dialogue. Dialogue is an indication of openness to one another. It shows that the participants are not bound by views, opinions, and judgments made prior to entering into conversation.

Martin Buber's view of communication sheds light on the nature of dialogue. He differentiates between three ways of communicating. The first is genuine dialogue where the intent is to establish mutual relationship and the participants are mindful of themselves and the other or others. The second is technical dialogue where the intent is to gain objective understanding. The third is monologue disguised as dialogue where the intent is not to communicate with others but which is self-centred.[122] Obviously, genuine dialogue, in which people are sensitive

120. Virginia Shabatay, "The Stranger's Story: Who Calls and Who Answers?" in *Stories Lives Tell: Narrative and Dialogue in Education*, ed. Carol Witherell and Nel Noddings (New York: Columbia University, 1991), 151.

121. Maurice Freedman, *The Confirmation of Otherness: In Family, Community, and Society* (New York: Pilgrim Press, 1983), 249-60.

122. Buber, *Between Man and Man*, 19-20.

and attentive to the sounds and silences of each other is the key to establishing an inclusive community.

Dialogue enables community members to develop meaningful ways of communication by opening new worlds of meaning across cultural, linguistic, faith, class, gender, age, and ethnic boundaries. Nothing and nobody is taken for granted. Dialogue facilitates the sharing of stories to continue unabated and thus nurture mutual trust in the community. Often one side of the participants may have to be more proactive, take the initiative to start dialogue, and mentor those who are just finding their voices and learning to articulate their stories. Dialogue is not primarily about getting our opinion across but about finding ways for inclusion and broadening our perspective. It implies that the dominant should initiate dialogue but listen more. As the relationship matures and the level of reciprocity increase, the players may mutually exchange stories.

As in any conversation, dialogue requires that the players or participants should take turns to listen and to speak. Dialogue establishes a powerful connection between the teller and the listener. The teller's story creates images for the listener to experience the story mimetically and the feedback received by the teller bonds them in a circular relationship. That relationship grows stronger as the listener reciprocates by telling back his or her own story. The experience of telling our story and listening to others' stories could be incredibly marvellous or gut-wrenchingly horrifying or any other human emotion. Whatever the case may be, the participants have an opportunity to reinvent their lives. As John Hoffman says, "Narrative, then, is a powerful means of transformation for weal or woe.... [S]tory offers the possibility of healing through its power to suggest new, more humane and creative ways to perceive ourselves, our people and the shared world."[123] If we tell good stories, if we listen even to those whose voices are faint, and if we engage in dialogue with openness, there is much hope for an inclusive community in which gender inequalities, racial prejudices, and class distinctions will be unknown. We will live and taste fuller lives and dream deeper dreams, then.

---

123. Hoffman, *Faith-Full Stories*, 42. Here, we should hope for a "better" transformation. A transformation for weal is a transformation that would upset the unjust social or religious structures and overturn the unequal opportunities between women and men. And a transformation for weal is one that would usher in creative decisions. However, such transformation will not take place if the stories are narrated to bring shame and belittle people.

Summing up Methodological Considerations

The method of research employed in this work is a combination of Narrative and Communication theory, which I categorise as a narrative communication approach. Narrative theory and communication theory are each very broad concepts that encompass a broad spectrum of critical theories. While integrating these two disciplines, I also seek to redefine and narrow the focus of both disciplines. Thus I pursue a definition of narrative that incorporates marginal narratives while its focus is narrowed down to storytelling. Likewise the definition of communication is to be understood in terms of communion and community.

By defining narrative communication in terms of narratives that create and foster community, a critique of narrative form becomes possible—does a particular narrative fulfil the purpose of communication for community formation? The assumption underlying such a critique is that narratives that fulfil their primary purpose, and theological purpose, one could add, will reinforce cohesion and loyalty within the community. Conversely, narratives that create disunity and conflict are obviously instances of communication that have been skewed or manipulated to serve vested interests. The brief survey of the positive consequences of storytelling above underpins the theoretical basis of narrative communication and establishes that storytelling is a feasible narrative means by which inclusiveness in community may be achieved.

Thus the method is not only a method but also an ideological standpoint from which I look at the elements of worship. It becomes the standard by which the content of worship may be assessed, critiqued, and judged. That is precisely what the next chapter will deal with. What are the factors that make gender segregation evident in worship? How can storytelling be applied to mend the great male-female divide?

3

APARTHEID IN WORSHIP

Defining Apartheid

Apartheid. Evil and ugly. The apogee of black suffering. An ideology akin to fascism. A brand of brutal humanity. The word encapsulates a terrible story of dehumanization.

The word *apartheid* is derived from the policy of racial segregation in South Africa legislated by the Nationalist Party (a coalition of two Afrikaner nationalist parties) when it came into power in 1948.[1] But its roots go further back to racist legislations from the 1890s to 1940s under British rule by means of which the white minority population exercised domination over the majority blacks. In Afrikaans, the literal meaning of apartheid is "separateness," which comes from the Dutch *apart* "separate" and *heid* (cognate of the English "hood").[2] Apartheid institutionalized racism and legalized racial discrimination. It classified people on the basis of colour. South Africa was divided into four racial groups. Whites came at the top, coloured (mixed race) and Indians came in the middle, and black Africans came at the bottom. However, the non-whites generally regarded themselves as a single group.

Apartheid laws made sure that the races were kept apart and that any form of resistance was effectively suppressed in order to entrench

---

1. John W. de Gruchy and Charles Villa-Vicencio, eds., *Apartheid is a Heresy* (Grand Rapids, MI: Wm B. Eerdmans, 1983); International Society for Human Rights, *Apartheid – How Much Longer? Report about the Journey of an ISHR Delegation to South Africa* (London: ISHR, 1986).

2. John Ayto, "Apartheid," in *Dictionary of Word Origins* (New York: Arcade, 1990), 29.

white minority control over the blacks and other races. Residential areas were segregated through forced removals and resettlement into group areas. Marriages and sexual intercourse between white people and people of other races were forbidden. In order to turn South Africa into a white man's country, African reserves were categorised as "homelands" or *Bantustans* where African people were allowed to "self-rule." Being members of autonomous homelands meant that the blacks lost their citizenship to South Africa. The homelands constituted about 13 percent of the most barren portion of South Africa's territory, in which approximately 21 million people had to find their livelihood whereas 87 percent of the land, rich in natural wealth, was occupied by the whites and others who constituted only about a quarter of the population. Blacks were not allowed to work in places designated as "white South Africa" unless they had a permit. Blacks were prohibited from attending "white" churches under the *Churches Native Laws Amendment Act* of 1957. Legislation was passed so that blacks and whites had separate syllabi of education and different wages for equal work. Most public facilities such as beaches, trains, buses, public toilets, and parks carried signboards saying "whites only."[3] Unlike other crimes against humanity, no one has ever been prosecuted for the crime of apartheid.

Apartheid is a blot in the conscience of humanity; more so in the white conscience than the coloured or black. When the United Nations eventually came round and passed a resolution on 6 November 1962 for economic sanctions against South Africa as a non-violent way of ending apartheid and bringing in political change, it was at the behest of Afro-Asian states. The resolution was opposed by the United States, Britain, Canada, Australia, and most of Western Europe except Scandinavia.[4] And in 1974, when a motion was passed to expel South Africa from the UN, it was vetoed by France, Britain, and the United States who were all

3. On the history and policies of segregation and apartheid in South Africa: William Beinart and Saul Dubow, eds., *Segregation and Apartheid in Twentieth-Century South Africa* (London: Routledge, 1995); Sean Connolly, *Apartheid in South Africa* (Oxford: Heinemann, 2001); Nancy L. Clark and William H. Worger, *South Africa: The Rise and Fall of Apartheid* (Harlow: Longman, 2004); John Allen, *Apartheid South Africa: An Insider's Overview of the Origin and Effects of Separate Development* (Lincoln, NE: iUniverse, 2005); Liz Sonneborn, *The End of Apartheid in South Africa*, Milestones in Modern World History (New York, NY: Chelsea House, 2010).

4. Mary Benson, *South Africa: The Struggle for a Birthright* (Harmondsworth: Penguin Books, 1966), 240.

benefitting economically from trading with South Africa.[5] It was only by the late 1980s, with growing international and domestic resentment against the racist regime of South Africa, that the United States and the United Kingdom began to impose selective trade sanctions against South Africa. But it was not until 1994 that general elections were held for the first time in South Africa and Nelson Mandela, leader of the African National Congress, was elected as its first black president.

How could a sane world allow, justify, and support the existence of such an immoral policy? The pages of history are very sobering places to visit. There were the Crusades, the Belgian genocide of the Congo, Hitler's Nazi Germany and the Jewish Holocaust, white supremacist Ku Klux Klan of USA, apartheid of South Africa, the Khmer Rouge of Cambodia, Islamic fundamentalism and 9/11, and many more. World history is a litany of human wickedness and intolerance. To be fair, the world produced Joan of Arc, Martin Luther King Jr., Dietrich Bonhoeffer, Marie Curie, Mahatma Gandhi, Mother Teresa, Rigoberta Menchu, and Nelson Mandela. But every time I look back at the past, I think: Why wasn't this madness stopped earlier? Why are humans so blind? Why don't people learn from history? I am sure countless millions of people have felt the same way. But here we are in the twenty-first century, no better than people of ages past, generally unaware that inhuman policies continue to exist in our time. One of the most disturbing is the kind of apartheid that is practised within the hallowed corridors of the churches and in the sacred space of worship. But I am getting ahead of myself. Let me go back to the definition of apartheid.

Although the dictionary meaning of the word apartheid is "separateness, apartness, or segregation," it carries with it a connotation of something stronger and more devastating than segregation. Writing during the time of an apartheid South Africa, Mokgethi Motlhabi notes how supporters of apartheid have distinguished its meaning from segregation:

> They see it as having farther-reaching implications than the latter. According to them, the old practice of segregation still offered black people some hope that through education and adequate assimilation of Western values they could become equals with whites and ultimately share with them in the government

5. Will Podmore, *British Foreign Policy since 1870* (Philadelphia: Xlibris, 2008), 180; South African Democracy Education Trust, *The Road to Democracy in South Africa*, vol. 2 [1970-1980] (Pretoria: University of South Africa, 2006), 63.

> of the country. Apartheid, on the other hand, does away with all such "false hopes" through its thoroughness and purposefulness in its concept of separation.[6]

What apartheid had in view was a permanent arrangement of racial relations. Thus it may be said that whereas the notion of segregation carries with it an element of hope that eventually people will become equals, apartheid is a reference to institutionalized discrimination whereby the status and destiny of people are irrevocably sealed on the basis of the colour of their skin. No wonder the word continues to be applied today in extreme contexts of systematic racial prejudice backed by government policies or by those who are in positions of authority. For instance, it is used to refer to Australia's policy against the aboriginal people. As late as October 2009, a member of the Northern Territory Opposition said, "welfarism and apartheid are killing Aboriginal people."[7] More strikingly, the Palestinian movement against the building of the walls in the West Bank and Gaza is called the "Palestinian Grassroots Anti-Apartheid Wall Campaign" and it calls on the international community to stop apartheid, end ghettoization of the Palestinians, and help end the siege of Gaza.[8]

Because the situation that women face in churches is a brutal denial of the full humanity of women and because women are kept apart by doctrine, liturgy, language, and practice of worship, I think apartheid is an accurate term to describe the situation. Adolphus Chinedu Amadi-Azuogu states:

> If the problem in South Africa hinged on racism, the problem in the Christian church hinges on sexism. And if the skin color of black folks was a liability for them, the gender of women is now their own liability in the *oikeíos tês písteôs* or *household of faith* (cf. Gal 6,10). What a pity! This highlights the bigotry of our age.
>
> In view of this comparison, it is unfortunate that many Christians do not know that by excluding women from the leadership of the church it is a *form of religious apartheid*. The reason for this is that it is *institutional segregation*, which was what defined apartheid in South Africa. This is even worse because

6. Mokgethi Motlhabi, *Challenge to Apartheid: Toward a Moral National Resistance* (Grand Rapids, MI: Wm B. Eerdmans, 1988), 1.

7. Iskhandar Razak, " 'Welfarism, Apartheid' Hurting Aborigines: CLP," http://www.abc.net.au/news/stories/2009/10/20/2718930.htm (accessed July 25, 2018).

8. Palestinian Grassroots Anti-apartheid Wall Campaign, "Stop the Wall," http://stopthewall.org/(accessed July 25, 2018).

> it is carried out in the name of God and on his [sic] behalf thereby playing down on the inevitable gender inequality.[9]

Discrimination against women is institutional violence perpetrated by the Church. There is nothing to indicate that this situation is meant to be a temporary thing but everything to show that women are expected to accept their secondary status by the fact of their birth as females. The powers that make worship an extension of male hegemony and the Church a bastion of male power must be overcome. It must be named and defeated. It must be named for subverting the worship of God and making it an adulation of masculinity. It must be named for hijacking the salvation of God and turning it into oppression. It must be named for systematically silencing women and denying them full humanity. I name it apartheid. From time to time, I will use the word segregation as well because segregation is an aspect of apartheid. But it is the cold and ruthless word apartheid that truly captures the systematic and institutionalized forms of gender segregation by means of which women are denied full participation in the ministry of the Church and in worship of God.

In this section, I will discuss how Christian worship is, at its core, apartheid. The exclusion and segregation of women in worship is carried on by doctrinal and theological discrimination against women. Certain biblical texts that curtail the participation of women in religious life and in worship have been presented as doctrinal and theological justification for denying women access to ministerial tasks. Besides that, the language of worship is replete with sexist terminologies. I will pay particular attention to God-language because the names given to God and the metaphors associated with God, in predominantly male categories, means that the women are further removed from God. Every sexist reference to God is a weapon of spiritual apartheid that excludes women, devalues their sexuality, and keeps them from authentic worship. The detrimental impact of sexist language on women, on their self-image, will be highlighted. I will begin with a brief overview of the history of sexism in the English language, which will be helpful to indicate how malespeak became dominant in the language of worship.

---

9. Adolphus Chinedu Amadi-Azuogu, *The Politics of Power and the Ordination of Women*, Gender and Power in the New Testament and the Church Today (Fairfax: Xulon Press, 2007), 142.

Sexism in the English Language

Language is the common code that a society uses to communicate between its members. However, across the male-dominated world, males have used their power to create a myth of male superiority and manipulated the evidence to substantiate a falsehood as truth. The construction of the male-dominated world makes use of language as a means for oppressing women.[10] According to Dale Spender, "If the rules which underlie our language system, our symbolic order, are invalid, then we are daily deceived."[11]

The rules of language do not incorporate women's symbolic meanings or their experiences. This does not mean that women are not allowed to use language; it means that women are compelled to use a language not of their own making. Women have to communicate in male terms. There is, within existing language, a tendency to make women invisible.[12] Thus language is inherently sexist or androcentric. Another way in which language is sexist relates to the ways in which language is used. Language can be used to ignore, demean, or deprecate. Very often this is manifested in the use of sexually derogatory terms to address women.[13] While all languages have sexist elements, the focus here will be on the English language. The reason for this is that tribal translations of the Bible were made from English versions. Thus sexism in English had a direct impact on the religious language and theological views of tribal communities in North East India.

Extensive studies have been made on sexism in English: Julia Penelope on language of "fathers' tongues";[14] Douglas R. Hofstadter on

---

10. Catherine A. MacKinnon, *Toward a Feminist Theory of the State* (Cambridge, MA: Harvard University Press, 1989).

11. Dale Spencer, *Man Made Language* (London: Routledge & Kegan Paul, 1980), 2-3.

12. This is very obvious in cases of woman-to-woman sexual violence since there is no word to name non-heterosexual acts of sexual harassment. Lori B. Girshick, *Woman –To-Woman Sexual Violence: Does She Call It Rape?* Northeastern Series on Gender, Crime, and Law (Boston: Northeastern University Press, 2002).

13. Robert Baker, "Pricks and Chicks: A Plea for Persons," in *Feminist Philosophies: Problems, Theories, and Applications*, ed. Janet A. Kourany, James P. Sterba, and Rosemarie Tong (Englewood Cliffs, NJ: Prentice Hall, 1992), 49-59.

14. Julia Penelope, *Speaking Freely: Unlearning the Lies of Fathers' Tongues*, Athene Series (New York: Pergamon Press, 1990).

the damaging effects of sexist language;[15] Deborah Cameron on non-sexist language;[16] and Anne Curzan on gender shifts in the English language.[17] Feminist writings cover such a wide range of interests that it is not possible to dwell on them here.

The fundamental point is that for centuries men have held power and that is reflected in language. For instance, the term "man" was regarded as the generic term for human beings, and it continues to be used in that sense very often. Therefore, people say, "Man is a social being." The absurdity comes out only when the same principle is applied to say, "Man breastfeeds his young." Similarly, masculine pronouns as generic terms for all human beings also contribute towards making women invisible.

Sexism is also apparent in the use of marked words to refer to women and unmarked words to refer first to men and then to both men and women. Therefore, people use "deacon" (unmarked) to refer to a male deacon, though it can also be used for a female deacon. The word "deaconess" (marked by the additional suffix -ess) is reserved specifically for a female deacon. The same is true for "actor" = "actress," "hero" = "heroine," "poet" = "poetess," and "men" = "women." Some terms such as "doctor" or "surgeon" are not gender based, yet these too are often used as though males are the first claimants for these designations. Therefore people say "lady doctor" or "woman surgeon" when the professional is a female.

Furthermore, male terms are regarded with honour whereas their female counterparts are without honour and sometimes used derogatorily. Thus "lord" is a title of distinction whereas its female equivalent "lady" can be used for anyone. Sentences such as "the lady holding the umbrella," or "the cleaning lady" are usual, whereas we have never ever heard it said "the cleaning lord." Similarly, "he is my master" and "she is my mistress" connote entirely different social statuses.

English is a natural gender language. This means that, unlike languages with grammatical gender, its nouns are not assigned genders.

---

15. Douglas R. Hofstadter, "A Person Paper on Purity in Language," in *Metamagical Themas: Questing for Essence of Mind and Pattern* (London: Penguin Books, 1987), 159-67; reprinted in idem, "A Person Paper on Purity in Language," in *The Feminist Critique of Language: A Reader*, 2nd ed., ed. Deborah Cameron (London: Routledge, 1998), 141-48.

16. Deborah Cameron, "Lost in Translation: Non-Sexist Language," in *The Feminist Critique of Language: A Reader*, 2nd ed., ed. Deborah Cameron (London: Routledge, 1998), 155-63.

17. Anne Curzan, *Gender Shifts in the History of English* (Cambridge: Cambridge University Press, 2003).

Now, English may be less gendered than German or Spanish, but in the context of North East India, it is necessary to assess the impact of the sexist elements in English language in vernacular translations. It is not that the Bible was free of sexism before its translations. Greek and Hebrew are also decidedly gender-based. Furthermore, biblical traditions developed in patriarchal contexts and these were written down and edited mostly, if not entirely, by male scribes. It is dominated by stories about men. Women do not figure at all in five of the Old Testament books, viz. Obadiah, Jonah, Habakkuk, Zephaniah, and Haggai. Of the approximately 1,400 people who are named in the Old Testament, only 151 are women. Only 48 women are named in the New Testament, which is proportionately much better than the Old Testament but still far short of the number of named men.[18] But the fact is the vernacular biblical translations of North East India were done not from Greek or Hebrew but from English versions.

On 24 February 1826, the Treaty of Yandaboo was signed between the British and the King of Ava (Burma) and a large portion of the present North East India was ceded to the British East India Company.[19] In due time, the region came to be administered by the British Crown although some "hostile" parts had to be designated as "unadministered area" due to stiff resistance from the indigenous people. Then the Christian missionaries came and opened the first formal schools.[20] To their credit, most of the missionaries applied a principle of "contextualization" to their work at a time when that concept was really unknown. The tribes of North East India had no written script until then. The missionaries to various tribes of the region were the first to study the language/s of their mission field and prepare primers, texts, and translations in the Roman script. Several of them also translated portions of the Bible into tribal languages.[21] But the fact remains that the earliest schools in the region were English medium schools. In Assam, the Assamese language

18. Cullen Murphy, *The Word According to Eve: Women and the Bible in Ancient Times and Our Own* (Boston, MA: Houghton Mifflin, 1998), 13.

19. Suresh K. Sharma, *Documents of North-East India: An Exhaustive Survey*, vol. 3, *Assam* [1664-1935] (New Delhi: Mittal Publications, 2006), 43-45.

20. Sajal Nag, *Contesting Marginality: Ethnicity, Insurgency and Subnationalism in North-East India* (New Delhi: Manohar, 2002), 55-57.

21. I have discussed this in the "Introduction" chapter. For a survey of the role of the missionaries and the impact of Christianity on North East India see Joseph Puthenpurakal, *Impact of Christianity on North East India* (Shillong: Vendrame Institute Publications, 1996).

was used in Schools and courts. Bengali was influential too. But in tribal areas that lay higher up on the mountains, English had greater influence. In due time, English became the standard for schools, universities, and offices in most tribal areas. The system established under the British rule continued after India gained independence. The ascendance of the United States of America as a culturally dominant force, made attractive by Hollywood movies and mass media and aided by its wealth, has also contributed to make English the preferred medium of education and communication in North East India.[22] In my tribe, we have our own language, known as A·chikku, but in our schools it is offered only as an optional subject. The upshot is that in translating our vernacular Bible, the translators depended on the *Authorized King James Version*. As far as I am aware, the translators of the vernacular Bibles did not translate from Greek or Hebrew texts. As someone has stated:

> The earlier versions were chiefly based on King James or Revised Version of the English rather than the originals. Even if those missionaries responsible for the project were well versed in the original languages their products show their great dependence on the English versions. The principle of translation they practiced is now known as "formal equivalent translation" or "literal translation." Every attempt was made to consistently translate the same original word into the same word once used in the receptor language, although the word might have different meaning in another context. Every word whether it has significant meaning or not is translated and so there are lots of ands, beholds etc. Sentence construction and clause forms were often reproduced. Only half-hearted attempts were made to split the more involved sentences into simpler sentences, because a verb or some other word has to be repeated or introduced which were not in English.[23]

Through this process, sexist language and practices have percolated down to my community. It has been the same with other communities of North East India and this has affected our theological concepts and our ways of worshipping God. Most modern vernacular translations, if

22. Nagaland, a state of North East India is the only state in India to have English as its official language. Ved Prakash, *Encyclopaedia of North-East India*, vol. 5 (New Delhi: Atlantic Publishers and Distributors, 2007), 2156.

23 Zairema Memorial Society, "Bible Translation in North East India: With Special Reference to Cultural Background," http://www.revzairema.com/?p=729 (accessed November 29, 2011). The same article is posted in http://nghakmawia.blogspot.com/2013/08/bible-translation-in-north-east-india.html (accessed July 26, 2018).

not all translations, in the region are based on *Today's English Version*, continuing the dominance of Western thought among tribal communities.

Most tribal languages of North East India have a common singular pronoun that is inclusive of both sexes. This is different from English which uses gender-specific pronouns.[24] Now I do not assume that languages with common gender have a higher degree of gender equality. But my view is that where language about God is concerned, gender-specific pronouns derived from the influence of English language have tended to impress tribals with androcentric notions about God. This has happened as a consequence of translation tribal Bibles from English and also due to the influence of western culture.

In the next section, I will discuss the intersections between a patriarchal Christianity, sexist language (particularly in the English language), culture that is oppressive towards women, and tribal life.

Apartheid Walls of Biblical Theology

The views of the bigoted, who argue against women leadership, continue to hold sway in the Church. Their argument is that the Bible teaches that men should exercise authority over women, that it forbids women to lead a church, and that women are spiritually weaker than men and cannot be trusted. Because Bible verses are given to support bigotry against women, ordinary Christians are often led to believe that the Bible teaches women to be subject to men. Mistranslation, misinterpretation, and quoting the Bible out of context are responsible for the prevalence of misogynistic biblical theology. But the biggest obstacle towards gender equality, in my opinion, is the male chauvinist who pretends to know the heart of Jesus, the mind of Paul, and the truth of the Bible.

Cover Your Head

The Pauline injunction in 1 Cor 11:4-6 states:

> Any man who prays or prophesies with something on his head disgraces his head, but any woman who prays or prophesies with her head unveiled disgraces her head – it is one and the same thing as having her head shaved. For if a woman

24. It is understood that tribal translators would face gender issues even if the vernacular translations were done from the original language manuscripts (Greek and Hebrew have grammatical gender).

> will not veil herself, then she should cut off her hair, but if it is disgraceful for a woman to have her hair cut off or to be shaved, she should wear a veil.

Because of this passage in the Bible, mothers tell their daughters: "*Sko illuruna nanga*" (your head must be covered). We, A·chik women, wear what we call "dakmanda chador." The dakmanda is a lower garment wrapped around the waist like a sarong, and the chador is an upper garment one end of which is tucked in at the waist and the other end comes up round the body to drape the shoulder. In the neighbouring state of Assam, Ahom women wear a similar two-piece suit called "mekhela chadar." The sari (also spelled saree and shari) and the salwar kameez (also spelled salvar/shalvar/shalwar kameez/qameez) are not traditional dresses of North East Indians, but they are also worn by women in some states such as Assam, Tripura, and Manipur, perhaps because the Hindu and Sikh cultural influence is greater in these states. The sari is a long strip of cloth one end of which is wrapped around the waist and the other end is draped over the shoulder. The loose end of the sari hanging on the shoulder is called the pallu or pallav. The salwar is a loose pair of trousers which is narrow at the ankle, and the kameez is a long shirt. The salwar kameez is worn with a chunni (sometimes shortened as unni or chunn; also called dupatta). Generally, the chunni is worn over the shoulder and it is regarded as a sign of a woman's modesty.[25] When a woman enters a church, she lifts up the chador/chadar/pallu/chunni, depending on what she is wearing, to cover her head. She does the same when she has to stand before a congregation to participate in the worship service and particularly when she reads the Bible.

Hindu and Sikh women cover their head when they are in a temple or a gurdwara, when they are in the presence of men who are not family members, and when they are in the presence of older or respected people. The practice appears to be similar to the covering of the head in ancient Jewish culture. In Gen 24:64-65, we read:

> And Rebekah looked up, and when she saw Isaac, she slipped quickly from the camel, and said to the servant, "Who is the man over there, walking in the field to meet us?" The servant said, "It is my master." So she took her veil and covered herself."

---

25. For an excellent survey of the sari and comprehensive account of regional attires see Linda Lynton and Sanjay K. Singh, *The Sari: Styles, Patterns, History, Techniques* (New York: H. N. Abrams, 1995).

Now, over the years I have come across various arguments with regard to 1 Cor 11:4-6.[26] One view is that Paul wrote this in order that new converts would not get the wrong idea about Christianity. According to this view, during the time of writing of 1 Corinthians, only prostitutes and women following fertility cults moved about in public without veils, and all decent Roman and Greek women wore veils as a sign of submission to authority. Thus Paul introduced this teaching to the Corinthian Christians out of consideration for the social customs and decorum of Grecian culture and Jewish law. The weakness of this view is that by the time 1 Corinthians was written, the notorious temple prostitute system had been destroyed (146 BCE) and Corinth was more a Roman than a Greek city. Furthermore, there is no explicit teaching in the Jewish Scriptures that women should pray with their head covered. Generally, women seemed to have moved about in public without wearing veils. In 1 Sam 1:12, Eli the priest could see Hannah's mouth while she prayed.[27] The problem of interpretation is further confused by the fact that in Jewish tradition, both women and men appear to have worn veils as a sign of humility and modesty.

In the talmudic era (c 200-500 C.E.), men covered their heads as a sign of reverence before God, especially while praying and studying mysticism (*b. Ḥag.* 14b; *b. Taʿan.* 20a).[28] The Babylonian Talmud refers to men covering their head during mourning (*b. Mas. Qet.* 24a), when raising their cup for blessing (*b. Ber.* 51a), and when in the presence of someone important (*b. Qidd.* 8a, 29b). It is said that Rav Huna "never walked four cubits without uncovered head, for he used to say: the Shekhina, God's

---

26. Gordon D. Fee, *The First Epistle to the Corinthians* (Grand Rapids, MI: Wm B. Eerdmans Publishing Company, 1987); Ben Witherington, *Women in the Earliest Churches*, SNTSMS (Cambridge: Cambridge University Press, 1988); Richard B. Hays, *First Corinthians*, Interpretation (Louisville, KY: John Knox Press, 1997); Raymond F. Collins, *First Corinthians*, Sacra Pagina 7, ed. Daniel J. Harrington (Collegeville, MN: The Liturgical Press, 1999).

27. This seems to indicate she was not wearing a veil when she was praying. Besides Gen 24:65, which is mentioned above, Gen 38:14-15 refers to Tamar covering her face with a veil and duping Judah into thinking she was a prostitute.

28. Joan E. Taylor, " 'The Woman Ought to Have Control over her Head because of the Angels' (1 Corinthians 11.10)," in *Gospel and Gender: A Trinitarian Engagement with Being Male and Female in Christ*, Studies in Theology and Sexuality, ed. Douglas A. Campbell (London: T & T Clark, 2003), 53, with reference to Alan Segal, *Paul the Convert: The Apostate and Apostasy of Saul the Pharisee* (New Haven: Yale University Press, 1990), 152-54.

Presence, resides above my head" (*Kid.* 31a, cf. *b. Qidd.* 31a and *b. Shab.* 118b). And Rav Nachman bar Yitchaq's mother tells him, "My son, cover your head completely, so that you will fear God, and always pray for his mercy, so that you should not be overcome by your evil impulses" (*b. Shab.* 156b).[29]

There is scarcely any information about women's headcovering in the Old Testament, but evidently in biblical times the uncovering of a woman's hair was a sign of humiliation and punishment (Isa 3:17; cf. Num 5:18; 3 Macc 4:6; Sus 32). Some scholars think that the law requiring women to cover their heads dates back to the second century BCE and that it derived the law from a biblical verse (*b. Ketub.* 72a).[30] But the reasons for covering women's head are neither simple nor straightforward. According to a Palestinian amoraic Midrash, God arranged the plaits of Eve's hair at her marriage (*Gen. Rab.* 18.1 with Gen 2:22). The same Midrash explains why a Jewish wife covers her head—because the sin and the shame brought by Eve. A question is posed: "Why does the man go forth with an uncovered head and the woman's head is covered?" And R. Yehoshua replies: "As one who committed a sin and is ashamed in public, so the woman goes forth with a covered head" (*Gen. Rab.* 17.8). The Midrash reflects the paradox of the covered head that calls attention to the hair by covering it. The headdress is something that exalts women while at the same time points to her lowly status.[31] Generally, however, women are told to cover their heads because their hair is sexually provocative. But strangely, veiling was required only of married women (*Ket.* 2:1). A husband could divorce his wife without paying her *ketubah* if she walked bareheaded in the street (*M. Ket.* 7:6; cf. *T. Ket.* 7:6; *y. Ket.* 7:7, 31b; *b.*

29. Leo Trepp, *A History of the Jewish Experience*, rev. and updated ed. (Springfield, NJ: Behrman House, 2001), 365; Dafna Shlezinger-Katsman, "Clothing," in *The Oxford Handbook of Jewish Daily Life in Roman Palestine*, ed. Catherine Hezser (Oxford: Oxford University Press, 2010), 374.

30. Abraham P. Bloch, *The Biblical and Historical Background of Jewish Customs and Ceremonies* (New York: KTAV Pub. House, 1980), 105. A discussion of the textual basis is found in Leila Leah Bronner, "From Veil to Wig: Jewish Women's Hair Covering," *Judaism* 42 (Fall 1993): 465-77.

31. Molly Myerowitz Levine, "The Gendered Grammar of Ancient Mediterranean Hair," in *Off with Her Head! The Denial of Women's Identity in Myth, Religion, and Culture*, ed. Howard Eilberg-Schwartz and Wendy Doniger (Berkeley: University of California Press, 1995), 106; Leila Leah Bronner, *From Eve to Esther: Rabbinic Reconstructions of Biblical Women*, Gender and the Biblical Tradition (Louisville, KY: Westminster John Knox Press, 1994), 32.

Ket. 72a-b).[32] Going bareheaded was considered a grievous transgression because according to the Talmud a woman's hair is comparable to her private parts (*b. Ber.* 24a). Thus a woman was expected to keep her hair hidden from all men except her husband. Because the allure of women's hair can distract men from their prayers, it was prohibited to recite the *shema* in the presence of a bareheaded woman. The Talmud reports of Kimchit, the mother of seven sons, who did not uncover her head even at home. When she was asked why she was blessed with so many eminent sons, she attributed it to her exceptional modesty and declared: "Because the beams of my house never saw my hair (*Yoma* 47a). The Zohar states that if a woman is careful in covering her hair: "Her children will enjoy increased stature over other children; moreover, her husband shall be blessed with all blessings, blessings of above and blessings of below, with wealth, with children and grandchildren."[33]

Yet even more confusing is Paul's argument that long hair is degrading for men (1 Cor 11:14) because this argument does not seem to be in conformity with Hebrew culture. The nazarite vow, which is an honourable action, required both women and men to shave their heads and then keep it uncut afterwards (Judg 16:17).

> A razor has never come upon my head; for I have been a nazirite to God from my mother's womb. If my head were shaved, then my strength would leave me; I would become weak, and be like anyone else.

Thus paintings of Jesus and other biblical characters with long flowing hair appear to be based on inferences from the historical study of biblical times.

Another view is that "head coverings" have nothing to do with submission to authority but all about investing women with authority. The text refers to the fact that women did actually pray and prophesy in the early Church. If Paul censures women who pray or prophesy with their head unveiled, he equally reproves men who pray or prophesy with their head covered. If some women of the Corinthian church had removed their veils in church while praying, it is also equally likely that some men had also worn their head-coverings while preaching or

---

32. Levine, "The Gendered Grammar," in *Off with Her Head*, ed. Eilberg-Schwartz and Doniger, 104-05; Shlezinger-Katsman, "Clothing," *The Oxford Handbook of Jewish Daily Life in Roman Palestine*, ed. Hezser, 373.

33. Ronald L. Eisenberg, *The JPS Guide to Jewish Traditions*, A JPS Desk Reference (Philadelphia, PA: Jewish Publication Society, 2004), 377.

praying. The important point here is that women were equal partners with men in the ministry of praying and prophesying. The notion that "head covering" is actually about empowering women is supported also by the cultural meaning imbued in the "veil." The head covering is a symbol of prestige, respect, and authority in eastern culture and especially in Israelite culture. In the Mosaic Law, vestments for the priesthood included a turban (Exod 28:4):

> These are the vestments that they shall make: a breast-piece, an ephod, a robe, a checkered tunic, a turban, and a sash. When they make the sacred vestments for your brother Aaron and his sons to serve me as priests.

In the visions of Zechariah, a clean turban and festal apparel represented the renewed honour that Israel would receive from God (Zech 3:4-5):

> The angel said to those who were standing before him, "Take off his filthy clothes." And to him he said, "See, I have taken your guilt away from you, and I will clothe you with festal apparel." And I said, "Let them put a clean turban on his head." So they put a clean turban on his head and clothed him with the apparel, and the angel of the Lord was standing by.

I understand that a head covering could be something similar to the turban worn by people in India and Pakistan. The turban is quite literally a man's crown, his honour (*izzat*), his self-respect, and his prestige.[34]

> A turban is never placed on the floor, for that would lower the prestige of the wearer. Similarly, it is a grave insult to step over a turban or take off another man's turban. The turban has several positive connotations. This can be seen in the tradition of publicly honouring an individual with a turban or a stole. Turbans are also presented at the time of weddings as a mark of respect to close relatives and the bridegroom and his family. A turban is so closely identified with the wearer and his standing in the community that it was, and, in some cases, it still is, accepted as collateral on a loan.[35]

From this context of turban use, it is possible to say that Paul's directive that women should cover their head is revolutionary because it signifies giving women the kind of dignity and respect that had traditionally belonged to men only.

---

34. Some Sikh Khalsa women wear the turban but generally speaking the turban is an article of men's dress.

35. Vandana Bhandari, *Costume, Textiles and Jewellery of India: Traditions in Rajasthan* (Mercury Books, 2005), 114.

The argument works both ways. It could be said that instead of prestigious headgear, women are being asked to wear a veil of subservience denoting their lower position in relation to men. From the controversies over the use of the burkha (also spelled burqa, burka, or burqua) or hijab by Muslim women in Canada, France, UK and other countries, we are more aware of the issues surrounding the use of veils. Some women consider it an honour to wear the burkha, others think of it as an instrument of repression.[36]

At this point, my intention is not to determine which interpretation is valid. I am more interested in *why* some tribal Christian women cover their heads in church when it seems to be alien to tribal culture. The main reason appears to be the cultural influence of neighbours who are different from tribal communities. In many places, tribal communities have become minorities in their own land. The dominant groups are the Hindus, Sikhs, and Muslims who have migrated to the region from other parts of India and from Bangladesh. Women from these religious traditions cover their heads with their pallu or chunni as a sign of respect to the deities and to elders. These religious and cultural practices of people from non-tribal communities impinge on tribal culture not only in the clothes that people wear but also in what those clothes signify.

Consequently, some tribal Christian women have picked up the custom of covering the head in church, particularly when they pray and when they read the Bible, as a religious practice. This practice perpetuates the idea of the subservience and inferiority of women because it comes from cultures that regard women as inferior beings. The use of the chador/chadar by A·chik women may be the result of Muslim influence. The geographical closeness and commercial ties that the A·chik Hills had with the Muslim-dominant Bangladesh neighbour for many years could have made an impact on A·chik culture. The chador/chadar is also worn by Ahom women in the neighbouring state of Assam where Bengali influence has been prominent from several generations back. The name chador/chadar is the same as the name for the full-length robe, also known as chador, worn by Muslim women (like the burqa) to keep

---

36. Bronwyn Winter, *Hijab and the Republic: Uncovering the French Headscarf Debate* (Syracuse, NY: Syracuse University Press, 2008); Katherine Bullock, *Rethinking Muslim Women and the Veil: Challenging Historical and Modern Stereotypes* (Herndon, VA: The International Institute of Islamic Thought, 2002); Clemens N. Nathan, "The Impact of Religious Symbolism in Europe: Wearing the Hijab and Burqha," in *The Changing Face of Religion and Human Rights: A Personal Reflection* (Leiden: Brill, 2009), 93-120.

the Islamic dress code of hijab. If the chador/chadar is the result of the influence of Islamic culture, then it follows that the chador/chadar may not be really the indigenous dress of the A·chik and Ahom people. Even today, among the A·chiks, when people dress up in traditional attire for dancing during festivals or for ceremonial purposes, it is not the chador that is worn but the turban, which is called *kotip*.[37] The *kotip* worn by A·chik women and men is a long band of cloth or *pagri* that is tied around the head. Long bird feathers, known as *do·me*, are stuck on it during festive occasions. The replacement of the turban, which signifies honour and prestige, with the chador, which signifies domicile submissiveness to male authority, in daily usage is not only unfortunate but catastrophic.

The practice of turban-wearing was forsaken with the advent of Christianity. Christianity came to the region with a pronounced patriarchalism, much more severe than the patriarchalism of tribal culture. However, wearing of the turban by women was something that did not convey the mistakenly perceived submissiveness required of women in various biblical passages. In its place, the chunni and the chador/chadar were introduced since they signified the subordinate status of women. Tribal women need to reclaim their turban and wear it as a statement of their self-assertion and self-respect.

Most of the tribal people of North East India are biblicists in the sense that people believe every single word in the Bible is the infallible word of God. People think that the Bible is directly given to humans in an act of verbal communication *à la* the tablets of stone presented to Moses on Mount Sinai. Thanzauva and R. L. Hnuni says, "The tribal Christians are mostly biblicists who try to use the Bible as a magical book to solve their problems."[38] Thus the Bible is considered holy as, most literally, the Word of God. In this bibliolatrous context, critical biblical exegesis and feminist readings of the Bible are regarded as corruptions of the absolute truth found in the Bible. Conversely, it is understood that if the Bible says women should cover their heads, there should be no argument against it.

Some tribal women cover their head in church because they have been led to believe it is biblical teaching. More accurately, it is a mixture

37. Women wearing a turban is a rarity among the tribal cultures of North East India. So the A·chik practice stands out.

38. Thanzauva and R. L. Hnuni, "Ethnicity, Identity and Hermeneutics: An Indian Tribal Perspective," in *Ethnicity and the Bible*, BIS 19, ed. Mark G. Brett (London: E. J. Brill, 1996), 347.

of biblical teaching and cultural influences that has given people in some circles the idea that women should cover their head when they pray or read the Bible. This combination has built a formidable wall of gender apartheid that is not easy to dismantle.

Do Not Speak

Tribal biblicism that I referred to above also leads to a belief, among some tribals, that women should not speak in the church. And just as the practice of headcovering by women is based on Pauline injunctions for women to keep silent, the silencing of women in Church is based on Paul's instruction that women should remain silent in Church:

> Women should be silent in the churches. For they are not permitted to speak, but should be subordinate, as the law also says. If there is anything they desire to know, let them ask their husbands at home. For it is shameful for a woman to speak in church (1 Cor 14:34-35).

This damning command is buttressed by another passage in 1 Tim 2:11-12:

> Let a woman learn in silence with full submission. I permit no woman to teach or to have authority over a man; she is to keep silent.

Among theologians and biblical scholars, the textual and literary difficulties of these passages are quite clear. For instance, there is a debate whether 1 Cor 14:34-35 came from Paul or is an interpolation by a post-Pauline editor.[39] Then there is a debate about what kind of silencing is meant. Some say that the passage is addressing a problem of abuse of

---

39. Supporting the view that 1 Cor 14:34-35 is an interpolation: Hans Conzelmann, *1 Corinthians: A Commentary on the First Epistle to the Corinthians*, Hermeneia Commentaries, trans. James W. Leitch, ed. George W. MacRae (Philadelphia: Fortress Press, 1975), 246; Fee, *The First Epistle to the Corinthians*, 699-702; and Hays, *First Corinthians*, 248. Supporting the view that 1 Cor 14:34-35 is authentically Paul's: Robert W. Allison, "Let Women be Silent in the Churches (1 Cor. 14.33b-36): What Did Paul Really Say, and What Did it Mean?" *Journal for the Study of the New Testament* 32 (1988): 44-53; Antoinette Clark Wire, *The Corinthian Women Prophets: A Reconstruction through Paul's Rhetoric* (Minneapolis: Fortress Press, 1990), 149-52; Curt Niccum, "The Voice of the Manuscripts on the Silence of Women: The External Evidence for 1 Cor 14.34-5," *New Testament Studies* 43 (1994): 242-55; and L. Ann Jervis, "1 Corinthians 14.34-35: A Reconsideration of Paul's Limitation of the Free Speech of Some Corinthian Women," *Journal for the Study of the New Testament* 58 (1995): 51-74.

spiritual gifts during ecstatic services.[40] Others say it is a prohibition of the evaluation of prophecy by women.[41] Still others say it is aimed at silencing women prophets of Corinth.[42] And some say the passage is limited to the context of asking irrelevant or disruptive questions in church.[43] What is common between all these various views is that each of them regards the passage as a response to a specific local problem and not a universal rule prohibiting women from speaking in public worship.

However, for the churches in my region, these two passages give the biblical reason for effectively curtailing the full participation of women in Church ministry. They reinforce the traditional view that women are inferior to men. Among the Khasi people, there is a saying, "When the hen crows the end of the world is near."[44] It means that women should not speak. Among the A·chik people, it is said, "*Do·nok wagam gri, me·chik gisik gri*," which means, "Just as the domestic fowl is toothless, so also the women do not have wisdom."[45] The implication is that women should not speak because their words are meaningless. Such notions of female inferiority found support in biblical passages like these two and armed the patriarchal Church to continue the oppression of women.

Generally speaking, in the churches of North East India, women are relegated to a supportive and secondary role in ministry. What is particularly daunting about the subject of women and speaking/preaching/teaching in church is that most churches do not have written policies stating that women are not allowed to preach or teach in public worship. Regardless of denominational affiliations, the struggle of women is against attitudes rather than printed policies. By their attitude, the men convey the message that women leaders and teachers are not wanted in the church.

---

40. Catherine Kroeger, "The Apostle Paul and the Greco-Roman Cults of Women," *Journal of the Evangelical Theological Society* 30 (1987): 25-38.

41. Craig Blomberg, *1 Corinthians*, NIV Application Commentary (Grand Rapids, MI: Zondervan Publishing House, 1995), 281; Wayne A. Grudem, *The Gift of Prophecy in 1 Corinthians* (Eugene, OR: Wipf and Stock Publishers, 1999), 251-55.

42. Wire, *The Corinthian Women Prophets*, 153-58.

43. Craig S. Keener, *Paul, Women and Wives: Marriage and Women's Ministry in the Letters of Paul* (Peabody, MA: Hendrickson Publishers, 1992), 80-88.

44. This is a common saying among the Khasi community and I have heard it from several people.

45. Marak, "Matriliny and the Status of Women in the A·chik Society," in *No More Sorrow in God's Garden of Justice*, ed. Longkumer, 88.

At Eastern Theological College, approximately 80-90 students graduate every year of which roughly 35-40 are women. Most male students are engaged by churches before they graduate as pastors and other top positions but the female students have to wait to be appointed in positions which do not require the exercise of authority. In most churches, male preachers take the pulpit Sunday after Sunday throughout the year. Only a few churches allow women to occasionally stand at their pulpit. Usually women speak only in women's fellowship and not in the main worship services.

The first two female theological graduates from the Khasi-Jaintia Presbyterian Synod graduated from Eastern Theological College in 1996. They could not find a placement in any church because their Church, the Presbyterian Church of India, does not allow women to preach or teach. Finally, they were assigned to teach at the John Roberts Theological Seminary in Shillong, which is the theological college of the Khasi-Jaintia Presbyterian Synod.

This episode made me also notice how other churches that are reluctant to appoint their women theological graduates to church positions are assigning them teaching positions in their theological colleges. In a strange paradox, local churches, church associations, and church councils are willing to let women train their pastors and leaders but do not want those same women to be ordained or made church leaders. There are signs of changes coming in as more and more theologically trained graduates assume positions of responsibility in church organizations but these are like small drops in a big pond.[46] Of course, it is also a fact that church leaders with theological training are not necessarily one in favour of women's leadership in their churches. This usually happens, though not always, when the leaders have graduated from conservative/fundamental theological seminaries.

Apartheid Language about God

God is captive to apartheid language. Our male only language for God has distorted our understanding of God. Hence, people are comfortable to call God "he" but would never agree to use "she" for God. Since language shapes our perception of reality, using exclusively male language for God leads people to assume that male dominance is divinely ordained.

---

46. Lalneihzovi, ed., *Changing Status of Women in North-Eastern States* (New Delhi: Mittal Publications, 2009).

Naming God

Language has a direct influence on how we perceive things. Our individual perception about God is determined by our language about God. Most people would agree that they believe the theological dictum that God is beyond both sex and gender. And again a good number of people probably miss the inconsistency of the statement—the fact that the word "God" is gender-specific. To the question, "Who is God?" I could respond, "God is the Creator of all things, ruler of the universe, transcendent, and Absolute being." But that answer does not take into account the image I have about God. Who do I *really* think God is? What does a person mean when s/he says, "I love God" or "I hate God"? Or what does an atheist mean when s/he says, "I do not believe in the existence of a God?" Can a person hate someone (God) he/she does not and can not really know fully? Does not the atheist really mean that s/he does not believe in the existence of what s/he conceives to be God?

What I am driving at is that the word "God" itself conjures up certain images. The word "God" is a masculine noun, the feminine noun being "Goddess," implying that God is a male. Val Webb notes:

> Part of our problem is the English translation "God." While the term God is supposedly generic as well as male, so long as we also use the word Goddess, God suggests the *male* variety of deity. Although the Creator God exhibited no sexuality, our English *language* gives God a gender with this term. Those who think this male label conveys a *generic* meaning only have to test "Goddess" as an alternative term and the assumed *maleness* of God becomes strikingly evident![47]

While describing a God who is infinite and beyond human words, I am still captive to finite images of God as a male. It needs some mental gymnastics to begin using the word God without picturing a male being. Unfortunately, in English, no equivalent word has been found for the word "God" without the shackles of human gender. Arts, such as Michelangelo's paintings in the Sistine Chapel, and masculine titles of God such as King and Father, have contributed to a perception of God as male.

In my community, the word for "God" is *Tatara Rabuga*, a name which has a male sound but with female attributes.[48] When people converted

47. Val Webb, *Why We're Equal: Introducing Feminist Theology* (St Louis, MO: Chalice Press, 1999),115.

48. Marak, "Tatara Rabuga: The Supreme Being of the A·chik People," in *Tribal Christian Theology*, ed. Lasetso and Vashum, 210-19.

to Christianity and the Bible was translated into A·chik language, a new word *Isol*, a corruption of the Bengali and Sanskrit *Ishwar*, was used instead of this traditional name. Since the A·chik Bible was translated from English versions, this appears to be an attempt to translate the masculine word "God" with a masculine name.

Among other tribes of North East India, the translators selectively picked masculine names for God. For instance, in the Ao Naga Bible, the word used for God is *Tsüngrem*. The word *Tsüngrem* is a generic term for spirit. In its original sense it denoted spirits in general without any specific attributes. This word was reconfigured by the missionaries and translators of the Ao Bible to incorporate all the ideas of a transcendent God of Christianity. In Ao Christian circles today, *Tsüngrem* has become so fully identified with the Christian concept of God that *Tsüngrem* can barely be distinguished, if at all, from the concept of God of the Bible.[49]

The traditional Gods of the Aos such as, *Lungkijingba* (stone house deity), who is also known as *Anung Tsüngrem* (Spirit of the firmament), and *Lijaba* (Chief of earth) were sidelined. Another deity called *Mojing* (Chief of departed spirits) is also well known but he is regarded as an evil deity.

In particular, *Lijaba* was regarded as a powerful God, the one who created the universe and everything in it. Limatula Longkumer states that "*Lijaba* is a fertility God in Ao religion."[50] But this definition is too narrow and misleading. *Lijaba* is not specifically concerned with human fertility, pregnancy, or birth. Neither is *Lijaba* associated with rites of sacral sexual intercourse that were typical in fertility cults of ancient societies, where phallic worship and human sacrifice were involved. People do seek *Lijaba's* blessing for good and abundant harvest, along with many other requests for blessings, but that is not sufficient reason to categorize *Lijaba* as a fertility God. In ancient times, *Lijaba* was conceived as an old man who is so immensely interested in the domestic affairs of human beings that he comes and lives with the people to fulfil all their needs. Thus he makes himself a member of the family.[51] This was the God who

49. For a study of the Ao concept of *Tsüngrem*, see, O. Alem Ao, *Tsüngremology: Ao Naga Christian Theology* (Aolijen, Mokokchung: Clark Theological College, 1994).

50. Limatula Longkumer, "Contextual Reading of the Bible: A Tribal Women's Perspective," in *No More Sorrow in God's Garden of Justice: Tribal Women Doing Theology*, Women Study Series 4, ed. Limatula Longkumer (Jorhat, Assam: Women Study Department, Eastern Theological College, 2007), 132.

51. C. A. B. Tirkey, *Religion, Primal Religions* (Delhi: ISPCK, 1998), 173.

was worshipped because he was inclined to bless human beings, although he could curse people too.

If the translators had not been overly concerned about what they perceived to be, mistakenly, the right attributes of God they would have picked *Lijaba* as the Ao name for God. Instead, they chose a general word for spirit as the name for God. The Angami Nagas are more fortunate in the sense that in the translation of their Bible the name for God is *Ukepenuopfü* or *Kepenuopfü*, their traditional name for God.[52] Literally, the name *Ukepenuopfü* means "the one who gave birth to us," a mother. However, under the influence of a patriarchal biblical theology, the Angamis began to think of *Ukepenuopfü* as a male God.

In the Hebrew Scriptures the most common words used to designate God are *El*, *Elohim*, and *YHWH*. All these terms for God occur in Deut 5:9, where we read: "I the Lord (*YHWH*) your God (*Elohim*) am a jealous God (*El*)."

The word *El* is found in the so-called E source (E=Elohist) of the four documentary hypothesis (JEPD). It is the Northwest Semitic word for deity. The name Allah is derived from its Arabic cognate *ilah* (*al* and *ilah*, which means "the God"). In the biblical tradition it became a generic word for God and is often accompanied by a suffix which defines it. *El Elyon*, "God Almighty" (Gen 14:19), *El Roi*, "a God of seeing" (Gen 16:13), *El-berith*, "The God of Covenant" (Judg 9:46), and most common of all, *El Shaddai*, "God Almighty" (Gen 17:1, 5-6; 28:3; 5:11; 43:14; 48:3-4 et al.).

Elohim occurs in the P source (P=Priestly) and E source (E=Elohist). It is a masculine plural noun, possibly an abstract noun but frequently used like a proper noun. Grammatically, it can be singular or plural depending on whether it is used with singular or plural verbs and adjectives. Some, such as Swidler, believe that the term probably arose in a polytheistic context as a reference to a confederation of divinities including the female *Eloah* (*Elah* in Aramiac), the male *El*, and other female and male deities.[53] About *Elohim*, Priests for Equality states:

> The cognate El is masculine, while the plural ending is feminine—so Elohim actually balances the feminine and masculine elements of God. This is difficult

52. Zhodi Angami, "Ukepenuopfü: An Exploration of the Goddess," in *Tribal Christian Theology: Methods and Sources for Constructing a Relevant Theology for the Indigenous People of North East India*, ed. Razouselie Lasetso and Yangkahao Vashum (Jorhat, Assam: ETC Programme Coordination, 2007), 231-41.

53. Cf. Swidler, *Biblical Affirmations of Woman*, 35.

to translate into English, so we have been careful to avoid pronouns of either gender when referring to God.[54]

While it is debatable whether the plural ending of *Elohim* is feminine or masculine, the fact remains that *Elohim* reflects a heavenly pantheon of male and female divinities. In any case, it is not an exclusive term of a male God. In 1 Kings 11:5 and 33, the word is used to refer to male and female divinities—to Astarte the goddess of the Sidonians, Chemosh the god of Moab, and Milcom the god of the Ammonites. English translations render this plural form with the singular "God." Genesis 1, which is from the Priestly tradition, would read very differently if it were read more literally, replacing "God" with "Gods" and thinking about "Gods" as inclusive of female deities. The plurality of *Elohim* seeps through at Gen 1:26: "And God said, "Let *us* make humankind in *our* image, according to *our* likeness."

YHWH, called the Tetragrammaton (four letters), is found in the J source (J=Yahwist). It is the closest there is of a proper name for Israel's God, a name so holy that human lips should not utter it. When the Torah was read, the Jews used the word *Adonai*, which means "my lords," in place of *YHWH*. The word *Yahweh* is an early Christian transliteration of *YHWH* but it is highly unlikely that this was how *YHWH* was vocalized in ancient times. *Jehovah* is yet another arbitrary vocalization of *YHWH* from the late medieval period, achieved by combining the four consonants with the vowels of *Adonai* (the vowel signs were placed by the Masoretes to indicate that the word *Adonai* should be read in its place). The NRSV and many other English versions of the Bible use "Lord" (big capital L and then small capitals) for *YHWH* and "Lord" (capital L and then lower-case letters) for *Adonai*. Sometimes *YHWH* is compounded with other words to define *YHWH*: *YHWH-yirah* means "the Lord provides" (Gen 22:8,14); *YHWH-nissi* means "the Lord is my banner" (Exod 17:15); *YHWH-shalom* means "the Lord is peace" (Judg 6:24); *YHWH-tsidkenu* means "the Lord is our righteousness" (Jer 23:6; 33:16); and *YHWH-rophi* means "the Lord is our healer" (Exod 15:26). *YHWH* is grammatically

54. Priests for Equality, *The Inclusive Psalms* (Brentwoord, MD: Priests for Equality, 1997), xvi. Also on Elohim as a feminine plural see S. L. MacGregor Mathers, *The Kabbalah Unveiled* (1887; repr., London: Arkana, 1991), 21-22.

male, but the Hebrew Scriptures provide feminine imagery about *YHWH*. This is seen particularly in the book of Isaiah.[55]

It is apparent from this brief survey of the "names" for God in the Hebrew Scriptures that God is one who is beyond names. The name *YHWH* is itself an ineffable name, made even more mysterious with the enigmatic declaration that *YHWH* is "I AM" (Exod 3:14-15). The God of the Hebrews is one who would rather be known as the one who was with their ancestors. *El*, *Elohim*, and *YHWH* are not actually names but descriptions of this God. A lot of theological meaning and conceptualization of God was lost to the English speaking world, and through it to many other language groups and communities, when *El* and *Elohim* were substituted by the masculine name "God" and *YHWH* and *Adonai* with the masculine "LORD" and "Lord" respectively. Unfortunately, these English words carry masculine connotations and they formalized a male image of God.

Feminist scholars have pointed out that the God of the Bible is a God who is revealed in many forms. The Bible depicts God as the Creator and Maker in Isa 44:

> Thus says the LORD, your Redeemer, who formed you in the womb:
> I am the LORD, who made all things, who alone stretched out the heavens,
> who by myself spread out the earth.

And in Job 10:8-11, we read:

> Your hands fashioned and made me ....
> You clothed me with skin and flesh, and knit me together with bones and sinews.

Feminine images of God occur in many places. In Deut 32:18, God is the woman who gave birth to her people.

> You are unmindful of the Rock that bore you;
> you forgot the God who gave you birth.

---

55. Irmtraud Fischer, "Isaiah: The Book of Female Metaphors," in *Feminist Biblical Interpretation: A Compendium of Critical Commentary on the Books of the Bible and Related Literature*, ed. Luise Schottroff and Marie-Theres Wacker (Grand Rapids, MI: Wm B. Eerdmans, 2012), 313-15; Susan Ackerman, "Isaiah," in *The Women's Bible Commentary*, ed. Carol A. Newsom and Sharon H. Ringe (Louisville, KY: Westminster/John Knox Press, 1992), 167-68.

Similarly, in Isa 42:14, God is the mother who cries out in labour pain. And in Isa 46:3, God is the one who bore Israel and carried them from the womb.[56]

> Listen to me, O house of Jacob, all the remnant of the house of Israel,
> who have been borne by me from your birth, carried from the womb;

In Isa 66:7-9, God is the midwife.

> Before she was in labour she gave birth;
> before her pain came upon her she delivered a son....

There is a strong allusion to God as mother in Hos 11.[57] She is, more explicitly, the nursing mother in Isa 66:12-13.

> ...and you shall nurse and be carried on her arm, and dandled on her knees.
> As a mother comforts her child, so I will comfort you;
> you shall be comforted in Jerusalem.

The Bible also portrays God as birds or animals. In Deut 32:11, God is a mother eagle:

> As an eagle stirs up its nest, and hovers over its young;
> as it spreads its wings, takes them up, and bears them aloft on its pinions,
> the Lord alone guided him; no foreign god was with him.

In Gen 49:9, God is lion/lioness:

> Judah is a lion's whelp; from the prey, my son, you have gone up.
> He crouches down, he stretches out like a lion, like a lioness – who dares rouse him up?

And in Isa 31:5 God is likened to mother birds hovering overhead protectively.

> Like birds hovering overhead, so the Lord of hosts will protect Jerusalem;
> he will protect and deliver it, he will spare and rescue it.

Images of God as inanimate objects such as fortress and rock also abound (Deut 32:4; 1 Sam 2:2; 2 Sam 22:2-3; Ps 18:2; 31:2-3; 62:2;

---

56. Phyllis Trible, "Journey of a Metaphor," in *God and the Rhetoric of Sexuality*, Overtures to Biblical Theology (Philadelphia: Fortress Press, 1978), 31-59.

57. Helen Schüngel-Straumann, "God as Mother in Hosea 11," in *A Feminist Companion to the Later Prophets*, ed. Athalya Brenner (Sheffield: Sheffield Academic Press, 1995), 194-218.

71:3; 91:1-2; 144:1-2). God is also a shield (Gen 15:1; Deut 33:29; Ps 3:3; 28:7; 33:20; 59:11; 84:9; 115:9; 119:114; 144:2). Thus a purely male image of God is contrary to the testimony of Scripture.

Talking about God in English and using the word "God" is unsettling. It presupposes that God is male—it is precisely God (male) and not Goddess. The use of the pronouns "he," "his," and "him" together with "God" makes it undeniably clear that the general concept of God in the English speaking world is not only masculine but male.[58] Viewed from this perspective, the incongruity of the statement in the preface of the NRSV Bible becomes apparent:

> The use of any proper name for the one and only God, as though there were other gods from whom the true God had to be distinguished, began to be discontinued in Judaism before the Christian era and is inappropriate for the universal faith of the Christian church.[59]

This statement is also myopic in that it does not think beyond the English language. It does not appreciate the fact the cultures in various parts of the world have been using proper names for God without in any way betraying the universal faith of Christians. The statement also demonstrates an audacity to presume that English is the norm for the whole world. It does not consider the fact that the word "God" belongs only to the English language. Granted, there are some other languages that share a close affinity to English. But there are vast numbers of language groups in the world which articulate the word "God" very differently.

My discussion about *Isol*, *Tsüngrem*, and *Ukepenuopfü* highlights the fact that in many cultures it is necessary to find an equivalent word for, or description of, "God." Ruether initiated the use of the term God/ess, "a written symbol intended to combine both the masculine and feminine forms of the word for the divine while preserving the Judeo-Christian

58. Rita M. Gross offers a refreshing look at God-talk using feminine pronouns that brings out the Goddess dimension and overcomes feminine stereotypes. She concludes, "One begins to sense that God, as well as Woman, has been imprisoned in patriarchal imageries. That discovery is at once scary, painful, and exhilarating." Rita M. Gross, "Steps toward Feminine Imagery in Jewish Theology," in *A Garland of Feminist Reflections: Forty Years of Religious Exploration* (Berkeley, CA: University of California Press, 2009), 177-88, here 188.

59. Bruce M. Metzger, "To the Reader," in *Holy Bible: New Revised Standard Version with the Apocrypha, Classics* (Peabody, MA: Hendrickson Publishers, 2004), ix.

affirmation that divinity is one."[60] Schüssler Fiorenza has attempted to highlight the inadequacy of language (especially English, I would add) to conceptualize the Divine and uses the spelling "G*d" to indicate that the God she refers to is neither masculine nor feminine. Likewise, she uses the word "the*logy" which is neither masculine (theology) nor feminine (thealogy).[61] Although I believe this is an effort in the right direction, I do not find Schüssler Fiorenza's coined words very convincing because they leave a problem about their pronunciation and it is not derived from any "living" language. Perhaps in time, and with usage, they will gain a life and significance of their own.

Models of God

Feminist scholars realize that naming God is risky, controversial, and provocative, but necessary. Is God he? Is God she? Is God both he and she? Is it appropriate to ascribe sexuality to God? Can God be a person and yet be asexual? These questions have been discussed, analysed, and argued over and over again.

There is no real consensus among feminists on how to deal with the patriarchal and androcentric language about God. Some try to balance the male-dominated language about God by proposing female metaphors; God is Father, but God is also Mother. Some look for feminine dimensions within the Divine. And some argue that both male and female images of God should be recognised as equally and independently valid.[62] Generally, these feminist studies stay within the biblical Christian tradition. Some feminist studies aim at going beyond the biblical tradition to cultures before goddesses were vanquished by

60. Ruether, *Sexism and God-Talk*, 46.

61. Elisabeth Schüssler Fiorenza started using "G*d" in her book *Jesus: Miriam's Child, Sophia's Prophet: Critical Issues in Feminist Christology* (New York: Continuum, 1994), 191n3. In her earlier works idem, *But She Said: Feminist Practices of Biblical Interpretation* (Boston: Beacon Press, 1992) and idem, *Discipleship of Equals: A Critical Feminist Ekklēsia-logy of Liberation* (New York: Crossroad, 1993), she had used the spelling "G-d." This is briefly noted by Schüssler Fiorenza in idem, "Feminist Studies in Religion and The*logy In-Between Nationalism and Globalism," *Journal of Feminist Studies in Religion* 21/1 (2005): 111-119, 111n1. https://muse.jhu.edu/article/183428/pdf (accessed July 26, 2018).

62. A discussion of these approaches is found in Elizabeth A. Johnson, "The Incomprehensibility of God and the Image of God as Male and Female," *Theological Studies* 45 (1994): 331-65.

male deities in order to show the Bible in an entirely new light.[63] Others seek resymbolization, i.e. using new symbols and new language for God based on women's experience. Yet others seek imageries for God that reflect a God who is without gender and not bound to male images alone.[64] Obviously, not all feminist literature will fit neatly into these categories but overlap.

Out of the huge body of literature that has been produced in feminist articulation of language about God, I will focus on a few significant indicators. For feminists, models of God are important. They understand that any human language is inadequate to address the immensity and enormity or capture the complete sense of who God is. We are using the limited means of human language to describe the divine. But how do we know God if God is beyond what we can imagine or describe? It is essential that humans talk about God and address God in ways that make God somehow knowable, however partially it might be. The way humans have always done that is by using metaphors drawn from life's experiences. Susan Ashbrook Harvey points to the necessity of metaphorical language to discuss the divine:

> How can we use human, limited language to discuss that which is divine and unlimited? What relation does a word bear to its object? Can language capture anything of the divine, or is all language for God meaningless? Given that the divine is by nature incomprehensible to us, in what ways can language help us comprehend something of God? For the ancients, as often for us, the only valid use of language to discuss the divine was metaphorical: we must never mistake the word for the reality when speaking about God. But words may offer a glimpse of an aspect of the divine, if we can understand words as metaphorical, as not limited in their meaning to a literal sense.[65]

---

63. Sarah B. Pomeroy, *Goddesses, Whores, Wives, and Slaves* (New York: Schocken Books, 1975); Merlin Stone, *When God was a Woman* (New York: Dial Press, 1976); Anne L. Barstow, "The Prehistoric Goddess," in *The Book of the Goddess, Past and Present: An Introduction to Her Religion*, ed. Carl Olson (New York: Crossroad, 1983): 7-15; Christine Downing, *The Goddess* (New York: Crossroad, 1984); Joseph Campbell and Charles Musès, eds., *In All Her Names: Explorations of the Feminine in Divinity* (San Francisco: HarperSanFrancisco, 1991).

64. Johanna W. H. van Wijk-Bos, *Reimagining God: The Case for Scriptural Diversity* (Louisville, KY: Westminster John Knox, 1995).

65. Susan Ashbrook Harvey, "The Odes of Solomon," in *Searching the Scriptures*, vol. 2, *A Feminist Commentary*, ed. Elisabeth Schüssler Fiorenza (New York, NY: Crossroad, 1994), 86-87.

Similarly, Sallie McFague says:

> Predicates such as omniscience, infinity, omnipotence, and omnipresence do not properly apply to God…for the meaning of all such language—knowledge, finitude, power, presence—applies properly only to our existence, not God's. All such predicates represent is an attempt to make human qualities limitless. In other words, how language, any language, applies to God we do not know; what religious and theological language is at most is metaphorical forays attempting to express experiences of relating to God.[66]

All God-talk, according to Sallie McFague, is metaphorical. By metaphorical, she means that language about God is indirect because God-language simply points towards God; there is no word to refer literally to God. Based on this theoretical position, McFague proposes models of God as mother, God as lover, and God as friend.[67]

McFague's models are alternatives to the traditional patriarchal models of addressing God. Another alternative to the male God and of the male Trinitarian concept is that of Sophia, a feminine symbol and the Jewish personification of Wisdom. Joan Chamberlain Engelsman makes a critical assessment of the repression of Sophia in the writings of Philo and in the New Testament to demonstrate how the feminine dimension of God was repressed in Christianity and how it made a comeback in Mariology, ecclesiology, and Christology.[68] The concept of Sophia was developed and pushed ahead by scholars such as Elizabeth A. Johnson who believes that,

> The mystery of God is properly understood as neither male nor female but transcends both in an unimaginable way. But insofar as God creates both male and female in the divine image and is the source of the perfections of both, either can equally well be used as metaphor to point to divine mystery. Both in fact are needed for less inadequate speech about God, in whose image the human race is created.[69]

---

66. Sallie McFague, *Models of God: Theology for an Ecological, Nuclear Age* (Philadelphia: Fortress Press, 1987), 38-39.

67. Sallie McFague, *Metaphorical Theology: Models of God in Religious Language* (Philadelphia: Fortress press, 1982); idem, *Models of God.*

68. Joan Chamberlain Engelsman, *The Feminine Dimension of the Divine* (Philadelphia: The Westminster Press, 1979).

69. Elizabeth A. Johnson, *She Who Is: The Mystery of God in Feminist Theological Discourse*, 10th Anniversary ed. (New York, NY: Crossroad, 2005), 55.

She finds the balance between masculine and feminine images of God in "Spirit-Sophia," "Jesus-Sophia," and "Mother-Sophia."[70] Sophia is associated with the ancient tradition of the Great Goddess Isis, the female personification of the God of Israel, and has re-emerged in feminist theology as a significant theological discourse.[71]

God "The Father"

The idea of a male God is further legitimized by the naming of God as Father. In the Hebrew Scriptures, father language is not very common but the context in which it was used is important.

In Exod 4:22, God is father of the covenant people: "Then you shall say to Pharaoh, 'Thus says the Lord: Israel is my firstborn son.'" In Deut 32:6, God is called father of Israel and Israel God's degenerate children: "Do you thus repay the Lord, O foolish and senseless people? Is not he your father, who created you, who made you and established you?" In 2 Sam 7:14 (also in 1 Chron 17:13, 22:10, and 28:6), God promises David an offspring and says, "I will be a father to him, and he shall be a son to me." Likewise in Hosea 11:1, Israel is the son whom God called out of Egypt: "When Israel was a child, I loved him, and out of Egypt I called my son." In Isa 63:16, a repentant Israel turns to God, calling God father and Redeemer: "For you are our father, though Abraham does not know us and Israel does not acknowledge us; you, O Lord, are our father; our Redeemer from of old is your name." In Isa 64:8, God is once again the father of Israel, as potter is to clay: "Yet, O Lord, you are our Father; we are the clay, and you are our potter; we are all the work of your hand." In the book of Jeremiah, the prophet takes issue with Israel for failing to call God "My Father":

> I thought how I would set you among my children, and give you a pleasant land, the most beautiful heritage of all the nations. And I thought you would call me, My Father, and would not turn from following me (Jer 3:19).

When Israel is restored and the exiles return, the Lord promises:

---

70. Johnson, *She Who Is*, part III; Cf. Phyllis Zagano and Terrence W. Tilley, eds., *Things New and Old: Essays on the Theology of Elizabeth A. Johnson* (New York, NY: Crossroad, 1999).

71. Mary Grey, *Introducing Feminist Images of God*, Introductions in Feminist Theology 7 (Sheffield: Sheffield Academic Press, 2001), chapter 8; Ninna Edgardh Beckman, "Sophia: Symbol of Christian and Feminist Wisdom?" *Feminist Theology* 16 (1997): 32-54.

> With weeping they shall come, and with consolations I will lead them back, I will let them walk by brooks of water, in a straight path in which they shall not stumble; for I have become a father to Israel, and Ephraim is my firstborn (Jer 31:9).

Malachi harps back on the covenantal relationship of Israel with God the father:

> Have we not all one father? Has not one God created us? Why then are we faithless to one another, profaning the covenant of our ancestors? (Mal 2:10).

Only in a few instances, such as in Ps 68:5, is God called Father without explicit reference to covenantal relationship: "Father of the orphans and protector of widows is God in his holy habitation."

A cursory reading of these passages is enough to know that the concept of God as Father in the Hebrew Scriptures has no connection with procreation. The father-son language is employed to metaphorically define the relationship between Israel and their God. It recalls the historical act of God in rescuing Israel out of slavery in Egypt and affirms the covenantal treaty God made with Israel. After observing Old Testament use of father language for God, Gail Ramshaw concludes, "The context of most Old Testament occurrences of Father suggests…that God's fatherhood is a gracious gift since it makes the covenant people, especially the king, God's children."[72] Thus the fatherhood of God is a concept that transcends sexuality and should not be unduly invested with exclusively male characteristics.[73] But that is exactly what people have done. Feminists reject the word Father because its masculine imagery distances women from God and reinforces the patriarchal oppression of women. Carol Christ asserts:

> To know ourselves as daughters of a Father God who claims to be the only parent is to be involved in a pathologically dependent relationship in which our strength and power as women can never be affirmed.[74]

The problem with calling God Father arises not so much from the use of the title in the Old Testament as from its repeated use in the New

---

72. Gail Ramshaw, *Worship: Searching for Language* (Washington, DC: The Pastoral Press, 1988), 170.

73. Claude Geffré, "'Father' as a Proper Name for God," *Concilium* 163 (1981): 69.

74. Carol P. Christ, *Laughter of Aphrodite: Reflections on a Journey to the Goddess* (San Francisco: Harper & Row, 1987), 93.

Testament and in the prayer Jesus taught his disciples to pray. Although few will admit it, the address to God as Father gives the impression that God is, in a mysterious way, the biological father of Jesus. It appears quite reasonable that if God is called the Father and Jesus is the beloved son there must be a genetic relationship between them. Since Mary is said to have become pregnant by the influence of the Holy Spirit, a further familial connection is made either to Mary or the Holy Spirit as the "mother," thus completing the father-mother-son circle. In my ministry as a church worker and a theological teacher I have come across a literal understanding of "father" countless times, although not stated as blatantly as I have done it here. The irony is that they believe they are being religiously pious and biblically correct whereas in reality they are merely displaying a disbelief of the mystery of the virgin birth of Jesus.

From "Father" to "Abba"

The word *abba* (ἀββα) occurs only once on the lips of Jesus, in his prayer in the Garden of Gethsemane (Mark 14:36).[75] It is found but twice in the rest of the New Testament, by Paul, with reference to the Spirit enabling believers to say "Abba, Father" (Rom 8:15; Gal 4:6). Yet, the Aramaic word *abba* has been accorded a lot of attention.[76]

Often I come across reflections on Jesus' addressing of God with the Aramaic word *abba* that romanticize the word as a new form of address to God, translating it as "daddy" or "papa." This came from an early idea suggested by the New Testament scholar Joachim Jeremias that *abba* came from children's baby talk.[77] James Barr highlighted the numerous problems associated with this view.[78] In fact, Jeremias retracted his earlier view and noted that the word *abba* was used by adults to address older people and teachers with respect.[79]

---

75. The term "Father" was used extensively by Jesus to address God in the gospels, but abba appears only three times in the entire New Testament.

76. In formulating the following discussion, I have relied partially on Marianne Meye Thompson, *The Promise of the Father: Jesus and God in the New Testament* (Louisville, KY: Westminster John Knox Press, 2000), 21-34.

77. Joachim Jeremias, *The Prayers of Jesus* (SCM Press: London, 1967), 62-63; idem, *New Testament Theology: The Proclamation of Jesus* (New York: Charles Scribner's Sons, 1971), 61-68. Jeremias did not say that *abba* meant "daddy" only that it was the language of small children for their fathers.

78. James Barr, "Abba isn't 'Daddy'," *Journal of Theological Studies* 39 (1988): 28-47.

79. Jeremias, *New Testament Theology*, 67.

We know now that *abba* was a common first century word for "Father."[80] Thus it falls well within the general usage of "Father" language in addressing God. The fact is that in Judaism, there had always been a sense of familiarity and intimacy in addressing God with familial language; God is the Father of Israel and Israel is God's son. Thus while it is a new form of address to God, Johnson is right in questioning its exclusivity and its frequency.[81]

Others like Phyllis Trible go even further and assert that there is no convincing evidence that Jesus actually used the word abba.[82] And Mary Rose D'Angelo also argues, "Abba cannot be shown to have been unique to Jesus, characteristic of Jesus, or even to have been used by Jesus."[83] As for me, I believe that Jesus probably used this word to address God during his life on earth. After all, Jesus' preferred term to address God is "Father." By and large, scholars do not dispute the fact that Jesus called God Father. *Abba* just happens to be the word for "father" in another language. What we have here is some kind of a linguistic conundrum. Do "Father" and *abba* convey very different meanings? Perhaps the difference was that one conveyed a greater level of intimacy than the other.

In tribal languages, close kinship relational terms are used to address each other. Very often, the closeness of familial relationship is expressed by compounding personal pronouns with a possessive case. A quick example is that of the Angami language, which is called *Tenyidie*. In *Tenyidie*, a father is called *apuo*, a mother is called *azuo*, and a friend is called *azieu*. The "*a*," which prefixes each of these names, is a possessive word meaning "my" and it is used for the name of every relative or acquaintance. Thus in the Angami society, a son or daughter of any age would always call her or his parents as "*my* father" and "*my* mother." Obviously, *puo* is "father"

80. However, James D. G. Dunn believes that Jeremias' initial conclusion was probably accurate. James D. G. Dunn, "Prayer," in *Dictionary of Jesus and the Gospels*, ed. Joel B. Green, Scot McKnight, and I. Howard Marshall (Leicester: InterVarsity Press, 1992), 618-19. Likewise, G. B. Caird states that abba was an address used at times by children to their father, indicating an intimacy and directness not contained in the formal abinu "our father." G. B. Caird, *New Testament Theology*, completed and ed. L. D. Hurst (Oxford: Clarendon, 1994), 400-01.

81. Johnson, *She Who Is*, 79-82.

82. Phyllis Trible, review of Hamerton-Kelly's *God the Father: Theology and Patriarchy in the Teaching of Jesus*, Overture to Biblical Theology 4 (Philadelphia: Fortress, 1979) in *Theology Today* 37 (1980): 116-19.

83. Mary Rose D'Angelo, "*Abba* and 'Father': Imperial Theology and the Jesus Traditions," *Journal of Biblical Literature* 111 (1992): 616.

and *zuo* is "mother" but these truncated words are never used to address people in practice. However, in the Angami Bible, the word Father for God is translated as *Puou*, without the possessive "*a*." This makes it sound as though God were a formidable being, and not like a father at all. The error is in translating the English word literally into *Tenyidie* thereby inadvertently promoting a Euro-Western concept of a distant, intimidating, and forbidding image of God.

Looking at the word *abba* from this perspective, it seems likely to me that it carried a connotation of greater intimacy and familiarity than the Greek word *pater* (πατήρ), father. This term alerts us to relationships and indeed transforms our understanding of Jesus' use of father language. Brian Wren contends that Jesus used *abba* in a patriarchal context in such a way as to question the patriarchal order:

> In Jesus' time, women had no hope of emancipation from male control, and to name God in female terms was not an option. It would have been an incomprehensible break with the past. "Father" was close enough to past usage to be accepted, but Jesus' characterization of Abba was innovative enough to provoke new insight. At that moment in history, seeing God in terms suggestive of a male head of household who risks himself in costly acts of unexpected love was a clear way of signaling radical change, from over-under relationship to a community of equals with only one Abba.[84]

Likewise Schüssler Fiorenza sees Jesus' use of "father" as a rejection of patriarchal structures and opening towards a new kinship relationship. She reconstructs Matt 23:9 thus:

> Call no one father
> for you have one father
> (and you are all siblings)

And she argues:

> The new kinship of the discipleship of equals does not admit of "fathers," thereby rejecting the patriarchal power and esteem invested in them…The "father" God of Jesus makes possible "the sisterhood of men" (in the phrase of Mary Daly) by denying any father, and all patriarchy, its right to existence.[85]

Similarly, Elizabeth A. Johnson observes:

---

84. Brian Wren, *What Language Shall I Borrow? God-Talk in Worship: A Male Response to Feminist Theology* (London: SCM Press, 1989), 186.

85. Schüssler Fiorenza, *In Memory of Her*, 150-51.

> Jesus' Abba, in other words, is not a patriarchal figure who can be used to legitimate systems of oppression, including patriarchal rule, but a God of the oppressed, a God of community and celebration. Everyone related to the one Abba stands in a relation of mutuality with one another.[86]

She bases this argument on the words of Jesus in Matthew's Gospel:

> You are not to be called rabbi, for you have one teacher, and you are all brothers and sisters. Call no man father on earth, for you have one Father, who is in heaven. Neither be called masters, for you have one master, the Christ. Whoever is greatest among you shall be your servant; whoever exalts oneself will be humbled, and whoever humbles oneself will be exalted. (Matt 23:8-12)

Johnson interprets this passage as an explication of the transformation of all teachers, fathers, masters, and great ones into servants of little ones, and the creation of new relationships of sisters and brothers.[87]

Apartheid Concepts about Jesus

Although they may be loath to admit it as boldly, some people regard the maleness of Jesus as more important than everything else about him. They do not regard the gender of Jesus as a mere accident but a divine choice (God chose to disclose himself as a man because God is male) and proceed to infer from it that only the male can represent the image of God.[88]

It is astounding how many biblical scholars, theologians, and pastors claim to be good and moral people and yet dedicate their time, energy and resources to preaching, teaching, and writing without any shame about their hatred for women. It is more astounding that many Christians believe and honour these hate-peddlers. Is the incongruity and absurdity not obvious? They say God has no sexuality and yet they insist that God is male. The analogy is taken literally. After establishing a lie as the truth, they declare that the maleness of the incarnation is soteriologiclly significant. To save humanity, they say, God did not become a *human* but a *man*. Hence, for them, Jesus is not just the Saviour, he is the *male* saviour.

---

86. Johnson, *She Who Is*, 81.

87. Johnson, *She Who Is*, 82.

88. The initial idea for the discussion that follows is derived from Hardesty, *Inclusive Language in the Church*, 40-51.

The Male Jesus

Jesus was a first-century Galilean Jew who lived in Palestine. We do not know what he looked like. It is unlikely that he looked like James Caviezel in the movie "The Passion of the Christ" directed by Mel Gibson. We know for a fact that he was a Jew of Davidic descent. So he must have looked like a Jew of that region, of that time—with sun-burnt olive complexion, broad weather-beaten face, brown eyes, short stature, thick beard, and dark brown hair. His hair could have been short and curly. Paul, who believed he saw Jesus, wrote that long hair is a disgrace to a man (1 Cor 11:14). On the other hand, Jesus' hair could have been long. He was regarded as a rabbi and a rabbi would have kept the Jewish law of not clipping hair or beard. As for his height, he could not have been more than 5 feet and a couple of inches tall. According to archaeologists, an average Semite male at the time of Jesus was about 5 feet 1 inch in height and about 110 pounds in weight.[89]

The imprint of the man in the Shroud of Turin, that is the cloth in which Jesus' body is believed to have been wrapped after his death, was about 5 feet 11 inches tall but I do not think the Shroud of Turin is a reliable piece of evidence about Jesus. If he had followed his father's trade before beginning his ministry, he might have been robust and muscular in build, which is usually the case for people who do strenuous physical work on a regular basis.

The prophet Isaiah who never laid eyes on Jesus may have got it right when he described the Messiah as one who had no beauty or majesty to attract us to him (Isa 53:2-5). Overall, he might have been unremarkable, just a dark and swarthy Middle Eastern man, like the one reconstructed by Richard Neave and his team with the aid of forensic anthropology.[90] We cannot be very certain about what Jesus looked like but we can be certain that he did not look like the tall, fair-skinned, light-eyed, finely-chiselled European depicted by artists. Yet Christians see nothing wrong in portraying Jesus like Graeco-Roman gods with long hair, bearded like Zeus, and wearing flowing royal robes. He probably wore very basic

---

89. Mike Fillon, "The Real Face Of Jesus: Advances in Forensic Science Reveal the Most Famous Face in History," *Popular Mechanics* 179/12 (2002): 68-71, https://www.popularmechanics.com/science/health/a234/1282186/ (accessed July 26, 2018); cf. Joan E. Taylor, *What Did Jesus Look Like?* (London: Bloomsbury T&T Clark, 2018).

90. Fillon, "The Real Face of Jesus," 3.

clothing: a knee length, one-piece tunic (John 19:23-24) and an undyed mantle (Matt 9:20; 14:26).

Jesus told his listeners: "Beware of the scribes, who like to walk around in long robes, and to be greeted with respect in the marketplaces" (Mark 12:38). He advocated that those who wish to follow him should give away their possessions to the poor (Matt 19:20-22). When he sent out his disciples, he commanded them to "take nothing for their journey except staff; no bread, no bag, no money in their belts; but to wear sandals and not to put on two tunics" (Mark 6:8-9). Jesus was a person who practised what he preached. Consequently, his appearance must have been consistent with his teaching. Origen states that the anti-Christian philosopher Celsus mocked the Christians, alleging that Christians tell people: "Believe that the person of whom I am telling you in God's Son, although he was most dishonourably arrested and punished to his utter disgrace, and though quite recently he wandered about most shamefully in the sight of all men [sic]" (Origen, *Contra Celsum* 6.10). While Celsus could have been wrong about the practice of the early Christians, it is possible he had some knowledge about the appearance of Jesus. According to Origen, the Jews held Jesus to be "a vagabond," and they accused him of being "an outcast who roamed about with his body disgracefully unkempt" (Origen, *Contra Celsum* 2.38). Jesus probably lived on alms, by begging and relying on donations, because a Jewish view claimed that he "obtained his means of livelihood in a disgraceful and importunate way" (Origen, *Contra Celsum* 1:62). All these point to the likelihood that Jesus not only associated with the poor and lowly people but he was one of them. In his lifestyle and appearance, Jesus was poor and scruffy—he was shabby like a street bum.[91]

Although the Western portrait of a White Jesus is the dominant image of Jesus, artists in other parts of the world have depicted Jesus as Black, Hispanic, Indic, Chinese, and other ethnic identities. In fact, Christology thrives on the portraits of Jesus that arise from diverse cultural and ethnic backgrounds. People can accept the idea that an Afro Jesus is one who can relate to the black community and an Asian Jesus to the Asian context. Thus they see no fundamental problem in separating Jesus from his Jewish identity.

But what happens when Jesus is presented as female? It becomes scandalous. Jesus as a non-Jew is not seen as a distortion of biblical

91. This idea comes from Zhodi Angami.

theology but Christa images are opposed for falsifying biblical narrative.[92] In the debate on women's ordination, the maleness of Jesus has often been cited by the Vatican as well as Protestant churches as the reason why women cannot be ordained—women cannot represent "the man" Jesus, "the image of the Eternal Father."[93] The argument against women's ordination is based on a male-dominant Christology that emphasizes "the male disclosure of a male God whose normative representative can only be male."[94]

Closely connected to this argument is the bridegroom and bride symbolism found in the New Testament. It is argued that since Christ the head and bridegroom of the Church is male, likewise those who represent him, priests, must be male because females cannot be bridegrooms. The inconsistency in this argument when all believers of Christ, including males, are called "bride" is overlooked.[95] Indeed many conservatives continue to hold the view that "the incarnation of the Logos of God into a male is not an historical accident but an ontological necessity. Just as Christ has to be incarnated in a male, so only can the male represent Christ."[96] It does not matter that Jesus was a Jew, that he never ate pork, and that he drank wine regularly. A person who is not a Jew, loves eating pork, and never drinks wine can be ordained. In fact, in the Baptist churches of North East India total abstinence is required in order for a person to be ordained. Changing the colour and ways of life of Jesus is not considered to be a distortion of biblical truth, but changing his sex is. To be very forthright, for many people the male genitalia of Jesus supersedes everything else about him. Because of this, they are unable to conceive of Jesus as a daughter of God.

---

92. As discussed in the Introduction.

93. This is explicitly stated as a reason for excluding women from priesthood in the Roman Catholic Church. Cf. "Declaration of the Congregation of the Faith on the admission of women to the ministerial priesthood" (*Inter insigniores*), Vatican City, 15 October 1976; "Apostolic letter of John Paul II" (*Mulieris Dignitatem*), 1988; and "Apostolic letter of John Paul II" (*Ordinatio sacerdotalis*), 1994. A conservation Anglican position is expressed by John Saward, *Christ and His Bride* (London: Church Literature Association, 1977). The protestant churches that I am familiar with do not bring up this argument but generally they believe that men have pride and honour to suitably represent Jesus whereas women are weak and imperfect and unfit to represent Jesus.

94. Ruether, *Sexism and God-Talk*, 125.

95. Ruether, *To Change the World*, 46.

96. Ruether, *Sexism and God-Talk*, 126.

It is understood that Jesus of history is a male but the resurrected Christ is beyond human gender.[97] But the problem is that the maleness of the human Jesus is always projected on the resurrected Christ. Brian Wren poses a few questions that allow men to understand why a male Saviour is a stumbling block for many women.

> How would we feel about praying to a female Savior? What would it mean for us if a woman had been crucified for our sins? How would it feel to be taught, from boyhood, that God became Woman for the salvation of all women, but that this includes men, even though – in the apt phrase – it just "goes without saying"?
>
> Asking myself these questions, I found a residual prejudice: the idea of God becoming incarnate in a woman startled me more than the idea of God becoming incarnate in a man.... I realize that if God's Anointed One was a woman, then however deeply saved and called I was by her life, death, and resurrection, I would always be aware that she was she and I was he. Her femaleness would highlight the differences between us and would be (potentially or actually) an obstacle to faith.[98]

In a practical exercise that highlights the problem of a male Jesus, Hardesty cites an article that endorsed the view that Jesus is a man's man. And then she asks the readers to reread the paragraph substituting female, her, she, femininity, girls, women, and Mother. This is the paragraph:

> It is helpful to look at the male aspect of Jesus Christ in his humanity, for he portrayed a theology of maleness. He was a picture of masculinity, a role model for boys to follow as they grow up learning to be men. His relationship to his Father, his understanding of himself, and his involvement with others paint for us a picture worth our study.[99]

Hardesty concludes:

> If Jesus does not offer a theology applicable to femaleness and a model for girls to follow as they grow up as well, then females might just as well start shopping for a different religion because they are excluded from this one. Many women, indeed, have come to this conclusion at precisely this point.[100]

---

97. Susan J. White, *Foundations of Christian Worship* (Louisville, KY: Westminster John Knox Press, 2006), 167.

98. Wren, *What Language Shall I Borrow?* 171.

99. Vivian Clark, "Was Jesus Christ a Man's Man?" *Christianity Today* 18 (February 1983), 16-18. Cited by Hardesty, *Inclusive Language in the Church*, 42.

100. Hardesty, *Inclusive Language in the Church*, 42.

I do not know why God chose to become incarnate as a man. Maybe it was because in the patriarchal society a man's voice would have been more authoritative than a woman's voice. Perhaps it was nothing more than an accident of history. But what is clear is that the Church has ascribed inordinate significance to the maleness of Jesus and uses it as an excuse for excluding women from ordained ministry or Church leadership.

The Son Jesus

Jesus was born as a male. That in itself poses a lot of problems for women, as we have just seen. Unfortunately, the male identity of Jesus is further stressed by the titles "Son of Man" and "Son of God." The reference to Jesus as "Son" is a serious problem for women. Both titles carry a connotation of "rightful heir" and "successor," something that a "daughter" does not have in a patriarchal society.

In patriarchal societies, particularly in Asian countries, sons are preferred to daughters, sons receive inheritance, and sons continue the family line. A daughter cannot have strong ties to her natal family for she is raised to be married and sent off to another family. Once married, she becomes an outsider, and she changes her name to take the family name of her husband. Among some of the communities of North East India such as the Ao tribe, women retain their family name. It is possible to argue that women in these communities have a higher status in the family than those who have to take their husband's name. But that assumption runs contrary to the fact that these communities are patriarchal societies. I believe that women who keep their family name are actually doubly marginalized as they cannot fully identify with their natal family or their husband's family. They are the outsiders, the perpetual homeless, who bear children for their husbands – children with whom she cannot even share a name. Thinking from a human perspective, what the world needed was a "daughter of God" who would take away the yoke of oppression that women suffer all over the world. But we received a Son instead. Granted this Son is different from other sons, indicated by the capitalizing of that title, but still unpleasant because of its maleness. Hardesty notes:

> Ironically the images of Son of God and "only begotten son" draw their power from patriarchal, patrilinear culture in which primogeniture, the right of inheritance of the firstborn son, influences all social relationships.[101]

In Hardesty's society, primogeniture is no longer the rule but it is among the societies of North East India. The Son language is therefore a thorny issue for women in communities of my region. The fact that the Saviour is born as "the only Son of God" makes it appear as though God was colluding with the patriarchal world to keep women in a subordinate position in relation to men. Sharon and Thomas Emswiler wrote: "If the society had been reversed and Palestine had been a matriarchy instead of a patriarchy, surely God would have sent her daughter." I understand the sentiment this statement is coming from but I am not certain that the statement is right. The God I am comfortable with is not one who sides with the powerful or the oppressor. Having said that, the problem with Jesus as Son is not primarily because he was male but because the churches use it as a basis to insist that Jesus is Son not symbolically or metaphorically but in biological terms.

While there is no guarantee that the situation of women would be different if Jesus had been female, it is worth pondering how an incarnate daughter could have eased the troubles of women and alleviated their position.

The Lord Jesus

"Lord" is a translation of the Greek *kyrios* (κύριος). According to a Greek-English Lexicon, the word is used to refer to one who possesses something, translated as "owner" or "master," such as the "owner" of a vineyard (Matt 20:8), the "owner/master" of a house (Mark 13:35), or the "owner/master" of a slave (Matt 18:31f). It is also used to refer to one who is in position of authority, translated as "lord" or "master," such as the position of a husband in relation to his wife (1Pt 3:6), or that of a father to his children (Matt 21:29). It is also used as a form of address to respected persons, translated as "sir," such as a high ranking official

101. Sharon Neufer Emswiler and Thomas Neufer Emswiler, *Women & Worship: A Guide to Nonsexist Hymns, Prayers, and Liturgies*, rev. and expanded ed. (San Francisco: Harper & Row, 1984), 45.

or ruler (Matt 27:63), or simply as an honorific title or an address of courtesy to a male stranger (Matt 25:11; John 4:11; 5:7; 12:21; 20:15).[102]

In the LXX, however, *kyrios* is used to extensively to translate *YHWH* and *Adonai*. Thus, Joseph Fitzmyer acknowledges its use as a divine title from a Palestinian-Semitic religious background: "It seems quite likely that there was an incipient custom among both Semitic- and Greek-speaking Jews of Palestine to call Yahweh *'ādōn*, *mārē'*, or *kyrios*."[103] Yet, the issue still remains whether it was used of the earthly Jesus as a divine title or it gained religious significance only after the resurrection. About this, Fitzmyer opines that "lord" may have meant only "sir" during Jesus' lifetime and it gathered dominical meaning "Lord" either in apostolic preaching or during the composition of the Gospels.[104]

Among the early Christians, the term "Lord" originally meant "Jesus is Lord" or "our Lord." However it has become a proper name for Jesus and in *Gloria in Excelsis* it is sung: "Lord Jesus Christ, only Son of the Father, Lord God, Lamb of God . . . ." There is so much authority in the word "Lord" that it would seem foolhardy to question it. But it must be questioned anyway because it perpetuates the sexism of traditional patriarchal society.

"Lord" is first and foremost a masculine term corresponding to the feminine "lady." The term "lord" is also reminiscent of the feudalism of medieval Europe, of feudal lords who exercised authority over vassals by granting them fiefs. The relationship between a lord and his vassal was that of "owner" and "owned."

---

102. Walter Bauer, W. F. Arndt, F. W. Gingrich, and F. W. Danker, *A Greek-English Lexicon of the New Testament and Other Early Christian Literature*, 3rd ed., ed. and rev. Frederick William Danker (Chicago: University of Chicago Press, 2000), 576-77, henceforth referred to as BAGD.

103. Joseph A. Fitzmyer, "New Testament Kyrios and Maranatha and Their Aramaic Background," in *To Advance the Gospel: New Testament Studies*, 2nd ed. (Grand Rapids, MI: Wm B. Eerdmans, 1998), 222.

104. Joseph A. Fitzmyer, "κύριος," in *Exegetical Dictionary of the New Testament*, vol. 2, ed. Horst Balz and Gerhard Schneider (Grand Rapids, MI: Wm B. Eerdmans, 1991), 329; idem, "New Testament *Kyrios* and *Maranatha* and Their Aramaic Background," in *To Advance the Gospel*, 227-28.

In the Indian subcontinent, a form of feudalism was experienced in the *Zamindari* (*zamin* "earth" and *dar* "holder) system.[105] The *Zamindari* system has its roots in the land tenure system in ancient India, going as far back as 300 CE. It flourished with the ascendancy of landed agricultural economy. *Zamindar* became the official name for a landlord in colonial India. Some of the biggest *Zamindars* were called "Maharaja" or "Raj" i.e., king, although they were not rulers. They were kept by the government of British India to serve the purpose of collecting taxes from the peasants. Tenants had to pay regular rent to *Zamindars* in order to keep their land rights, and *Zamindars* in turn had to pay annual rents to the government. Unscrupulous *Zamindars* charged rents that were beyond the capacity of poor peasants. Peasants, who were illiterate and had no idea how to keep financial accounts, lost everything they owned. Many were caught in debt traps and "sold" themselves and their future generations to the rich landlords. Women suffered more than men because they were regarded like nothing more than livestock, to be traded and bartered as the men desired. The system was abolished after Indian independence. Yet, despite various land reform acts, landlordism continues to exist in various parts of India. Thus in certain contexts, the term "lord" is synonymous with notions of oppression and exploitation.[106]

The androcentrism of the title "Lord" is obvious. It is another gendered Christology that emphasizes the maleness and masculinity of Jesus.

Rethinking the Gender of Christ

Feminist scholars point out that in his teachings and in his life, the human Jesus was critical of the social customs and religious practices of his day. In fact, it is a common understanding in New Testament scholarship that the early movement initiated by Jesus countermanded class, ethnic, and gender boundaries. Many New Testament scholars have presented

105. Irfan Habib, *The Agrarian System of Mughal India (1526-1707)* (Delhi: Oxford University Press, 2000); Gian Chand Chauhan, *Origin and Growth of Feudalism in Early India: From the Mauryas to AD 650* (New Delhi: Munshiram Manoharlal Publishers, 2004); R. S. Sharma, *Indian Feudalism, c. AD 300-1200*, 3rd ed. (New Delhi: Macmillan India, 2006).

106. However, the argument can be reversed. Christ as "Lord" may be used subversively in a post-colonial context to imply that no human master is Lord except Christ Jesus. I think the problem with the use of the word Lord is not primarily because of the sense of the word itself but its association with other terms such as Shepherd, King, and Son all of which emphasise the maleness of Christ.

extensive studies of Jesus variously as a Millenial prophet, as a radical wisdom prophet, as a Mediterranean peasant, as a social reformer, and many other images.[107]

The common denominator in these studies is that most of them depict Jesus as one who castigated the religious leaders and political leaders alike for their duplicity and corruption and as one who strove for an egalitarian society. Thus, the life and teaching of Jesus is not a problem but rather a resource for enriching feminist theology. The difficulty for feminist theologians is the maleness of Christ; here the word "Christ" is used as a reference to the resurrected One, in contrast to the flesh and blood "Jesus" of first-century C.E.

Ruether asked, "Can a male Saviour save women?"[108] Jann Aldredge-Clanton calls for an inclusive Christology because, "Seeing Christ in exclusively male images places external and internal limits on Christ's living within and ministering through women."[109] A male saviour, one who is still tied to the male biological identity even in the new resurrected body, is a serious theological challenge.

On the surface, Christian theology, following the Chalcedonian assertion, is against fusing or confusing the two natures of Christ – the human and the divine natures.[110] Yet the easy use of male metaphors for the divine and perceiving female metaphors as deviant indicate that the maleness of Jesus had been mixed with the divinity of Christ. In fact, by calling Christ "God from God" with the belief of a male Christ has also reinforced the impression that God is also male. Mary Daly's accusation

107. Dale C. Allison, *Jesus of Nazareth: Millenarian Prophet* (Minneapolis, MN: Fortress Press, 1998); Marcus J. Borg, *Jesus, A New Vision: Spirit, Culture, and the Life of Discipleship* (San Francisco: Harper & Row, 1987); idem, *Jesus in Contemporary Scholarship* (Valley Forge, PA.: Trinity Press International, 1994); idem, *Meeting Jesus Again for the First Time* (San Francisco: HarperSanFrancisco, 1994); John Dominic Crossan, *The Historical Jesus: The Life of a Mediterranean Peasant* (San Francisco: HarperSanFrancisco, 1991); idem, *Jesus: A Revolutionary Biography* (San Francisco: HarperSanFrancisco, 1994); B. D. Ehrman, *Jesus: Apocalyptic Prophet of the New Millennium* (Oxford: Oxford University Press, 1999); Fiorenza, *In Memory of Her*; Richard A. Horsley, *Jesus and the Spiral of Violence: Popular Jewish Resistance in Roman Palestine* (San Francisco: Harper & Row, 1987).

108. Ruether, *To Change the World*, 45-56.

109. Jann Aldredge-Clanton, *In Search of the Christ-Sophia: An Inclusive Christology for Liberating Christians* (Mystic, CT: Twenty-Third Publications, 1995), 5. This work includes resources for worship.

110. Cf. Carter Heyward, *Speaking of Christ: A Lesbian Feminist Voice*, ed. Ellen C. Davis (New York, NY: Pilgrim Press, 1989), chap. 1 and 2.

that "If God is male, then the male is God"[111] has been proven over and over every time the Church associated priesthood and maleness. It has been precisely the identification of Christ with maleness working in conjunction with a male-identified God that has been used as an excuse for excluding women from ordained ministry in many churches. It is clear that a male Saviour cannot save women. Rather, Christian theological history is a litany of oppression against women and not redemption for women.

Mary Daly gave her damning indictment against a male-dominant theology and a male saviour by removing herself from the Roman Catholic Church.[112] Daphne Hampson, formerly a member of the Church of England, chooses a genderless God in place of the masculine Christian God and writes, "Feminism represents the death-knell of Christianity as a viable religious option."[113] And Naomi Goldenberg passes a harsh verdict against Christianity's masculine divinity:

> Jesus Christ cannot symbolize the liberation of women. A culture that maintains a masculine image for its highest divinity cannot allow its women to experience themselves as the equals of its men. In order to develop a theology of women's liberation, feminists have to leave Christ and Bible behind them .... Feminist theology must cease depending on the metaphor of Jesus *himself*.[114]

Likewise, other feminists have also found the male God of Christianity and feminist struggle for human equality so incompatible that they felt they had no other option than to renounce Christianity. Some of them have gone over to primal and nature religions associated with the worship

---

111. Mary Daly's critique of the patriarchal Church appears in her earlier works. Daly's *The Church and the Second Sex*, is a response to the Second Vatican Council. Idem, *Beyond God the Father: Towards a Philosophy of Women's Liberation* (Boston: Beacon Press, 1973). In *Beyond God the Father*, Daly rejects the patriarchal God of Scripture and tradition as incompatible with and unredeemable for the liberation of women. Mary Daly's new religious philosophy appears in idem, *Gyn/Ecology: The Metaethics of Radical Feminism* (Boston: Beacon Press, 1978) and idem, *Pure Lust: Elemental Feminist Philosophy* (Boston: Beacon Press, 1984).

112. Ruether, *To Change the World*, 47. A part of the discussion and bibliographical references here are drawn from John W. Cooper, *Our Father in Heaven: Christian Faith and Inclusive Language for God* (Grand Rapids, MI: Baker Books, 1998).

113. Daphne Hampson, *Theology and Feminism* (Oxford: Basil Blackwell, 1990), 1.

114. Naomi Goldenberg, *Changing of the Gods: Feminism and the End of Traditional Religions* (Boston: Beacon Press, 1979), 22, 25; cited in Thompson, *The Promise of the Father*, 6n11.

of the Goddess.[115] Others have stayed within the Christian theological tradition and continue to try to change the unfair structures from the inside. Part of that effort is seen in developing a Christology which will enable women to encounter Christ as female, as sister and mother.

From the early Church to the Middle Ages, and through the Medieval period to the present, there is a long, if fragile, tradition of reflecting on Christ as mother or sister.[116] In *Oratio* 65, Anselm refers to Christ's suffering on the cross as the labour pains of giving rebirth to humanity in him as Mother. Similar theologies have been expressed by Richard Rolle and the Carthusian prioress Marguerite of Oingt. But one of the most striking writings on Christ as Mother comes from the meditations of Julian of Norwich, the anchorite of Norwich. Julian received her divine revelations in May 1373 and she spent years developing a theology of Christ as Mother. Christ is mother because: 1) He gives spiritual birth to us. 2) He is present at our original creation. 3) He persuades and guides us to our spiritual birth.[117] The value of Julian's writings, and others like hers, is that they indicate an ongoing desire to envision Christ, and also God and Spirit, in female categories.

Apartheid Ideas about the Holy Spirit

The Holy Spirit is the third person in the doctrine of the Trinity. The confession of God as "three in one," as Father, Son, and Holy Spirit is a foundational element of Christian belief. Yet the Holy Spirit is usually sidelined in theological discourse. Johnson points out that many theologians have acknowledged the Holy Spirit to be "the forgotten God." She notes the colourful language used by various theologians in reference to the Spirit: "faceless" (Walter Kasper), "shadowy" (John Macquarrie), "ghostly" (Georgia Harkness), or "anonymous," the "poor

115. Miriam Starhawk, *The Spiral Dance: A Rebirth of the Ancient Religion of the Great Goddess* (San Francisco: Harper & Row, 1979); Christ, *Laughter of Aphrodite.*

116. Eleanor McLaughlin, "'Christ My Mother': Feminine Naming and Metaphor in Medieval Spirituality," *St. Luke's Journal of Theology* 18 (1975): 367-86. In fact in the medieval period, more men than women used female imagery for Christ. Carolyn Walker Bynum, *Jesus as Mother: Studies in the Spirituality of the High Middle Ages* (Berkeley: University of California Press, 1982).

117. Noragh Jones, "Motherhood of God," in *An A to Z of Feminist Theology*, ed. Lisa Isherwood and Dorothea McEwan (Sheffield: Sheffield Academic Press, 1996), 149-52, esp. 150; Cf. E. Colledge and J. Walsh, eds., *Julian of Norwich: Showings, Classics of Western Spirituality* (London: SPCK, 1978).

relation" in the Trinity (Norman Pittinger), the "unknown" or "half-known" God (Yves Congar). She also notes that the Holy Spirit has been analysed as "homeless" in the West (Joseph Ratzinger) and "watered down" (Wolfhart Pannenberg), and the doctrine of the Spirit as the "Cinderella" of theology (G. J. Sirks).[118]

Coming after Father and Son in the sequence of persons in the Godhead, the Holy Spirit became susceptible to unfortunate assumptions, which have been exploited in order to destabilize the position of women in religious life. The first assumption is that the placement of the Holy Spirit in the third position also establishes the status of the Holy Spirit in a hierarchy of the Godhead. Another assumption is inferred from the male terminologies that are clubbed together with the Holy Spirit. It is often understood that since "Father" is a male term, and "Son" is also a male term, the Holy Spirit must be male too; after all, the spirit of a male God must logically be male. This understanding has been further validated by the use of masculine pronouns when referring to the Holy Spirit.

Although, as Ruether states, "The figure of the Holy Spirit picks up many of the Hebraic traditions of the female *Sophia* and *Hokmah* (spirit)"[119] it has not been enough to shake the traditions of the androgyny of God. Rebecca Button Prichard makes an insightful reflection of the association of Christian spirituality and Hebrew Scriptures. She states:

> Human being is a wholeness, heart and soul, body and spirit, and mirrors the wholeness and holiness of God. Ruach, the feminine noun that means breath, wind, and spirit, speaks of human as well as divine life. Its semantic field overlaps in places with heart and soul; it encompasses both heaven and earth, and it is the word used to name God's Holy Spirit.[120]

Of course, Prichard clarifies that she does not mean Hebrew thinking was good and it was replaced by corrupt Greek thought. She believes that the earliest Christian authors were Jewish and that the wholeness and integration of Hebrew poetics and language are not entirely lost in

---

118. Johnson, *She Who Is*, 130. Cited by Nicola Slee, "The Holy Spirit and Spirituality," in *The Cambridge Companion to Feminist Theology*, Cambridge Companions to Religion, ed. Susan Frank Parsons (Cambridge: Cambridge University Press, 2002), 171.

119. Ruether, *Sexism and God-Talk*, 59.

120. Rebecca Button Prichard, *Sensing the Spirit: The Holy Spirit in Feminist Perspective* (St. Louis, MO: Chalice Press, 1999), 15.

Christian Scripture.[121] Yet it is also true that in the Church traditions have repressed the feminine images of the Holy Spirit and whenever female imagery is associated with the Holy Spirit, the Holy Spirit gets marginalized.

Besides making the Holy Spirit a male spirit, the Church has also managed to limit the interpretation of the dimension of the Holy Spirit. The Council of Nicea (325 CE) condemned Arianism, which claimed that Christ was less than God, and stated that Christ was of the same substance as God and thus equal to God. However, the Nicene Creed left the Holy Spirit in an ambiguous situation by stating that the Holy Spirit proceeds from the Father. Not long after the Council of Nicea, the Council of Constantinople (381 CE) extended the formula of the Nicene council, adding the so-called *filioque* clause, which subordinated the Holy Spirit in relation to the Father and the Son: "And we believe in the Holy Spirit, the Lord and Giver of life, who proceeds from the Father [and the Son; *filioque*]." The text of these two councils made it sure that the Spirit that had hitherto been regarded in Hebrew thought as the life-giving breath (*ruah*), as the energy that brought forth the whole creation at the beginning of time, lost that identity. The spirit that was previously understood as the universal entity of all forms of life came to be available only through the Son.

Thus in theory the Holy Spirit is fully God and equal to the Father and Son, but in practice it is limited only to those who accept the Son, Jesus Christ.[122] The Church continues to insist that the three persons in one God are equal in spite of obvious contradictions that belie that affirmation. For instance, the custom of praying to God "through" Jesus Christ actually implies that Jesus is a medium for reaching God. And in Pentecostalism, the experience of being "filled by the Holy Spirit," manifested by speaking in tongues and other ecstatic charisma, when a person receives Jesus and is "born again" implies a Holy Spirit who is subservient to the purpose of God and Jesus Christ.

If left to themselves, male chauvinist theologians would most probably continue marginalizing the Holy Spirit. Perhaps they unconsciously fear the potential the concept of the Holy Spirit has to overturn the patriarchal construction of God. Conversely, feminist theologians have

---

121. Prichard, *Sensing the Spirit*, 16-17.

122. Sallie McFague, "Holy Spirit," in *Dictionary of Feminist Theologies*, ed. Letty M. Russell and J. Shannon Clarkson (Louisville, KY: Westminster John Knox Press, 1996), 146-47.

found, in the Holy Spirit, ample ammunition to challenge masculine images of divinity.[123] They see the Holy Spirit as the feminine divine. For instance, Eleanor Rae and Bernice Marie-Daly regard the Holy Spirit as the feminine divine who is present and active where unjust structures are challenged and transformed. Thus they seek to rediscover the Holy Spirit:

> We will rediscover Her as those who have gone before us have found her: as Wisdom; as the Mind of God/ess; as Relationship; as Love; as the feeling aspect of God/ess; as Creator; as Ruler; as Mother, Daughter, Sister, the New Eve; as the Presence of God/ess; as Radical Freedom; as the Embodiment of God/ess in the Universe. And in names yet to be revealed.[124]

Feminists have also attempted to retrieve ancient traditions about the Holy Spirit.[125] Ruether mentions a few Apocryphal texts that refer to the Spirit as female. In the Gospel of Hebrews the Holy Spirit is mother: "Even so did my mother, the Holy Spirit, take me by one of my hairs and carry me away onto the great mountain of Thabor." In the Acts of Thomas, blessing on the gifts for a Eucharist uses female language: "Bread of life ... we name over thee the name of the mother of the ineffable mystery of the hidden dominions and powers; we name over thee the name of Jesus." And the Gospel of Philip states that the female Holy Spirit could not have impregnated Mary: "Some said: 'Mary conceived by the Holy Spirit.' They are in error. They do not know what they are saying. When did a woman ever conceive by a woman?"[126] Ruether believes that early Christianity got it right when it used female imagery for the Spirit and states that this understanding of the Spirit held sway until it was marginalized and repressed by a victorious Greco-Roman Christianity.

---

123. For an overview of feminist challenge to traditional ways of interpreting the Holy Spirit see Veli-Matti Kärkkäinen, *Pneumatology: The Holy Spirit in Ecumenical, International, and Contextual Perspective* (Grand Rapids, MI: Baker Academic, 2002), 164-69.

124. Eleanor Rae and Bernice Marie-Daly, *Created in Her Image: Models of the Feminine Divine* (New York: Crossroad, 1990), 28.

125. Yves Congar, *I Believe in the Holy Spirit*, vol. 3 (New York: Seabury Press, 1983); Leonardo Boff, *The Maternal Face of God: The Feminine and Its Religious Expressions* (Maryknoll, NY: Orbis Press, 1987); Donald Gelpi, *The Divine Mother: A Trinitarian Theology of the Holy Spirit* (Lanham, MD: University Press of America, 1984); Alwyn Marriage, *Life-Giving Spirit: Responding to the Feminine in God* (London: SPCK, 1989). These references are taken from Slee, "The Holy Spirit and Spirituality," in *Cambridge Companion to Feminist Theology*, ed. Parsons, 171n2, 185.

126. Ruether, *Sexism and God-Talk*, 59.

Other evidences also indicate that the early Christians thought of the Holy Spirit as being female. In the oldest Syriac version of the Bible, Jesus uses the feminine pronoun to refer to the Holy Spirit. This occurs in John 14:26 while Jesus was comforting his disciples before his crucifixion. The Syriac text reads: "The Spirit, the Paraclete, She shall teach you everything." The word for "Spirit" in Syriac is feminine in gender and thus the Holy Spirit was always referred to as feminine. However, under the influence of Greek theology, translators of the fifth-century Syriac version, *Peshitta*, changed "She" to "He."[127]

Another argument for a feminine Spirit, as Jann Aldredge-Clanton points out, is found in the New Testament image of the Spirit giving new birth (John 3:6 et al.). The implication is unmistakeable. Giving birth is a female function. Thus the use of the masculine pronoun with the Holy Spirit is not an accurate translation.

If we wish to be very literal, the Greek word for Spirit is *pneuma*, which is neuter in gender. The preferred pronoun should have been "It." The problem is that "It" is not compatible with Christian theology as God is conceived as a personal God. Thus a choice has to be made between "He" and "She," of which "She" ought to be chosen because of the internal and external evidences discussed above. Ideally, an inclusive singular personal pronoun would have been most appropriate but English does not have any such word.[128]

While pointing out ideas of the "feminine dimension" or "feminine side" of God, many feminists have struggled with the fact that "the highest symbol of divine sovereignty still remains exclusively male."[129] Out of growing awareness that feminizing the Spirit is not going to take the feminist enterprise very far, a new strand of feminism evolved that focused on articulating new God language that would be truly inclusive. The dramatic and controversial presentation of the Holy Spirit by the South Korean theologian Chung Hyun Kyung at the Seventh Assembly of the World Council of Churches in Canberra in which she mixed East Asian Philosophy, Korean Shamanism, and Buddhism to interpret the Holy Spirit demonstrated the possibilities for women if the Spirit is

---

127. F. Crawford Burkitt, *Early Eastern Christianity: St. Margaret's Lectures 1904 on the Syriac-Speaking Church* (London: John Murray, 1904), 88. Referred to by Jann Aldredge-Clanton, *In Whose Image? God and Gender*, rev. and expanded ed. (New York: Crossroad, 2001), 37.

128. Aldredge-Clanton, *In Whose Image?* 38.

129. Ruether, *Sexism and God-Talk*, 61.

unleashed from patriarchal shackles. Chung Kyung invoked Kwan Yin, the Buddhist Goddess of compassion and wisdom, as feminine image of the Holy Spirit.[130] In similar manner, feminist theologians from various cultural and historical backgrounds are renaming the Spirit by allowing dialogue between Christian tradition and other heritages.

The radical approach of Elizabeth Johnson is also noteworthy. Johnson is not happy with simply naming the Spirit as female for that reduces the Trinity to two male persons and an obscure female still subordinate to the male.[131] Therefore, she proposes looking at all three persons of the Trinity through the theme of divine sophia. Her theological starting point is the Spirit, "God's livingness subtly and powerfully abroad in the world."[132] And she develops a systematic Trinitarian theology of Spirit-Sophia, "divinity drawing near and passing by," Jesus-Sophia, "wisdom made flesh," and Mother-sophia, "unoriginate origin," based on women's experience of the Spirit. Johnson's theological construction of divinity is a significant step towards conceptualising God in equally feminine and masculine categories. Jann Aldredge-Clanton raises a daring question: "If God can include three persons, can't God include two genders?"[133] The answer is easy: "yes."

Apartheid Hymns

About God in hymns, Jim Obelkevich writes:

> With God represented as a remote, powerful, sometimes martial figure, a father, king, lord or judge, the cardinal virtues are a childlike submissiveness and obedience. The hymns legitimate existing political authority and the social hierarchy; they recommend charity rather than justice and they defer the rewards of the righteous poor to the afterlife. Though portraying the relation between man [sic] and God in erotic terms, they reject sexuality and reveal a masochistic streak, as if to justify pain and suffering.[134]

---

130. Chung Hyun Kyung, "Come, Holy Spirit – Renew the Whole Creation,' in *Signs of the Spirit: Official Report, Seventh Assembly*, ed. Michael Kinnamon (Geneva: World Council of Churches, 1991), 37-47.

131. Johnson, *She Who Is*, 50.

132. Johnson, *She Who Is*, 122.

133. Aldredge-Clanton, *In Whose Image?* 63.

134. Jim Obelkevich, "Music and Religion in the Nineteenth Century," in *Disciplines of Faith: Studies in Religion, Politics and Patriarchy*, ed. Jim Obelkevich, Lyndal Roper, and Raphael Samuel (London: Routledge and Kegan Paul, 1987), 554.

These are strong words. Obelkevich's focus is on social and political issues, but here also the point is made – hymns have been made tools of gender apartheid. The pernicious influence of such gender-biased hymns that congregations have sung ever since they can remember cannot be measured. Most people can sing the hymns without looking at their words; they have been singing the hymns so often that they have inadvertently memorised the words. We can be sure that the theology of the hymns has also been memorised and internalised.

When I took charge of the women's hostel at Eastern Theological College as Hostel Superintendent, my house was just a few metres away from the hostel. During the evenings, when they gathered for prayers or for some social occasion, they would sing hymns and choruses. One song I heard them singing often was the chorus, "Father Abraham had many sons; Many sons had father Abraham. I am one of them, and so are you. So let's just praise the Lord!" Needless to say, at the first opportunity I got, I expressed to them the incongruity of females singing they were "sons" of Abraham. It did not occur to them that the song is inappropriate for them to sing. And I presume most females are like that. Social conditioning makes us oblivious to the most blatant forms of patriarchalism and sexist language. Some women have expressed how they felt out of place in church worship services. But the sensitivity, the feeling of isolation and of exclusion in male-dominant worship arises, in most cases, only after we become aware of it through some accident or have been told by somebody else. Until then, we happily sing we are "sons of Abraham," "sons of God," "brothers," and "men."

For many years, in a theological college, I myself sang traditional hymns like "Rise up, O men of God ....Bring in the day of brotherhood .... As brothers of the Son of Man," "Faith of our fathers," "Jesus shall reign where'er the sun .... And all the sons of want are blessed," "This is My Father's World," and "Christ the Lord is risen today, Alleluia! Sons of men and angels say: Alleluia!" without any thought of what these hymns mean to me, a woman. Looking back, I think I was not uncomfortable with singing these hymns and others like them because they "speak" the same language I hear outside the church, a language that takes no notice of the presence of women and makes women invisible. I had no reason to doubt that these hymns are anything but totally good. They had been sung by Christians for centuries. They were sources of blessings for countless people. What I did not know then was that the traditional hymns that are sung most often in churches were composed in contexts that were blatantly patriarchal. Their use in worship over centuries has imbued them with an aura of divine authority.

The "truth" of hymns is almost synonymous with the "truth" of scripture. They are called "sacred" hymns, "spiritual" songs, and the like, and many people do not want to entertain the idea that there might be anything wrong in them. Questioning the morality of hymns is almost like challenging the integrity of Scripture. Therein lies the problem with regard to hymns. The problem is twofold: the sexist language of the hymns and the sense of immutability with which Christians view them. This problem cannot be overemphasized since hymns express the theology of the Church, its faith, and its mission. When the hymns that are at the core of Christian experience are skewed, promote distorted views about female humanity and male humanity, and exclude sections of underprivileged people, the theological ramifications are disastrous indeed. The purpose of singing hymns is to involve members, unite the congregation as equal worshippers, experience the graciousness of God, and embody the power of God's salvation, but that purpose cannot be met when hymns are androcentric.

The examples of apartheid hymns I have named are obvious ones. When we really get down to it, the majority of traditional hymns in our hymn books are inappropriate for any kind of worship. In North East India, where the subject of non-sexist hymnals has not been broached except in a minority circle, people love the old hymns with the "thee," "thy," "thine," "thou," "art," "wouldst," and suchlike. Strange as it may seem, the old King's English is being treasured by pockets of communities outside the so-called "English-speaking" nations.

The language of liturgy and hymns has changed in many parts of the English-speaking world, in conformity with the changes taking place in society and particularly in conformity with the movement for the use of inclusive language. The Language and Liturgy Task Group of the Australian Council of Churches produced *Out of Darkness*, a worship resource to encourage and inspire the use of inclusive language in worship.[135] There are some useful suggestions in this resource book. For instance, it is suggested that substitutions can be made to hymns to make them more inclusive; "all" for "men," "people" for "brothers," "people" for "mankind," "humankind" for "all mankind," "Maker" for "Father," "The Word" for "His Word," "God" for "He," "You" for "He," and "The

135. Frances Ford, et al., eds., *Out of the Darkness: Paths to Inclusive Worship* (Sydney: Australian Council of Churches, 1986).

Christ" for "The Lord." The Task Group also suggested that "He" can be alternated with "She," and "Father" with "Mother."[136] The proposals made in the book are invaluable. They exemplify what can be done to make worship more inclusive.

However, the easy substitution of words for changing hymns is like doing patchworks; they are imperfect. It may be just me, but the substituted words appear clumsy for the tongue to sing. In some instances they affect the rhyme and metre of the songs. I deem the rewording of traditional hymns as proper for an interim arrangement, something to be used until new hymns that are appropriate to the theological climate of the times find their place in worship. Some of the traditional tunes that people cherish can be supplied with new lyrics (not changing a few words) and used for worship. But in general, I think that it is better to place the seriously flawed hymns in the archives, remembering them as historical landmarks representing an age that is long gone. Nevertheless, these suggestions will act as eye-openers for Christian communities in North East India, although many will probably regard these ideas as outrageous.

The theologies of the beloved old hymns have a stranglehold on women that they are unaware of. The examples of sexist hymns are too numerous to list down here. For the sake of convenience, I will only refer to some common Christmas carols. In the song "While Shepherds Watched," we sing: "...glad tidings of great joy I bring to you and all mankind ....goodwill henceforth from heaven to men begin and never cease." In "Joy to the World," we sing: "...let men employ their song." In "Hark! the Herald Angels Sing," we sing: "...Pleased as Man with man to dwell .... born that man no more may die, born to raise the sons of earth." In "God Rest Ye Merry Gentleman," we sing: "And with true love and brotherhood each other now embrace." In "Good Christian Men, Rejoice," we sing: "He hath ope'd the heavenly door, and man is blest for evermore." In "O Little Town of Bethlehem," we sing: "...and peace to men on earth." In "Love Came Down at Christmas," we sing: "Love to God and all men." These samples from a few pages of worship hymnal show very clearly that all the rejoicing of Christmas belongs to men. Some might argue and say that the word "man" is a generic term for "human beings." However, the use of "man" and "men" together with

136. Ford, et al., eds., *Out of the Darkness*, 71.

"gentlemen,""brotherhood," and "son" indicate that far from being generic these are actually male-exclusive terms.

The feminist insistence on using inclusive language for songs is so that women (and men) can sing wholeheartedly and with conviction. It is a search to worship God without pretending to be men, which is difficult when male imagery dominates Christian worship and hymnody. Brian Wren suggests that "the regal Christ sitting with God almighty is an idol."[137] Renaming and reimagining God in worship and using inclusive language is not meant to pitch women against men, but to facilitate a genuine encounter with God. Brian Wren says:

> God-talk in worship is of the utmost importance, because it slants and shapes our conceptions of God from early childhood. One reason it is so powerful is that worship looks for an encounter with God and therefore aims not to criticise language, but to open us to meet God through it.[138]

As well, Elizabeth J. Smith writes:

> Hymnody can help to change worshipers' expectations about the kinds of language and images that will speak of a liberating God who is calling the Church to move beyond patriarchal structures and habits.[139]

One prominent terminology in developing inclusive hymns is "emancipation." Marjorie Procter-Smith offers three ways of responding to androcentric language: using non-sexist language (avoiding gender specific terms), being inclusive (balancing male and female terms), and employing emancipatory language (transforming language and challenging stereotypical gender references.[140] The feminist hymn write Ruth Duck takes a different approach called "expansive language" – expanding liturgical language. According to her, expansive language "seeks not so much to eliminate traditional masculine imagery as to place it among a broad range of other metaphors from Scripture, tradition,

137. Wren, *What Language Shall I Borrow?* 233.

138. Wren, *What Language Shall I Borrow?* 5.

139. Elizabeth J. Smith, *Bearing Fruit in Due Season: Feminist Hermeneutics and the Bible in Worship* (Collegeville, MN: Liturgical Press, 1999), 206.

140. Marjorie Procter-Smith, *In Her Own Rite: Constructing Feminist Liturgical Tradition* (Nashville, TN: Abingdon Press, 1990), 63; Robin Knowles Wallace, *Moving Toward Emancipatory Language: A Study of Recent Hymns* (Lanham, MD: Scarecrow Press, 1999), 55.

and faith experience."[141] Expansive language aids in including everyone by applying appropriate metaphors for race, disability, and gender and also broadens our understanding of God. In her hymns, Duck uses feminine pronouns for God supplemented by persistent feminine imagery. In one of her hymns, God is "Sister Wisdom."[142] In another hymn, the Trinitarian image is modified as the Maker, Christa, and Spirit.[143] Feminist approaches may differ, but eventually all the efforts are leading towards greater appreciation of the feminist argument for equality and deeper understanding of the worlds of sense and images that may be used to honour God.[144]

The Search for Inclusive Language

Whether it is discussion about God language, or Christological terminologies, or hymns, I keep encountering the problem of sexism in the English language. I have to keep realigning the perspective from which I look at things from my particular linguistic and cultural background with the sense I get when I read texts in English. I am not alone in this. On many occasions, I have found that other people from North East India and people with apparently similar linguistic characteristics as my own confuse the pronouns "he" and "she," using them interchangeably and indiscriminately. We often find ourselves using "he" while referring to a woman and "she" while referring to a man.

Gendered personal pronouns are not used often in tribal languages and so learning to use gender-differentiating pronouns with every reference to a person can prove to be challenging. I myself did not notice this basic difference between English and my own A·chik language probably because I started learning English from nursery school. However, I can understand the shock that some people experience when they are exposed to the English language. Satoko Yamaguchi, a Japanese feminist theologian expresses the experience of hearing androcentric language

141. Ruth C. Duck, "Expansive Language in the Baptized Community," in *Primary Sources in Liturgical Theology: A Reader*, ed. Dwight W. Vogel (Collegeville, MN: The Liturgical Press, 2000), 292.

142. Ruth C. Duck, *Circles of Care: Hymns and Songs* (Cleveland: The Pilgrim Press, 1998), 7; Cf. idem, *Dancing in the Universe: Hymns and Songs* (Chicago: GIA Publications, 1992), 14.

143. Duck, *Circles of Care*, 17.

144. Further on women's contribution in hymnody Janet Wootton, ed., *This is Our Song: Women's Hymn Writing* (London: Epworth Press, 2010).

when she arrived in the United States in a way that the tribal communities of my region would easily identify with:

> I was astounded by the use of male personal pronouns in reference to G*d in the English language. For example, people would speak about G*d as follows, "God is love. He loves you." My first impression was, "Oh, No! G*d is *male* in this culture!" It seemed strange to me that gendered personal pronouns would be used for G*d, since G*d was not a human being and thus neither female nor male. In Japanese, G*d is always *kami* (G*d), never "She" or "He." Before coming to the United States, I had never thought about G*d as "He."

Yamaguchi then reasons:

> If a woman has to identify herself with "he" always and everywhere in her daily life, how extensively might her self-identity be hurt and distorted? I thought, "What a horribly violent language English is!"[145]

Since we know and perceive things through language, an androcentric language such as English must surely impact women in a negative way, making them feel lesser than men. The impact cannot be anything but catastrophic when that same linguistic culture is allowed to intrude into biblical theology, into language about God, into concepts of Jesus, and into the language of worship.

In my experience, the local cultures have actively promoted theological expostulations aimed at subjugating women. There is an unholy alliance between culture and Scripture in the denial of ordination to women, enforcing covering of the head, and prohibiting women from preaching. There is a need to expose the patriarchalism in the Bible and the patriarchalism of our cultures. Knowing that the Bible is a patriarchal product means knowing that there are passages in the Bible that are sexist and discriminatory. This could be controversial, but I believe it is appropriate to regard the Bible as context specific, each segment being people's perception of God and God's activity during their time. We actually do this all the time without stating it. Why else would we adore a God who demanded that entire nations should be wiped off, including women, children, and animals? Why else would we regard some commandments as binding and others as meant for Israel and that only for a specific period of Israel's history? It is because we believe

145. Satoko Yamaguchi, "Father Image of G*d and Inclusive Language: A Reflection in Japan," in *Toward a New Heaven and a New Earth: Essays in Honor of Elisabeth Schüssler Fiorenza*, ed. Fernando F. Segovia (Maryknoll, NY: Orbis Books, 2003), 201.

God is working in a different way in our time. It is also because we believe our knowledge of God is imperfect and that our capacity to perceive God is limited. Thus our ethics, our moral values, and our sense of where God is leading us, will guide us in our interpretation of Scripture. Feminist exegetes will show the hidden part of biblical tradition, they will remember the forgotten, but there will be places where even the best exegete can do nothing. That is when we have to rely on our God-given conviction of justice and goodness, and God's graciousness, to do what is right in our unique context.

Translating the Bible with inclusive language is a step towards toppling apartheid in worship. The process is essential for changing our biased perceptions of God, for making liturgy holistic, and for writing new hymns. An important inclusive language Bible is *The Inclusive Bible: The First Egalitarian Translation* published in 2007. In this particular Bible, care has been taken to distinguish between modern sexist biases and sexism within the text itself. If the sexism is due to linguistic conventions, it is more easily corrected by adopting alternatives that are non-sexist. If the sexism is part of sacred scriptures, the task becomes more difficult but an attempt is still made to render the text in the best way possible without perpetuating the sexism and without destroying the actual text either.[146] When referring to language about God the translators make substitutions as follows:

> Where the usage is descriptive, we use "Most High," "Most High God," "Almighty," and "Sovereign One" in place of the sexist and classist form "Lord." Where "Lord" is a form of address, we use "Adonai" in Hebrew scripture readings and either "Rabbi" or "Teacher" in Christian scripture readings about

146. Priests for Equality, *The Inclusive Bible: The First Egalitarian Translation* (Lanham, MD: Rowman & Littlefield Publishers, 2007). This continues their earlier work idem, *The Inclusive New Testament* (Lanham, MD: Rowman AltaMira, 1996). Some of the significant previous publications on the inclusive Bible include: Burton H. Throckmorton, ed., trans., *The Gospels and the Letters of Paul: An Inclusive Language Edition* (Cleveland, OH: Pilgrim Press, 1992); Cross Cultural Publications, *The New Testament of the Inclusive Language Bible* (Notre Dame, IN: Crossroads Books, 1994); Victor Roland Gold, et al., *The New Testament and Psalms: An Inclusive Version* (New York: Oxford University Press, 1995). Other publications of interest include: National Council of the Churches of Christ in the USA, Inclusive Language Lectionary Committee, *An Inclusive Language Lectionary* (Atlanta, GA: John Knox Press, 1983-1988); Hymn Society in the United States and Canada, *Holding in Trust* (Carol Stream, IL: Hope Publishing, 1992); and United Church of Christ, *The New Century Hymnal* (Cleveland, OH: Pilgrim Press, 1995).

> Jesus' public ministry. We use "Abba" for "Father," where it expresses a close, familial relationship. We also used the phrase "Loving God" as a substitute for "Father" ....
>
> In referring to Jesus, we use "Only Begotten," "God's Own," and "Eternally Begotten" in place of "Son of God." "Son of Man" is a difficult problem because it has so many different shades of meaning .... We use "Chosen One" when it seems to refer to Jesus' self-understanding of his prophetic mission, and "Promised One" when Jesus appears to be speaking about his self-identity as an apocalyptic figure....
>
> The title "Lord," especially when it refers to Jesus, is hard to replace because it is confessional .... To avoid sexist and classist connotations, we use substitutes for Lord that are meaningful in our own confessing of Jesus, such as Sovereign, Savior, and Jesus Reigns.[147]

The value of *The Inclusive Bible* is that it goes beyond mere substitution of a few words and actually works at recovering meaning from sexist phrases and customs. For instance, "Whore of Babylon" in Rev 17 is translated as "Great Idolater" because the word which is translated as "prostitute" or "whore" implies selling sex in the modern context whereas the original meaning of the word in the Mediterranean world connotes idolatrous defilement. Another example is found in the genealogies, where the translators include Sarah with Abraham, Rebecca with Jacob, and Leah and Rachel with Jacob. And throughout the Bible, feminine imagery is emphasized.

Feminist insistence on the use of inclusive language in religious life has taken on new and unexpected trajectories as it has given voice to other marginal groups whose perspectives have been missed out in the contemporary language scene. Inclusive language is not just about our struggle for our right but about rendering equal justice to all people regardless of their gender, sexual orientation, age, physical and mental condition, economic position, political view, religious belief, and ethnic background. Some aspects of growing sensitivity towards these issues appear in a recent publication called *The Edge of God*, which covers various aspects of worship vis-à-vis people living at the margins.[148]

In this book, Susanna Snyder, in her article, "'Strangers' in the Sanctuary," discusses two kinds of approaches to asylum seekers in the context of British society: 1) welcoming them to standard Sunday services,

147. Priests for Equality, *The Inclusive Bible*, vi.

148. Stephen Burns, Nicola Slee, and Michael N. Jagessar, eds., *The Edge of God: New Liturgical Texts and Contexts in Conversation* (London: Epworth, 2008).

and 2) creating liturgies that support asylum seekers. Both approaches, according to Snyder, have merit but neither is adequate on its own. So she suggests an approach that will combine the best of both by looking at worship as an invitation to be transformed by strangers.[149] Several essays of the book also deal with the perspective of the disabled. Most church liturgies seem to assume that a gathered group of worshippers comprises solely healthy men. What about women and children? What about the disabled? Frances Young, whose son is unable to use language to communicate, stresses the importance of incorporating people with extreme disabilities in worship for the body of Christ embraces impairments.[150] And Jane E. Wallman-Girdlestone, who is visually impaired, makes a passionate plea on behalf of vulnerable people and people with disabilities. She uses her encounter with edges as a blind person as a metaphor for liturgical edges and proposes that blurring the edges, smudging liturgy, mingling experience, and blending diversity would enrich the liturgical and spiritual life of the Church.[151] Another perspective on liturgy comes from a dialogue about food between Claire Carson and Nicola Slee.[152] Claire's perspective is based on her struggles with being anorexic while for Nicola food had been something positive – symbolising generosity, sensual pleasure, and communion – although she is familiar with bodily frailty due to her own ill health. They argue that the Eucharist, with its emphasis on food symbolism, can exclude and cause pain to those who struggle with eating disorders. They then proceed to develop alternative liturgical resources that acknowledge the experiences of people with eating disorders, migraine, chronic fatigue and other bodily experiences, and create space for them in worship.[153]

While these essays are not specifically about the use of inclusive language, they are associated with the issue as inclusive language is all about being sensitive to everyone regardless of their physical or mental condition. John M. Hull's article deals more directly with language as he

149. Susanna Snyder, "'Strangers' in the Sanctuary: Asylum Seekers, Faith and the Church," in *The Edge of God*, 73-87.

150. Frances Young, "Songs without Words: Incorporating the Linguistically Marginalized," in *The Edge of God*, 91-103.

151. Jane E. Wallman-Girdlestone, "Blurring the Edges: Finding Commonality by Smudging our Differences," in *The Edge of God*, 104-16.

152. Taking my clue from their references to themselves using their first name, I do the same in my following references to them.

153. Claire Carson and Nicola Slee, "Brokenness, Love and Embrace: Eating Disorders and the Eucharist," in *The Edge of God*, 134-50.

analyses hymns from the perspective of the deaf and the blind. He cites several hymns as examples to show that metaphors and language often disparage deaf and blind people and alienate them. To drive home his point, he concludes with a verse from John Newton's "Amazing Grace."

> Amazing grace, how sweet the sound
> That saved a wretch like me;
> I once was lost but now am found,
> Was blind but now I see.

He suggests this altered version:

> Amazing grace that set me free
> And brought me to the light;
> I once was blind but now I see,
> Was black but now I'm white.

Hull argues, "Most people today would, I imagine, find the last line objectionable. So why not the second last line?"[154]

The issues raised by these writers matter to feminist scholars because inclusivity is not only about women but all those who have been excluded by language and practice. Many churches are comfortable with their established patterns of worship, with their cosy communities, and with their familiar liturgies. For the Church to truly become the body of Christ, it needs to become uncomfortable, experience the unfamiliar, expand its horizon, welcome everyone, and minister to all.

---

154. John M. Hull, "'Lord, I was Deaf': Images of Disability in the Hymn Books," in *The Edge of God*, 117-33, quote is from 131.

4

TRINITARIAN KOINONIA AND SPIRITUAL RENEWAL

In this chapter, I wish to take forward the discussion about the theological bases for community and communion. Christians can seek unity on the basis of such sayings of "that all may be one" (John 17:21) or the Church conceptualised as the "body of Christ" (Rom 12:5; 1 Cor 10:7; 12:27; Eph 4:12; 5:23; Col 1:24), or the fact that all have been baptised into "one Lord, one faith, one baptism" (Eph 4:5).[1] However, one of the strongest bases for unity, for koinonia or communion comes from the revelation of God as the Trinity. The formulation of God as three beings existing in God's own self is ground for a profound hope because it shows that diversity does not prevent unity but rather is the basis for relationship.

While the first section of this chapter is focussed on retrieving the significance of ancient Trinitarian dogma, the second section is based on tribal experience of the Holy Spirit as the basis for inclusive community. Feminists point to the fact that Spirit is a feminine noun in Hebrew. Thus the Holy Spirit portrays the feminine dimension of God. But my reason for discussion of the Holy Spirit is not primarily because of that theological notion. It is because in tribal history of Christianity, God has been most intimately experienced as the God who comes and dwells in us as the Holy Spirit. The communion or koinonia experienced during spiritual revival movements, when the presence of God in the community is felt to be real and visceral, is the basis for an inclusive community.

1. Cf. Everett Ferguson, *The Church of Christ: A Biblical Ecclesiology for Today* (Grand Rapids, MI: Wm B. Eerdmans, 1996), 401-06.

Trinitarian Koinonia and Christian Koinonia

Koinonia is a concept fundamental to the theological and doctrinal expression of the Church as an egalitarian community. Koinonia encapsulates the relationship of the Father, Son, and Holy Spirit, which is the basis for the relationship between churches of various denominations and also of a Christian's relationships with the triune God and with fellow human beings. My interest here is not just to restate the theological discussion about koinonia. My focus is on how to translate the theological principles surrounding koinonia into concrete expressions of faith that reflect the egalitarian and communitarian nature of community. But I will begin by defining koinonia and its biblical foundations, and then suggest overtures for developing Christian koinonia.

The Meaning of Koinonia

The word "koinonia" itself is a transliteration of the Greek word κοινωνία. Its Latin equivalent is *communio* and in English it is translated as "communion" and "fellowship." Koinonia in its Greek political context meant "partnerships created by holding things in common."[2] The Greek noun koinonia (κοινωνία) derives from the adjectival root word koinos (κοινός), meaning "communal," "common." In its noun form koinonia (κοινωνία), the word koinonia means "association," "communion," "fellowship," and "close relationship"; "generosity," "fellow-feeling," and "altruism"; "sign of fellowship," "proof of brotherly (sic) unity," "gift," and "contribution"; and "participation" and "sharing." In its verbal form koineneo (κοινωνέω), it means "to share," "to have a share," "to give/contribute a share." Koinonos (κοινωνός) is "a companion," "a partner," or "a sharer." And koinonikos (κοινωνικός) is one who is "liberal" or "generous."[3] The use of the word both in its transliterated form as well as in its translation with the use of a multitude of words is a clear indication that the word does not have an exact equivalent in English. That being the case, the use of just one word in English such as "fellowship" puts

---

2. Jeffrey T. VanderWilt explains: " 'Goods in common' might mean land or commodities or it could refer to social ideals, like 'beauty,' 'balance,' or 'harmony.' Sharing goods, the Greeks thought, is the foundation of human society." Jeffrey T. VanderWilt, *A Church Without Borders: The Eucharist and the Church in Ecumenical Perspective* (Collegeville, MN: The Liturgical Press, 1998), 10.

3. BAGD, 551-53.

the word in too narrow a frame which does not do justice to the richness and diversity of its meaning.

In the New Testament, the term koinonia occurs nineteen times.[4] Koinonia and its cognates appear primarily in the Pauline Corpus (Rom 15:26; 1 Cor 1:9; 10:16 [twice]; 2 Cor 6:14; 8:4; 9:13; 13:13; Gal 2:9; Phil 1:5; 2:1; 3:10; Philem 6) although it also appears in the Johannine epistles (1 John 1:3 [twice], 6, 7), Hebrews (13:16), and in the Acts of the Apostles (2:42). In the gospels, the term itself is not found but its derivatives appear in Matthew (23:30) and Luke (5:10).

Trinitarian Koinonia

To be sure, the term koinonia is not used in the New Testament to describe the relationship of the persons within the Godhead. It is also not used to express the relationship of the Father to the Son. In fact, koinonia is not even purely a religious or Christian term. It comes from the Roman idea of a legal contract known as *societas*. These were consensual contracts not based on getting profit out of each other but on an idea of partnership.

Unlike sale or hire, it is not a transaction in which the parties' performances are reciprocal. A *socius* does not give or do anything *in order to* receive a counter performance from his fellow *socii*. *Societas* is thus not based, primarily, on an antagonism of interests; its essence is the pooling of resources (money, property, expertise or labour, or a combination of them) for a *common purpose*. *Socii*, in the words of Daube, are not bent on getting the utmost out of each other; they are, in the first place, "friends", pursuing their common interests against third parties.[5]

---

4. George Panikulam, *Koinōnia in the New Testament: A Dynamic Expression of Christian Life*, Analecta Biblica 85 (Rome: Biblical Institute Press, 1979), 2. However, Panikulam says that the term koinonia occurs 18 times in the New Testament. But the terminology appears nineteen times. See Lorelei Francis Fuchs, *Koinonia and the Quest for an Ecumenical Ecclesiology: From Foundations through Dialogue to Symbolic Competence for Communionality* (Grand Rapids, MI: Wm B. Eerdmans, 2008), 9. Fuchs adds that including related terms and cognates in other parts of speech increases the appearance of the word to sixty-four times.

5. Reinhard Zimmermann, *The Law of Obligations: Roman Foundations of the Civilian Tradition* (Oxford: Oxford University Press, 1996), 451. The details of the law of societas are discussed in chap 15 of this work (451-76). The reference to Daube is from David Daube, "Societas as Consensual Contract," *Cambridge Law Journal* 6 (1938): 381-403, esp. 391.

Paul evidently borrowed this secular word and used it to refer to Christian practices in his letters.[6] In the Septuagint, the term koinonia appears only three times (Lev 5:21; Wis 8:18; 3 Macc 4:6). In all these instances, the reference is to the relationship between humans and never for the relation between God and humans.[7] Yet in Christian theology, the term koinonia has been found to be appropriate to define the mystical union of the Trinity.

According to Fuchs:

> In Christian understanding, trinitarian koinonia is the foundation for all koinonia. This theological language is suggestive of image and symbol, not of the literal and factual. That is to say, it is analogical language. Taken in this way, the language of the koinonia concept understands the communion of the trinity to be at the source of communionality and the competence thereof, precisely because the trinity is the archetype of Christian relationship.[8]

Scriptural support for trinitarian koinonia is found in reciprocal abiding of the Father, Son, and Spirit, which is the leitmotif of John 14-17. These four chapters spell out the mutual indwelling of the Father and the Son. Max Turner observes that within John 14-17, "it emerges that the essence of salvation consists in 'knowing' the Father and the Son (17.3)." Thus, "Salvation *is* communion."[9] The Father and the Son share a mystical union that is highly suggestive of koinonia although the word itself is not used by the Evangelist. The Gospel speaks not only of the love and unity that exist between the Father and the Son but also of the horizontal unity between the community of faith and the vertical unity between the community of faith and the Father-Son through the Spirit.

In John 14, Philip asks Jesus to show them the Father. Jesus replies, "Whoever has seen me has seen the Father" (14:9), "I am in the Father and the Father is in me" (14:10). Jesus urges them, "Believe me that I am in the Father and the Father is in me" (John 14:8-11). What makes the Father and the Son so completely identified with each other? The answer is scattered throughout the chapters. It is the Son's total submission to

6. J. Paul Sampley, *Pauline Partnership in Christ: Christian Community and Commitment in Light of Roman Law* (Philadelphia: Fortress Press, 1980).

7. Panikulam, *Koinōnia in the New Testament*, 4.

8. Fuchs, *Koinonia and the Quest for an Ecumenical Ecclesiology*, 26-27.

9. Max Turner, "The Churches of the Johannine Letters as Communities of 'Trinitarian' Koinōnia," in *The Spirit and Spirituality: Essays in Honour of Russell P. Spittler*, Journal of Pentecostal Theology, Supplement Series 24, ed. Wonsuk Ma and Robert P. Menzies (London: T & T Clark, 2004), 58.

the task of glorifying the Father, (14:13) and the Father's love for the Son and the Son's love for the Father and abiding in the love of the Father (14:31; 15:10), which ties them in a uniting bond that is an expression of koinonia at its deepest level. The Spirit is part of the union.

It is the Paraclete, the Holy Spirit, whom the Father will send, who will remind the disciples of what Jesus had taught them (14:26). The Paraclete will also be sent by Jesus (16:7) and the Paraclete will guide the disciples into all the truth and glorify Jesus (16:13-14). Thus the Holy Spirit is closely associated with the Father and the Son as one who is sent to reveal God to the disciples. In fact, the Spirit is the medium of mutual indwelling of the Son in the Father, the disciples in the Son, and the Son in the disciples (14:20). Jesus promises the disciples that he would not leave them orphaned and keeps that promise by coming to them and abiding in them through the Spirit.

The clearest feminist articulation of Trinitarian koinonia comes from Elizabeth Johnson. According to her, the Trinity "evokes a sense of ultimate reality highly consonant with the feminist values of mutuality, relation, equality and community in diversity."[10] She speaks of the triune God as a "Mystery of Relation." Johnson writes: "At the heart of holy mystery is not monarchy but community; not an absolute ruler, but a threefold *koinonia*."[11] In order to explicate the significance of the Trinity, Johnson relates it to women's experience of true friendship, which is not based on possessiveness but mutuality, as a metaphor for divine communion or koinonia.

> The love of friendship is the very essence of God. Hidden Abyss, Word and Spirit mutually indwell in a companionable communion of unimaginable strength. In Simone Weil's evocative words, "Pure friendship is an image of the original and perfect friendship that belongs to the Trinity, and is the very essence of God." In this living friendliness the hypostases are not determined by their point of origin or rank in the order of procession but exist in each other in genuine mutuality.[12]

The dynamic unity between the Father, the Son, and the Spirit is the model for the unity within the community of believers. In other words, the trinitarian koinonia invites all Christians to become, to use Fuchs' terminology, a "communionality." In his petitions to the Father Jesus

10. Johnson, *She Who Is*, 211.
11. Johnson, *She Who Is*, 216.
12. Johnson, *She Who Is*, 218.

asks that the disciples may all be "one" (17:21). That oneness is possible when through the Spirit the disciples are in reciprocal abiding in God just as the Father is in the Son and the Son is in the Father.

Overtures for Christian Koinonia

It is surprising then, that use of "koinonia" has been largely limited to the pursuit of ecclesiastical unity while its application for gender equality in the Christian community at large has not been sufficiently explored.[13]

The trinitarian koinonia is a powerful model for reshaping the relational aspect of the community; it is the theological *raison d'être* for an egalitarian community. Consider the mutual indwelling by which God is revealed to humanity. The mutual indwelling does not lead to a fusion of personalities or loss of self identity. Rather, mutual indwelling is made possible because each is a person and continues to be a person. Each person of the Godhead is who they are precisely because the other persons are who they are. "They are personal and communal because the persons of the trinity are distinct, and yet do what they do only because of their being in communion with one another."[14] One is not lesser nor greater than the other. Earthly koinonia that is called and inspired by the trinitarian koinonia ought to be a community in communion. A community in communion shares a common life – not subject to the dictates of culture or tradition and not established on unjust structures.

That brings the discussion from the theological basis of koinonia to the meaning of koinonia in practice. To the believers at Ephesus, Paul writes:

> Lead a life worthy of the calling to which you have been called, with all humility and gentleness, with patience, bearing with one another in love, making every effort to maintain the unity of the Spirit in the bond of peace. There is one body and one Spirit, just as you were called to the one hope of your calling, one Lord, one faith, one baptism, one God and Father of all, who is above all and through all and in all. (Eph 4:1b-6)

---

13. For its application with regard to ecclesiastical unity, see for instance, Thomas F. Best and Günther Gassmann, eds., *On the Way to Fuller Koinonia: Official Report of the Fifth World Conference on Faith and Order*, Faith and Order Paper 166 (Geneva: WCC Publications, 1994). See however, Leonardo Boff, *Holy Trinity, Perfect Community*, trans. Phillip Berryman (Maryknoll, NY: Orbis Books, 2000), who explores the significance of trinitarian koinonia and perichoresis (shared trinitarian life) for egalitarianism both in church and in society.

14. Fuchs, *Koinonia and the Quest for an Ecumenical Ecclesiology*, 28.

This passage is usually quoted as Scriptural support for Church unity as in the ecumenical unity of different denominations. Often, it is quoted as the basis for the unity of all believers regardless of ecclesiastical and doctrinal divisions. However, in its proper context, the letter is addressed to the Christian community and not to churches of different denominational affiliations. Of course, the message of the text applies to church bodies but there is clear misapplication when the interpretation of the text does not include the unity between individual Christians who constitute the body of Christ. The unity of the community is built on the unity of God who is "one" God. This unity is expressed in diversity. The same Spirit that indwells the believers and unites them in God also distributes varieties of gifts, services, and activities (1 Cor 12:1-11), thus calling forth unity in diversity.

The practicalities of koinonia are evident in Luke's description of the sharing of material goods and breaking of bread:

> They devoted themselves to the apostles' teaching and fellowship [κοινωνία], to the breaking of bread and the prayers.
>
> All who believed were together and had all things in common [κοινὰ]; they would sell their possessions and goods and distribute the proceeds to all, as any had need. Day by day, as they spent much time together in the temple, they broke bread at home and ate their food with glad and generous hearts, praising God and having the goodwill of all the people. (Acts 2:42, 44-47a)

Monetary contribution is considered as a koinonia in Romans 15:26:

> Macedonia and Achaia have been pleased to share [κοινωνίαν] their resources with the poor among the saints at Jerusalem.

Thus in koinonia there is mutual exercise of spiritual gifts as well as sharing of resources so that the needs of the community are met and the community stays healthy and grows. But the full implication of koinonia really comes out in the breaking of the bread, in the celebration of the Lord's Supper.

> The cup of blessing that we bless, is it not a sharing [κοινωνία] in the blood of Christ? The bread that we break, is it not a sharing [κοινωνία] in the body of Christ? Because there is one bread, we who are many are one body, for we all partake of the one bread. (1 Cor 10:16-17)

The κοινωνία, "sharing" in the Lord's Supper symbolizes the unity of the believers as one body for they partake from one bread. But its significance is not just symbolic; the outward unity symbolically performed in the sharing of bread and wine denotes a spiritual uniting of the believer with other believers as they share what Christ has given, his flesh and blood. Furthermore, the communion of the Lord's Supper is one by which the community receives God's grace and mercy as revealed in the Son. And because God's mission is to the whole world, koinonia also becomes the model for the transformation of the world into living agape.

So, what does koinonia imply for women? Koinonia means that women share equal dignity and partnership in the oikoumene of God. They belong to God's household and are beneficiaries of what God has given through Christ. Reality, however, is different. In order not to repeat what has already been said earlier, I will state this briefly. There is injustice in the Church. Women have been disinherited from the household of God and their share has been claimed by men. They are treated as inferior beings not fit for leadership in the Church and the ministry of priesthood. They have been silenced by a combination of narrow interpretation of Scripture, tradition, and culture.

Schüssler Fiorenza is one of the few who have looked at the concept of koinonia from a feminist perspective. Although she does not state it explicitly, her definition of koinonia is evidently derived from the *societas* – implied in her reference to J. Paul Sampley who, in a study of Paul's letters, referred to koinonia as a Greco-Roman legal term. Schüssler Fiorenza translates koinonia as "shared partnership and commitment," which is a "consensual partnership" that operates when partners are of the "same mind."[15] Writing in the context of the synod of bishops of 1985, Schüssler Fiorenza contends that "the synod was a splendid manifestation of patriarchal church."[16] A theme proposed by the synod, "church as *koinōnia*/communion" offers an opening for Schüssler Fiorenza to raise two incisive questions: "Does the 'salvific love of God for the world' include women? Have Christian women entered into the consensual partnership with God, Christ, and the Holy Spirit in the church for the salvation/well-being of everyone?"[17] Schüssler Fiorenza then makes two practical suggestions:

> First, as long as the college of bishops is restricted to men, that of cardinals should become restricted to women. Since the college of cardinals does not go back to Jesus nor stand in apostolic succession nor require ordination, no

15. Fiorenza, *Discipleship of Equals*, 272.
16. Fiorenza, *Discipleship of Equals*, 270.
17. Fiorenza, *Discipleship of Equals*, 272.

> theological obstacle can be fabricated that would prohibit the implementation of such a suggestion. If it were adopted, the next synod or council of the Roman Catholic Church would then be able to live and model koinonia, consensual partnership on an international and ecumenical level....
>
> Second, the synod declares "reciprocal dialogue between bishops and theologians" as necessary "for the building up of the faith and its deeper comprehension." Such a permanent reciprocal dialogue between bishops and feminist theologians ought to be instituted on a national and international level to foster a deeper comprehension of the church as a discipleship of equals in consensual partnership.[18]

Not only the Catholic Church but in any church, the leaders who hold the church in their power-greedy paws are not ready to notice the wisdom in Scripture nor to hear the cries of the daughters of God. But it is not for "men" to give women what is their due. Salvation is God's work. Koinonia cannot be forced or imposed. If I have a little grain of faith, it is to believe that God will bring transformation and is bringing change already in the Church. People, regardless of ethnic identity, gender, or status, are becoming one body. It is true women are not wanted – certainly not as leaders and ministers – by those who are comfortable with their theological and cultural excuses. These people will have to learn anew. They will have to let their reluctant fingers release their hold on the reins of power. But they need not fear because there is space for them in the new order; there is space for everyone. True communion does not exclude anyone.

The Significance of the Spirit in the Community

Pneumatology is not an easy thing to pin down. There is a variety of positions among the New Testament writers, doctrinal outlook varies greatly between various churches, and theological opinions are even more diverse. In this section, I do not intend to enter into a discussion of the doctrine of the Holy Spirit. Rather, my objective here is to highlight some aspects of the Holy Spirit from the perspective of the experience of the Holy Spirit in the churches of North East India. I will be drawing my conclusions from the book of Acts and the experience of the Holy Spirit by the people of North East India.

---

18. Fiorenza, *Discipleship of Equals*, 273-74. She refers to these suggestions as "practical" but for the Church it is anything but.

Pentecost and After

According to the writer of Luke Acts, the Church began with the coming of the Holy Spirit on the day of Pentecost. This event was something the prophets foretold in the Hebrew Scriptures:

> ... until a spirit from on high is poured out on us, and the wilderness becomes a fruitful field, and the fruitful field is deemed a forest. (Isa 32:15)

> For I will pour water on the thirsty land, and streams on the dry ground; I will pour my spirit upon your descendants, and my blessings on your offspring. (Isa 44:3)

> ... and I will never again hide my face from them, when I pour out my spirit upon the house of Israel, says the Lord God. (Ezek 39:29)

> Then afterward I will pour out my spirit on all flesh; your sons and your daughters shall prophesy, your old men shall dream dreams, and your young men shall see visions. Even on the male and female slaves, in those days, I will pour out my spirit. (Joel 2:28-29)

The Acts of the Apostles describes how after the resurrection and ascension of Jesus, the disciples of Jesus and certain women including Mary the mother of Jesus were constantly praying together:

> All these were constantly devoting themselves to prayer, together with certain women, including Mary the mother of Jesus, as well as his brothers. (Acts 1:14)

The author of Acts goes on to say that a group of believers, numbering at least one hundred and twenty people, were also with the disciples and took part in electing Matthias to be added to the eleven disciples. The Greek text uses the terms *adelphon* (ἀδελφῶν) and *andres, adelphoi* (ἄνδρες, ἀδελφοί) for this group of believers (1:15-16). The NIV and the NRSV translate *adelphon* in 1:15 as "believers" with the note that *adelphon* in the Greek is "brothers." As for *andres adelphoi*, the NIV translates it simply as "brothers" without any accompanying note, whereas the NRSV translates it as "friends" with the note that Greek has "Men, brothers." However, the BAGD lexicon maintains that while the singular is essentially a reference to "a male from the same womb as the reference person, *brother*," the plural *adelphoi* can mean "brothers and sisters" although there is room for uncertainty in some cases.[19] The vocative *andres* and *adelphoi* in apposition occurs frequently in Acts. Henry J. Cadbury maintained that *adelphoi* and *andres adelphoi* is used in Acts by the Jews and Jewish Christians to address fellow Jews.[20] Paul Trebilco observed that Luke delayed using *adelphoi* for Gentile Christians until Acts 15:1 and 15:22-23 in order to express that Jewish and Gentile Christians became truly "brothers and sisters" after the Jerusalem Council accepted the Jewish Christians as legitimate members of the movement without needing circumcision and without them keeping the whole law.[21] Thus the use of *adelphoi* and *andres adelphoi* does not mean that the group comprised males only, rather they refer to the Christians as a community.[22] What is remarkable about this description of the first recorded business of the Christian Church is that the election of an apostle was not left to the coterie of disciples but referred to the entire community.

On the day of Pentecost, when "they" were all together in one place, the Holy Spirit came upon them (2:1-4). Again, there is good reason to assume that "they" included both women and men. However, because the presence of women is mentioned in 1:14, but not in 2:1-4, it is often assumed that the women were no longer there when the Holy Spirit came to indwell the followers of Jesus on the day of Pentecost. That assumption is called into question in 2:17-18, where Peter quotes the Prophet Joel to explain what had happened:

> In the last days it will be, God declares, that I will pour out my Spirit upon all flesh, and your sons and your daughters shall prophesy, and your young men shall see visions, and your old men shall dream dreams. Even upon my slaves, both men and women, in those days I will pour out my Spirit; and they shall prophesy. (Acts 2:17-18)

Unless it can be claimed that Joel's prophecy was only partially fulfilled and that only "sons" received the Spirit, Peter's speech clearly supports

---

19. BAGD, 18.

20. Henry J. Cadbury, "Note XXX. Names for Christians and Christianity in Acts," in *The Beginnings of Christianity, Part 1: The Acts of the Apostles*, vol. 5: *Additional Notes to the Commentary*, ed. Kirsopp Lake and Henry J. Cadbury (London: Macmillan and Co., 1993), 379.

21. Paul Trebilco, "The Significance of the Distribution of Self-Designations in Acts," *Novum Testamentum* 54 (2012): 35.

22. Cf. Ben Witherington, *The Acts of the Apostles: A Socio-Rhetorical Commentary* (Grand Rapids, MI: Wm B. Eerdmans, 1998), 120n21. According to Witherington, the language of family is used here and elsewhere to refer to Christians.

the view that women received the Holy Spirit and spiritual ability along with male believers. Thus from its very beginning, Christianity has been a movement of the Holy Spirit.

> Throughout Acts, the presence of the Spirit is seen as the distinguishing mark of Christianity – it is what makes a person a Christian. Acts 2:21 indicates that the giving of the Spirit is not just for ecstatic speech or gifts, because it enables one to confess the Lord's name from the heart and be saved in the first place. The Spirit, then, is the *sine qua non* for being a Christian, not merely a means by which one gets a spiritual booster shot subsequent to conversion.[23]

The indwelling of the Holy Spirit among the believers enabled women to take up roles and duties that would have been denied to them otherwise. In his exegesis of the scene in Acts 2, N. T. Wright points out an important line of reasoning. He notes that the Pentecost account of Acts 2 and the Baptism of Jesus in Luke 3 are structured on a similar theological framework, and makes this observation:

> Just as Jesus' baptism and anointing with the Spirit in Luke 3 is to be understood as standing behind and explaining everything else, from his "messianic" proclamation in Luke 4 to his messianic death and resurrection, so the coming of the Spirit in Acts 2 is to be understood as standing behind and explaining everything else that the church then does, particularly its worship, its mission, and its bold stand in obeying God rather than human authorities.[24]

Viewed from the perspective of this new insight, the life of the early Christian communities, especially the role of women, becomes all the more significant. Leadership was not limited to men. Women served as evangelists, teachers, and deacons. All the four virgin daughters of Philip exercise the gift of prophecy (Acts 21:9). Priscilla and her husband Aquila led a house church and they are referred to as colleagues of Paul in Corinth and Ephesus (Acts 18:2-3; cf. Rom 16:3-4; 1 Cor 16:19). Priscilla and Aquila also had the authority to explain the "Way of God"

23. Witherington, *Acts of the Apostles*, 140. Witherington notes that Paul's view of the Holy Spirit in or by which believers become the body of Christ (1 Cor 12:13) is similar to Luke's view. In both, spiritual baptism has nothing to do with achieving spiritual superiority.

24. N. T. Wright, "Worship and the Spirit in the New Testament," in *The Spirit in Worship – Worship in the Spirit*, ed. Teresa Berger and Bryan D. Spinks (Collegeville, MN: Liturgical Press, 2009), 6. Further on the parallels between the inauguration of the ministry of Jesus in Luke and the beginning of the church in Acts, see Graham H. Twelftree, *People of the Spirit: Exploring Luke's View of the Church* (Grand Rapids, MI: Baker Academic, 2009), 30-32, 75.

to Apollos, a prominent leader in the early Church (Acts 18:26). Tabitha (Dorcas), the only person on record to have been raised to life by an apostle, was a "disciple" devoted to good works and charity (Acts 9:36). Lydia, "a dealer of purple" and hence a businesswoman, was converted and baptized along with her household in Philippi, and this began the Church in Europe (Acts 16:14-15, 40).

Thus women were apostles, disciples, deacons/bishops, evangelists, prophetesses, presbyters, and house church leaders. All this sharing of responsibilities and leadership was made possible by the presence of the Spirit, because the presence of the Spirit is also the presence of the living God in the life and works of the community. Patriarchal barriers were broken. Gender considerations did not get in the way of serving God, serving the community, and ministering to the world.

Comparing the New Testament accounts with the context of the tribal churches in North East India, the presence of so many prominent women in the early Christian movement is remarkable. The contrast is very stark. The picture of the ways of the early Christians, where women were active as apostles, evangelists, teachers, deacons, leaders, and co-workers with other disciples is unrecognisable in contexts where women have to be submissive and silent. The account of the active participation of women in the Church is strange not because people did not read those passages; it is because those passages were always shown through the optic of patriarchy. Thus even when women read those early stories, they assumed the women were helping men and giving them support, not leading or teaching men about Scriptures.

It is significant that in the Acts account the Holy Spirit continued to be manifested in the life of the Church after the Pentecost event. In Acts 4:31, the Holy Spirit comes and fills the followers of Jesus; it is accompanied by a shaking of the place where they were gathered in a prayer meeting. In Acts 8:17, Samaritans, who had been baptized, but on whom the Holy Spirit had not fallen, receive the Holy Spirit by the laying-on of the apostles' hands. In Acts 9:17-18, Ananias lays his hands on Paul and Paul is filled with the Holy Spirit, and something like scales fell from Paul's eyes and his eyesight was restored. In Acts 10:44-47, the Holy Spirit is poured out on Gentiles, who had not yet received water baptism, in the house of Cornelius in Caesarea while Peter was preaching, and they spoke in tongues and praised God. In Acts 19:6, twelve disciples at Ephesus, who were baptized but had not received the Holy Spirit, received the Holy Spirit when Paul laid his hands on them, and they spoke in tongues and prophesied.[25] From these accounts, it is possible to ascertain that for the early Christians the indwelling of the Holy Spirit meant a call to mission, the Spirit gave them ability to speak boldly about the work of God in and through Jesus. The ecstatic manifestations that accompanied the filling with the Holy Spirit appear to have served as a witness to believers and non-believers alike to the power that the Holy Spirit imbued the believers with (Acts 1:8; 6:3, 8; 10:38).

In Pauline writings too, we see the prominent role played by women in the early Church. Women in the early Church were involved in praying and prophesying (1 Cor 11:4-5). Phoebe was a deacon of the church in Cenchreae (Rom 16:1-2). Junia and Andronicus were an important missionary couple, compatriots of Paul, and in Paul's words, "they are prominent among the apostles" and he acknowledged that they were prior to him in their faith (Romans 16:7). Euodia and Syntyche were evangelists and Paul's co-workers (Phil 4:2). Apphia "our sister" was one of three leaders of a house church (Phlm 2). Chloe was a leader of a house church (1 Cor 1:11) and so was Nympha of Laodicea (Col 4:15).

The impartiality and egalitarianism seen in the early spirit-filled Church of the first century lost its impetus as the Church became more and more male-oriented and hierarchical in succeeding centuries. As Kirsty Thorpe notes:

> Women's status in the Church changed significantly between the first and the second centuries. By the later period, women's leadership survived only on the Gnostic edges of the early Church, and the main roles for women in the mainstream Christian community were marriage and martyrdom. This is a familiar pattern which has been replayed throughout church history. In times of change, when the authority of the Holy Spirit has been recognized, women's leadership has flourished. As the ferment has died down, however, and the authority of spiritual gifts has been replaced by that of the Church as an institution, the role of women has once again been restricted and downplayed.[26]

The observation that the role of women in the Church has been proportionate to the emphasis placed on the Holy Spirit is particularly true of North East India. As I will soon show, something similar to the Pentecost and the history of Christianity after the Pentecost has been replayed in North East India.

---

25. A discussion of the passages mentioned here and a few others can be found in, Twelftree, *People of the Spirit*, 69-70, 84-100.

26. Kirsty Thorpe, "Women's Ministry – a Developing Story," in *This is Our Story: Free Church Women's Ministry*, ed. Janet Wootton (Peterborough: Epworth, 2007), 40.

Pentecostalism and the Revival Movements in NEI

Perhaps modern pentecostalism and charismatic movements are indicative of the Christian search for their roots in the Holy Spirit along the lines of the experience of the Holy Spirit in Luke-Acts. The Pentecostal Church is the fastest growing church of modern times, but pentecostalism is not confined to it.[27] Pentecostalism is being felt across denominational affiliations from the Catholic Church to the Anglican, from the Lutheran to the Baptist. While the mainline churches, by and large, continue to seek to silence women, one can see that many women influenced by charismatic movements and/or pentecostalism have found their voices.

I do not mean to imply that pentecostalism alone is responsible for the greater freedom and egalitarianism that women have in churches in modern times. What I intend to show is that pentecostalism and charismatic movements that emulate the Luke-Acts Pentecost experience subvert patriarchal theology. In his study of the rise of pentecostalism, Harvey Cox makes an accurate statement when he says: "Pentecostalism is unthinkable without women." He notes that "women have continued to play a disproportionately prominent place in the pentecostal movement." I assume that by "disproportionate" Cox means "disproportionate to men" in the sense that there are more leading women than men in the pentecostal movement. Cox adds that "the salience of women in this movement has resulted in a dramatically different conception of who God is, and the quiet subversion of centuries of patriarchal theology."[28]

People of North East India are familiar with the experience of the Holy Spirit as manifested through charismatic gifts such as speaking in unknown tongues, seeing visions, and prophecy. During 1905-1906, the Khasis experienced a spiritual revival during which four thousand people converted to Christianity in one year alone. This was apparently

---

27. Murray W. Dempster, Byron D. Klaus, Douglas Petersen, eds., *The Globalization of Pentecostalism: A Religion Made to Travel* (Oxford: Regnum Books Intl., 1999); Donald M. Lewis, ed., *Christianity Reborn: The Global Expansion of Evangelicalism in the Twentieth Century*, Studies in the History of Christian Missions (Grand Rapids, MI: Wm B. Eerdmans, 2004).

28. Harvey Cox, *Fire from Heaven: The Rise of Pentecostal Spirituality and the Reshaping of Religion in the Twenty-first Century* (Reading, MA: Addison-Wesley Publishing, 1995), 121.

an effect of the Welsh Revival of the Presbyterian churches in Wales from whence missionaries had come to the Khasi Hills.[29]

At that time, the Welsh Presbyterian missionaries David Evan Jones (called "Zosaphluia," or the "old" missionary in Mizo; a term of respect as Jones was only thirty years old when the Mizos started using this name for him) and Edwin Rowlands (called "Sapthara" in Mizo) were working in the North of Mizoram and established in Aizawl, and the Scottish Baptist missionaries James Herbert Lorrain (called "Pu Buanga" in Mizo) and Frederick W. Savidge (called "Sap Upa" in Mizo) were working in the South of Mizoram and stationed in Serkawn (not the same as Serkawr or Saikao, which was the station for mission to the Mara people; Serkawn continues to be the headquarters of the Baptist Church of Mizoram), near Lunglei. The Northern and Southern region of Mizoram were then called North Lushai Hill District and South Lushai Hill District.

Hearing about the revival in the Khasi hills, Jones and Lorrain decided to send a joint delegation to Mairang, in the Khasi Hills where the annual Khasi Presbyterian Assembly was to be held in March 1906 in order to have a first-hand experience of the revival. The team from the North had seven members, of which three were women (Siniboni, Pawngi, and Thankhumi/Thangkungi) and four were men (Khuma, Thanga, Chawnga and Vanchhunga). Lorrain sent four members from the South, but one had to drop out because of an injury and only three went (Thankunga, Parima, and Zathanga). One of the women, Siniboni who was actually a Khasi woman, was the leader of the team of ten people.[30] They encountered many unusual things during the journey and in the Assembly too. On their long trip back home through dense forest, the team stopped before reaching Aizawl to offer a prayer of thanks. As each of them said a prayer, they had an amazing experience. Zathanga, one of the ten, said: "While the first of us was praying I was aware of a streak of flame, very high above us. And, as each one prayed in turn, the flame descended lower and lower and, as the last one prayed, it disappeared. I am sure it went inside us!"[31]

---

29. J. Meirion Lloyd, *History of the Church in Mizoram: Harvest in the Hills*, Gospel Centenary Series, 1 (Aizawl, Mizoram: Synod Publication Board, 1991), 88-89.

30. Lloyd, *History of the Church in Mizoram*, 89-90.

31. Lloyd, *History of the Church in Mizoram*. 94.

After the contingent returned from the tour, the expected revival did not happen on their Sunday public meetings. However, as a farewell meeting was being conducted on Monday at the Aizawl schoolhouse for the contingent members from the South returning home, something strange happened while the hymn "God be with you till we meet again" was being sung. A euphoric state possessed the congregation. They sang it again and again and other hymns as well with great fervour. Soon it was time for school, and children carrying their books and slates came and joined the meeting. The meeting went on spontaneously for hours. They said prayers and sang hymns alternately. Sometimes the whole congregation prayed together in "mass" prayer—all the members saying their petitions aloud at the same time—and it sounded like the crashing of the waves of the sea on the shore. If someone kept on praying too long, the congregation would start singing a hymn. People, including school children, stood up on their own accord and confessed their sins and dedicated themselves to Jesus. The sound of the revival reached the people in two neighbouring villages and people from those villages hurried to the Aizawl schoolhouse. The doors and windows of the schoolhouse were flung open as the congregation kept growing in number. The enthusiasm of the gathering was such that it took some effort to persuade people to go home to eat food. An open-air meeting on a nearby hill was promised for the afternoon. This was the first of similar meetings that was conducted every day for weeks, and sometimes these meetings continued till midnight. A great revival swept across the Mizo country. Very often, people in the congregation would fall unconscious as the Holy Spirit descended upon them. Some of them would utter prophecies while in a trance. Others would see visions during their trance and recount them after regaining consciousness.[32]

A second wave of revival occurred among the Mizos in 1913. A third wave followed in 1919. And a fourth wave began in the early 1930s. The fourth wave kindled missionary zeal much more intensely than the previous revivals. Ever since then, mission work has been a major emphasis of the Christians of Mizoram. Even sixty years later, that enthusiasm has not diminished in the least. By 1994, the Mizoram Presbyterian Church was supporting 1,763 missionaries. Most of them were working in the neighbouring tribal areas and other communities

32. Lloyd, *History of the Church in Mizoram*, 94-96.

in India, and 190 were working in mission fields outside India.[33] The Baptist Church of Mizoram is equally enthusiastic about mission work. For instance, in its annual budget of 2002-2003, the Baptist Church of Mizoram set aside 40 percent of its funds, amounting to more than thirty one million rupees, for outreach mission work.[34] These figures are remarkable considering that the Mizo population is less than a million. It is unlikely that any community in the world can compare to the Mizos in the proportion of missionaries and financial resources they invest in missionary activities.

From the Mizo hills, the fires of the revival spread to Manipur around 1922, reaching first the Kuki tribes, who share ethnic affinity with the Mizos, and then moving to the Tangkhul Nagas. The revival was marked by prolonged prayer meetings, ecstatic utterances, dreams and visions, and millennial ideas. These were considered excessive and condemned by the American Baptist missionaries in Manipur.[35] The Nagas of Nagaland also experienced a series of revivals in 1956, 1966, and 1972. The revival of 1972 coincided with, and was perhaps set off by an evangelistic crusade of Billy Graham and Akbar Haqq, an associate of Billy Graham, which was attended by about 500,000 people.[36] At the height of the 1972 revival, people became so enthusiastic about worship that they were reluctant to go home. Household activities were forgotten and crops lay unattended in the fields. People brought blankets to church so they would not need to go home. They stayed for weeks in church, constantly praying, singing hymns, and reading and sharing from the Bible. Thousands upon thousands of people dedicated their lives to the Saviour and many of them dedicated their yet-to-be-born and even their yet-to-be-conceived children to the service of God.

---

33. Zari Malsawma, "The Mizos of Northeast India: Proclaiming the Gospel to their Neighbors Near and Far," *Mission Frontiers* (Nov-Dec 1994), http://www.missionfrontiers.org/issue/article/the-mizos-of-northeast-india (accessed Aug 28, 2018).

34. Baptist Church of Mizoram, "Outreach Missions," https://www.mizobaptist.org/outreach-missions/ (accessed Aug 28, 2018).

35. John Parratt and Saroj N. Arambam Parratt, " 'Kabui Messiah': The Jadonong Movement in Manipur," http://thohepou.wordpress.com/2007/08/22/kabui-messiah-the-jadonong-movement-in-manipur/ (accessed Aug 28, 2018).

36. Manpreet Singh, "The Soul Hunters of Central Asia," *Christianity Today* (Feb 1, 2006), http://www.christianitytoday.com/ct/2006/february/38.51.html (accessed Aug 28, 2018).

Wherever revivals struck, the religious composition of the population was completely transformed. Indeed, it would not be remiss at all to declare that the tribal churches of the hills of North East India were born in the fires of revivals of the Holy Spirit. Foreign missionaries did the initial work but it was the power of the Holy Spirit that shook the tribal communities and turned them into Christians. According to the Indian population census of 2011, the number of Christians is 74.59 percent in Meghalaya, 87.16 percent in Mizoram, 41.29 percent in Manipur, and 87.93 percent in Nagaland. The figures are very different where no revival, or no revival of significance, had occurred: 30.26 percent in Arunachal Pradesh, 3.74 percent in Assam, 9.91 percent in Sikkim, and 4.35 percent in Tripura.[37]

A striking feature of these revival movements is that they enabled women to gain greater freedom in society. Revivals are a culture-changing phenomenon. Societies that would not normally tolerate a woman opening her mouth in the presence of men and that would not allow a woman to become a leader of the community whatever her abilities might be changed with the arrival of revival. Women were the recipients of the gifts of the Holy Spirit along with men. In fact, very often, more women than men were exercising the gifts of seeing visions, prophesying, and speaking in tongues and interpreting tongues. Women were central figures in the mission of the Church and provided spiritual leadership. Revival strengthened egalitarian outlook because in a revival meeting anyone, regardless of age or gender, can be filled with the Holy Spirit and see visions, pray in tongues, utter prophecies, or share testimony. When a message comes directly from God in the Holy Spirit, no one dares to challenge it; after all, a Spirit-filled person is not acting of his or her own volition but under the influence of the power of God.[38] Since the events of the revivals in North East India and the history of early pentecostalism appear to share similar characteristics, I offer this quote

37. Census Population 2015 Data, "Christian Religion Census 2011," https://www.census2011.co.in/data/religion/3-christianity.html (accessed Aug 28, 2018). The percentage of Christians in Nagaland fell from 89.96 percent in the 2001 census to 87.93 percent in the 2011 census. Conversely, Arunachal Pradesh had 18.72 percent of Christians in the 2001 census and it rose to 30.26 percent in 2011.

38. The same has been the case in churches where the Holy Spirit is given greater importance. Thorpe, "Women's Ministry – a Developing Story," in *This is Our Story*, ed. Wootton, 31: "Within Free Church traditions, which stress the work of the Holy Spirit, the occasional presence of women carrying a strong sense of God's call to preach and teach has been more difficult to silence and overlook."

from Cox who observes, after visiting Pentecostal churches in many parts of the world, that women always play some leading role and participate fully in worship:

> They sing and testify, prophesy and heal, counsel and teach. In fact, it often appeared that the part men play in pentecostal churches is more shadow than substance. It also became evident to me that women, far more than men, have been the principal bearers of the pentecostal gospel to the four corners of the earth.[39]

But Cox also notes that pentecostalism has not always been supportive of women's leadership.

> But pentecostalism has not always adhered to this [egalitarian] momentum. Ever since the beginning of the modern movement, both men and women have tried to undercut the Spirit's gender impartiality. And they have met with considerable success, especially where pentecostals have drifted into theological alliances with fundamentalists who insist on enforcing the dictum from Corinthians 14:34 which says that women should be silent in church. But wherever the original pentecostal fire breaks through the flame-extinguishing literalist theology, women shine.[40]

It was the same in the revival movements of North East India. Substitute "pentecostals" with "Revivalists" in the above quotes, and the statements would fit as though Cox were speaking of the Revivalists in North East India. As time went by and the fires of the revivals began to dwindle, the call to organise the Church along conventional lines became more strident. Spirit-led and gift-wielding leadership gave way to election and ordination of Church leaders, and women and men who had naturally emerged as leaders of the community were pushed to the sidelines. The Holy Spirit that was poured freely upon all, which did not discriminate between sons and daughters, was replaced by a domesticated Holy Spirit, or more precisely, a cautious "use" of the Holy Spirit, a Holy Spirit that is restrained by cultural beliefs and principles of Church governance and dogmas that make leadership available only for males. Women lost their place in the life and ministry of the Church.

In Mizoram, three men namely Rosema, Dala, and Darchhinga were odained as elders in the first Presbytery held in 1910 at the Aizawl church.[41] This was followed by the ordination of the first Mizo Pastor,

39. Cox, *Fire from Heaven*, 125.
40. Cox, *Fire from Heaven*, 125.
41. Lloyd, *History of the Church in Mizoram*, 124.

Chhuahkhama, in 1913.[42] From then until today no woman has ever been ordained as an elder or pastor in the Presbyterian Church of Mizoram. The other major denomination in Mizoram, the Baptist Church of Mizoram (BCM), which has very close historical ties with the Presbyterians and which has a centralized system of government like the Presbyterians, bucked a century of patriarchal bias and ordained R. L. Hnuni as its first woman minister in 2012. However, according to reports, the ordination was given with the rider that she will not ask to become the pastor of a church. Thus while there is a movement to make the church more inclusive, opposition to the inclusion of women in ministry is really strong. So long as men alone continue to hold positions of power in the church, this will continue to be the case. In the Presbyterian Church of the Khasi and Jaintia Hills of Meghalaya, leadership and church ministry is still held solely by males. Among the Nagaland Baptist Church Council and the Manipur Baptist Church, patriarchal ideals have held sway until very recently when a few women have been ordained. Only a negligible number of women are in ordained ministry and they constantly face sexist behaviour from people.

During the revivals in the North East, the appeal for restraining the "excesses" of emotional and ecstatic outbursts came from devout Christians who felt that the practice of gifts should conform to what the Bible says about it. Theologically, the ones calling for rational, biblical, orderly worship were fundamentalists or Biblicists who were of the view that the Bible must be interpreted literally. The theological discord between those who wanted to follow traditional Christianity and those who felt that the Holy Spirit supersedes everything else grew until congregations splintered into new denominational groups. The theological difference between the extremists/charismatics and the rationalists/conservatives/fundamentalists may be summed up in the words Cox uses to describe the antagonism between Pentecostals and fundamentalists:

> What clearly bothered the fundamentalists more than anything else was the same issue that has divided them from the pentecostals ever since [the antipentecostal attacks in the first decade of pentecostal history]: the question of spirit versus letter. While both parties claimed to believe that both the Bible and the Holy Spirit are sources of authority, clearly the pentecostals put much more weight on the Spirit than the fundamentalists do. In their growing emphasis on the authority of the letter, fundamentalists soon began to teach that every

42. Lloyd, *History of the Church in Mizoram*, 163-64.

> single word of the Bible was verbally inspired and that to differ with them on this novel view of scripture was to read oneself out of Christianity altogether.[43]

The gain of fundamentalist theology in North East India is a great loss for women. Revival had opened opportunities for women and enabled women to tell their stories in their community churches. It would appear that women are consistently drawn to pentecostalism and charismatic movements because these movements allowed them space to tell their stories—through sharing their testimony and through expressions of their visions and prophecies. Telling stories, after all, is of utmost importance for all humans and especially for women, as argued in chapter 1. All this changed when Biblical teaching was offered by fundamentalists as the reason women should be silent in the churches. There were no definite lines separating the fundamentalists from the charismatics; almost everybody had experienced the same spiritual passion brought about by the revivals that swept across the hills. But the inconspicuous conflict between those who gave more importance to the ecstatic elements of the Holy Spirit and those who supported a literal interpretation of the Bible shook the foundations of the churches.

In the context of North East India, especially of Mizoram, it is necessary to distinguish between the revivalism that swept across the region in the early twentieth century and the sectarian groups that sprang up later on. There are over eighty religious sects in Mizoram. Some of the sects are so radical that the major Christian denominations hold them in contempt while some are barely Christian.

For instance, one sectarian group was started by a man named Lalzawna in the 1980s. Lalzawna claimed he saw a vision of a huge rock rolling from the East in order to punish the people because of their sins. He found many followers and together they migrated eastward and settled near a place called Champhai. Vanawia Pawl, founded by Vanawia, also arose during that same period. The teachings of this sect are based upon writings on the arm of Laldiheli, wife of Vanawia, which were regarded as divine text. They are nudists and live in a colony in the forest. Another strange sect was established by Ziona who saw himself as something of a Solomon. He married 39 wives and has 94 children. At present, he is said to have 33 grandchildren and many daughters-in-law. This group is named after Ziona's late father Chana, and is called Chana Pawl. Ziona has a following of about 400 families and they live

43. Cox, *Fire from Heaven*, 75-76.

in a village of their own. They are experts at making wooden furniture and adept at producing utensils with aluminium. There are some other sects who do not believe in secular education and do not send their children to schools. Yet another religious group is called Bnei Manashe, "children of Manashe." This group believe they are one of the lost tribes of Israel and converted from Christianity to Judaism. They have been accepted as such by the Jewish authorities of Israel and many of them have migrated to Israel.[44]

Unlike revival movements that are based mainly on the experience of an outpouring of the Holy Spirit, these pseudo-revival groups are not based on any experience of the Holy Spirit. Furthermore, unlike revival movements that result in numerous conversions, these sectarian groups are small groups which have no significant impact on the community at large. In these later movements, women are denied leadership positions within the sect.

In Nagaland, the post-revival breakup of the church has not resulted in scores of splinters as in Mizoram. The Naga Christians essentially broke up into two distinct groups. The majority of the people remained in the Baptist group but a small group broke away and formed a new denominational church called the Christian Revival Church. The worship of the Christian Revival churches' is marked by speaking in unknown tongues, interpretation of tongues, visions, and prophecies. Besides these elements, the Revivalists also adopted some other obligatory rituals. One practice they adopted is the repetition of the phrase "Praise the Lord," or "Jihovah Tshe" (Angami for "Praise Jehovah"). The phrase is repeated three times at the beginning and at the conclusion of prayers, before and after sermons, and practically everything else during worship. Another characteristic of Revivalism in Nagaland is the use of the word "Halleluyah," which punctuates their prayers, sermons, and talks.

Both the Christian Revival churches and the Baptist churches believe in the Holy Spirit, but the difference is in their emphasis and on what they think the Bible says about spiritual gifts. For the Revivalists, Mark

44. Zodin Sanga, "Mizos' Migration to Myanmar, Israel – All for Faith," *Heritage Explorer*, July 2012, 11, http://www.heritagefoundation.org.in/Download/heritage_explorer/2012/heritage_july_2012.pdf (accessed on July 30, 2018). The sectarian divisions, however have not became a serious issue because the majority of the Christians have continued within the major denominational groups: 66% Presbyterian, 15.6% Baptist, 6.5% Salvation Army, 5.5% United Pentecostal Church, 2.3% Roman Catholic, 2.1% Seventh Day Adventist.

16:17-18 is primary statement of faith and is said in unison in worship services.

> And these signs will accompany those who believe: by using my name they will cast out demons; they will speak in new tongues, they will pick up snakes in their hands, and if they drink any deadly thing, it will not hurt them; they will lay their hands on the sick, and they will recover. (Mark 16:17-18)

For the Baptists, the teachings of the Apostle Paul in 1 Cor 14:18-19 is put forward as support for the lesser degree of emphasis on ecstatic gifts:

> I thank God that I speak in tongues more than all of you; nevertheless, in church I would rather speak five words with my mind, in order to instruct others also, than ten thousand words in a tongue. (1 Cor 14:18-19)

In fact, 1 Cor 12, 13, and 14 are interpreted by the Baptists as evidence that the ecstatic gifts of the Holy Spirit are not more important than other gifts of the Holy Spirit (1 Cor 12:28 – first, apostleship, then prophecy, teaching, deeds of power, gifts of healing, forms of assistance, forms of leadership, and last of all, various kinds of tongues) and certainly not greater than the greatest gift of all, love (1 Cor 13). Baptists also believe that worship should be orderly (1 Cor 14:26-40) in order that God is glorified and that this does not happen when some people steal the limelight by drawing attention to their ecstatic gifts.

Then again, the Revivalists regard the worship of the Baptists as well as the Roman Catholic Church, which is another major Christian denomination in Nagaland, as "lifeless" and devoid of the active presence of the Holy Spirit. They place emphasis on millennial doctrine and think that ecstatic religious manifestations are a sign of their spiritual superiority.

But the fact is that revival in Nagaland had already died down by the time the split occurred. And no one denomination can claim spiritual superiority. The claim of the Christian Revival Christians that Baptists neglect the Holy Spirit is not an empty claim because cultural prejudices and patriarchal ideology dominate Baptist theological thinking. On the other hand, the Revivalists claim to have the Holy Spirit yet the Holy Spirit they display is a mere shadow of the reality, a poor imitation of the primal Christian pentecostal experience. They have a domesticated Holy Spirit, one who can be summoned at the will of the holder of the so-called spiritual gift, a far cry from the outpouring of the Holy Spirit experienced during revivals.

Yet the impact of revival is still visible in the deep spirituality of the people. Today, over seventy-five percent of the population of Nagaland are Baptist. Revivalists, Catholics, Pentecostals, Assembly of God and other denominations including one called Baptist Revivals, constitute about fifteen percent of the total population. Only about ten percent of the people are non-Christians and these are mostly non-Nagas who have settled in Nagaland. According to some estimates, less than 0.3 of ethnic Nagas of Nagaland are non-Christians, who still follow tribal traditional religion.[45]

On the basis of the experiences of women in the tribal churches of North East India, I find that the Holy Spirit is needed to move the people once again to reverse the disempowerment of women. Unfettered, the Holy Spirit will infuse the people with a sense of the mission of God and override petty human squabbles. I am not primarily looking for revivals of the outpouring of the Holy Spirit and manifestation of ecstatic gifts. Scripture says that the Spirit is mysterious like the wind and nobody can tell where it comes from and where it goes (John 3:8). Thus it is possible to pray for revival but it is impossible to make it happen out of human will. But there is something else that can be done and that is to articulate faith in terms of the Holy Spirit in such a way that the activity of the Holy Spirit becomes visible in the life of the Church and in the life of those who constitute it.

Developing a Pneumatology for Empowering Women

The preceding discussion has shown that the presence of the Holy Spirit in the community builds up the community because the Holy Spirit breaks down traditional and cultural barriers that segregate women from the

---

45. New World Encyclopedia, "Nagaland," http://www.newworldencyclopedia.org/entry/Nagaland (accessed July 29, 2018). However, I am not very confident about the accuracy of this information. It carries a number of wrong information. For instance, it says that the Indian epic, the Mahābhārata, refers to Nagaland. That hypothesis is tenuous at best. Then it claims that the Nagas embraced "the teaching of British Baptist missionaries," whereas it was the American Baptist missionaries who introduced Christianity to the Nagas. Furthermore, the website refers to the traditional religion of the Nagas as "animist." This is not true. Animism is the belief that a spirit exists in every object, be it animate or inanimate, and in natural phenomena. I believe it is invalid to use the term animism to designate tribal religion; animism is not really a religion in itself but its elements can be found in many religions of the world.

community because of their gender. For North East Indian Christians, perhaps their experience of revivals can be the basis to formulate a theology of the Holy Spirit which promotes the inclusive nature of the community.

One aspect of the Holy Spirit that is felt in a real way during revival is its mystery. The Holy Spirit is a mystery that becomes a reality in the life of people and yet remains mysterious. The Holy Spirit is beyond human control, and moves on its own volition, as God wills.

Another aspect is the power of the Holy Spirit. In the beginning of the creation of the cosmos, God's spirit, a mighty wind, was at work (Gen 1:1-2; cf. Job 26:12-13; 33:4; Ps 104:27-31). During the escape of the Hebrew people from slavery in Egypt, they experienced the Spirit of God working in a powerful way on their behalf. For God pushed back the sea by "a strong east wind" that blew all night, turning the sea into dry land, and parting the waters (Exod 14:21; 15:8-10). When Israel was in Babylonian captivity, the prophet Isaiah proclaimed that "the breath of the Lord" will destroy that empire like the blast of the desert wind withers the grass and the flowers (Isa 40:7). In Ezekiel's vision, dry bones are brought to life by the breath of the four winds (Ezek 37:9-10) which is further explained as the spirit of God bringing the house of Israel to life (Ezek 37:14).

In the revivals of North East India, people experienced the overwhelming power of God that can transform the villages and towns of the hills and mountains and valleys like no other force could. But perhaps the most important lesson the people can learn from the revival experience is that the Holy Spirit comes without any discrimination. Women, men, or children, all can come under the influence of God's spirit.

Complementarians believe that men alone have been given the authority to lead in the family, church and society. Yet there are so many occasions in the Bible where God bypassed husbands and other male members of the family to speak to women, empower them, and give them authority to act—without seeking the permission of men. For instance, in Judges 13, an angel of God revealed God's plan for the deliverance of Israel to Manoah's wife. Then there are women with spiritual insight and fortitude such as the unnamed wise woman of Abel Beth Maacah who saved her town from being destroyed (2 Sam 20:14-26), and the Shunammite woman who brought blessing to her family by welcoming the prophet Elisha (2 Kgs 4:8-37). God has not conferred spiritual authority to men alone.

For women, the stories of women in the Judeo-Christian Scripture who have done deeds of greatness under the influence of the spirit of God can serve as models for their empowerment in the present time. At the time of the deliverance of the Hebrews through the Sea of Reeds,[46] Miriam the prophet took her tambourine and led all the women in playing their tambourines and dancing. Under an anointing by God's spirit, Miriam sang: "Sing to the Lord, for he has triumphed gloriously; horse and rider he has thrown into the sea" (Exod 15:20-21).[47]

Much, much later, another woman bearing the same name as her and also filled by the spirit of God would become the mother of the Saviour and sing a glorious song of praise. Miriam's actions are similar to the spirit-filled and newly anointed King David who danced before the Lord (2 Sam 6:14-15).

Hannah, having been blessed with a child in answer to her prayers, praised God in an inspired song of thanksgiving: "My soul exults in the Lord; my strength is exalted in my God..." (1 Sam 2:1-10).[48] Huldah, prophet and wife of Shallum, keeper of the wardrobe, declared the coming judgment of God upon Judah for the king of Judah and its inhabitants had abandoned the Lord (2 Kings 22:14-20).

---

46. Although we are more familiar with the name "Red Sea," the Hebrew text of Exodus 13:18 is *Yam Suph* which means "Sea of Reeds" or "Reed Sea." The name "Sea of Reeds" is probably derived from the fact that plant life abounded in the area where the crossing of the sea occurred. There are no reeds on the shores of the red Sea. Later Jewish and Christian tradition developed the idea that the Israelites crossed the Red Sea during the exodus from Egypt.

47. Miriam's song is attributed to Moses in Exod 15:1. Yet research indicates that Exod 15 is more likely a song of Miriam than of Moses. There has been extensive discussion on this. See the various articles in Pt. 3 of Athalya Brenner, ed. *A Feminist Companion to Exodus and Deuteronomy*, ed. Athalya Brenner (Sheffield: Sheffield Academic Press, 1994), 166-258; Frank Moore Cross and David Noel Freedman, "The Song of Miriam: Exodus 15," in *Studies in Ancient Yahwistic Poetry*, Society of Biblical Literature Dissertation Series (Grand Rapids, MI: Wm B. Eerdmans, 1975), 31-45.

48. J. Gerald Janzen, "Prayer and/as Self-Address: The Case of Hannah," in *A God So Near: Essays on Old Testament theology in Honor of Patrick D. Miller*, ed. Brent A. Strawn and Nancy R. Bowen (Winona Lake, IN: Eisenbrauns, 2003), 127. Janzen sees Hannah's song as well as Samuel's epoch making role in Israel as consequences of Hannah's prayerful travail in 1 Sam 1. Borrowing Paul's words in Rom 8 he states: "In its internal thundering, inaudible to the ears of Eli, one may also hear her *śîaḥ* [meditation] as the echo within her own heart of the Spirit of God who, with unutterable groanings, makes intercession for her and her people. The outcome, of course, in Hannah's case, is the song of thanksgiving in 1 Sam 2:1-10."

Then there is Deborah, judge and prophet, who led Israel to victory, and enabled the land to rest for forty years (Judg 5:31). The Scriptures do not record an instance when the spirit falls on her. But some traditions name her, along with Miriam, Anna, and Huldah, as being filled with the Spirit of God.[49] Her song of victory is preserved in Judges 5.

To this list of women who danced before God, sang, prayed, prophesied, and achieved glorious deeds by the power of God's spirit, many other names can be added such as the wise Abigail (1 Sam 25:2-42), the unnamed prophet wife of Isaiah (Isa 8:3), the prophet Noadiah (Neh 6:14), the courageous Vashti (Esth 1), and the judicious Esther (Esth 2:7 et passim).[50]

But the most powerful model for a pneumatology of women's empowerment comes from the story of the young woman who becomes the mother of our Lord by the power of the Holy Spirit. Luke tells us of this brave woman who made the radical decision to allow the will of God to be fulfilled through her. The angel comes to her and tells her: The Holy Spirit will come upon you, and the power of the Most High will overshadow you" (Luke 1:35). She responds: "Here am I, the servant of the Lord; let it be with me according to your word" (Luke 1:38). And while visiting her cousin Elizabeth, she breaks out in song,

49. The *Apostolic Constitutions*, a fourth-century document, which has liturgical and disciplinary writings from the first three centuries, has this prayer for the ordination of a deaconess: "O eternal God, the Father of our Lord Jesus Christ, the Creator of man and of woman, who did fill with the Spirit Miriam, Deborah, Anna, and Huldah (Exod 15:20-21; Judges 5; Luke 2:36-38; 2 Kings 22:14-20), who did not deem unworthy that your only-begotten Son should be born of a woman, who also in the tent of witness and in the Temple ordained women as keepers of your holy gates, now look upon this your servant who is being ordained as a deaconess [sic], and give her the Holy Spirit, and purify her from any defilement of the flesh and spirit (2 Cor 7:1), so that she may worthily accomplish the work entrusted to her and to your glory and the praise of your Christ, with whom and to you and to the Holy Spirit be glory and adoration forever. Amen!" *Didascalia et Constitutiones Apostolorum*, ed. F. X. Funk (Paderborn, 1905) II, 26, 6, 105, as cited in Elizabeth Clark, *Women in the Early Church* (Wilmington: Michael Glazier, 1983), 177.

50. In rabbinical literature, Sarah, Miriam, Deborah, Hannah, Abigail, Huldah, and Esther are regarded as female prophets (*b. Meg.* 14a). E. Earle Ellis, *The Gospel of Luke*, NCB (London: Oliphants, 1974), 84.

like the spirit-filled female singers of her ancestors: "My soul magnifies the Lord, and my spirit rejoices in God my Savior ..." (Luke 1:46-55).[51]

The Protestants, especially those in North East India, have been overly critical of the Mariology of the Roman Catholic Church. In being so, they are theologically poorer, for a celebration of the person of Mary really throws light on an aspect of the work of God in human life. It is a basis for women today to assert that as equal recipients of the Holy Spirit women have equal place in the service of God. Now, lest I be misunderstood, let me make clear here that I do not think it is right to deify Mary, I do not subscribe to the cult of the Virgin Mary, I do not believe in the Marian appearances all over the world that actually discredit the Church and Christian faith, and I do not deem it right to model womanhood after the person of Mary. I am particularly averse to the Mary who is a figment of ecclesiastical imagination and the ideal Mary of patriarchal interpretation wherein she is depicted as superhuman, co-redemptrix, co-mediatrix, Queen of Heaven, icon, perfect mother, spotless womb, passive, and all those models which no real woman can follow or emulate. That said, it is not important for us to agree about Mariology to agree that Mary has a special place in salvation history. There is, then, no reason why the doors of Church ministry should be closed to women when God had deemed it appropriate to have the Holy Spirit come upon Mary and work the salvation of humanity through a woman.

Conclusion

Retrieving the ancient Trinitarian dogma for formulating an inclusive community takes into account the experiences of the diverse community. Trinitarian koinonia is not based on uniformity but on mutual relationality. The distinctiveness of each person is not lost by its mutual abiding with the other persons but heightened. Trinitarian koinonia values differences. It invites us to become a community of different yet equal partners. There is no domination involved in the Trinity. Similarly, discrimination and subordination of some members of the community would destroy the

51. For a powerful theological assessment of Mary and of her song, Elizabeth A. Johnson, *Truly Our Sister: A Theology of Mary in the Communion of Saints* (New York: Continuum, 2006), 209-304. For a brief feminist perspective on the Spirit and women of the Bible, Kristin Johnson Ingram, "Shekinah – The Glory of God," in *The Wisdom of Daughters: Two Decades of the Voice of Christian Feminism*, ed. Reta Halteman Finger and Kari Sandhaas (Philadelphia, PA: Innisfree Press, 2001), 46-48.

mutuality and synergy in the community and community would no longer be community. Communion and koinonia exists in the orbit of mutual and equal relations.

Now, for the tribals of North East India, the outpouring of the Holy Spirit experienced during the early twentieth century is the most trustworthy sign of the communitarian nature of the community called forth by the Spirit. Spirit baptism, then, was a personal experience but it was lived out in the community. The gifts of the Spirit were also exercised in the community. Tribal Christians ought to remember that when the Spirit took birth in the depths of their soul, they did not consider gender, or social status, or education as significant for participating in the life and ministry of the Church. They ought to remember that those became obstacles only when they allowed their awareness of the presence of God to become faint and indistinct.

5

THE CHURCH AS AN INCLUSIVE COMMUNITY

God Calls "All" to Worship

During the triumphant entry of Jesus into Jerusalem some of the Pharisees tried to stop the people's victorious chant and praise of God, to which Jesus replied, "If these were silent, the stones would shout out" (Matt 19:40). It seems to me that God calls every woman, man, and child to ascribe glory to God in worship. Indeed God calls all to worship. The Westminster Shorter Catechism, completed in 1647-1648 by the Westminster Assembly and used by many Presbyterian churches, captures the theology of humanity as a worshipping community. Question 1 of this catechism asks: What is the chief end of man [sic]? The answer is: Man's [sic] chief end is to glorify God (Ps 86:9; Isa 60:21; Rom 11:36; 1 Cor 6:20; 1 Cor 10:31; Rev 4:11), and to enjoy him [sic] forever (Ps 16:5-11; 144:15; Isa 12:2; Luke 2:10; Phil 4:4; Rev 21:3-4).[1] The language of this doctrinal statement is androcentric. It refers only to "man" as the standard for all human beings and to God as "him," but otherwise there is substance in this small question and brief answer. It conveys joyful glorifying of God as the primary purpose for humanity, which leads to a celebration and enjoyment of God.

The expression of praise to God is articulated in worship of God. As Karen Baker-Fletcher states,

1. Center for Reformed Theology and Apologetics, "Westminster Shorter Catechism: With Proof Texts," www.reformed.org/documents/wsc/ index.html (accessed 27 July 2010).

> We are created for the purpose of God's enjoyment. We are created to enjoy God. The purpose of creation is to glorify God, not to glorify itself. A moral life glorifies God through praise and worship of God.[2]

According to the New Testament, human failure to live up to God's purpose has the effect of making the whole creation groan in universal travail, awaiting the redemption of humanity on which hinges the salvation of the whole creation.

> For the creation waits with eager longing for the revealing of the children of God, for the creation was subjected to futility, not of its own will but by the will of the one who subjected it, in hope that the creation itself will be set free from its bondage to decay and will obtain the freedom of the glory of the children of God. We know that the whole creation has been groaning in labour pains until now; and not only the creation, but we ourselves, who have the first fruits of the Spirit, groan inwardly while we wait for adoption, the redemption of our bodies (Rom 8:19-23).

Evidently, the entire universe is tied up together in sharing a common purpose (to give glory to God) and a common hope (adoption and redemption). Nature, in its beauty and power, glorifies God. But it is human beings, made in the image of God, who have a responsibility to express praises to God in worship. Human failure to live according to God's purposes has placed both humanity and the creation into bondage, susceptible to death and decay. Striving for the communion and shared community of all creatures is integral to the realization of God's purposes for creation. Worship is one space of human activity where humans can put a life of shared communion and community into practice.

Humanity has been engineered by God to be a worshipping community.[3] Before Christianity, God's dealing with human beings, as seen in Jewish Scriptures, is based on the notion of an elect people of God. No doubt the individual has a place but the community took precedence over the individual. Israel was a federation of tribal groups and each tribe was an alliance of houses and families tied together in kinship relationship. A similar tribal configuration exists among people of my region. In the following discussion, I will look at the implications of

2. Karen Baker-Fletcher, *Dancing* with *God: The Trinity* from a *Womanist Perspective* (St. Louis, MO: Chalice Press, 2006), 67.

3. Brent D. Peterson, *Created to Worship: God's Invitation to Become Fully Human* (Kansas City, MO: Beacon Hill Press of Kansas City, 2012). 67.

tribal identity and tribal ways of life in worship and in tribal perspective on community.

Tribal Identity, Community, and Worship

Tribal people of North East India identify themselves first by their clan, then by their tribe, and then by their ethnic group. In this cultural setting, the honour of the family, clan, and tribe stands above everything else. Tribal life, as I know it, is communitarian. The achievement of an individual is regarded as bringing prestige and honour to the larger community (of family, clan, and tribe). Thus individual initiative is encouraged but the individual lives with the awareness that her/his life shapes the community and s/he is in turn shaped by her/his community. Talking about the spirit of community among tribal people, Ezamo Murry states that a tribal is the prototype of a social being. He says that in tribal community, shame and sin are not experienced in the mind or inner conscience but from the community's judgment. According to Murry, right and wrong conduct of a person is based on the community's way of thinking. The individual's identity and self-esteem is formed out of the person's experience in groups in the community.[4]

The communitarian ethos of traditional tribal life was transferred into the churches of the tribal people. Tribals found in Christianity a life of community familiar to them, although there are positive and negative effects.

Tribal feelings run deep. The churches in North East India are primarily based on tribal divisions. Take the Baptist churches of Nagaland for example. The local churches belonging to a particular tribe form a particular tribe's "association" of churches (some use the term council). As noted in the introductory chapter, there are twenty such associations in Nagaland. These associations come together to form a "council" (called "convention" by some other states of the region) called the Nagaland Baptist Church Council. Thus the association of churches is based on tribal identity and the Nagaland Baptist Church Council is based on ethnic grouping. But as the denomination is Baptist, the administration

4. Ezamo Murry, "Bible and Culture: A Model of Christian Acculturation of Tribal Culture," in *Doing Tribal Christian Theology with Tribal Resources: Cultural Resources from North East India*, Tribal Study Series 18, ed. Razouselie Lasetso and Eyingbeni Hümtsoe (Jorhat, Assam: ETC Programme Coordination, 2009), 15.

is not centralized. Churches of the associations and councils/conventions are only loosely connected.

Local churches are passionate about their tribal identity. The tribalism (or tribal pride) of the churches is often manifested in churches trying to outdo each other in building churches that are more expensive and more magnificent than others, and celebrating church jubilees and centenaries in a grander fashion than others.[5] Poor villagers have to make huge sacrifices to build big churches they can ill afford. A village will often have a big church surrounded by comparatively tiny shacks. Tribalism can be a big burden for the poor. But the good thing about it is that tribal pride also makes people very generous. They try to outdo each other as much in showing off their wealth as in generosity and mission works. Thus the positive and the negative impact of incorporating tribal communitarian ethos into Christian life intertwine.

On the positive side, the Church became an institution where tribals could continue to do the things they love most; sharing whatever they have and being together like a family. They found in the Church an avenue to express their unique identity. The Church as a community (a tribal community) reflects the sharing of ministries, koinonia, and the first bloom of the egalitarianism of the early Christian Church as seen in New Testament passages like Gal 3:26: "For in Christ Jesus you are all children of God through faith." One sharp contrast between tribals of North East India and people from other parts of India is that tribal societies of North East India do not have beggars, which is unusual for poverty stricken India. Writing about the North East tribal people, Ambrose Pinto notes:

> They live and work as members of one community in their fields, not as individuals but as a community. It is a socialist life for each of those tribes there with hardly any beggars on the streets of Kohima, Aizal [sic Aizawl], Shillong or other cities where the tribals inhabit the place. If there are any beggars in that part of India, they are mostly those who have come there from other parts of the country.[6]

In tribal society, if anyone falls into economic difficulties the relatives and clan of that person invariably come to the rescue of the one facing

5. Cf. Phuveyi Dozo, *The Cross over Nagaland* (Guwahati: Christian Literature Centre, 1983), 42.

6. Ambrose Pinto, "Exodus of the North-East People: Do Our Cities Alienate Them?" *Mainstream* L/38 (September 8, 2012), http://www.mainstreamweekly.net/article3679.html (accessed September 1, 2018).

trouble. It is shameful for the relatives and clan members if they allow one of their own to suffer. Not only that, but the entire community shares a common responsibility to take care of one another across familial and clan divisions. Thus if someone wants to build a house, some would bring timber for erecting posts, some would come with straw for the roof, and many would join in building the house. Because of living as community, traditional tribal houses do not have doors or locks; if some keep a barrier it is to keep pigs or chickens out and not because of fear of thieves. Because members take care of one another, there has never been any need for orphanages or destitute homes. Tribal community itself functions like a welfare society. In recent times, the sense of community is dwindling. Yet the positive communitarian value of tribal culture has enriched the Church's understanding and practice of koinonia.

Conversely, the Church has copied the patriarchal bias of traditional tribal culture, continuing the marginalization of women, and now with the excuse of "divine" sanction. The patriarchalism of the Church did not come from tribal culture alone; it also came via Christian tradition. The New Testament Church was already showing signs of structuring itself in hierarchical orders with the male being dominant as leaders and decision makers.[7] Over the years, the Church has lost more and more of the egalitarianism of the early years and has become more and more parochial, segregating people, privileging a few, and denying others who seem to be different. Eventually, the Christian tradition received by tribal Christians is steeped in patriarchalism and the Church structure is based on a hierarchical order. And some aspects of patriarchalism in the Church are our own inventions.

In a community based culture, the impact of conservative theology is felt deeply. My grandfather was an ordained Baptist minister. His ordination was revoked because one of his daughters married a non-Christian. He did not endorse the marriage, but he was found guilty by association. I cite this unpleasant story from my family closet as an example of how from a tribal community perspective, the virtue of a person cannot be reckoned apart from his/her family and relatives. Even today, the procedure for ordination among the Baptist churches (associations and councils) involves a careful appraisal of the life of the

7. Schottroff, *Lydia's Impatient Sisters.* Referred to by Bernard J. Cooke, "Body and Mystical Body: The Church as *Communio*," in *Bodies of Worship: Explorations in Theory and Practice*, ed. Bruce T. Morrill (Collegeville, MN: The Liturgical Press, 1999), 40.

candidate for ordination as well as the candidate's immediate family. An ordination committee would have second thoughts about recommending a candidate for ordination if someone from the candidate's immediate family has a disagreeable background.

The inextricable link between an individual and his/her family is also evident in the norm for accepting new converts in the Baptist churches of Assam. Baptists, in general, require that a convert seeking baptism should be mature enough to make a personal decision—hence "believer's baptism." But in Assam there is another requirement that must come together with a confession of faith in Jesus, and that is a "no objection certificate" from the would-be convert's family. Consequently, people from other religious traditions who wanted to convert to Christianity have been unable to do so because their family refused to give a no objection statement. Thus the regional churches have allowed a narrow interpretation of community to determine its practice.

Not only do churches interpret community in a narrow sense, but they also misuse people's need for community. This is seen in the practice of excommunication. Withdrawal of fellowship from a member of a church who has offended the laws of the church is an accepted practice among the Baptists.[8] The rule of excommunication is based on the command in 1 Cor 5:13: "Drive out the wicked person from among you."[9] The interpretation of the passage is not easy. Some commentators think that Paul's view is based on Lev 18:8 and 20:11 which stipulates that if a man has sexual relations with his father's wife, both the man and the woman must be put to death. Similar instructions are found in Deut 22:30 and Deut 27:20, prohibiting a man from marrying his father's wife. Others reckon that Paul was appealing to Deut 17:7, which pronounces the death penalty for those who worship other Gods. Paul reinterpreted the Jewish Scriptures by substituting execution with excommunication.

Excommunication may be necessary to discipline believers who are engaged in serious, unrepentant sin, so that they may comprehend the gravity of their sin and repent. However the rule should not be misused, it is not the duty of the Church to "police" sin. Christians should not

8. Theodore Gerald Soares, *A Baptist Manual: The Polity of the Baptist Churches and of the Denominational Organizations* (Philadelphia: American Baptist Publication Society, 1911), 46-52.

9. A thorough investigation of the exclusion of sinners from the Corinthian Church is found in Brian S. Rosner, *Paul, Scripture and Ethics: A Study of 1 Corinthians 5-7* (Leiden: E. J. Brill, 1994).

become self-righteous defenders of Church discipline as though they are perfect and sinless. Excommunication is not meant to be retributive punishment for people's sin. As far as possible, the focus should be on guiding the erring ones back to faith and restoring them to communion.

Among the Baptists of the region, cases of excommunication are mostly for fornication or adultery. Church leaders have led people to think that this as in accordance with biblical teaching. However, they forget that the text refers not only to the sexual immoral but also to the greedy, the idolater, the reviler, the drunkard, or the robber. As far as I know, except for fornication/adultery and drunkenness no one has ever been excommunicated for the other reasons given in 1 Cor 5:13.

In tribal villages where community is more close-knit than other cultures, there can be nothing worse than excommunication as a means of discipline.[10] Therefore the rule of excommunication ought to be considered thoroughly before a member is excommunicated. On the occasions when it becomes absolutely unavoidable and the rule is applied with much sadness, it should be employed in such a way that it does not give the impression that sexual sin is greater than embezzlement of funds, extortion of money, kidnapping, robbery, or murder (practices which are common in North East India). It should be kept in mind that the Church is not only meant to build up community but it is a community itself. Communion, community, and communication are what the Church is supposed to aim towards, not ex-communication.

Because of the instinctive inclination for sharing and a communitarian way of life in tribal societies, I see great possibilities for living out a theology of the Church as community in North East India.[11] However, the persistence of patriarchalism and conservative theology stands in the way of realizing true community. Instead of tapping into kinship relationship in tribal society as a way of strengthening the Church, the Church has allowed itself to be sidetracked by smaller issues in order to

---

10. "The individual's identity is found in the village community and in the age group ["age group" refers to the division of groups to which each individual is assigned according to age. These groups organize themselves to work in each other's fields and group activities during festivals, village road clearing events, and other social occasions.] The village is the guardian of the individual. To be banished from the village, therefore, is the greatest punishment and humiliation for any individual." Murry, "Bible and Culture," in *Doing Tribal Christian Theology with Tribal Resources*, ed. Lasetso and Hümtsoe, 15.

11. K. Thanzauva, *Theology of Community: Tribal Theology in the Making* (Aizawl, Mizoram: Mizo Theological Conference, 1997).

exercise power over its members. As such, culture is used as an excuse to discriminate against and to deny equal participation. That brings me back to the discussion about worship because the Church's theology and practice has a direct impact on worship. Is there a correct way of worshipping God? Is it still worship if some of the members have places of honour and others have none? Is worship happening when women are segregated and silenced? How is God glorified if those who are different, or are minority, are counted out?

What worship is in the Church and what it ought to be appears to be different. Writing from a Catholic perspective about Vatican II's emphasis on communio in Lumen gentium, Bernard J. Cooke points out that the council stressed the collegiality of the ordained, the communio of all the baptized as one body of Christ, and the sharing in one eucharistic celebration.[12] Vatican II is, of course, revolutionary. And yet while speaking about all the baptized as the body of Christ, sharing in the one Spirit, the Bishops and the Presbyters are assumed to have greater "saintliness" than the ordinary folk. This is not so among the Baptists and those who have descended from the Anabaptist tradition. Consider in particular to the doctrine of the "priesthood of all believers" (1 Peter 2:5-9), which was a cardinal principle of the 16th century Reformation.[13] This doctrine is vociferously upheld by the Baptists as a "Baptist distinctive." It stands on the democratic conviction that all human beings, whether ordained or not, are equal. It asserts that humans do not need priests or mediators to have access to God, to interpret Scripture, or to serve in the ministries of the Church. Thus Baptists' understanding is that salvation cannot be brokered through human mediators for it is the responsibility of the individual. Unfortunately, this doctrine has been reduced to individualism and theological expediency in North East India (and other places) so that any dispute or disagreement results in the formation of a new church, or even a new denomination. The Baptist principle of the "autonomy of the local church," has further added to the disorganization and schisms

12. Cooke, "Body and Mystical Body," in *Bodies of Worship*, ed. Morrill, 41-42.

13. Cyril Eastwood, *The Priesthood of All Believers: An Examination of the Doctrine from the Reformation to the Present Day* (1960; repr., Eugene, OR: Wipf & Stock, 2009).

among the Baptists in the region.[14] Actually, the priesthood of all believers had more to do with collective responsibility than with the position or status of the individual. A good interpreter of Luther says:

> Luther never understands the priesthood of all believers merely in the sense of the Christian's freedom to stand in a direct relationship to God without a human mediator. Rather he constantly emphasizes the Christian's evangelical authority to come before God on behalf of the brethren and also of the world. The universal priesthood expresses not religious individualism but its exact opposite, the reality of the congregation as a community.[15]

And of course, the nonconformists accepted Luther's articulation of the priesthood of all believers. The difference between Luther and the nonconformists was that the nonconformists wanted to go further than Luther to apply the grounding concept religious liberty to remake the Church, and not simply reform it.[16]

North East Indian Baptists should look back to their nonconformist heritage and begin to regard the priesthood of all believers as a call to live in true community rather than in the complacency of individual privilege. Of course, true to their doctrine, they have never regarded ordained ministers or pastors as having more saintliness or as being holier than ordinary people. According to Baptists, ordination does not establish a hierarchical authority of the minister over the congregational members. Ordination is not seen as a ceremonial consecration into a sacred office by which the clergy are sacerdotally separated from the laity but as an appointment to a ministerial office.[17]

---

14. By this, I do not mean to imply that the autonomy of the local congregation is an undesirable principle. This principle affirms the Baptist belief that the Church is composed of believers and not organized religion governed by various ranks of priests (Baptist pastors and ordained ministers are to guide and teach their congregation and not rule over them). It is also consistent with the Baptist belief of the "competency of the soul," which means that every individual is responsible to God. But it is wrong to turn religious liberty into anarchy. Local self-rule is to be exercised in submission to Christ, the true head of the Church.

15. Paul Althaus, *The Theology of Martin Luther* (Philadelphia, PA: Fortress Press, 1966), 314.

16. Michael H. Montgomery, "Non-Conformist Ecclesiologies," in *The Routledge Companion to the Christian Church*, ed. Gerard Mannion and Lewis Mudge (New York, NY: Routledge, 2008), 217-33.

17. Cf. Edward T. Hiscox, *Principles and Practices for Baptist Churches: A Guide to the Administration of Baptist Churches* (1894; repr., Grand Rapids, MI: Kregel Publications, 1980), 344-64.

Nevertheless, while eschewing priestly hierarchy, the Baptist churches of the region have abdicated their responsibility and their right, on matters like ordination, to their associations or councils. Consequently, even if a local Baptist church wishes to ordain a woman, it is unable to do so unless the association or council approves it (the convention in some cases). The role of the local church is simply to recommend the name of the candidate they wish to ordain to the council or association. This is one reason why the ordination of women in the Baptist churches of North East India is confined to a handful of associations or councils. Of course there is a solid theological reason why a council should be involved in the ordination of a minister—the ordained ministry has a direct relation to the whole denomination and to the universal Church.

> The minister has relations at once that are wider than those to the local church. Hence the counsel of the churches is sought in ordination, and the act is one of denominational significance.[18]

The need to receive the counsel of the churches is met by calling a council of churches to ordain a minister. In North East India, this process has somehow led to some accruement of power to the councils and associations, whose leaders have decided that women cannot be ordained. Unfortunately, most of the leaders of the associations and councils under CBCNEI are against the ordination of women. The fact is that the parent body of the CBCNEI, the American Baptist Churches in the USA (ABC-USA), had been ordaining women as early as 1882. In 2005, ABC-USA had 410 women who served as pastors.[19] This piece of information is something the leaders of the associations and councils would love to hide from the churches. The Southern Baptist Convention (SBC) also ordained women. The first woman to be ordained by SBC was in 1964. There were 232 ordained women by 1986, although only a few of them were serving as pastors. However, in 1984, following a change in leadership, SBC resolved to exclude women from pastoral functions and ordination.[20]

The exercise of power by the associations or councils that override the wishes of the local congregations is contrary to the Baptist polity in which the local congregation is supposed to be the base of power. Authority is

18. Soares, *A Baptist Manual*, 54.

19. Robert E. Johnson, *A Global Introduction to Baptist Churches* (Cambridge: Cambridge University Press, 2010), 372.

20. Johnson, *A Global Introduction to Baptist Churches*, 372.

meant to seep upward from the local congregation to the associations or councils rather than downward from the associations or councils to the congregation. The churches should have insisted on the autonomy of the local church especially with regard to ordination. In which case, the officials of the councils and associations could be invited to participate and give their blessings in the ordinations of the local churches.

Paul's teaching about one body with many members (1 Cor 12:12-31) points towards the equality of all the members; one is not better than the other. The equality of all members does not mean that each individual can claim to be self-sufficient. Rather, it means that we have to live in mutual interdependence. The "offices" appointed by God — apostles, prophets, teachers, deeds of power, gifts of healing, forms of assistance, forms of leadership, various tongues—point towards some form of structure for governance in the Church. And indeed all churches need some form of structure, with leaders, assistants, and committees, to be able to function coherently. Yet the context of the passage—all being baptized into one body because all drank of one Spirit—makes it clear that the offices do not connote a hierarchical "pecking order" in the Church. It is important to note that the spiritual gifts are not gendered.[21] This implies that gender-based distinctions cannot apply in Church leadership. First Corinthians 12 in no way precludes women from holding office. Rather the body metaphor for solidarity anticipates that all women should function as members of the one body. In this body, "If one member suffers, all suffer together with it; if one member is honoured, all rejoice together with it" (1 Cor 12:26). That is one good reason why women should not be dishonoured. The denial of the offices of the Church to women is inconsistent with the notion of the Church as the body of Christ.

On the surface, there is no dispute about the fact that God calls everyone—men, women, children, and indeed all creatures great and small—to worship God. An overwhelming number of Scripture passages refer to God's call to all nations and all the earth to worship. The Psalmist calls all the peoples and all the earth to worship God:

> Ascribe to the Lord, O families of the peoples,
> ascribe to the Lord glory and strength.
> Ascribe to the Lord the glory due his name;
> bring an offering, and come into his courts.

---

21. Kristina LaCelle-Paterson, *Liberating Tradition: Women's Identity and Vocation in Christian Perspective* (Grand Rapids, MI: Baker Academic, 2008), 71.

> Worship the Lord in holy splendour;
> tremble before him, all the earth (Ps 96:7-9).[22]

The prophet Isaiah, in an oracle, declares that all flesh will worship God:

> From new moon to new moon, and from Sabbath to Sabbath,
> all flesh shall come to worship before me, says the Lord (Isa 66:23).

The issue in dispute is not about whether someone can worship God but about what should constitute true worship. In Rom 12:1, the apostle Paul appeals to Christians to present their bodies as a living sacrifice, holy and acceptable to God, which is their reasonable worship. Here Paul addresses his recipients as "brothers." This is merely a patriarchal usage, which actually means "brothers and sisters." The writer of Hebrews talks of service that is pleasing to God: "Through him, then, let us continually offer a sacrifice of praise to God, that is, the fruit of lips that confess his name. Do not neglect to do good and to share what you have, for such sacrifices are pleasing to God" (Heb 13:15-16). In the Gospel according to John, Jesus tells the Samaritan woman: "The hour is coming when you will worship the Father neither on this mountain [Mount Gerizim] nor in Jerusalem...But the hour is coming, and is now here, when the true worshippers will worship the Father in spirit and truth, for the Father seeks such as these to worship him" (John 4:21-23). These and many biblical passages teach of the ideal worship as something that is not dependent on rites and rituals nor on art and architecture or on people and place but on selflessness, altruism, sharing, and community.

It is in sharing, fellowship, and koinonia of community that humans are able to experience God. Worship, as it is generally understood, is an experience of God which leads one to give "worth" to God.[23] One cannot give "worth" to God unless one experiences God in some way, even if without fully understanding how and whence. God, as revealed in the biblical tradition, is a God who is revealed in community. There is a personal and inward dimension in human experience of God, but the individual experience must find its expression and articulation in community. The Baptist understanding of worship, in general, emphasizes the inner experience of the individual.

---

22. Other notable psalms include Ps 67, 84, 95, 100, 117, 148, and 150.

23. This idea is evident in the word "worship," which comes from the Middle English "weorth-scipe" as in ascribing honour and worth to God. White, *Foundations of Christian Worship*, 2.

> In Baptist writings about worship, the primary concern has been not so much about the ordering of worship as about a concern for the integrity of the worshippers. From the celebration of faith and discipleship in the baptism of believers to the prizing of extempore prayers, Baptists are concerned more about sincerity and the "spiritual" aspect of worship than about the way in which certain activities in worship might be undertaken. What they call "simple" worship is often "abstract," with a focus on intellect and interior feelings; recognition of the importance of the devotional dimension is essential to understanding Baptists. John 4:24 has been regarded as a crucial text: "God is spirit, and those who worship him must worship in spirit and in truth."[24]

My experience of worship in the Baptist churches is a mixture of the personal and the corporate. People's idea of worship, especially in small group worship conducted in member's houses, is influenced by the Bible verse which says that where there are two or three gathered in the Lord's name, the Lord is there among them (Matt 18:20). While it is true that the Baptists give credit to the interior experience of the individual, the Baptists of my region are greatly influenced by communitarian codes. Worship is seen as a community activity. Attending church worship on Sunday is something everyone does, not because they feel obligated or compelled in some way to do so but because church worship is simply a way of life in the community. A conspicuous cultural element seen in the local churches of North East India is the practice of "mass prayer." Mass prayer refers to audible and loud spontaneous prayers that are said by all the worshippers at the same time. Baptists have less regard for prayers that are written, viewing them either as not inspired by the Holy Spirit or as not coming from the heart of the person.[25] Those who are unaccustomed to hearing mass prayers would probably be disoriented by the cacophony of the noise of a thousand different spontaneous prayers being said at the same time. However, for those who are used to it, worship feels empty and lifeless without it. Thus for those who grew up in churches that practise mass prayer, it is a special moment of opening

---

24. Christopher Ellis, "Baptists in Britain," in *The Oxford History of Christian Worship*, ed. Geoffrey Wainwright and Karen B. Westerfield Tucker (New York, NY: Oxford University Press, 2006), 571.

25. What Christopher Ellis says about this from the context of Britain is also true of the Baptists in North East India. Ellis, "Baptists in Britain," in *Oxford History of Christian Worship*, Wainwright and Tucker, 571: "Most prayer is still offered by someone speaking spontaneously on behalf of the congregation. This is regarded both as an expression of the person's devotion, and therefore sincere, and as a dependence on the Holy Spirit and therefore Spirit-filled."

your heart to God—to seek forgiveness, to petition, to thank, to praise—that transforms the bare church into a sacred space where God is present and God's people are gathered.

The idea of corporate worship is taken beyond the walls of the church. Prayer meetings in houses and localities are fairly common as are retreats and youth camps away from home. Christmas and Easter celebrations, the two festivals that are taken seriously (unlike other festivals like Pentecost, which are not generally observed), spill over from the church to a public place, such as the local football field, where the celebration continues in the form of community feasts.

Baptists are sceptical of liturgical rituals.[26] Liturgical robes are generally not used, although a few ministers now use a robe for performing marriage ceremonies. In fact, the word "liturgy" is not used, as it appears to connote text-based ritualism, and "service" or "ceremony" is used in place of the word "liturgy." Baptists are wary of the word "creed" because they are reminders of the persecution of dissenters. They claim that there is no creed other than the Bible. Other terms associated with Catholic/Episcopal language such as "narthex," "chancel," and even "pews" are not part of the Baptist vocabulary. Simpler terms like "veranda," "stage," "pulpit," "lectern," and "benches/seats" are used. The Baptist preference for ordinary words rather than technical ecclesiastical terminologies goes back to the rejection of sacramental institutions in the 16th century Reformation. Thus worship is de-sacralised. Ordinary, non-technical words are used.

Whereas the Roman Catholic, Eastern Orthodox, and some Protestant churches use the term "sacraments" to refer to baptism and the Lord's Supper, Baptists prefer to call them "ordinances." Baptists do not recognise the five other sacraments of the Roman Catholic Church. The Baptist preference for "ordinances" is based on their theological rejection of the sacerdotal position of the Catholic and Orthodox churches. The word "sacrament" comes from the Latin word *sacramentum*, which was used by Tertullian to translate the Greek word *mysterion* (μυστήριον), which means "secret" or "mystery."[27] While *mysterion* was derived from the initiatory rites of mystery cults, *sacramentum* came not only from the initiatory rites of the Roman army but also from the money placed in a sacred place by litigants. The Catholic Church holds that the sacraments

26. Johnson, *A Global Introduction to Baptist Churches*, 406.

27. Joseph Martos, *Doors to the Sacred: A Historical Introduction to Sacraments in the Catholic Church*, expanded ed. (Liguori, MO: Liguori Publications, 1991), 29.

are efficacious, that in themselves they are means or instruments of grace to people, seals assuring people of God's grace. And all these come through the priests who administer them. By contrast, "ordinances" implies that the observance of baptism and the Lord's Supper are done as an act of obedience to Christ, because they were ordained by Christ (Matt 28:19; Luke 22:19; 1 Cor 11:23-25). Baptists believe that the ordinances have no inherent power in themselves, but they are symbolic acts of our union with Christ, signs that point to the Gospel.[28] This is yet another Baptist heritage that can be meaningly employed to place emphasis on the communitarian nature of corporate worship. It is neither the minister nor the ordinances that bring God's grace, but the community living in communion (baptising into one body and eating bread together) that makes God's grace evident.

Baptist practice of letting go of all sacerdotal baggage is also noticeable in their worship service. Worship programmes, whenever printed, contain nothing more the basic outline of worship. A typical worship service would have the following elements:

1) Call to Worship – Not common but followed by some. No prelude or processional.

2) Invocation – Said by the worship leader or a member of the congregation.

3) Hymn – Not necessarily just one hymn. Unplanned hymns and songs may be called out by the worship leader or members of the congregation and everybody joins in singing together. This extended time of singing serves as a preparation for the worship.

4) Bible reading – One or two passages, selected by the speaker.

5) Announcements (Notices/Intimations) – Anything that might be necessary for the congregation to know is announced, such as upcoming weddings, new births, special offering, Sunday evening programme, next Sunday's programme, prayer meetings, Bible studies, youth and women's weekday fellowship, latest news or information from the mission department or some committee of the church, or matters of

28. A helpful discussion from the Baptist perspective is found in Charles L. Quarles, "Ordinance or Sacrament: Is the Baptist View of the Ordinances Truly Biblical?" *Journal for Baptist Theology and Ministry* 1/1 (Spring 2003): 47-57, http://www.baptistcenter.net/journals/JBTM_1-1_Spring_2003_04_Ordinance_or_Sacrament.pdf (accessed September 3, 2018).

public concern.[29] Announcements are made by anyone who has matters of importance to inform the congregation. Sometimes announcements alone may take more than half an hour, because of that and also in order to avoid disruptions in worship, some churches now make the announcements at the beginning before the formal beginning of the worship service.

6) Special Numbers – Solos, group, or choral songs.

7) Offering and Offertory – People's money offering, monthly tithe, thanksgiving offering for some achievement or new birth, first-fruits offering, and harvest offerings are collected and a prayer of dedication is said by the leader or by a member of the congregation. Some big churches place their collection boxes at the entrance as collecting offering during the service will take up too much of the worship time.

8) Prayer – Intercessory prayer, petition prayer, pastoral prayer, or mass prayer. A prayer said by a member of the congregation, a deacon, or the pastor. This may take anything between one to ten minutes. Most of the time, prayers are lengthy because they are extemporaneous, covering a wide range of concerns: petition for various blessings, confession of sins, thanksgiving for mercies, prayer for the nations and leaders, prayer for the Church, prayer for the sick, and anything else that might occur to those praying on behalf of the congregation.

9) Sermon – Usually delivered by the pastor but a deacon or any member of the congregation can also bring the sermon. The sermon is considered the most important part of the service and thus the rest of the worship is a movement towards the delivery of the sermon.

10) The Lord's Supper – Most churches do this once a month. In the past, when ordained ministers were few, the Lord's Supper was rarely celebrated.

11) Hymn – A closing hymn serving as a form of congregational response to the sermon.

---

29. In the churches I attend in Assam, announcements often include the information of somebody offering for a birth of a baby or a success in some project. The amount is usually small. For instance, on a few occasions I have heard contributions of Rs 10 being announced, which is approximately 0.25 AUD (enough to buy two cups of coffee in India). I realised the purpose of the announcement is not to let the people know how much money has been offered as thanksgiving, but to let the community share the good news of the one making the offering.

12) Benediction – Said either by the leader or speaker or a member of the congregation.[30]

This sample of a typical Baptist worship service indicates the easy sharing of ministry between lay people and ordained ministers. Almost everything that an ordained minister does can be done by a lay member of the congregation because Baptists believe in the priesthood of all believers. Thus while an ordained minister is regarded as being specially called to Church ministry, it does not make a minister holier than a lay person.

As Baptists emphasize the people more than the building, church building designs are rather plain. A prominent, unadorned wooden cross is found in every church. Besides the cross, paintings and icons of any kind are almost totally nonexistent. Most Baptists think that putting up images of Jesus or other biblical characters is inappropriate as they consider it close to idolatry. Nevertheless, some churches do place pictures on the walls and face little or no opposition. Plenty of fresh flowers are used to add some beauty and colour to the church and not for any religious significance. A pulpit and a table, for the Lord's Supper, occupy the front. Theologically, Baptists of North East India have been resistant to the ecumenical movement, labelling it a tool of Satan, whereas evangelical and charismatic elements have been welcomed.

An issue raised earlier is what should constitute worship in spirit and in truth. My detour into a discussion of worship in Baptists churches provided an indication not only of where my views have been forged but also of the views back home against which I have to wrestle. From my Baptist perspective, the rites and rituals and the artificial accoutrements that surround worship distract from true worship rather than enhance the human experience of God. At the same time, because of my exposure to other churches and having listened to the stories of others who come from other traditions, I begin to appreciate the fact that rites and rituals are not empty acts but recreations of the stories of the lives of people. And architecture, whether plain or complex, is not a distraction but designed to resonate with human perception of the divine. Music likewise, in various forms, can tell human stories and touch people deeply and spiritually.

30. For examples of Baptist worship see Frederick S. Downs, *Manual of Worship* (Gauhati: Christian Literature Centre, 1975). However, it is to be noted that the *Manual* does not really represent actual worship in local churches, which have some routine and yet are freestyle and do not follow any strict formal pattern.

Equality in Worship

Studies of worship during the New Testament period show that gender was not a factor in the worship life of the early Christians. In fact, besides the Lord's Prayer, two of the most known prayers come from the lips of two New Testament women. One is Mary's song of praise known as the "Magnificat" (Luke 1:46-55) and the other is Elizabeth's blessing of Mary, "Blessed are you among women, and blessed is the fruit of your womb" (Luke 1:42), which is incorporated in the prayer known as the Hail Mary recited regularly by those in the Catholic Church. Other women are also described as praying and praising God. They include the prophet Anna (Luke 2:38), "certain women" (Acts 1:14), and the four daughters of Philip who prophesy (Acts 21:9).[31] Among many, John Wijngaards presents incontrovertible evidence that the early Church ordained women to full sacramental ordination as deacons. From Paul (c. AD 58; Rom 16:1-2, which names Phoebe as a deacon of the church at Cenchreae), Timothy (c. 100; 1 Tim 3:8-11), Pliny the Younger (112), Clement of Alexandria (c. 150-215), Origin (185-255), to numerous ancient texts such as *The Ecclesiastical Canons of the Apostles* (c. 250?), *The "Didascalia" of the Apostles* (c. 250), and *The Apostolic Constitutions* (c. 380), Wijngaards traces the history of women's full ordination into Church ministry to show that since the Church ordained women in the past, it can do so now.[32]

The initial egalitarianism of the early years was lost as the Church gradually allowed itself to embrace patriarchal structures and principles. It is apparent that the current practices of Church worship are inherited from narrow cultural influences over two millennia. There is valid ground therefore for feminists to be critical of the denial of clerical office to women and the clericalization of the sacraments:

> The sacraments have traditionally functioned to legitimate male power (by restricting sacramental or consecratory power to men), to value men's bodies as being more "like Christ" than women's (by denying or limiting women's access to ordination), to value men's will and initiative over women's (by giving men control over not only the sacraments themselves but also access to the

31. Teresa Berger, "Women in Worship," in *The Oxford History of Christian Worship*, ed. Geoffrey Wainwright and Karen B. Westerfield Tucker (New York, NY: Oxford University Press, 2006), 758-59.

32. John Wijngaards, *No Women in Holy Orders? The Women Deacons of the Early Church* (Norwich: Canterbury Press, 2002).

> sacraments), and to sacralise men's bonds and heritage (especially through a male celibate priesthood, but also more subtly in defining sacramental ministry as a male vocation to which women can be admitted only under carefully controlled circumstances).[33]

Baptist churches have not been faithful to their belief in the priesthood of all believers. If believers were truly equals, distinctions would not be made between males and females in ministry. There would not be such strong and vehement opposition to the ordination and ministry of women either. Most Baptist leaders appear to believe only in the priesthood of men. In fact, the eschatological age ushered in by and through Jesus does away with the need for a priest to act as mediator between God and humans because Christ, our priest and mediator, has accomplished it for us. From this perspective, the differences between clergy and laity vanish.

Discussing the Lutheran concept of priestly ministry, Eugene L. Brand notes that the priestly concept derives from baptism and as such all baptized people are included in the priesthood of all believers.[34] Brand also notes that in the New Testament the word priest is never used for those disciples and apostles and all those who later came to be known as clergy. The word laity comes from the word Greek word *laos* (λαὸς), which means people. 1 Peter 2:9 calls all Christians as "a chosen race, a royal priesthood, a holy nation, God's own people [a people for his possession]." This implies that all Christians are called to be the laity, i.e. the people of God. The word for clergy comes from the Greek word *kleros* (κλῆρος). The term means "lot" or "portion." It appears in 1 Pet 5:3 where it means "the portion allotted to each individual elder."[35] Therefore the word does not imply that those who are *kleros* possess something which other Christians don't have. Thus Brand feels that clergy and laity refer to the same people and concludes, "that the offices of bishop and presbyter (and deacon) should become a separate ruling class in the church

33. Procter-Smith, *In Her Own Rite*, 138.

34. Eugene L. Brand, "Vocation and Ministry," in *In Search of a Round Table: Gender, Theology & Church Leadership*, ed. Musimbi R. A. Kanyoro (Geneva: WCC Publications, 1997), 13-15.

35. Brand says 1 Pet 5:2, but this is probably a typographical error. The word translated "in your charge" in v 2 is *episkopountes* ("look upon," "care for," "oversight") whereas the word which is also translated "in your charge" in v 3 is *klērōn* ("heritage," "inheritance," "lot," "portion").

is clearly in violation of NT teaching."[36] A concept of an authoritarian sacerdotal clergy developed later in the Church as a consequence of a sacerdotalizing of the ordained ministry.

The Protestant Reformation questioned the power of the Church. Reinterpreting priesthood, Martin Luther said "all Christians are priests, and all priests are Christians."[37] I think, on this point, that Luther's position is consistent with the New Testament teaching in general and Paul's preaching that "there is no longer Jew or Greek, there is no longer slave or free, there is no longer male and female; for all of you are one in Christ Jesus" (Gal 3:28). What Paul preached and what God appointed is however kept in abeyance as *men* continue to control the Church, subjugate and silence women and minority groups.

Baptist churches of North East India are deeply evangelical. Camps or retreats for the youth, men, or women, Vacation Bible School for children, and other programmes of that kind are considered an important aspect of Christian ministry. These programmes are aimed at bringing nominal Christians to experience new birth in Christ, refreshing the faith of the people, and giving opportunity for making a commitment to join the ministry of the Church. People also like to hold big meetings, called "rallies," in open fields where thousands upon thousands of people can come and hear inspiring messages, renew their faith, reaffirm their commitment, and respond to God's call to join the Christian ministry.

I've often wondered why the preachers (usually males), whether in Bible camps and retreats or in "rallies," don't preach what is really in their mind when they make altar calls for those who wish to join the Church ministry. I've wished that they would come straight out and say that when they say "*anyone* who wishes to serve God," or "*anyone* who wishes to commit his or her life to God's work and study theology," what they really mean is "*any man* who wishes to serve God," and "*any man* who wishes to commit his life to God's work and study theology." I've wished they would be upfront about what they think about women studying theology—that women can study theology but should not hope to receive a ministerial position in a church after they have gone through the rigour of theological training. Because the evidence is that in most cases that is what happens. Women answer God's call to ministry and they go through the same process as their male counterparts in

36. Brand, "Vocation and Ministry," in *In Search of a Round Table*, ed. Kanyoro, 15.

37. Cited by Brand, "Vocation and Ministry," in *In Search of a Round Table*, ed. Kanyoro, 16.

attaining theological education. But when they graduate, they are not offered ministerial positions, if they are offered anything at all. I have seen this happen year after year in the life of my students. What would happen if all the facts are laid out in the open from the time the preacher makes the altar call? Would women still go for training in theological colleges? And if women realized the full extent of the stranglehold that men have on Church governance and ministry, would they continue to attend church as they do now?

When there is so much inequality in the Church, the worship of the Church cannot be anything more than a caricature of true worship. Worship cannot be true when the worshippers cannot come before God as equals. How is God glorified when men come to worship with pride about their maleness and act as though that alone privileges them to positions of power and influence? And how is God honoured when women come to worship with diffidence and distrust of their self-worth, because they have been conditioned into thinking they are inferior?

Worship requires community. Worship entails unencumbered communication. To be at worship the community must be in communion, and communion is a spiritual union of equals. Even in marriage, the Bible teaches us not to be unequally yoked (2 Cor 6:14). I realise that the Corinthian passage can be debated variously and could be problematic from a pluralistic perspective. The theological basis for this Pauline injunction comes from Deut 22:9-11 and especially 22:10: "You shall not plow with an ox and a donkey yoked together." The principal for this law comes from the Genesis account of creation in which God established order and boundaries for creation. From this perspective, I read 2 Cor 6:14 as signifying that marriage is the union of two equals and not an unethical, contrary-to-creation, yoking together of a superior or stronger and an inferior or weaker creation.

How much more so the Church should seek equality in worship. A new understanding of Church ministry as service and not power is needed. The idea of a round table captures the idea of equality in Church, and by inference, in worship. Christine Grumm states, "it is no longer enough that we have a place at the table: now we need to be involved in actually reshaping that table to accommodate our presence."[38] A round table has no sides, no "head," and no preferred seating. The inspiration

38. Christine Grumm, "In Search of a Round Table," in *In Search of a Round Table: Gender, Theology & Church Leadership*, ed. Musimbi R. A. Kanyoro (Geneva: WCC Publications, 1997), 28.

for a round table comes from a poem—*In Search of a roundtable*.[39] A roundtable changes the physical and spiritual configurations of how people worship. It has no dais or throne, and no head from where priests would preside. It has no sides unlike "narrowlong" churches that resemble the cross but do not emulate it. Roundtabling implies being together rather than "them" and "us" or "first" and "last."

The imagery of a round table is helpful in articulating a notion of Church ministry that is not based on the exercise of power but on genuine fellowship. Spiritual union, and thereby communion, is not possible unless worshippers see themselves as equally sinful and equally saved before God. The idea of redefining, redesigning, redoing, and rebirthing the Church is particularly relevant because it portrays a Church which is transformed from the inside out. Often churches assume enough has been done when two or three women are ordained and two or three women are included in the church committees. Self-satisfied, they go on with business as usual. The structure and organization of the church remains unchanged.

Ultimately, the feminist agenda is not to replace male priests with female priests, or to have 50 percent male deacons and 50 percent female deacons in every church. The feminist objective is to transform the Church so that there is no big and small, no high and low, and no superior and inferior but all serving and being served—one in Christ and one in Spirit. Is this kind of equality possible in the Church? Some theologians see inequality as an inevitable and necessary aspect of Church governance.

> The Christian view of justice does not confuse the personal equality due to all members of the church and of society because they are created in God's image with the necessarily hierarchical inequality of gifts, offices, and kinds of status required for a community to achieve the common good of its members and to permit the maximum participation by all.... Consequently, it is not unjust but the realization of true justice that the church has a hierarchical structure, and that only persons possessing the qualifications for an office, even when this qualification is one of gender, are admitted to it.[40]

Not surprisingly, this view comes from someone who enjoys a high office in the Catholic Church. The author purports to be speaking the language of justice, but it is anything but. For instance, he concludes

39. Chuck Lathrop, cited in Grumm, "In Search of a Round Table," in *In Search of a Round Table*, ed. Kanyoro, 28-29.

40. Benedict M. Ashley, *Justice in the Church: Gender and Participation* (Washington, DC: The Catholic University of America Press, 1996), 164.

that the priesthood can be conferred only to males because "maleness is essential to Christ's revelation of the nature of God as Father, Son, and Holy Spirit." He adds that the exclusion of women from the priestly office "is not a denial of personal equality because males are also excluded from a complementary role in the church fulfilled by consecrated virgins."[41] His argument does not convince. Rather it typifies the opposition to the realization of gender justice and equality from those in "narrowlong" churches.

Teaching about worship, Jesus taught his followers: "When you are offering your gift at the altar, if you remember that your brother or sister has something against you, leave your gift there before the altar and go; first be reconciled to your brother or sister and then come offer your gift" (Matt 5:23-24). This passage is significant not only because it teaches that the worshipper's heart and mind should be right before making an offering to God but also because of the underlying principle it embodies; that things that happen outside the immediate act of worship have a direct correlation with worship. The issue of women's ordination, the constraints placed on women in pastoral and other Church ministries, the male oriented organization of the Church, the segregation of the minority, and indifference towards the weak and the poor are all barriers that stand in the way of worship. They impede the community's experience of the grace of God and keep the community from truly becoming community.

Building up Community Through Worship

In my consideration of the Church as an inclusive community of believers, I have discussed the linkages between tribal identity, community and worship, the egalitarian and communitarian aspect of koinonia inspired by the mutual abiding of the Trinity, and the significance of the presence of the Spirit for empowering women. In this section, I wish to discuss the place of worship in building up community, to extend the notion of community and inclusivity to worship. My focus will be on baptism and the Lord's Supper to highlight ways in which worship can and should foster inclusive community. I do not mean to imply that these two aspects of worship are the most important elements by means of which the sense of inclusive community may be communicated to members of the Church. Notions of koinonia and trinitarian koinonia, the presence of

41. Ashley, *Justice in the Church*, 165-66.

the Spirit in worship, the language of liturgy, and sermons and prayers are all pertinent. Most of these have, however, been touched upon in previous discussions. Thus my discussion here will be based on the Lord's Supper and baptism to draw out the principles of community building in worship. I will be adding a feminist or a tribal perspective whenever it seems appropriate. My selection of the Lord's Supper and baptism for discussion is primarily because Baptists observe these two ordinances. I think my case can be suitably covered by a discussion of these two observances of the Church rather than all the sacraments maintained by other Christian denominations but which are not observed by the Baptists.

The Lord's Supper

Holy Communion, Eucharist, Mass, or the Lord's Supper is a matter of deep theological division in the global Christian community. It was one of the most serious controversies during the Protestant Reformation. Prior to the Reformation, at the fourth Lateran Council in 1215 the belief in transubstantiation was defined as *de fide* of the Catholic Church.[42] The doctrine of transubstantiation holds that the Eucharist is an encounter of the mystery of the Lord's "real presence" because the substance of the bread and wine are converted into the body and blood of Christ when the priest uttered the words of consecration, "This is my body" (Latin *hoc est corpus meum*). During the Reformation, the doctrine of transubstantiation was rejected by all the prominent reformers. However, the reformers did not share the same theological view about the Lord's Supper and this caused a very public controversy among the reformers. Martin Luther maintained that the real presence of Christ was at the table.[43] However, he rejected transubstantiation and attacked it in his work *On the Babylonian Captivity of the Church* (1520), where he also stated his view:

---

42. Gary Macy, *Treasures from the Storeroom: Medieval Religion and the Eucharist* (Collegeville, MN: The Liturgical Press, 1999), 81-120. Later, in the Council of Trent of 1562, Rome supplemented transubstantiation with the doctrine of the Eucharist as a propitiatory sacrifice, leading to fierce objections by Protestants as well as the Eastern Orthodox churches.

43. Basil Hall, "Hoc est Corpus Meum: The Centrality of the Real Presence for Luther," in *Luther: Theologian for Catholics and Protestants*, ed. Gregory Yule (Edinburgh: T & T Clark, 1985), 112-44. See also Althaus, *Theology of Martin Luther*, 375-403.

> For my part, if I cannot fathom how the bread is the body of Christ, yet I will take my reason captive to the obedience of Christ [II Cor. 10:5], and clinging simply to his words, firmly believe not only that the body of Christ is in the bread, but that the bread is the body of Christ.... What does it matter if philosophy cannot fathom this? The Holy Spirit is greater than Aristotle. Does philosophy fathom their transubstantiation? Why, they themselves admit that here all philosophy breaks down.[44]

Luther's position is often identified as "consubstantiation" but he did not use that word. His point is that philosophical explanations such as transubstantiation or consubstantiation are inadequate to express Christian faith. Ulrich Zwingli, the Swiss reformer was much more radical than Luther. He felt that Luther's view is too close to the Catholic view and unpurged of the sacramentalism which Luther was fighting against. A letter written by Cornelisz Hoen in 1522 arguing for a figurative explanation of the Lord's Supper had an influence on Zwingli.[45] Hoen himself was in turn influenced by the humanist Wessel Gansfort. Zwingli promoted Hoen's ideas and adopted it to oppose Luther's interpretation of the Lord's Supper. Zwingli held the view the Lord's Supper is a symbolic memorial of the suffering and death of Jesus.[46] Zwingli argued that it is not possible to eat the actual body of Christ by faith:

> Observe, therefore, what a monstrosity of speech this is: I believe that I eat the sensible and bodily flesh. For if it is bodily, there is no need of faith, for it is perceived by sense; and things perceived by sense have no need of faith, for by sense they are perceived to be perfectly sure. On the other hand, if your

---

44. Martin Luther, "The Babylonian Captivity of the Church" [1520], in *Martin Luther: Three Treatises - From the American Edition of Luther's Works*, 2nd ed., trans. A. T. W. Steinhäuser, rev. Frederick C. Ahrens and Abdel Ross Wentz (Philadelphia: Fortress Press, 1970), 150-51.

45. Matthew R. Crawford, "On Faith, Signs, and Fruits: Martin Luther's Theology of the Lord's Supper," in *The Lord's Supper: Remembering and Proclaiming Christ Until He Comes*, NAC Studies in Bible and Theology 10, ed. Thomas R. Schreiner and Matthew R. Crawford (Nashville, TN: B & H Publishing Group, 2010), 210.

46. Helpful sources for Zwingli's view of the Lord's Supper are: Zwingli, "On the Lord's Supper," in *Zwingli and Bullinger*, Library of Christian Classics 24, ed. G. W. Bromiley (London: SCM Press, 1953), 176-238; Bruce Ware, "The Meaning of the Lord's Supper in the Theology of Ulrich Zwingli (1484-1531)," in *The Lord's Supper: Remembering and Proclaiming Christ Until He Comes*, NAC Studies in Bible and Theology 10, ed. Thomas R. Schreiner and Matthew R. Crawford (Nashville, TN: B & H Publishing Group, 2010), 229-47.

> eating is a matter of belief, the thing you believe cannot be sensible or bodily. Therefore what you say is simply a monstrosity.[47]

Interpreting 1 Cor 11:25-26, he insisted that the Lord's Supper is "a commemoration of Christ's death, not a remitting of sins for that is the province of Christ's death alone."[48] To support his argument that the elements signify the body and blood of Christ, Zwingli pointed out that there are many places in Scripture where the verb "is" stands for signification and not substance. So when Jesus said, "this is my body," in Matthew 26, he used the word "is" for "signifies"[49]

Luther and Zwingli, along with Oecolampadius and Philip Melanchton, met at the Marburg Colloquy in 1529 to hold a debate and resolve their disagreements.[50] However the debate did nothing to change their opposing views. The controversy cooled down after the death of Zwingli two years later. Melanchton, Martin Bucer, and John Calvin continued to grapple with the knotty issue of the Lord's Supper, yet the theological disputes proved to be irreconcilable and remain so to this day.

All the major reformers such as Luther, Zwingli, and Calvin clung to infant baptism and also the union of church and state. They also would not take the radical step of handing ecclesiastical authority to the people in local churches.[51] On such grounds the Anabaptists broke with them. The Anabaptists felt that the reformers failed to uproot Romanism from the Church and establish a true Church consistent with the testimony of the New Testament. For this reason, some Baptists do not like to be called "Protestants" in the same sense it is applied to other denominations.[52]

---

47. Ulrich Zwingli, *Commentary on True and False Religion*, ed. Samuel Macauley Jackson and Clarence Nevin Heller (1929; repr., Durham, NC: The Labyrinth Press, 1981), 213-14.

48. Zwingli, *Commentary on True and False Religion*, 228.

49. Zwingli, *Commentary on True and False Religion*, 227.

50. Martin E. Lehmann, trans., "The Marburg Colloquy and the Marburg Articles," in *Luther's Works*, vol. 38 (Philadelphia: Fortress Press, 1971), 3-89.

51. This was why the radical reformer Andreas von Bodenstein Karlstadt called those in Luther's circle at Wittenberg "the new papists." Andreas Karlstadt, "Whether One Should Proceed Slowly" [1524], in *The Radical Reformation*, Cambridge Texts in the History of Political Thought, ed. Michael G. Baylor (Cambridge: Cambridge University Press, 1991), 66; Calvin Augustine Pater, *Karlstadt as the Father of the Baptist Movements: The Emergence of Lay Protestantism* (Toronto: University of Toronto Press, 1984), 63.

52. Robert A. Baker, *The Baptist March in History* (Nashville, TN: Convention Press, 1958), 38.

There is not sufficient space here to offer more than a thoroughly abridged summary of the controversies over the Lord's Supper at the time of the Reformation. Yet these remain highly relevant for Christians today. Thus it is proper to try to define the fundamental meaning of the Lord's Supper. For the purpose of this study, I wish in particular to revisit the so-called "words of institution" found in 1 Cor 11:23-26 and discuss what Jesus meant when he said "Do this in remembrance of me."[53]

> For I received from the Lord what I also handed on to you, that the Lord Jesus on the night when he was betrayed took a loaf of bread, and when he had given thanks, he broke it and said, "This is my body that is for you. Do this in remembrance of me." In the same way he took the cup also, after supper, saying, "This cup is the new covenant in my blood. Do this, as often as you drink it, in remembrance of me." For as often as you eat this bread and drink the cup, you proclaim the Lord's death until he comes.

The meal and this instruction took place in a Passover setting.[54] And the words used in the liturgy such as "cup of blessing" (1 Cor 10:16) reflect the Passover celebration. But did Jesus mean to say, "Do this to remember me whenever you celebrate the Passover"? The followers of Jesus did not understand it in that sense. Passover is celebrated only once in a year but the followers of Jesus did not observe the meal in memory of Jesus as an annual event. What Jesus meant then, and what his followers understood him to mean, was "Do this to remember me whenever you have your common meal."

Consequently, Luke records that the disciples and followers of Jesus, including the three thousand first converts of the Pentecost, "devoted themselves to the apostles' teaching and fellowship, to the breaking of bread and the prayers" (Acts 2:42). Further to that, Luke adds: "Day by day, as they spent much time together in the temple, they broke bread at home [or from house to house] and ate their food with glad and generous hearts" (Acts 2:46). The common meal became a way of life of

---

53. The following discussion is based on John Howard Yoder, *Body Politics: Five Practices of the Christian Community before the Watching World* (Nashville, TN: Discipleship Resources, 1992).

54. The gospels do not agree about the precise day. The synoptic Gospels regard it as a Passover meal (Matt 26:17-30; Mark 14:12-25; Luke 22:7-23). On the other hand, John 13:1 (cf. John 19:31) implies that it took place before the festival of the Passover, on the day of Preparation. John's date is evidently motivated by his presentation of Jesus as the Passover Lamb. In either case, a connection with the Passover is clear.

the early Christians. The sharing at a common table paved the way for the formation of an egalitarian and economic community.

> Now the whole group of those who believed were of one heart and soul, and no one claimed private ownership of any possessions, but everything they owned was held in common. (Acts 4:32)

> There was not a needy person among them, for as many as owned lands or houses sold them and brought the proceeds of what was sold. They laid it at the apostles' feet, and it was distributed to each as any had need. (Acts 4:34-35)

Yoder believes that the "common purse" of the church in Jerusalem was a common table and not a purse. He reasons that the sharing of food at a common table extended normally into the sharing of all things in common. The common meal, Yoder argues, was not a new development in the post-pentecostal church but a resumption of the practice of Jesus and his itinerant band of disciples who were fed and cared for by supporters that included women and people healed by Jesus.

The notion of God feeding the people and people eating together is highlighted in Jewish scriptures in the narrative of the provision of manna during the Israelites sojourn in the wilderness. Further, the mosaic law of jubilees, calling for the periodic reallocation of land ownership every fifty years (Lev 25; Deut 15),[55] underlines God's ultimate ownership of all the land. Indeed the principle underlying the mosaic law of jubilees foreshadows the sharing of all possessions among the disciples of Jesus and in the Jerusalem community. Jesus declared it as his manifesto at the beginning of his ministry as "proclaiming the year of the Lord's favour" (Luke 4:18-21). Thus the messianic age envisioned by Jesus is one characterized by an equal sharing of all resources and the realization of personal well-being. John the Baptist, who also declared the coming of the Kingdom of God told his hearers how they could best prepare themselves: "Whoever has two coats must share with anyone who has none; and whoever has food must do likewise" (Luke 3:11). Jesus refused

55. Evidently, this law may not have been followed in ancient Israel. However, it reflects a Jewish theological understanding of God as the owner of the land. This is an important theological principle for tribal theology. For a discussion of the importance of land in tribal theology see A. Wati Longchar, "Dancing with the Land: Significance of Land for Doing Tribal Theology," *Indian Journal of Theology* 38/2 (1996): 16-28; and A. Wati Longchar and Yangkahao Vashum, eds., *Tribal Worldview and Ecology*, Tribal Study Series 2 (Jorhat, Assam: Tribal Study Centre, 1998).

to make bread at the behest of the devil (Luke 4:3-4). But during the later part of his mission, of his own will, he multiplied bread, enough to feed five thousand on one occasion and four thousand at another time and many baskets were left over on both occasions (Matt 14:13-21; 15:13-39; Mark 6:30-44; 8:1-11; Luke 9:10-17; John 6:1-14). In doing so, he gave a foretaste of the messianic banquet. After his resurrection, Luke reports, Jesus took time to sit at the table and eat bread with the disciples at Emmaus (Luke 24:28-35). Luke also reports that the resurrected Jesus appeared to his disciples and asked for something to eat. They gave him a piece of broiled fish and he ate it in their presence (Luke 24:36-43). And John notes specifically that Jesus ate fish and bread with his disciples after he was raised from the dead (John 21:9-14).

Therefore, the common meal, on which the Lord's Supper is based, is not an innovation but a recapitulation of a principle of egalitarian sharing demonstrated in many instances in the life of the Israelites and in the life of Jesus.

One of the earliest decisions of the Christian community concerned a complaint from the Hellenists against the Hebrews because their widows were not being treated fairly in the daily distribution of food (Acts 6:1-6). Seven leaders were then appointed to take care of the distribution of food. This account confirms the importance of the common meal and that it was a daily event. What is significant though is that the early Christian community reorganized their leadership structures in order to make it sure that non-Hebrew widows would not be neglected in the distribution of daily food. Yoder goes on to argue that the church council held at Jerusalem (Acts 15) arose from the conditions of table fellowship and it laid the foundation for a missionary policy that welcomed Gentiles into the fold. Paul's instructions in 1 Corinthians dealt extensively with issues of table, regarding food offered to idols (1 Cor 8, 10) and segregation at the table fellowship (1 Cor 11). Paul warned the Corinthians that if their table fellowship was conducted in an unworthy manner, that is, if they did not overcome social stratification at the common meal, they would "eat and drink judgment against themselves" (1 Cor 11:29).

The interpretation of the common meal as a religious ceremony, a ritual to be observed occasionally, has divested the table fellowship of its social and economic significance. Furthermore, the theological debate about the symbolic significance of the elements has taken attention away from the basic meaning of the common meal. Scripture witness is clear that the early Christians regarded the bread as the body of Christ and the wine as the cup of the new covenant in the blood of Christ (cf. 1 Cor 11:23-26). The significance of the so-called words of institution does not rest upon whether the bread and wine become the actual flesh and blood of Jesus when a priest says the right prayer over it. The greatest significance of the text, as I see it, is that Jesus is as indispensable as the food and drink people need to keep them alive. Bread and wine does not merely stand for something else, it is real bread and wine too. Eating and drinking together is not merely a symbolic act but the actual way of life in community, a life of social and economic solidarity. Remember, Jesus' Nazareth manifesto (Luke 4:18-19) is about bringing a sea of change to the poor, the captives, the blind, and the oppressed. Certainly, the apostles and early disciples of Jesus saw the common meal and its extension into a common economics as a way of realizing the objective of the Nazareth manifesto. The Scriptures envision the eschatological age in terms of a great messianic feast in which the poor and the hungry are fed (Ps 107:9; Isa 25:6-9; 49:10; 55:1-3; Luke 13:29; cf. Josephus, Jewish Wars 2.129-31). The daily breaking of the bread in the community prefigures the great banquet when the whole world, especially the poor, crippled, blind, and lame eat together in a lavish feast of food for all (Matt 22:1-14; Luke 14:15-24). The full implication of this teaching will never be known unless it is recognised that the main element in a banquet is actual food and that sharing it anticipates the fullness of life in God's realm.

A North East Indian tribal perspective of the Lord's Supper can arise from the interpretation of the Lord's Supper based on traditional tribal practices of community feasts.[56] Feasts are central to tribal culture. Traditionally, we held feasts to welcome a new season, to celebrate the harvest, to honour certain people with feasts of merit, to celebrate our festivals, and to observe rites of passage. The traditional inclination to have feasts is seen today in tribal fondness for celebrating Christian festivals such as Christmas and Easter with big community feasts, in celebrating church centenary and silver, gold, and platinum jubilees, and in regarding any significant event as an opportunity to have community feasts. If the Lord's Supper is a transformation of the well-known communal meal

56. It is noteworthy that feminist Christians are celebrating the Lord's Supper at meals, emulating the early Christians. Diann L. Neu, "Feminist Eucharists at Wisdom's Many Tables," in *New Feminist Christianity: Many Voices, Many Views*, ed. Mary E. Hunt and Diann L. Neu (Woodstock, VT: SkyLight Paths Publishing, 2010), 190-205.

following a sacrifice at the Temple of Jerusalem, as Bernhard Lang posits,[57] it stands to reason that tribal people should look to their own communal meals to understand the Lord's Supper from a tribal perspective.

Sharing food is important to tribal people. As a young girl I often accompanied my parents when they went visiting people in villages. One pleasant autumn afternoon, we visited a place called Araimile. It was a village back then, but now it is a part of New Tura town. The headman of the village, called the Nokma, happened to be my father's friend. Soon after we arrived, there was a hustle and bustle. A goat was slaughtered in our honour. Most of the villagers appeared to have turned up. Some of them started cooking. The goat's brain was carefully placed in a bamboo to be cooked over the fire. The brain preparation is a special item called *brenga*. Since the small brain is not sufficient to distribute among all the people, it was mixed with some rice on a bamboo winnower and a portion was distributed to everyone, including the children. On occasions like this, it is apparent that tribal ethos respected every member of the community especially with regard to the sharing of food.

A few decades back, in traditional tribal communities, food was scarce. People grew vegetables such as pumpkin, yam, chilli, ginger, maize, tapioca, sweet potatoes, and beans, and cultivated crops such as rice and millet in their fields. They kept a few domestic animals such as dogs, goats, chickens, cows, and buffaloes. These were not sufficient to feed the family so people relied a lot on wild herbs, shoots, and roots that they foraged for in the forest for their daily consumption. For meat, they hunted animals and birds. They caught fish, crabs, field rats, locusts, crickets, and all kinds of crawling or flying insects. They did not have a lot but whenever they had feasts, you wouldn't notice they were poor. Feasts were always a lavish communal affair. Everybody, regardless of their economic or social status, participated in these feasts. There would be plenty of rice, which is the staple food of the people, and meat in abundance. The rich opened their granaries, those who had cattle slaughtered them, brewed wine flowed freely, and everybody gave whatever they could. There would not be the sequence of rituals that the ancient Israelites followed in the Jerusalem Temple, but there would be other rituals and prayers honouring God and thanking God for blessings received. In tribal people's worldview, God is intimately involved in their daily life. Thus when they meet for feasts, God is viewed as being present and in many communities food

57. Bernhard Lang, *Sacred Games: A History of Christian Worship* (New Haven: Yale University Press, 1997), 215-233.

is offered first to God before people begin to eat. A Garo prayer of thanksgiving goes like this:[58]

Tatara Rabugana,	For Tatara Rabuga
Dakgipa Rugipana	For Creator and Maker
Misina Saljongna,	For Misi Saljong
Me·enma Rokimemana	For Me·enma Rokimema
Patigipa Ra·rongipana	For the one who blesses and shares
Ge·songgipa Ge·botgipana	For the one who has made to grow
Nang·ni patia, Nang·ni ra·rona	For you blessed and you shared
Jako rakuja, Ku·o pilkuja	I have not taken yet, I have not eaten yet
Nang·nan on·chengenga	I am offering you first
Nang·nan chin·chengenga	I am taking it out for you first
Cha·pabo ine, ringpabo ine	Please eat, please drink
Misia Saljonga	you Misi Saljong
Kiri Rokimeara…	you Kiri Rokime

A discussion of bread and wine in tribal context appears to be appropriate at this point. Bread is not a traditional tribal food. It has no place in tribal food culture or life. On the other hand, rice is a fundamental aspect of tribal life. From growing and harvesting to cooking and eating it, rice occupies tribal life and activity. Thus other people from Asian cultures whose primary food is rice have suggested that bread should be interpreted contextually as rice. A Korean poem written by freedom fighter and poet Kim Chi Ha has theological resonance for North East Indian tribals:

rice is heaven
as we cannot go to heaven alone
we should share rice with one another.
as all share the sight of the heavenly stars,
we should share and eat rice with one another.
rice is heaven
when we eat and swallow rice
heaven dwells in our body.
rice is heaven
yes, rice is the matter
we should eat together[59]

58. Mihir N. Sangma, *Some Important Festivals and Ceremonies of the Garos: Hundred Drums Wangala Festival* (Tura: Narayan Group, 2001), 11.

59. Quoted in Samuel Rayan, "Give Us this Day Our Daily Bread," in *The Challenge of Basic Christian Communities*, ed. Sergio Torres and John Eagleson, trans. John Drury (Maryknoll, NY: Orbis Books, 1981), 221-22.

Rice, for tribals, evokes the back-breaking labour that brings it to the table. It brings to mind the entire year's work, no matter rain or sunshine: clearing of the fields, tilling the soil, preparing it for plantation, planting, keeping the water-course clear, clearing the weeds, harvesting, winnowing, carrying the loads of harvest on backs, putting out under the sun, and pounding the rice in handfuls. Every grain of rice is important. My parents taught me not to waste food, to eat up every grain of rice on my plate. Tribal perspective about food is thus critical of Western culture of wasteful living that has resulted in global warming and contributed towards the poverty of poorer countries around the world.

According to a report released by the Food and Agriculture Organization of the United Nations (FAO), the International Fund for Agricultural Development (IFAD), the United Nations Children's Fund (UNICEF), the World Food Programme (WFP), and the World Health Organization (WHO), in the year 2016 about 815 million people, or one of every ten people, around the world are affected by chronic hunger.[60] This gargantuan problem of world hunger is not because of food shortages but because the rich people see hunger as a problem of the poor. Advances in biotechnology offered hope for solving global hunger. Yet genetic engineering and commercial agriculture destroyed local food cultures and brought disastrous consequences on the Indian farmers.[61] There is no concerted attempt to end world hunger. George Kent points to the structural violence in the global economic system in which the poor feed the rich—food flows from poor countries to rich countries. In the current trading system it is the rich countries who benefit because it is tilted in their favour.

> The global marketplace is not an equal-opportunity marketplace. Many countries stay stuck on the bottom no matter how much outsiders try to help them. To some extent that is due to forces within the country such as armed conflicts, rapid population growth, and corrupt leaders. To some extent it is the result of international political and economic forces that keep them down. For example,

---

60. FAO, IFAD, UNICEF, WFP and WHO, *2017: The State of Food Security and Nutrition in the World 2017—Building Resilience for Peace and Food Security*, https://docs.wfp.org/api/documents/WFP-0000022419/download/?_ga=2.268521401.974489353.1506032202-1929593996.1506032202 (accessed September 10, 2018).

61. Vandana Shiva, *Stolen Harvest: The Hijacking of the Global Food Supply*, Culture of the Land (Lexington, KY: University Press of Kentucky, 2016); idem, *The Violence of the Green Revolution: Third World Agriculture, Ecology, and Politics*, Culture of the Land (Lexington, KY: University Press of Kentucky, 2016).

> massive subsidies of agricultural products in richer countries result in their dumping large quantities of these products in poorer countries, undermining those countries' agricultural sectors. Sometimes poor countries cannot get access to the markets of rich countries to sell their export products, and then they can do that only if they sell at rock-bottom prices. Not only individuals but also entire countries have, in effect, become unemployed, totally marginalized by the global economic system.[62]

Food, and the way it is shared, ought to be respected. "Eating," says David Andrews, "is a moral act."[63] He is right. Food, bread, or rice is at the heart of the prayer Jesus gave us. Whether we are eating at our family tables or faith tables, our eating of food should not leave some people hungry or excluded.

In sharp contrast to bread, wine is a ubiquitous component of tribal life. Rice brew or millet brew called "zu," "chu bitchi," and many other names, is traditionally regarded as food. It is consumed daily by men, women, and children. Although it is a fermented drink, drunkenness is not common among villagers as people know how to drink in moderation. The traditional brew is taken as a tonic for health. It is drunk in plenty especially during feasts and festivities. Whether during weddings or funerals or a ceremony for the healing of a sick person, wine is essential. However, drinking wine, including the traditional tribal brew, is forbidden by the protestant churches of the region. When Western missionaries came to the region they told the people that their traditional drink was evil. The North American Baptist missionaries were products of the temperance movement in their home country. They prohibited the tribals from drinking their traditional brew once they converted to Christianity. Two basic things were required of converts: abstention from work on Sundays (called "Robibar mania" in A·chik language) and total abstinence from drinking wine or liquor. In recent years, some have started questioning the prohibition of drinking traditional wine. Indeed the cultural casualties brought about by the demonizing of a traditional way of life are undeniable. Whereas non-Christians continue to drink the brew as part of their daily food, many Christians drink it in secret. Consequently, many Christians have become alcoholics. Alcoholism has

62. George Kent, *Ending Hunger Worldwide* (London: Paradigm Publishers, 2011), 7-8.

63. David Andrews, "The Lord's Table, the World's Hunger: Liturgy, Justice, and Rural Life," in *Liturgy and Justice: To Worship God in Spirit and Truth*, ed. Anne Y. Koester (Collegeville, MN: Liturgical Press, 2002), 71-73.

become a bigger problem where drinking is prohibited than where it is accepted. Until tribals restore their traditional attitude towards drinking rice brew, churches of the region will continue to give the impression to their congregations that Jesus drank unfermented grape juice. Churches will continue to avoid the fact Jesus ate food and drank wine regularly, which gave cause for his enemies to charge him as being a glutton and a drunkard (Matt 11:18-19).

Communitarianism was expressed most eloquently in the sharing of food and drink during feasts. This outlook about sharing whatever you have for the community is still alive in tribal societies today. A notion of the Lord's Supper as a community feast would evoke the sense of community associated with feasts. Breaking bread together in community shatters social and economic barriers and gender segregation. Importantly, from a tribal perspective, a community meal is never confined to a group but to every person in the village and, in the case of big feasts, also to people of neighbouring villages. From this viewpoint, the Lord's Supper is really the great leveller. A member cannot be satiated and satisfied with food while another stays hungry. Food has to be shared. But the Lord's Supper is not only about food. It is also about sharing the life of Jesus, following the life he lived. It is about sharing status, of serving one another, and of regarding men and women as equals. The Lord's Supper is really a harbinger of the messianic age, experienced in the church but looking forward to its fulfilment in the wider world. The presence of God in the celebration of the Lord's Supper is not because of a prayer but because the community is doing God's will by sharing food and drink, and more importantly, living in communion.

Baptism

Baptism is a matter of deep theological and doctrinal importance to the Church. Agreement about its theological implications and its implementation is sometimes seen as a factor that could bring greater unity among churches of various denominations.[64] But such a unity is easier on paper than in reality because baptism is a fractured issue and a divisive practice. I will begin this section by pointing out the

64. Susan K. Wood, *One Baptism: Ecumenical Dimensions of the Doctrine of Baptism* (Collegeville, MN: The Liturgical Press, 2009); Michael Root and Risto Saarinen, eds., *Baptism and the Unity of the Church* (Grand Rapids, MI: William B. Eerdmans, 1998).

basic elements in the practice of baptism in various church traditions. Because this will be a broad treatment, my statements will be general observations and will not take into account specific local practices. The purpose is not to point out the wrong or right of church practices but to highlight the difficulties for churches to recognise each other's baptisms in a mutual way.[65] I will then discuss some of the specific areas that hinder churches from mutually accepting each other's baptism as equally valid. Following this, I will attempt to develop a theological perspective for viewing baptism as a means for realising inclusivity in the community. My perspectives arise mostly from my Baptist background, which means that my criticism could be directed more towards Baptist practices, but I expect the conclusions to be of wider significance.

The Practice of Baptism in Various Churches

The Catholic Church has three catechumenal programmes.[66] The catechumen for adults, called the *Rite of Christian Initiation of Adults* (RCIA), which sprang from the reforms initiated by the Second Vatican Council, is meant for new converts and for Christians joining the Catholic Church from other churches. Along with this, there are also programs for the baptism of infants who lack the use of reason (under 7 years of age—*Rite of Baptism for Children*) and for children who have the use of reason (ages 7-17 - RCIA).[67] Such baptism is generally done by the sprinkling of baptismal water (aspersion), but baptism by pouring (affusion) and baptism by dipping under the water (immersion) are also acceptable. The main rituals of baptism include the litanies of the saints, blessing of the water, the renunciation of sin, and the profession of faith. Then comes the actual baptism by immersion or pouring water three times over the head with the words "in the name of the Father,

65. For some studies in this area see Paul Meyendorff, "Toward Mutual Recognition of Baptism," in *Baptism Today: Understanding, Practice, Ecumenical Implications*, Faith and Order Paper No. 207, ed. Thomas F. Best (Collegeville, MN: Liturgical Press, 2008), 195-206.

66. Philippe Larere, *Baptism in Water and Baptism in the Spirit: A Biblical, Liturgical, and Theological Exposition*, trans. Patrick Madigan (Collegeville, MN: The Liturgical Press, 1993), 37-42.

67. John M. Huels, *The Catechumenate and the Law: A Pastoral and Canonical Commentary for the Church in the United States* (Chicago, IL: Liturgy Training Publications, 2003), 25; Maxwell E. Johnson, *The Rites of Christian Initiation: Their Evolution and Interpretation*, rev. and expanded ed. (Collegeville, MN: Liturgical Press, 2007), 375-450.

and of the Son, and of the Holy Spirit." For adults, baptism is followed immediately by the sacrament of confirmation and the unction with chrism. The bishop anoints the neophytes with perfumed oil on the forehead with the words, "Receive the mark of the Holy Spirit which is given to you." Thus baptism may conclude with confirmation but confirmation may also be postponed until later.[68] Following baptism, a white garment is given to signify that the believer has put on Christ and become a new creation. And then a lighted candle is presented to indicate that the newly baptised must walk as children of light. If it is a child who is being baptised, the parents or godparents speak on behalf of the child and commit themselves to the formation of the child. Once baptised the neophytes receive communion for the first time.

Within the Orthodox churches a variety of baptismal rites are followed depending on linguistic and cultural characteristics.[69] According to the Byzantine rite the sacrament of infant baptism includes prayers and elaborate ceremonies that touch on the deliverance of the mother, her churching on the fortieth day, name-giving on the eighth day, entrance into the catechumenate, baptism and confirmation, washing on the eighth day after baptism, and tonsure. In the case of an adult, various exorcisms are pronounced followed by a renunciation of sin with the recitation of the Nicene Creed. The words for both exorcism and renunciation are repeated three times. The baptistry is incensed and blessed. The water is exorcised three times and sanctified with a thrice-repeated formula. Then the person is baptised by a triple total immersion in the baptismal font with the words, "The servant (name) is baptised in the name of the Father." This is followed by confirmation, the Eucharist, and chrismation.[70]

In the Presbyterian and Reformed tradition too, there is baptism for adults as well as infants.[71] The ceremony for baptism begins with the

---

68. Post-baptismal anointing with chrism is performed only when confirmation does not follow immediately. James F. Puglisi, "Rite[s] of Baptism in the Catholic Church: A Theological-Pastoral Community," in *Baptism Today: Understanding, Practice, Ecumenical Implications*, Faith and Order Paper 207, ed. Thomas F. Best (Collegeville, MN: Liturgical Press, 2008), 36. *Baptism Today* carries a good number of commentaries on Baptism in churches not covered in my discussion.

69. Larere, *Baptism in Water and Baptism in the Spirit*, 54-57.

70. See further Johnson, *Rites of Christian Initiation*, 269-308.

71. Larere, *Baptism in Water and Baptism in the Spirit*, 42-48; Martha Moore-Keish, "Baptism in the Presbyterian and Reformed Tradition," in *Baptism Today: Understanding, Practice, Ecumenical Implications*, Faith and Order Paper No. 207, ed. Thomas F. Best (Collegeville, MN: Liturgical Press, 2008), 63-71.

reading of the institution of baptism by Jesus (Matt 28:19-20). Then the baptismal candidates join the congregation in reciting the Apostles' Creed. Following this, the minister prays a prayer of thanksgiving over the water. Baptism is done either by aspersion, affusion, or immersion. The baptismal formula is always, "(name), I baptise you in the name of the Father, and of the Son, and of the Holy Spirit." The newly baptised member is then welcomed to take part in the Eucharist. Like other protestant churches, there is no blessing of the water or anointing with oil. If it is a child who is being baptised, the parents act on behalf of the child and commit themselves to the spiritual instruction of the child and promise to show by example of a life following Christ. For parents who prefer not to baptise their child, provision is given to present their child in the church. Whether presented or baptised, the child will later be confirmed after completing his or her religious instruction and after having professed his or her faith. The non-baptised who have only been presented are baptised with the baptismal formula during confirmation. Unlike the Catholic and Orthodox churches, where confirmation is a sacrament, confirmation in the Reformed tradition is not a sacrament.[72] Congregationalists believe that baptism is complete without confirmation; the infant receives the blessing of the Holy Spirit through the faith of the congregation.

The Baptists only baptise those who profess their faith in Jesus Christ as Saviour.[73] This is known as "believers' baptism." Sometimes it is mistakenly referred to as adult baptism, whereas children can be baptised in believers' baptism if they are old enough to profess faith in Jesus. The Baptist perspective goes back to the Anabaptists who vehemently opposed infant baptism—in sharp contrast to Martin Luther, John Calvin, Ulrich Zwingli, Martin Bucer, Heinrich Bullinger and others who variously justified infant baptism—and insisted that Baptism is a mark of faith. Baptists do not baptise those who have not experienced conversion and have faith in Jesus. Consequently, infants who are not capable of personally professing their faith are not baptised. Children can

72. More on confirmation practices in Protestant churches, Richard Robert Osmer, *Confirmation: Presbyterian Practices in Ecumenical Perspective* (Louisville, KY: Geneva Press, 1996).

73. Larere, *Baptism in Water and Baptism in the Spirit*, 48-52; Paul Fiddes, "The Baptism of Believers," in *Baptism Today: Understanding, Practice, Ecumenical Implications*, Faith and Order Paper No. 207, ed. Thomas F. Best (Collegeville, MN: Liturgical Press, 2008), 73-80.

be presented in the church so that the church can thank God and pray for them and their families. Baptists also believe that baptism should be by immersion and not by aspersion or affusion. Immersion baptism is conducted either in the baptistry built within the church or outside the church, or in a water source like a river or lake. Immersion is preceded by the words, "On the profession of your faith before God and before his Church, into the death and resurrection of Jesus Christ I baptise you, in the name of the Father, and of the Son, and of the Holy Spirit." Baptists do not believe that baptism is a means for salvation, but an act of obedience to the Word.[74]

While most Christian denominations practice water baptism, there are a few who do not. The Salvation Army,[75] and the Quakers,[76] neither baptize nor take the Lord's Supper. And the so-called hyper-dispensationalists or untra-dispensationalists differ among themselves on the baptism and the Lord's Supper; some accept both, some reject both, while others repudiate baptism but keep the Lord's Supper.

Thus there are vast differences between the churches with regard to the practice of worship. These differences are not only liturgical but deep-seated theological viewpoints as well. Despite these differences there is room for some form of consensus among churches because the baptismal formula, "in the name of the Father, the Son, and the Holy Spirit," is used by almost all the churches in administering baptism. Unfortunately, this sentence is so infused with male imagery and patriarchal bias that some other alternative must be found before any meaningful dialogue can begin. This is an area that we cannot afford to avoid because unity

---

74. The *Southern Baptist Statement on Baptist Faith and Message*, VII (2000) states: "Christian baptism is the immersion of a believer in water in the name of the Father, the Son, and the Holy Spirit. It is an act of obedience symbolizing the believer's faith in a crucified, buried, and risen Saviour, the believer's death to sin, the burial of the old life, and the resurrection to walk in newness of life in Christ Jesus. It is a testimony of his faith in the final resurrection of the dead. Being a church ordinance, it is prerequisite to the privileges of church membership and to the Lord's Supper."

75. Earl Robinson, "A Salvation Army Perspective on Baptism: Theological Understanding and Liturgical Practice," in *Baptism Today: Understanding, Practice, Ecumenical Implications*, Faith and Order Paper 207, ed. Thomas F. Best (Collegeville, MN: Liturgical Press, 2008), 173-80.

76. Janet Scott, "Baptism and the Quaker Tradition," in *Baptism Today: Understanding, Practice, Ecumenical Implications*, Faith and Order Paper 207, ed. Thomas F. Best (Collegeville, MN: Liturgical Press, 2008), 81-88.

based on injustice will never be real unity. However, I will have to keep that issue aside and move on to areas of discord that make the phrase "one baptism" nothing but empty words.

Areas of Discord

One of the most important documents with regard to baptism in modern times is the *Baptism, Eucharist and Ministry* (Faith and Order Paper No. 111), which is an ecumenical statement developed by the Faith and Order Commission of the World Council of Churches and published in 1982. This document highlighted the meaning of baptism from biblical images and from the liturgy of the Church: participation in Christ's death and resurrection; conversion, pardoning and cleansing; the gift of the Spirit; incorporation into the body of Christ; and the sign of the kingdom. These dimensions of baptism offer theological basis for churches to find common ground and discover convergences of convictions and perspectives. Importantly, this document also highlighted problem areas. In Commentary (6), it noted:

> The inability of the churches mutually to recognize their various practices of baptism as sharing in the one baptism, and their actual dividedness in spite of mutual baptismal recognition, have given dramatic visibility to the broken witness of the Church. The readiness of the churches in some places and times to allow differences of sex, race, or social status to divide the body of Christ has further called into question genuine baptismal unity of the Christian community (Gal. 3:27—28) and has seriously compromised its witness. The need to recover baptismal unity is at the heart of the ecumenical task as it is central for the realization of genuine partnership within the Christian communities.[77]

Furthermore, the document identified the disagreement between those who insist only on believers' baptism and those who practise infant baptism as a critical area of ecumenical concern. Commentary (12) encouraged churches to recognise that "both forms of baptism embody God's own initiative in Christ and express a response of faith made within the believing community."[78] I can only applaud this comment.

77. World Council of Churches, *Baptism, Eucharist, and Ministry*, Faith and Order Paper No. 111 (Geneva: World Council of Churches, 1982), 2. This document is available online at the WCC website: http://www.oikoumene.org. An account of the history of the document is found in William G. Rusch, " 'Baptism, Eucharist and Ministry' – and Reception," in *The Search for Visible Unity*, ed. Jeffrey Gros (New York: Pilgrim Press, 1984), 129-42.

78. WCC, *Baptism, Eucharist, and Ministry*, 4.

The recognition only of believers' baptism ignores the fact that one who is given believers' baptism requires continuing Christian nurture just as infants require spiritual nurture in their Christian formation.

Baptist insistence on believers' baptism has led to a theological and doctrinal paucity with regard to children and infants. Clearly, Baptists need a deeper theological understanding of the spirituality of children and program for their spiritual nurture. The command of Jesus in Mark 10:14, "Let the little children come to me," is not fulfilled simply by bringing children to church and teaching them Christian songs and telling them Bible stories. The invitation must be seen as an invitation to share the gift of life in Jesus Christ, and partake in the blessings and the grace of the new humanity.

Jesus' invitation to children is the same invitation that is given to the poor, the outcast, the oppressed, and the "sinner," even before they are able to understand or respond to the invitation. Some might see the invitation to children as different from the invitation to adults because adults eventually respond whereas infants are unable to do so. However this would mean that adult humans save themselves with their faith and not because of God's grace.

Similar convoluted debates have been going on for centuries because Scripture can be persuasively argued from both sides. This is precisely why I wish to place the debate in the context of Jesus' call for an inclusive community. Baptists need to recognise that an inclusive community based on the practice of Jesus and animated by his death and resurrection must include not only women and men but small children and infants too. I am not advocating infant baptism, but rather encouraging a greater degree of openness and concession in relation to the practice of other churches.

Conversely, the Orthodox, Catholic, and Reformation churches could have greater appreciation of the difference between baptism that is imposed upon an infant and baptism from personal choice. Is baptism an instrument of salvation or is it a reflection of the reality of new life in Christ? If it is a means of attaining salvation, will everyone baptised be "saved" even without faith?

I realise that these issues will always be debatable. For instance Martin Luther argued against the Anabaptists:

> They want to make this [Mark 16:16] to mean that no one should be baptized before he [sic] believes. I say they have ventured a very great presumption. For if they want to follow such a belief they must not baptize before they know for certain that the one to be baptized believes. How and when do they always

> intend to know this? Have they now become gods that they can see in people's hearts whether they believe or not?"[79]

But in defence of Baptists, I must say that believer's baptism is not based on the measure of a person's faith but on profession of faith, something infants are unable to do. Baptists consider personal confession of faith in Jesus supported by a godly lifestyle as proof enough that the person believes in Jesus.

Believer's baptism, in my opinion, gives some reasons for churches that practice indiscriminate infant baptism to reflect on the consequences of baptism and the significance of conversion or profession of personal faith in the community of the new creation.

Another area of discord identified in the document is that of repeating baptism. It unambiguously states in Commentary (13) that baptism should not be repeated:

> Churches which have insisted on a particular form of baptism or which have had serious questions about the authenticity of other churches' sacraments and ministries have at times required persons coming from other church traditions to be baptized before being received into full communicant membership. As the churches come to fuller mutual understanding and acceptance of one another and enter into closer relationships in witness and service, they will want to refrain from any practice which might call into question the sacramental integrity of other churches or which might diminish the unrepeatability of the sacrament of baptism.[80]

The churches of the Reformed tradition have the practice of accepting a person from the Catholic or Orthodox churches into full communion with a ceremony of reception, without requiring the person to be baptised again. This is made possible because of a common Trinitarian theology and certain doctrinal agreements.

In the Catholic Church too, re-baptism is explicitly disallowed by Canon law. Canon 845 §1 of the Catholic Church states: "Since the sacraments of baptism, confirmation, and orders imprint a character, they cannot be repeated." The Catholic Church adheres to this rule and does not rebaptise non-Catholic Christians who seek full communion in the Catholic Church, provided the validity of the baptism is found

79. Quoted in John W. Riggs, *Baptism in the Reformed Tradition: An Historical and Practical Theology*, Columbia Series in Reformed Theology (Louisville, KY: Westminster John Knox, 2002), 104.

80. WCC, *Baptism, Eucharist, and Ministry*, 4-5.

to be satisfactory. Baptism with water together with the Trinitarian formula, and a baptismal certificate with the name of the minister on it are considered important to prove the validity of a baptism. Conditional baptism is given to those whose baptism cannot be proved satisfactorily. As for those whose baptism is recognised, they are required to take confirmation, except for the Eastern churches, the Old Catholic, Old Roman Catholic and Polish National churches.[81]

On its part, the Orthodox Church accepts the baptism of the Catholic and Reformation churches as valid, but does not fully recognise the baptism of other churches. It recognises, on principle of "economy," baptisms outside the Orthodox Church so long as it is done with water and in the name of the Trinity. This essentially means that it does not baptise again those who join it from those churches whose baptisms are recognized although it does not fully accept the other baptisms.[82] Baptised protestant converts are therefore not baptised again. Instead they are given anointing and accepted as members of the church.

Baptists differ from the majority in that they consider the differences so critical that if someone comes from another church, they require the person to be baptised again. Of course, Baptists are divided about their attitude towards baptism outside the Baptist churches. Certain Southern Baptist churches say that the only valid baptism is a Baptist baptism. Some Baptists accept any immersion baptism, even if performed by non-Baptists. And some think that non-Baptist immersion is irregular but not invalid.[83] For Baptists, baptising a person who has been previously baptised by sprinkling or pouring water is not considered rebaptism because the first baptism was not a valid form of baptism. But this is a myopic view that disregards the theological and biblical basis for other forms of baptism that are as strongly attested as baptism by immersion.

Rebaptism is not practised in churches where there is a secondary level of initiation such as anointing or confirmation; it is practised in churches like the Baptist and independent protestant churches which do

81. Huels, *Catechumenate and the Law*, 21-24.

82. Cf. Paul Turner, *When Other Christians become Catholic* (Collegeville, MN: The Liturgical Press, 2007), 10-11. By code of canon law (Canon 844), Catholics are forbidden to receive the Eucharist from ministers of other churches except for ministers of the Eastern Orthodox Church and those who maintain the apostolic succession. Jeffrey T. VanderWilt, *Communion with Non-Catholic Christians: Risks, Challenges, and Opportunities* (Collegeville, MN: The Liturgical Press, 2003), 40.

83. H. Leon McBeth, *The Baptist Heritage* (Nashville: Broadman Press, 1987), 697. Referred to in Wood, *One Baptism*, 79-80.

not have chrismation or confirmation. This in itself indicates that churches, whether they have rebaptism or not, have difficulty fully accepting each other's baptisms as equally valid. Churches are able to affiliate closely with, and maintain a certain degree of mutuality, with those churches which share similar theological and doctrinal outlook. But there is no relation between churches that have a greater degree of difference in their ideas about baptism.

Based on the responses of hundreds of churches to *Baptism, Eucharist, and Ministry*, two more Faith and Order documents, *The Nature and Mission of the Church* and "Called to be the One Church," were published. *Nature and Mission of the Church* noted that there was a high degree of agreement about baptism. But a perusal of the areas of contention reveals that in fact no progress has been made in all the major issues. In fact the list of areas of conflict is considerably longer.[84] The inability to find common ground is testament to the fact that baptism is viewed more as an initiatory rite for membership into a denominational body rather than into the body of Christ, the universal Church. Such a view of baptism falls short of the apostolic proclamation of the "new creation" or "new humanity" envisaged in the act of baptism.

Feminist Critique of Baptism

Feminist rethinking of baptism goes beyond the ecumenical concerns and touches its theological foundation. Part of feminist focus has been on the Trinitarian baptismal formula, which is baptism "in the name of the Father, the Son, and the Holy Spirit."

> Does this mean that baptism is only valid if it is understood as into a male-defined church identified by its relationship with a God that can only be spoken about in terms of male Trinity? Or is a rereading of the Trinitarian formula possible as divine being in relation, which could also be seen as God, for example, Mother, Lover and Friend?[85]

84. World Council of Churches, *The Nature and Mission of the Church: A Stage on the Way to Common Statement*, Faith and Order Paper No. 198 (Geneva: World Council of Churches, 2005), 20-21; idem, "Called to be the One Church," The Porto Alegre Ecclesiology Text (Geneva: World Council of Churches, 2006). These documents are available online at the WCC website: http://www.oikoumene.org.

85. Natalie K. Watson, *Introducing Feminist Ecclesiology*, Introductions in Feminist Theology (London: Sheffield Academic Press, 2002), 83.

Thus feminist thinkers have searched for alternatives in liturgical language so that it is sex-inclusive.[86] Sometimes, the alternative is to use "Mother" or "Father and Mother" for the first person of the Trinity. Frequently, the triadic "Creator, Redeemer, Sustainer" is proposed. Yet this is not entirely satisfactory. First, it refers only to the action of God and not to the person of God. Second, a "functionalist" approach ignores the relationship within the Godhead.[87] Another formula was formulated by James F. Kay and used at Riverside Church, New York: "I baptize you in the name of the Father and of the Son and of the Holy Spirit, one God, Mother of us all."[88] These alternatives may not be perfect but they are important for they point to the inadequacy of the traditional Trinitarian formula and the need to faithfully name God as we have experienced God. Conversely, Catherine Mawry LaCugna has argued that it is unnecessary to repudiate the Trinitarian formula. She maintains that "Living what we promise in baptism and becoming a community of inclusiveness ultimately may have less to do with language than with ourselves."[89] I believe that the male imagery of the traditional Trinitarian formula is much more sexist and patriarchal than LaCugna acknowledges. But I agree with her that the priority should be on how to develop a theology of baptism that helps in creating an inclusive community.

Closely linked to the feminist objection to the Trinitarian baptismal formula is the issue of baptism itself. Is baptism necessary for salvation? Churches that practice infant baptism do so primarily because of the belief that baptism is a means of God's grace, necessary for human salvation. In such a context, baptism signifies the new birth separating the child from its natural birth through its mother. Watson states:

> Therefore serious questions of a praxis of infant baptism arise. If baptism is interpreted as a rite of spiritual rebirth which supersedes the natural birth by a woman mother, I want to ask whether this adds to the denial of relationships

86. Ruth C. Duck, *Gender and the Name of God: The Trinitarian Baptismal Formula* (Cleveland, OH: The Pilgrim Press, 1991).

87. White, *Foundations of Christian Worship*, 168.

88. Bryan D. Spinks, *Reformation and Modern Rituals and Theologies of Baptism: From Luther to Contemporary Practices* (Aldershot: Ashgate Publishing, 2006), 159.

89. Catherine Mowry LaCugna, "The Baptismal Formula, Feminist Objections and Trinitarian Theology," *Journal of Ecumenical Studies* 26/2 (Spring 1989): 250; further idem, *God For Us: The Trinity and Christian Life* (San Francisco: Harper & Row, 1991).

> such as between mother and daughter which is hardly mentioned at all in the Christian tradition.[90]

In fact, feminists think that baptism in its current form is a male usurpation of the acts that women do naturally. Women give birth, but the "real" birth is given by male priests in baptism. Christine Gudorf asserts:

> Limitation of sacramental administration to men functions as a claim for men that they—not women—have exclusive power to create and sustain real life, spiritual life, through representing Jesus, the source of life. This claim implements a separation between ordinary natural life nurtured by women, and spiritual life nurtured by a male elite who serve as symbols for all men.[91]

Similarly, Anne McClintock states:

> The male ritual of baptism—with its bowls of holy water, its washing, its male midwives—is a surrogate birthing ritual, during which men collectively compensate themselves for their invisible role in the birth of the child an diminish women's agency.[92]

A search for an inclusive Trinitarian articulation of baptismal understanding has to take these concerns into consideration. Replacing a few words or tacking a word here and there is not the ultimate solution. Using "Mother and Father" for the first person of the trinity is not enough to change the existing systems. Our attention has to shift beyond words and rituals to the things they enact. Baptism is performance of birth. Men are simply not the right gender to take up the role of birther. But it is also important to draw men into the experience of birthing without at the same time diminishing the role of women. How can we be community of women and men in Church, and how can we know rebirth in the womb of baptism?

90. Watson, *Introducing Feminist Ecclesiology*, 83.

91. Christine E. Gudorf, "The Power to Create: Sacraments and Men's Need to Birth," *Horizons* 14/2 (1987): 297, cited in Susan A. Ross, *Extravagant Affections: A Feminist Sacramental Theology* (New York, NY: The Continuum International Publishing Group, 2001), 193.

92. Anne McClintock, *Imperial Leather: Race, Gender, and Sexuality in the Colonial Contest* (New York: Routledge, 1995), 29.

Baptism and an Inclusive Community

Writing to explain his practice of allowing Jews and Gentiles equally into the same community, for which he was being criticised from both sides, Paul argues:

> For the love of Christ urges us on, because we are convinced that one has died for all; therefore all have died. And he died for all, so that those who live might live no longer for themselves, but for him who died and was raised for them. From now on, therefore, we regard no one from a human point of view (κατὰ σάρκα); even though we once knew Christ from a human point of view (κατὰ σάρκα), we know him no longer in that way. So if anyone is in Christ, there is a new creation: everything old has passed away; see, everything has become new! (2 Cor 5:14-17)

Paul is arguing here that baptism initiates a person into a new humanity and a new world where the values of the old world no longer have any significance. Yoder adds new insight to the text by proposing that the Greek phrase κατὰ σάρκα "according to the flesh," which is translated in the NRSV as "from a human point of view," really means "ethnically."[93] Following Yoder's proposal, I can now translate v 16 as: "From now on, we regard no one as a Jew or Greek (ethnically); even though we once knew Christ as a Jew (ethnically), we know him no longer in that way." The statement that "there is a new creation" is rightly translated as "there is a new world" in the New English Bible. It is not only the individual who has become new but the whole world. This outlook is not confined to the Corinthian letter but is echoed in Galatians and Ephesians.

> For in Christ Jesus you are all children of God through faith. As many of you as were baptized into Christ have clothed yourselves with Christ. There is no longer Jew or Greek, there is no longer slave or free, there is no longer male and female; for all of you are one in Christ Jesus. And if you belong to Christ, then you are Abraham's offspring, heirs according to the promise. (Gal 3:26-29; cf. 4:5-7)

Baptism brings about a new identity where ethnic differences, socio-economic status, and gender distinctions have no meaning for all become "children of God" because they are "in Christ Jesus." The statement that anyone who belongs to Christ is an offspring of Abraham is radical. The belief that they are children of Abraham is integral to Jewish identity. To open that to the Gentiles, so that they can also claim a personal

93. Yoder, *Body Politics*, 28-29.

relationship with Abraham, is to give what the Jews believed to be theirs alone to others outside their community. This is part of the new world brought about by baptism. When Gal 6:15 is read in the light of Gal 3, the notion of "new creation" in 6:15 is a consequence of baptism: "For neither circumcision nor uncircumcision is anything; but a new creation is everything." The passage in Ephesians makes the same argument with the words "peace" and "new humanity":

> For he is our peace; in his flesh he has made both groups into one and has broken down the dividing wall, that is, the hostility between us. He has abolished the law with its commandments and ordinances, that he might create in himself one new humanity in place of the two, thus making peace. (Eph 2:14-15)

In all these passages, there is a consistent contention that baptism breaks down the basic barrier between Jews and Gentiles, and eventually breaks down all barriers that segregate, discriminate, and victimize people. Yoder asserts:

> In all three epistles [2 Cor, Gal, and Eph], then, in different language, the functional affirmation is the same: Baptism celebrates and effects the merging of the Jewish and the Gentile stories. A people with the law and a people without, a people walled off from the world and a people open to it, become a single community, melding the legacies of both.
>
> It is not enough to say that each of us is individually born again and baptized, with the result that all the born-again individuals are collected in one place, commanded by God to love one another and plant churches, with no reason for discrimination. Paul says more than that; he says that two peoples, two cultures, two histories have come to flow into one new humanity, a new creation.[94]

Thus in Yoder's view baptism is one that overarches patriarchal, ethnic, and class distinctions. Baptism is the creation of a new world order, a new society, a plural community, that brings together diverse communities and makes them one. Associating this with the practice of communal meals, discussed earlier, we can confidently assume that in the New Testament period, beginning with baptism, people from diverse cultures adjusted their dietary habits in order to eat together at the same table. This presents to us a model of the eschatological world. Baptism as a repudiation of patriarchy and imperialism, as a realisation of the

94. Yoder, *Body Politics*, 29-30.

breakdown of ethnic, sexual, and class distinctions, and as a means for eating at one table has been lost.

Baptism as a reconciliation of cultures and peoples fits in with feminist interpretations of baptism. But in feminist thought, the emphasis is not on Jews and Gentiles but on female and male. According to Ruether, baptism is a conversion from ideologies that allow persons to perpetuate the exploitation of themselves and others. Conversion, she maintains, is disassociation with the evil and the sin of sexism that has distorted human relationship and robbed women of full selfhood.[95] Relating conversion to baptism, Ruether says it is a recovery of a person's authentic potential for human life.

> Baptism signifies our disaffiliation from patriarchy and all its claims to social necessity and divine legitimacy, and our commitment to a new order.[96]

One can imagine that this will not be an easy thing. Patriarchy is internalised both in women and men. Confronting it, women may begin to view all men as evil and demonic and lose sight of the humanity of the males. Women have to resist a reversed egoism and focus on, in Ruether's words, "a grounded self." On their part, men have to face the fact that they are the oppressors who have robbed women of their dignity and selfhood. I have encountered men who say they need a "male-nist" theology because they are also discriminated against. They often cite examples of women who beat their husbands, women who are given privileges because of their sex, and other such isolated examples. This attitude is a denial of the historical reality of apartheid against women. Men have to learn to understand women's perspective and enter into solidarity with them, not with condescension but with the knowledge that in women's liberation they too will be liberated.

Baptism is a sign of the new world God is bringing, a world where ethnicity, gender, age, class, physical ability, sexual preference, and all distinctions are superseded by the common identity of an inclusive community of the body of Christ. However, the elusive unity that churches seek and never find will continue to be unachievable so long as baptism is viewed as a form of initiation into an exclusive community. Unless the Church shows by one baptism that baptism is incorporation into the one body of Christ, it cannot witness to the world that it is an

95. Ruether, *Sexism and God-Talk*, 159-92.

96. Rosemary Radford Ruether, *Women-Church: Theology and Practice of Feminist Liturgical Communities* (New York: Harper & Row, 1985), 125.

expression of the new community initiated by Jesus. In the institution of baptism (Matt 28:19-20), baptism is associated with "going out," "making disciples," and "teaching them," indicating that baptism is not a rite that is to be confined to an established community. It both anticipates and demands a movement outward to the world beyond the Church. Paul explains that this outward movement, marked by baptism in the name of the Trinity, radicalises the world, makes it a new world. This is a world where there is no Jew or Greek, no male or female, and no slave or free. This is how baptism will make the world new.

Conclusion

A community is not a group of people who share similar interests or have compatibility because of similar ethnic, tribal, social, or economic background. A community, as envisioned in the Christian scripture, is not defined so much by its social or ethnic composition as by its practice of relationship. Community is a relationship like that which is found in a family, a tribe, or a village. But true community transcends tribal, ethnic, economic, social, and religious barriers. A community cannot be brought into being by a decision passed in a meeting. It cannot be built by organising "community" events or by conducting seminars to talk about it. A community is created by choices people make in their day to day life, by choosing to be generous, to share, and to be sympathetic to others, especially to those who are different from us. The Christian community, in fact, best expresses itself in welcoming the stranger, the outsider, without drawing attention to it. I think this is inclusivity at its best.

Inclusivity is not found in having fifty percent women and fifty percent men deacons in a church, or having an equal number of males and females represented in church committees and church association or convention offices. Inclusivity is not even in having leadership divided equally between gay, lesbian, bisexual, transgender, questioning, and intersexed, between male and female, or equally between various social and ethnic groups—although that might be an improvement from the present structures. But true inclusivity is in looking beyond gender and sexuality to the person, in regarding each other as equals, in seeing each other not as competitors but as members of the same body.

The language of worship must reflect the full spectrum of inclusivity. Indeed without language to express what inclusivity means, it is not possible to know community or have true communion. But inclusive language alone is not sufficient to engender inclusive community. There is need to move beyond languages, to probe sexist attitudes that promote exclusive language and heal those kind of attitudes from the roots. At the same time, there is need to merge the realm of worship, and the activities we regard as worship, with the realm of ordinary life, and the activities we regard as belonging to our day to day life, so that humans are seen as one whole rather than bipolar individuals. For tribal Christians the ordinances/sacraments of the Church make the most sense when they are viewed not as routine rituals that are incomprehensible but as reflections of community values and recalling life in the community.

6

STORYTELLING MODELS OF WORSHIP

In the preceding chapters, we have discussed the many ways in which worship is being held to ransom by sexual differentiation. Christian worship misses its true potential when it allows gender apartheid to prevail, when the language for worship is sexist, and when Scriptures are distorted to silence women and deny them a place in the ministries of the Church.

The consequence of gender apartheid is tragic for women. Because they are unable to tell their stories in a patriarchal Church dominated by male narratives, they find themselves unable to communicate, to express themselves, or to discover themselves in worship. Women in many churches find themselves on the margins of the community, excluded from full communion because they are not allowed to administer the Lord's Supper and unable to exercise their gifts of leadership and other gifts for ministry.

Storytelling in worship is an attempt to discover worship that allows people to cross boundaries, to pursue worship that is inclusive, which recognizes that God has called all humanity to worship, regardless of class, gender, tribe, ethnicity, opinion, or religious belief. It is an attempt to harness the implications of koinonia and live out the presence of the Holy Spirit who knows no discrimination. Storytelling in worship implies moving beyond mere patchwork on the liturgy that aims simply to "add" women's stories to the existing worship liturgy while the rest continues as usual. The initiative requires us to overhaul liturgy and transform it from the roots.

In this chapter, I explore ways by which women can tell their stories in worship. This is part of the liturgical movement that seeks to repair centuries of Church liturgies that gave no space to women in worship. Some call it the "Feminist Liturgical Movement,"[1] some call it the "Women's Liturgical Movement,"[2] and others call it the "feminist ritual project."[3] All these classifications are interconnected. Storytelling is a feminist proposal but it also belongs within the purview of women's liturgy and feminist ritualizing. However, from a Baptist perspective, these labels are not fully acceptable. As noted in the previous chapter, Baptists recoil from the word "liturgy." Their visceral aversion and suspicion of the word arises from its association of the word with Roman Catholicism, which continues to be regarded as a perversion of Christian faith. "Liturgy" connotes, for the Baptists, set ritualism, which is contrary to the Baptist notion that Spirit-led worship should not follow a prescribed order of service. Baptists expect sermons to be spontaneous, unscripted, and prayers "from the heart" to be extemporaneous. Rituals, too, are seen with much distrust. This is why in worship Baptists avoid all obvious rituals (or what are perceived to be ritualistic) of the "high" churches such as lighting candles and burning incense, using vestments and other worship accoutrements, reading from a lectionary and praying from an official prayer book, and following a Church Year.

Thus, the terms "liturgy" and "ritual" are to be avoided as a label for the present enterprise, although I will be employing them extensively during my discussion. "Women's worship initiative" would be an appropriate label for the Baptists of North East India. The term "feminist" could be used but only with a proviso that it is being employed in distinction from the feminist theory of white North American and European women. A fitting tag for a project that specifically considers women's place in worship would be "Women's worship initiative."

This project begins with an understanding that women are often rendered storyless. Commenting about American political tradition and the absence of a philosophy in the nation to inspire community, Michael Sandel says:

---

1. Procter-Smith, *In Her Own Rite*.

2. Teresa Berger, *Women's Ways of Worship: Gender Analysis and Liturgical History* (Collegeville, MN: Liturgical Press, 1999).

3. Mary Collins, "Principles of Feminist Liturgy," *Women at Worship: Interpretations of North American Diversity*, ed. Marjorie Procter-Smith and Janet R. Walton (Louisville, KY: Westminster/John Knox Press, 1993), 17-24.

> There is a growing danger that, individually and collectively, we will find ourselves slipping into a fragmented, storyless condition. The loss of the capacity for narrative would amount to the ultimate disempowering of the human subject, for without narrative there is no continuity between present and past, and therefore no responsibility, and therefore no possibility of acting together to govern ourselves. Since human beings are storytelling beings, we are bound to rebel against the drift to storylessness.[4]

This observation holds true for women. Society and Church have silenced us, wiped out our stories. Our storyless condition leads to our disempowerment. The solution, then, is to remember our stories, to create new ones, and tell them.

Storyless

Both Matthew and Mark carry the account of a woman in Bethany who came to Jesus with an alabaster jar of expensive ointment, broke it and poured it on Jesus' head as he sat at the table. The men who were present were angry and scolded her for wasting the ointment. But Jesus intervened and told them that by her act she has prepared his body for burial. Then he said: "Truly I tell you, wherever this good news is proclaimed in the whole world, what she has done will be told in remembrance of her" (Matt 26:13; Mark 14:9). However, contrary to Jesus' promise that what she had done would be associated with the proclamation of the gospel, her name was forgotten even before the gospels came to be written down. And the Church liturgies do not remember her. Not only is her name forgotten, but the significance of her ritual performance has been lost. She is an example of the failure of the Church to remember the stories of women, especially of women whose stories challenge the principles of a male-dominated society. Thus Procter-Smith notes that the Church has not really forgotten women but rather chosen to remember selectively those that show women as troublesome or dangerous, or docile or useful.[5]

The story of this woman in Bethany whose memory is made to slip into oblivion is a reflection of the circumstance of women in the Church whose stories remain untold in the worship of the Church. We do not have stories of our own. Like the woman in Bethany, the stories of our foremothers have been pushed to the edges. Our stories have been lost

---

4. Michael J. Sandel, *Democracy's Discontent: America in Search of a Public Philosophy* (Cambridge, MA: Belknap Press of Harvard University Press, 1998), 351.

5. Procter-Smith, *In Her Own Rite*, 39.

in the pandemonium of male narratives that drown female voices. But our storylessness itself can be our story. The woman forgotten by the Church can be remembered as one who performed a liturgical act. Ancient baptismal rites included anointing with oil to signify initiation into the Messianic royal priesthood.[6] Proposing a recovery of this woman's liturgical-prophetic act, Procter Smith states: "We can only imagine what Christianity would look like if all baptismal anointings were performed "in memory of her."[7]

In chapter one, I noted, that we are the stories we tell. But our stories are not just stories about our individual lives, they are also stories of our life in community, and stories we have been told. All these are our stories. Our stories enable us to relate to the world and the world to relate to us. But women have been unable to tell their stories in worship. Rendered storyless by traditional liturgy, we have not been ourselves but shadows of the men in our lives. Without stories of our own we are unable to define ourselves, unable to understand our lives, and unable to communicate either collectively or individually. Thus instead of defining ourselves, we have been defined by the narratives of patriarchal culture as temptress, sinner, frail, silly, wife, mother, daughter, child-bearer, dumb, and the like. Formulating a female narrative is a way of reclaiming our identity, to turn our silence into speech, to ritualize women's experiences, and to concretise our pain and pathos. Carolyn Heilbrun states:

> What matters is that lives do not serve as models; only stories can do that. And it is a hard thing to make up stories to live by. We can only retell and live by the stories we have read or heard. We live our lives through texts. . . . Whatever their form or medium, these stories have formed us all; they are what we must use to make new fictions, new narratives.[8]

By her statement that lives do not serve as models Heilbrun means that "there will be narratives of female lives only when women no longer live their lives isolated in the houses and the stories of men."[9] Our life is our script. In rediscovering and retelling it we will reinvent ourselves. Women storytelling in worship is essential for creating narrative plots

6. Gabriele Winkler, "The Original Meaning of the Prebaptismal Anointing and Its Implications," *Worship* 52 (1978): 24-45, referred to in Procter-Smith, *In Her Own Rite*, 57.

7. Procter-Smith, *In Her Own Rite*, 58.

8. Carolyn G. Heilbrun, *Writing a Woman's Life* (New York: Ballantine Books, 2002), 37.

9. Heilbrun, *Writing a Woman's Life*, 47.

to challenge traditional metanarratives of liturgy and for overcoming the storylessness of women. Women's stories, Marjorie Procter-Smith maintains, are sacred stories:

> Telling one's story in the community is telling it to God. But telling one's story also is a means of making God present to others. Thus the stories become not only our personal stories but God's stories, sacred stories.[10]

Our personal sacred stories ought to be narrated in church worship and acted out in its rituals. In the following discussion, I will attempt to suggest women's ways of worship which will allow women to find their voices. The ways of women's worship are in fact ways of telling our stories and the stories we have heard and read. Women's narrative cannot repeat the mistakes of the patriarchal narratives that have dominated church worship for centuries. Thus men will not be excluded from our narrative. We will not impose a metanarrative as a universal narrative for all. Rather, we will listen while we speak. Because male-oriented liturgy has pushed women outside the sphere of sacred liturgy, we will hallow our own space in the ritual of gathering together to celebrate our stories. We will respect that our stories will be diverse because our narrative plots are shaped by our cultural and historical contexts. We will be sensitive to the fact that for many of us, telling our story will be difficult because of life-long social conditioning that made us think speaking out is improper for women. We will focus on healing rather than hurting. And we will not claim a truth but rather appreciate truths that punctuate our experiences of knowing and feeling God.

Finding Sacred Space for Women's Narrative

During my studies at Melbourne, my family and I attended a vibrant Baptist church. Sometimes the worship of the church was organised by women. This happened when the pastor was on leave. In that church, the church secretary was a woman and all the Sunday School teachers were also women. Thus when the pastor was away, women organised the worship service. From observing them, I understood that women's idea of worship is very different from men's. I find that women are much less formal. Participation is emphasised. The selections of songs cover a range of interests. There are small choruses to which small children can

10. Marjorie Procter-Smith, *Praying with our Eyes Open: Engendering Feminist Liturgical Prayer* (Nashville, TN: Abingdon Press, 1995), 59-60.

beat their musical instruments. And there are traditional hymns that the older folks can enjoy singing. Instead of the usual sermon, members are given opportunity to share their thoughts about the theme/s of the day. Members, young and adults alike, are involved in prayers, readings, and collecting offerings. Women, it appears to me, tend to think of the church like a family. They want to involve everybody in its activities, to see to it that everybody is comfortable, and everybody is made to feel needed.

The earliest Christian communities met for worship in private homes, space that was conventionally regarded as belonging to women. In this congenial environment women were important members of the community, forming churches in their homes and functioning as their heads. As noted in chapter three, Priscilla, Phoebe, Tabitha, Lydia, Junia, Euodia, Syntyche, Apphia, Chloe, Mary, Nympha, and many other women of the early Church held important positions as apostles, disciples, bishops, evangelists, presbyters and leaders of house church. But when church worship moved into the public sphere in the fourth century, it proved to be disadvantageous to women. Women found themselves being pushed away from the altar and from the presiding celebrant. Teresa Berger notes that by this time women clergy were often more disadvantaged than lay men.[11] There is thus a direct correlation between physical space and liturgical space. Down through the ages women continued to be distanced from the heart of worship. In some monastic communities of the thirteenth century, women were placed so far away from the altar that they could not see it during the celebration of the Eucharist.[12] The degree of exclusion of women from the liturgical centre differs according to ecclesial structures and social contexts. Throughout Christian history there have been exceptions. Some women were able to cross over from the domestic sphere into the public sphere with great success. However, a few exceptions cannot be used to generalise the situation of women in the Church.

Obviously, the community is more faithful to the teachings of Jesus in spaces which are natural, such as a home. The teachings of Jesus were radical in his cultural context. He taught and practised equality of men and women, slave and free, and Jews and Gentiles. This egalitarian

11. Berger, *Women's Ways of Worship*, 19.

12. Berger, *Women's Ways of Worship*, 19, 33; referring to Caroline A. Bruzelius, "Hearing Is Believing: Clarissan Architecture, ca. 1213-1340," *Gesta* 31 (1992): 83-91, and Roberta Gilchrist, *Gender and Material Culture: The Archaeology of Religious Women* (New York: Routledge, 1994), 104f., 109.

principle is best emulated in the house churches of the early centuries. Therefore, I propose that we begin our stories by redefining the physical worship space from women's perspective.

Physical Space

Women see space differently from men. If we take some time to ponder upon the arrangements of a church, traditionally designed by men, we feel awkward. Churches are designed to focus attention on the action taking place up front. It is as though worship is designed to make the worshipper feel small. Churches are not arranged like a place for the community to come and share their stories and experience koinonia. The physical layout and atmosphere is such that we sit rigidly, facing the front. We are unable to see the faces of other members who are worshipping together with us. Someone's back is to us, our back is to someone else. We feel uncomfortable. We would love to see each other's faces, whether strangers, friends, or family members.

Given the opportunity, we would rather sit in a circle. A circle not only enables us to communicate face to face, it also signifies that everybody gathered is equals.[13] A round arrangement has no head. It gives no privilege to any person as being holier than others or closer to God. Leaders are facilitators, not a boss or a director.[14] We want our place of worship to be not just a building we go to on Sundays, but a space made holy by mutual respect for one another and acknowledging God's presence. A place for worship, from a woman's perspective, should be like a living room filled with things we cherish—photos of family, friends, and places, mementos from important events in our life, and our religious symbols. These things stir up our memories, inspire creative imagination, and remind us of the various stories that comprise our lives.

For instance, think of what new ways of communicating our stories would happen if a tribal worship space included tribal paintings. Our life is often captured in paintings. Tribal people of North East India have turned to this medium not only to tell their stories of the present time but also to recapture the stories of the past. Seyiekielie Tepa's *Sophfüno* recaptures the ancient story of an Angami woman who was driven out of home into *Sophfüno* the darkness of night by her drunken husband.

13. Berger, *Women's Ways of Worship*, 128.

14. Janet R. Walton, *Feminist Liturgy: A Matter of Justice*, American Essays in Liturgy (Collegeville, MN: Liturgical Press, 2000), 36-37.

Taking her small child, her basket, a burning torch, and a bamboo stick she made her way through the deep forest to her parent's house. She did not reach there. An evil spirit had attacked her and killed her. When a search party went to look for her they found only a pair of oval shaped stones—one big, one small. Mother and child. The stone is still to be seen in Rüsoma, her village.[15] Now, we do not believe in evil spirits, not in the same sense as the ancient people did, but the painting has contemporary relevance. There are, of course, husbands who are drunkards and who abuse their wives. Beyond that, *Sophfüno* reveals the plight of women in male-dominated cultures. Another painting by the same artist, untitled, relates to the burning of a Naga village called Mima. It depicts an old woman holding her two grandchildren and running away from her burning village. The painting recollects not only the courage of women during Indo-Naga conflict and it also their fearless effort to bring peace and reconciliation in a trouble-torn region. Another untitled painting depicts a mother and daughter. The daughter is evidently pulling out grey hair from her mother's head on a *genna* day (a day of rest due to an unusual occurrence—villagers used such days to relax and do small things at home). Mothers not only use such moments to bond with their daughters but also to pass their wisdom to their daughters. This is subversive. The traditional role of the father has been taken by the mother. But of course, women have always filled the tedium of domestic activities such as grooming each other's hair, or cooking, or cleaning to narrate their stories. Such ways of telling stories are outside the "normative" ways of storytelling which are controlled by men. A sculpture by the same artist has a mother in a kneeling position holding a baby in her arms and with a basket on her back, looking at her baby as though the sight of her baby has erased all thoughts of the heavy load on her back.[16] The sculpture illustrates the reality of women's life—taking care of family and baby, and doing work in the fields. It also provides room for its viewers to find parallels with Mary and discover a tribal Mary (or, according to Akhrieno Savi, "the feminine face of God"). In the contemplation of such

---

15. Akhrieno Savi, "Through the Eyes of a Painter: A Naga Woman's Perspective," in *No More Sorrow in God's Garden of Justice: Tribal Women Doing Theology*, ed. Limatula Longkumer (Jorhat, Assam: Women Study Department, Eastern Theological College, 2007), 50-53.

16. Savi, "Through the Eyes of a Painter: A Naga Woman's Perspective," in *No More Sorrow in God's Garden of Justice*, ed. Limatula Longkumer, 53-60.

works, women's stories and stories of the community that have potential for transformation are communicated without a word being uttered.

Liturgical Space

Liturgical space is at the heart of worship. Liturgical space means a reorientation of the liturgy. A huge body of liturgy for women is available, but often these liturgies aim at feminist liturgical communities or women-church gatherings. While it is necessary for women to meet together in solidarity and share their experiences, it is vital that we claim liturgical space in the whole church. This space is controlled by men so it is necessary for men to identify with women (not easy in a patriarchal society) and give space to women to tell their stories. This cannot be achieved by giving women a few minutes of women time in worship. A simple add-women-and-stir is not going to serve the purpose.

In this connection, the growth of non-traditional liturgy, including feminist liturgy, is invaluable. What we can notice is that these liturgies challenge the traditional hierarchical Church structure without being too obvious. They incorporate feminist concerns but are aimed at the whole community. One example is the Iona Community. The Iona Community is based on Celtic spirituality and works for peace and social justice, rebuilding of community, and the renewal of worship. Its Wild Goose Resource Group works for the revitalisation of worship by developing new forms of relevant and participative worship. These resources are used by churches and groups worldwide.[17] It is also worth mentioning the Prayer Book of the Anglican Church in Aotearoa, New Zealand and Polynesia, *A New Zealand Prayer Book – He Karakia Mihinare O Aotearoa*. This Prayer Book uses inclusive language and other Anglicans are borrowing extensively from it.[18] Such authorized Prayer Books that show a commitment to inclusive language are a response to the voices

17. Wild Goose Publications are available at http://www.ionabooks.com/ (accessed June 18, 2019).

18. Church of the Province of New Zealand, *A New Zealand Prayer Book – He Karakia Mihinare o Aotearoa* (Auckland: Collins, 1989). Referred in Smith, *Bearing Fruit in Due Season*, 140, where a related article is also mentioned; Susan Adams, "Towards Partnership: Race, Gender, and the Church in Aotearoa/New Zealand," in *No Easy Peace: Liberating Anglicanism: A Collection of Essays in Memory of William John Wolf*, ed. Carter Heyward and Sue Phillips (Lanham, MD: University Press of America, 1992), 91-102.

and worship activities of women that have found their way into liturgical revisions because they were in sync with the biblical witness.

Women's liturgical arrangement may be termed horizontal as opposed to vertical. Horizontal gatherings emphasise the relationship between the members of the community whereas vertical arrangements stress the relationship between the individual and God, in some cases, through the priest or pastor. Northup asserts: the "inherent horizontality of religious rituals experienced by, developed by, and reclaimed by women frees it from the bonds of verticality and allows it to spread out."[19]

Liturgical space for women requires the liberation of liturgy from the clutches of patriarchal culture. All that I have discussed in the previous chapters about androcentric language of the Bible, words used to signify divinity, and sexist hymns applies here.[20] But any glossological change will be ineffective unless people learn to think from the perspective of the other and become sensitive to the nuances of language, both subtle and obvious. Liturgical space for women implies a new way of reading the Bible, new emphases in preaching, new songs, new images and symbols, new ways of relating, and new ways of telling. I will briefly highlight a few aspects of the implications of liturgical space for women, especially from the tribal perspective of North East India.

Names for Divinity

Feminist theologians have suggested many names for God—Mother, Sister, Sophia, Friend, and many other feminine as well as non-feminine names.[21] The creativity and imagination which feminists use to name God in a way they can relate to, can inspire tribals to use their own cultural

19. Lesley A. Northup, "Claiming Horizontal Space: Women's Religious Rituals," *Studia Liturgica: An Ecumenical Review for Liturgical Research and Renewal* 25/1 (Spring 1995): 98 cited in Berger, *Women's Ways of Worship*, 128.

20. Some resources dealing with language in worship are: Casey Miller and Kate Swift, *Words and Women: New Language in New Times*, rev. ed. (San Francisco: HarperCollins, 1991); Heather Murray Elkins, *Worshipping Women: Reforming God's People for Praise* (Nashville, TN: Abingdon Press, 1994); Gail Ramshaw, *Liturgical Language: Keeping it Metaphoric, Making it Inclusive* (Collegeville, MN: Liturgical Press, 1996).

21. For proposals of various names for the Divine: Mary Kathleen Speegle Schmitt, *Seasons of the Feminine Divine: Christian Feminist Prayers for the Liturgical Year, Cycles A-C* (New York: Crossroad, 1993-1995); Julie Howard, *We are the Circle: Celebrating the Feminine in Song and Ritual* (Collegeville, MN: Liturgical Press, 1993); and van Wijk-Bos, *Reimagining God.*

roots to name God. From the Angami tribe, we get the image of the Goddess giving birth. She is *Kepenuopfü*. The name of God is "Birthing Spirit." She is the mother. She is the earth. But "She" is also "He" the Sky. For the Angami prayer starts like this: "Sky my father, earth my mother, *Ukepenuopfü* my sovereign, have mercy on me today."[22] From the Garo tribes, we get the image of the Goddess who hatches and gives birth. Her, or his, name is *Tatara Rabuga*, the Creator, Moulder, Shaper and Binder, Setter of limits, Fixer of edges, Mother Goddess Shadow, Owner of Life, and Root of Soul.[23] From the Khasi tribe, we have Planner and Creator (*U Nongbuh U Nongthaw*), Giver and Dispenser of Life (*U Nongsei U Nongpynlong*), Creator and Architect of Humankind (*U Nongthaw-bynriew U Nongbuh-bynriew*), Giver of Wealth (*U Bleilong-spah*), Goddess of the Clan (*Ka 'Leilongkur*). The usual Khasi designation for God is *U Blei*, "*U*" signifying masculine gender, but as *'Leilongkur* or *'Leilongjaid* God is termed *Ka Blei*, "*Ka*" signifying feminine gender.[24] The male God is *U Blei Nongthaw*, the Creator, and the female Supreme Goddess is *Ka Blei Synshar*, Perpetuator, and Goddess Who Makes Crops Prosper. Thus in the religious background of many tribes, God is conceived with both male and female attributes without any apparent contradiction. With more than three hundred linguistic communities in North East India, the possibilities for meaningful names of God are limitless. The sad part is that in tribal Christian language about God, the traditional understanding and terminologies about God have been forsaken and replaced by words that seemingly fit the Western concept of a male God. It is time tribal Christians begin to name God with honesty, being true to the God of their experience—as they have felt, tasted, and known God.

Work of Christ

During the past few decades several tribal theologians and biblical scholars of North East India have shown an interested in articulating

22. Angami, "Ukepenuopfü: An Exploration of the Goddess," in *Tribal Christian Theology*, ed. Lasetso and Vashum, 236.

23. These characteristics of *Tatara Rabuga* are expressed in the translation of the incantation: "Dakgipa Rugipa, Stugipa Pantugipa, Suulgipa Imbanggipa, Ma·gipa Jagring, Janggini Nokgipa, Jamani Biambi." Dewansing Rongmuthu, comp., *The Folktales of the Garos* (Gauhati: Department of Publications, University of Gauhati, 1960), 355, 369.

24. Cf. H. O. Mawrie, *The Khasi Milieu* (New Delhi: Concept Publishing, 1981), 29-32.

a Christology that would be relevant for the tribal context.[25] One area of discussion has been the reference to Christ as "the Lamb of God." This is easily understood in the context of the sacrificial system in the biblical world. But, tribal scholars ask, how can "the Lamb of God" be explained to people who have never seen a lamb? Because lambs are unknown in this part of the world, tribal scholars have suggested that a more fitting substitute would be "the Cock/Rooster of God."[26] I am not fully convinced by this proposal, and I will give the reason below, but first it is necessary to point out why scholars suggest replacing "Lamb" with "Cock/Rooster." This proposal was made because many tribes practice cock sacrifice in their traditional religion. Tribal people also sacrifice other animals and things, but the preference for "Cock/Rooster" came about through the influence of a Khasi story.

According to Khasi folklore the Sun is the sister of the Moon. Once they attended a festival and danced together but they were mocked by the creatures. The Sun was hurt and hid herself in a cave thereby plunging the world in darkness. Neither humans nor birds or animals could plead well enough with the Sun to come out and shine again. Finally, the meek and humble cock who lived in a sacred grove called the Sun out. Darkness is a metaphor for sin and the Sun is a metaphor for God. The cock was found to be the only one who could represent human beings and stand before God on their behalf.[27]

The Cock/Rooster is also of significance for the Kukis. Among the Kuki tribes, the cock is believed to be invested with sacred power of keeping time and its wings have cosmic powers to summon paddy (rice

25. O. M. Rao, *Focus on North East Indian Christianity* (Delhi: ISPCK, 1994), 45.

26. J.L. Roy, "Primal Vision and Hermeneutics in North-East India – A Protestant Tribal View," *Indian Journal of Theology* 31/3-4 (July-Dec 1982): 314-22; Felix H. Kharkongor, *The Revealed Christ of the Khasi Religion* (Worthing: Loxwood, 1994), and others.

27. Fuller story in Appendix E: "The Story of the Sun and the Cock." Fowl sacrifice is common among various tribes of North East India. Other animals such as the mithun, pig, and goat are used in sacrificial rituals based on a belief that they have powers for curing sickness and for restoring the fertility of the soil. I believe that the symbolism of these animals may be used to interpret the sacrificial work of Christ particularly when tribal myths or legends give them significance.

still in the husk) from the left and right of the mountain ridge.[28] As rice is the main food of the tribal people, the ability of the Cock/Rooster to provide paddy/rice is particularly significant.

Despite the appeal of "the Cock/Rooster of God" as substitute for "the Lamb of God" among tribal scholars in North East India, I am hesitant about endorsing it. Tribal scholars, particularly women scholars who want to further the cause of gender equity, have to be discriminating about religious language. From a woman's perspective, I find the gender-based "Cock/Rooster" inadequate as a substitute for "Lamb." Instead of more gender-based terminologies we have to look for neutral categories that recall the work of God in nurturing and redeeming humanity.

Thus I would propose "Sacred Grove," or "The Big Tree" to talk about Christ. The basis for "Sacred Grove" comes from the forest areas called *Law kyntang*, *Law Lyngdoh*, or *Law Niam* in Khasi language, which are found at the outskirts of almost every Khasi village and held to be sacred ground. The trees cannot be cut nor fruits or flowers picked from these groves.[29] Garos have preserved groves (called *A·song Kosi*), believed to be the dwelling place of *Kalkame Kalgra*, from where the streams and brooks originate.[30] The sacred groves signify the presence of God in different places in order to bless the community. In some places they have been turned into village reserve forests.[31] The basis for "The Big Tree" comes from Khasi folklore. According to the Khasis, in ancient days a tree grew on top of *U Lum Sohpetbneng* (the Naval Peak of Heaven), which touched heaven. This tree formed a golden bridge (*Jingkieng ksiar*) of communication between the sixteen clans of earth (*Trep ki*

28. Satkhokai Chongloi, "The Unseen Christ among the Kuki People," in *Garnering Tribal Resources for Doing Tribal Christian Theology*, Tribal Study Series 16, ed. Razouselie Lasetso (Jorhat, Assam: Eastern Theological College Programme Coordination, 2008), 183-84.

29. Cf. Rekha M. Shangpliang, "Ecological Basis of Khasi Ethno-Cultural Traits," in *Christianity and Change in Northeast India*, ed. T. B. Subba, Joseph Puthenpurakal, and Shaji Joseph Puykunnel (New Delhi: Concept Publishing, 2009), 219-31.

30. Cf. Paulinus R. Marak, *The Garo Tribal Religion* (Delhi: Anshah Publishing House, 2005), 31.

31. Limatula Longkumer, "Response to Ecological Problem by Women of North East India," in *No More Sorrow in God's Garden of Justice: Tribal Women Doing Theology*, ed. Limatula Longkumer (Jorhat, Assam: Women Study Department, Eastern Theological College, 2007), 39-40.

Khathynriew Skum) and God.[32] I do not mean that these terminologies should substitute Christ, Jesus, Lamb or any such title. Mere substitution of theological terminologies will create more problems rather than solve them. But I do mean that worship would be much enhanced when creative names and phrases are used to address Christ—particularly names that convey wholesome, inclusive, human-affirming notions of divinity.

Prayers

Women like to pray with beautiful words; words that not only express coherent thoughts but also convey emotions. The most pleasing phrases and poetic language is used in prayer. Women also like to pray using conversational language. They see prayer not as theological statements but as conversations with God. In tribal communities, women are very articulate in praying. They like to pray about everything around them. Nothing is too trivial, nothing too weighty that they cannot bring it to God in prayer. A child's fever, a neighbour's trouble, a husband's negligence, everything is reason to say a prayer.

Prayer gives space to women in a constricted world. In society, tribal women are told not to speak when men are making decisions in village council meetings. They are told not to speak out of turn anywhere. And in the church, they are expected to be quiet listeners. But prayer is a different space. During prayers nobody can silence women. Women are free in their prayers to share their fears and uncertainties, to bemoan the ills that befall them, to cry out their unhappiness, to express hopes and desires, and to give thanks for blessings. They are able, in prayers, to voice their innermost thoughts unreservedly and wholeheartedly. They speak to God as to an intimate friend, a counsellor. This is particularly true in Baptist and other protestant churches of the region where spontaneous prayer is expected. Consequently, women have found their voices in prayer. In most tribal churches, women are known for praying "spiritually" and people facing difficulties seek them out to give them prayer requests. However, this is not in the context of the worship service. This is not necessarily a bad thing. If women simply duplicate the way men pray (official prayers) in the place men pray (church pulpit) they will become captive to the patriarchal pattern. Taking prayer to roadsides, to homes, and to the fields redefines sacred space and claims it as new non-hierarchical sacred space.

---

32. Fuller story in Appendix F: "The Navel of Heaven." Mawrie, *The Khasi Milieu*, 33-34.

Women's ways of praying challenge the official liturgical celebrations not only because they are not part of the liturgical calendar but also because they see prayer differently.[33] For instance, feminist liturgical scholars argue against the practice of kneeling to pray and/or receive communion from the priest. They opt rather to sit or stand.

The feminist argument not to kneel is not entirely new. During the 16th and early 17th centuries the Puritans rejected the signs and symbols of domination in worship which had been retained by the Church of England from Catholicism, including wearing clerical garb and kneeling to receive communion. Their ministers would not wear surplices and the parishioners received communion standing or sitting, which Puritan features were continued by nonconformists and form the basis of Baptist worship.[34] For these principles, nonconformists and Baptists suffered deprivation, imprisonment, and loss of livelihood. Some died for their belief.[35] Baptists do not practice kneeling to receive the elements of the Lord's Supper, although some kneel for the laying on of hands during ordination. I believe Baptists can contribute towards women's worship initiative not only through adopting liberating postures for receiving communion or discarding garbs of hierarchical domination but also through espousing religious liberty and equality in worship.

Nonetheless, in recent years, in a number of Baptist associations of North East India there has been a trend to let the ordained ministers wear stole, cassock, clerical collar, badge, and other such distinguishing attire. With the adoption of such practices, Baptists of the region stand to lose a substantial portion of their hard-earned theological heritage.

Feminists also argue against praying with eyes closed and invite women to pray with their eyes open. Postures of kneeling and closing eyes have political connotations of power and domination. The meanings of physical postures are often overlooked because of years of conditioning but they are nevertheless present and affect women subliminally.

---

33. Miriam Therese Winter, *Woman Prayer, WomanSong: Resources for Ritual* (Oak Park, IL: Meyer-Stone Books, 1987).

34. Alan Betteridge, *Deep Roots, Living Branches: A History of Baptists in the English Western Midlands* (Leicester: Matador, 2010), 2-4; Justo L. González, *The Story of Christianity*, vol. 2, *The Reformation to the Present Day* (San Francisco: Harper & Row, 1985), 150.

35. Keith E. Durso, *No Armor for the Back: Baptist Prison Writings, 1600s-1700s* (Macon, GA: Mercer University Press, 2007); O. M. Rao, *Baptist Distinctives: With Special Reference to the Churches of the CBCNEI* (Gauhati: Christian Literature Centre, 1980), 11-18.

Insisting that prayer is a political act, Procter-Smith argues that prayer, especially public prayer, engages the participants in a web of oppression and subjugation. She notes that women who have been victims of various forms of violence cannot close their eyes to pray in church. Women do not feel safe to close their eyes. Closing eyes is like putting oneself in personal danger.

> Most traditional postures of prayers are postures of submission: kneeling, prostration, head bowed, eyes closed. They literally place the person in a physically vulnerable position. No subversive reading of this posture is possible to a woman who is regularly raped and beaten by her husband.[36]

Similarly, Janet Walton reasons:

> Closing one's eyes is dangerous in an unjust society. Though we presume we are safe in our gatherings, we do not repeat actions that have historically limited, demanded, or hurt us.
>
> . . . when women kneel to receive Communion or a blessing from men, rather than promoting an experience of reverence, it can be a reminder of sexual violation or subservience. Since women are frequently victims of violence at the hands of men, we practice standing and sitting rather than kneeling.[37]

And Nicola Slee writes:

> We must pray with eyes wide open, refusing to see nothing of
> what is hidden, secret – blatant lies.
>
> We must pray with heads held high, refusing to bow in
> obsequiousness to prelate, priest or pope . . .
> We must pray with bodies known, bared: touching our own
> knowledge, knowing our instinctual wisdom, refusing to be
> violated or shamed.
> We must denounce false ways of praying, false names for God,
> false myths and images and stories.
> We must accuse our God of all that has abused us, crippled us,
> Maimed us. We must drag deity to court, testify against him,
> lay the charge at his feet, bring forward many witnesses and see
> what he will answer. We must refuse all excuses, justifications,
> legitimations. We must insist on the charge, 'Guilty'.
> We must lament our lost history, liturgy, story. We must bewail
> our betrayed bodies, knowledge, beauty. We must reproach our
> abandoned altars, mourn our overturned tables, weep for the

---

36. Procter-Smith, *Praying with our Eyes Open*, 48.
37. Walton, *Feminist Liturgy*, 38.

> broken vessels: the sacred chalice scattered, scattered in a
> thousand pieces.[38]

Women's prayer can become a catalyst for reclaiming sacred space in worship. It cannot and should not emulate public corporate prayer. Public prayers tend to be fixed theological statements that expound the discourse of the powerful. This is uncomfortable for women, especially those who have been betrayed by those who hold power both outside the Church and within the Church. For tribal women, prayer is best when it is not structured. It is not necessary to start with an address to God, highlighting titles and attributes of God, and to end with a fixed formula. Prayer can be made in the form of a relationship with God. Thus the language of prayer can be drawn from daily life, like having a conversation. We can pray with our eyes open. God knows we feel insecure. We can pray with poetry, with dance, with music. We can pray rebelliously. We can pray to express anger and frustration. We can pray without words. Whichever way we pray, our stories are embedded in our prayers. One thing is for sure, we won't be praying to a male God. Our prayers can draw upon the prayers of our forebears who saw God both as father and mother.

> *Vohpi dekon nasah bangin neihinsan.*
> *Kelchal kiheh nasah bangin neihinsan. . . .*
> *Eihinsan, eihin sasol hih in,*
> *eihin bolsol hih in.*
> *Kumtin ju napenge,*
> *kumtin sa napenge.*
> *Kapu houvin eihin san,*
> *kapa houvin eihin san.*
> *Pathen nun eihin san,*
> *Pathen pan eihin san. . . .*

In English translation:

> Bless me the way you have blessed the slant fore-headed mother pig.
> Bless me the way you have blessed the curly horned he-goat. . . .
> Bless me, do not overlook me, do not create deformity in me.
> I will worship you throughout the year with wine and meat offerings.
> Bless me, O God of my grandfather,
> Bless me, O God of my father.
> Bless me, O Mother-God,

38. Nicola Slee, *Praying Like a Woman* (London: SPCK, 2004), 1.

Bless me, O Father-God.[39]

Obviously, the poetic form and melody and rhythm of the Kuki version is lost in the English translation. Lest the prayer be misunderstood, it must be noted that "God of my grandfather" and "God of my father" do not mean the God of the ancestors in chronological time. The grandfather-father combination implies time without beginning or end, that is, eternity.

Tribal ways of praying can be a facilitator for actualising a worship that is liberated from the doctrinal approaches. It invites further storytelling. Whether a prayer is for confession, supplication, adoration, thanksgiving, or intercession, it is an opportunity to tell stories. A prayer is also a time for truth-telling, for people cannot tell lies to God who knows everything. Thus in truthful prayers, the oppressed and the discriminated can tell of the injustice of society and the Church against them. Likewise, the oppressors will have to acknowledge their role in reducing the worth of others by their prejudices. A redefined prayer that not only connects the individual to God but also unites the members of the community will change the face of worship as we know it.

Songs

Songs are sacred components of tribal way of life. People express their joys and sorrows through songs. Whether it is about the birth of a child or the death of a dear one, or of falling in love or of being jilted, the human stories are told through songs. It is right that we should bring the songs of our life to our worship space. Consider the song of a tribal woman whose husband went to war:[40]

---

39. Chongloi, "The Unseen Christ among the Kuki People," in *Garnering Tribal Resources for Doing Tribal Christian Theology*, ed. Lasetso, 187-89. I have rearranged the Kuki version to highlight its harmony and rhythm and edited the English translation. The mother pig with the slanted forehead, the curly horned he-goat, and various things such as a bamboo bangle, a small gourd, a spear, a knife, a basket, and a cord are materials that are symbolic of *Indoi*, the means by which the presence of *Pathen*, God, is known in the Kuki household.

40. Eyingbeni Hümtsoe, "Women's Experience of 'Sorrow' as a Source for Doing Theology from Naga Perspective," in *No More Sorrow in God's Garden of Justice: Tribal Women Doing Theology*, ed. Limatula Longkumer (Jorhat, Assam: Women Study Department, Eastern Theological College, 2007), 5.

> Where are you? Why are [you] so late in coming home? All your friends have returned home.
> I asked them, "Where is the boy's father [?]" They said, "He may be on the way."

Finally, when the woman realizes that her husband must have been killed, she continues:

> I waited and waited. Our son is weeping; crying for you.
> I came to meet you on the way with *zütsü* (rice-beer), and our baby on my back,
> But you never came...

The woman who sung this belonged to a patriarchal tribal culture that celebrated war and "trampled womanhood on the way of achieving manhood."[41] Yet through her song she is able to express her deepest anguish.[42] Furthermore, in the gaps and pauses between the words of her song, within her personal lament, we can read her read her commentary on the futility of war and killings. Tribal Christians can apply songs like this to counter ethnic violence and other forms of conflict in the community. Also imagine juxtaposing such a song with that of biblical narrative to retell Jesus' parable of the lost coin (Luke 15:8-10), the lost sheep (Matt 18:12-14; Luke 15:1-7), or the prodigal son (Luke 15:11-32).

In traditional tribal societies, while going to the fields at the beginning of the day or coming back from the fields after the day's work, women and men express their thoughts and feelings through song. These songs are often spontaneous verses sung by two parties in turns like a conversation. Two aspects of this way of singing are noteworthy. The first is the dialogical method of singing. Dialogue is essential for developing rapport, for building understanding, and for getting rid of misconceptions. The second is the content of the songs. In traditional tribal songs, women

---

41. Hümtsoe, "Women's Experience of 'Sorrow,' in *No More Sorrow*, ed. Longkumer, 6.

42. "The songs that we sing in worship should express our deepest and widest emotions.... When we are in a strange land, and we are tormented, our song should reflect the pain of our present condition [Ps 137:1-4].... We are to be ready with a song that comes from the recesses of our faith experience....At other times, when we as individuals are unable to sing, we should ask the community to sing on our behalf." C. Randall Bradley, *From Memory to Imagination: Reforming the Church's Music* (Grand Rapids, MI: Wm B. Eerdmans Publishing, 2012), 94.

are spoken of with love and honour.[43] Mutual respect is always evident. As an example, I offer a traditional A·chik love song called "*Nanggorere.*"

Refrain: *Nanggorere goserong*
Oe nanggo goserong

Men: *A·baoni jalikko maina min·chichotata*
Angni mikchagipako maina mikchi ong·ata?

Women: *Chiringoni ro·ongko pileng pileng ga·mana*
Angni mikchagipako pil·e pil·e nimana.

Women: *Susimeni do·mesal pringo gisikatchenga*
Marak pante da·siwal angko chame jikchenga.

Men: *Salgisako bilgipa do·reng ong·ja do·masa*
Angko ja·chapronggipa Marak ong·ja Sangmasa.

A free translation into English:[44]

Refrain: (The words cannot be exactly translated but they are expressions of agreement with one another)

Men: Why did you let the chillies of the hillside overripen?
Why did you let my beloved cry?

Women: Just as the stones turn when I step on them while crossing the stream
So I turn my head again and again to look at my lover.

Men: The bird flying in the sky is not a kite (a bird of prey) but a *do·masa* (a wild bird)
The one who is always going alongside me is not a Marak (clan) but a Sangma (clan).

Women: Early in the morning the wild fowl of Susime (goddess, giver of wealth) crowed
Last night a young Marak (clan) man proposed to me to be his love.

Such responsive songs can be used to engage women and men in dialogue. It is untenable to presume that worship songs should always have God's

43. Though not an exact parallel, it is pertinent to point out that Mujerista theology derives its inspiration from Hispanic love songs and protest songs in which women are called *mujer* – woman. Isasi-Díaz, "*Mujeristas*: A Name of Our Own," in *The Future of Liberation Theology*, ed. Ellis and Maduro, 410.

44. Translation is mine.

name in it. Can we not think of love songs and songs from daily life as equally valid to sing in worship? Of course, there is something good about singing praises to God and that should always be an essential part of worship. However, we need to relate not only to God but with each other. And our songs of love and community can fulfil that aspect of worship.

Sermons

Procter-Smith points out the use of symbols and gestures of dominance prevalent in churches. Some of these are the practice of preaching from a physically elevated space (the pulpit), the preacher standing while others sit, the use of official clothing, and monological style of preaching. Then there are the assumptions that the sermon is the word of God and that it is above criticism. The close association of the sermon with the reading of Scripture reinforces these assumptions. The reading of Scripture is itself surrounded by gestures of dominance, such as bringing it into the worship space with processions and acclamations, restricting access to it, and using formulae such as "the word of God" to convey its authority.[45]

Women's perspective on preaching reflects women's overall view about ministry. Traditionally, the liturgical role of the male priest/preacher has been based on power, special knowledge, and consequently, authoritarian style of leadership. Women ministers, on the other hand, want to be "more vulnerable and more compassionate."[46] Women's compassionate personality and direct approach is seen in their sermons.[47] Carol M. Norén talks about the distinctive style of preaching by women. According to her, women preachers tend to disclose themselves in the pulpit through their

---

45. Procter-Smith, *In Her Own Rite*, 131-32.

46. Spoken by an Anglican woman priest in an interview with Uta Blohm. Another says (about an authoritarian style of leadership), "It's not ours, you know, you always think, there's this old fashioned picture of our vicar sort of running the parish and everyone else sort of just feeding into that and I can't go with that." Uta Blohm, *Religious Traditions and Personal Stories: Women Working as Priests, Ministers and Rabbis*, Studies in the Intercultural History of Christianity 137 (Frankfurt am Main: Peter Lang, 2005), 175 and 179.

47. For collections of sermons by women: Helen Gray Crotwell, ed., *Women and the Word: Sermons* (Philadelphia: Fortress Press, 1978); *Spinning a Sacred Yarn: Women Speak from the Pulpit* (New York: Pilgrim Press, 1982); David Farmer and Edwina Hunter, eds., *And Blessed Is She: Sermons by Women* (San Francisco: Harper & Row, 1990).

illustrations, autobiographical references, and nonverbal communication.[48] She also points out that women often pick up familiar biblical passages for their sermons, but call attention to aspects of it that escaped notice or were thought unimportant before.

Christine Smith also accepts that sermons crafted and delivered by women have a distinctive quality.[49] She uses the metaphor of weaving for preaching in a feminist perspective, relating each element of preaching to a corresponding element of weaving.[50] Christine Smith proposes feminist preaching to be prophetic. Being prophetic implies being critical of traditional God language, Christology, and biblical hermeneutics. She also regards feminist preaching as a vision for transforming the world by a commitment to peace and disarmament and harmony with all creation. She believes that feminist spirituality is essential for prophetic preaching because it aims for social transformation, affirms and celebrates the human body, and appreciates diversity of spiritual disciplines and perspectives. She states:

> Until all preachers are willing to open themselves to the voices in the communities and to be changed by those voices and insights, the preaching act will remain individualistic in nature, and the content of sermons will be less than inclusive, isolated from the needs and wisdom of the whole people of God.[51]

Procter-Smith says that feminist preaching must be emancipatory. In order to be emancipatory, preaching must replace gestures of domination with gestures of mutuality and reciprocity. The community has to be enabled to actively participate in the process of preaching. Emancipatory preaching, Procter-Smith outlines, has to be: 1) based on a sense of accountability to women, conscious of and committed to women's struggle against patriarchy; 2) based on women's experiences of struggles for emancipation in church and society; 3) dialogical, communal, and participatory; 4) empowering of all women to speak up and out for

---

48. Carol M. Norén, *The Woman in the Pulpit* (Nashville, TN: Abingdon, 1991). Chap 4.

49. Christine M. Smith, *Weaving the Sermon: Preaching in a Feminist Perspective* (Louisville, KY: Westminster John Knox Press, 1989), 9.

50. Another metaphor used for feminist preaching is that of "voice." Mary Donovan Turner and Mary Lin Hudson, *Saved from Silence: Finding Women's Voices in Preaching* (St. Louis, MO: Chalice Press, 1999).

51. Christine M. Smith, *Weaving the Sermon*, 123.

themselves; and 5) able to claim from Scripture the authority of women to speak and act on our own behalf.[52]

A feminist approach to preaching in worship is offered by Elizabeth J. Smith:

> Feminist preaching may be characterized by gender inclusive language, modified theology and Christology, new images for God, relational approaches to authority, and personal storytelling, as well as the use of feminist biblical hermeneutics.[53]

Smith dwells particularly on the importance of feminist biblical hermeneutics in feminist preaching and says:

> Feminist preachers are "canonically transgressive" in order to compensate for biblical silences attentively discerned and to correct the painfully recurrent misrepresentations of women in the canonical Scriptures. For the sake of women's flourishing, feminist interpretation for preaching moves to and fro across the boundaries of the biblical text, telling women's personal stories, recounting community stories as seen through women's eyes, making poetry, paraphrases, and prayers to be proclaimed in women's voices.[54]

Feminist views about preaching, such as those expressed by Christine M. Smith, Procter-Smith, and Elizabeth J. Smith, challenge traditional liturgical practices that are androcentric and patriarchal.[55]

In the context of North East India, it seems too early to speak about women preaching sermons. What is the point when the pulpit is not available to women?[56] In our churches, the pulpit has been reserved for men. Logically, the focus should first be on how to make the pulpit

---

52. Procter-Smith, *In Her Own Rite*, 132-34.

53. Elizabeth J. Smith, *Bearing Fruit in Due Season*, 105

54. Elizabeth J. Smith, *Bearing Fruit in Due Season*, 117.

55. Cf. Katie G. Cannon, "Womanist Interpretation and Preaching in the Black Church," in *Searching the Scriptures*, vol. 1, *A Feminist Introduction*, ed. Elisabeth Schüssler Fiorenza (New York: Crossroad, 1993), 326-37; Majorie Procter-Smith, "Feminist Interpretation and Liturgical Preaching," in *Searching the Scriptures*, vol. 1, *A Feminist Introduction*, ed. Elisabeth Schüssler Fiorenza (New York: Crossroad, 1993), 313-25.

56. This has been discussed in Chapter 1. Baptist churches do not have any established rule that women cannot preach, but the majority of churches are not favourable towards women preachers. The situation is worse among the Presbyterian churches of North East India where women are fully excluded from the Pulpit. Cf. T. Vanlaltlani, "Participation of Women in the Church – With Reference to North East India," in *Changing Status of Women in North-Eastern States*, ed. Lalneihzovi (New Delhi: Mittal Publications, 2009), 139-40.

accessible to women and then only we can talk about what and how women may preach. However, because there are a few churches that accept women preachers and because there are a few women who are ministering in churches, it is pertinent to talk about preaching by women. And indeed the big number of women theological graduates from North East India, who, we hope, will eventually preach in churches, makes the issue urgent.

The one element that is found in women's discussion about preaching is that of justice.[57] Our sensitivity towards issues of justice and fairness arises from our own experiences of being treated unjustly and unfairly. We know how demeaning and unpleasant it is to be ordered around. So when we preach we rarely use the imperative. We do not tell people what to do.[58] Rather we invite reflection and contemplation. When we do biblical exegesis we do not detach ourselves from the text. We relate ourselves and our experiences to the text. In particular, our specific context invites us to use storytelling to interpret the Bible, critique traditional practices, and communicate how we see the world. Storytelling is something tribal women will find in common with their sisters in other cultures.

Elaine J. Lawless found that women relied a lot on storytelling:

> I felt a concerted effort on their part to make the scriptures relevant to modern audiences, not in an ahistorical way, but by bringing the scriptures and people's lives into praxis through storytelling.[59]

And Christine M. Smith observes:

> It appears that many women use story for two purposes: to name reality from a woman's perspective and to serve as a means of self-disclosure. I believe that for women, story and narrative theology are more than a means of effective theologizing or a type of imaginative communication. Story and narrative theologizing represent a powerful and important way of naming reality for women, and naming is clearly a critical feminist issue. Women have relied on

57. Christine M. Smith, *Preaching as Weeping, Confession, and Resistance: Radical Responses to Radical Evil* (Louisville, KY: Westminster John Knox Press, 1992); Kathy Black, *A Healing Homiletic: Preaching and Disability* (Nashville, TN: Abingdon Press, 1996); L. Susan Bond, *Trouble With Jesus: Women, Christology, and Preaching* (St. Louis, MO: Chalice Press, 1999); Mary Catherine Hilkert, *Naming Grace: Preaching and the Sacramental Imagination* (New York, NY: The Continuum International Publishing Group, 2006).

58. So Christine M. Smith, *Weaving the Sermon*, 14.

59. Elaine J. Lawless, *Women Preaching Revolution: Challenge for Connection in a Disconnected Time* (Philadelphia, PA: University of Pennsylvania Press, 1996), 87.

> oral tradition throughout time as a means of preserving their "herstory" and remembering their identities as women.[60]

Narrative preaching came into prominence in the 1980s and has been influential since.[61] Narrative scholars, of course, differ on what they mean by narrative preaching. But generally speaking, narrative preaching and storytelling are regarded as two different things altogether. A story (such as illustrations and anecdotes) may be part of a sermon but it is not the whole sermon. Narrative preaching refers to the whole sermon. It is a storytelling style of preaching, of structuring the sermon like a story with setting, characters, and plot.[62] Thus strictly speaking, storytelling in women's preaching does not fit the definition of narrative preaching (defined as a sermon structured like a story). The standard definition of narrative preaching is too narrow and labelling women's storytelling in preaching as narrative preaching will not only be restrictive to women's ways of preaching but also create confusion. This will arise because narrative preaching is not interested in storytelling but in the structure of the sermon or in narrative art form. Women can and should use narrative preaching. And narrative preaching should give importance to women's stories and keep and open ear to hear to stories of women within the biblical text and other spheres of life. As well, Barbara K. Lundblad says:

60. Christine M. Smith, *Weaving the Sermon*, 14.

61. On narrative preaching: Fred B. Craddock, *As One Without Authority*, 3rd ed. (Nashville, TN: Abingdon Press, 1979); Frederick Buechner, *Telling the Truth: The Gospel as Tragedy, Comedy, and Fairy Tale* (San Francisco: Harper & Row, 1977); Eugene L. Lowry, *The Homiletical Plot: The Sermon as Narrative Art Form*, Expanded ed. (Louisville, KY: Westminster John Knox Press, 2001); idem, *Doing Time in the Pulpit: The Relationship between Narrative and Preaching* (Nashville, TN: Abingdon Press, 1985); idem, *How to Preach a Parable: Designs for Narrative Sermons*, Abingdon Preacher's Library (Nashville, TN: Abingdon, 1989); idem, *The Sermon: Dancing the Edge of Mystery* (Nashville, TN: Abingdon Press, 1997); Richard L. Eslinger, *A New Hearing: Living Options in Homiletical Methods* (Nashville, TN: Abingdon Press, 1987); John S. McClure, *Other-wise Preaching: A Postmodern Ethic for Homiletics* (St. Louis: Chalice Press, 2001).

62. Fred B. Craddock, "Story, Narrative, and Metanarrative," in *What's the Shape of Narrative Preaching?* ed. Mike Graves and David J. Schlafer (St. Louis, MO: Chalice Press, 2008), 87-98; David Buttrick, "Story and Symbol, the Stuff of Preaching," in *What's the Shape of Narrative Preaching?* ed. Mike Graves and David J. Schlafer (St. Louis, MO: Chalice Press, 2008), 99-113.

> Consideration of narrative preaching is not only a matter of how the narrative moves, but which narratives are worth hearing and preaching. This is true whether the narrative is in the Bible, in contemporary literature, film, public media, or in people's lives.[63]

The other term for storytelling approach to preaching is called "story-preaching." This approach has been advocated by Edmund A. Steimle, Morris J. Niedenthal, and Charles Rice[64] and by Richard A. Jensen.[65] This term is also inappropriate for using as a label for women's storytelling form of preaching although it can be used as a form of conversational preaching as discussed by Lucy Atkinson Rose.[66] "Story preaching" refers to a sermon as a single story. Perhaps it is best to think of women's storytelling in preaching without labels. It is simply a way of preaching that uses story to move to and fro from stories of people's lives, to narratives of biblical text, to stories of the community—making one impact and transform the other and vice-versa.

Stories in women's sermons are not amusing anecdotes meant to give the listeners a break from the monotony of the sermon. Nor are they illustrations to clarify or amplify a point. There is nothing wrong with using stories in this way. But for women stories mean much more than that. Storytelling, for women, implies using stories of abuse, violence, and injustice as homiletical material.[67] It means regarding women's experiences as an authoritative perspective from which Scripture can be interpreted. Stories may be told as oral narrative. However, stories also make a strong impact when they are enacted in drama, skit, dance, or some other style of performance. Whatever way stories are told, the storyteller and the listeners together experience the story as it is narrated. They live afresh, episode by episode, the story of the oppressed, the raped, and the abused. By reliving the experience of the storyteller, the listeners are able to identify with the pains, struggles, and hopes of the storyteller.

---

63. Barbara K. Lundblad, "Gasping for Breath: Women Listening, Women Telling Stories," in *What's the Shape of Narrative Preaching?* ed. Mike Graves and David J. Schlafer (St. Louis, MO: Chalice Press, 2008), 159.

64. Edmund A. Steimle, Morris J. Niedenthal, and Charles L. Rice, *Preaching the Story* (Philadelphia: Fortress Press, 1980).

65. Richard A. Jensen, *Telling the Story: Variety and Imagination in Preaching* (Minneapolis: Augsburg, 1980); idem, *Thinking in Story: Preaching in a Post-Literate Age* (Lima, OH: CSS Publishing, 1993).

66. Lucy Atkinson Rose, *Sharing the Word: Preaching in the Roundtable Church* (Louisville, KY: Westminster John Knox Press, 1997), 116-17.

67. Procter-Smith, *In Her Own Rite*, 131.

Both the teller and the listeners will experience emancipation; the narrator by telling her story and the listeners by enabling her to find her voice.

Rituals

Stories and rituals are interconnected. Rituals have their origin in stories—stories enacted over and over again eventually become rituals. The identity of family, tribe, and community is formed around stories that accompany rituals. Our rituals tell us who we are, what is important to us, what we consider good, and what we consider bad. Ritual both creates and expresses meaning. In a sense, our rituals are like our narratives.[68] Rituals of worship are no different. Every ritual that is performed in worship has a story or stories attached to it. In a real sense, worship ritual weaves together the human narrative and God's narrative into a single web. Herbert Anderson and Edward Foley argue that "public worship is a privileged ritual moment" in which "the communities who gather for worship must give evidence that divine coauthorship is rehearsed and confirmed in their life together."[69] But often, people find their story missing in worship rituals. The marginalized, Anderson and Foley observe, may find their isolation intensified in the rituals and stories of worship.

This is particularly true of women. The rituals of worship are performed by men. Male priests administer the sacraments. Baptism, meant to initiate members into the community, instead inducts a person into a patriarchal ecclesial set-up. Baptismal rites have no room for plurality or diversity in personal faith. "Do you believe in one God, Father, Son and Holy Spirit?" "Do you confess Jesus Christ as your Lord and Saviour?" "Do you turn from sin, renounce evil, and intend to follow Christ?" These are the standard questions asked in Baptist churches at baptism. It is not so much different in other churches. The candidate can only respond "I do." The questions and the candidate's responses are fixed. There is no room for diversity which would not have been the case if the candidate were asked instead to tell his or her story, to express what, how and why he or she believes.

We have to lament the abandonment of conversion narrative, or sharing testimony of faith, during baptism by many evangelical churches

---

68. Herbert Anderson and Edward Foley, *Mighty Stories, Dangerous Rituals: Weaving Together the Human and the Divine* (San Francisco, CA: Jossey-Bass, 1998), 20-35. This work is a very cogent articulation of the interconnectedness between story, narrative, and ritual.

69. Anderson and Foley, *Mighty Stories*, 44.

despite the fact that it was integral to evangelical spirituality.[70] Although researchers have been unsuccessful in locating its precise origin, conversion narrative probably emerged around 1634 in New England, through the influence of a minister named John Cotton, from where it was exported back to England.[71] Certainly, it was an important element in the Puritan gathered churches. Conversion narrative, the sharing of the story of being "born again," in its historical context, is based on the nonconformist understanding of individual responsibility. So in conversion narrative "conscious understanding was to replace what the reformers viewed as 'Popish' mumbling and babbling of set prayers and recitations."[72] Churches need to recover conversion narrative; drawing from the Puritan, Reformed, Wesleyan, Anabaptist heritage. The experience of faith is to be taken seriously for it is through shared experience that the community will know mutuality and respect amidst differing perspectives and practices.

Like baptism, the Lord's Supper, is also administered by male priests. Originally a communal ritual for sharing food and resources generously, it has been turned into a ritual that excludes and segregates the minority and deprives them of community. Feminists have drawn attention to the exclusivism of these rituals and have insisted that there should be open commensality at the table and in the total life of the Church. Some, such as Procter-Smith, explore ways by which baptism and Eucharist may be emancipatory.[73]

---

70. Roger M. Payne, *The Self and the Sacred: Conversion and Autobiography in Early American Protestantism* (Knoxville: The University of Tennessee Press, 1998); D. Bruce Hindmarsh, *The Evangelical Conversion Narrative: Spiritual Autobiography in Early Modern England* (Oxford: Oxford University Press, 2005); Gordon T. Smith, *Transforming Conversion: Rethinking the Language and Contours of Christian Initiation* (Grand Rapids, MI: Baker Academic, 2010); Kathleen Lynch, *Protestant Autobiography in the Seventeenth-Century Anglophone World* (Oxford: Oxford University Press, 2012). For Methodist conversion narratives David Hall, *Worlds of Wonder, Days of Judgement: Religious Belief in Early New England* (Cambridge, MA: Harvard University Press, 1989). For Baptist conversion narratives Susan Juster, *Disorderly Women: Sexual Politics and Evangelicalism in Revolutionary New England* (Ithaca, NY: Cornell University Press, 1994).

71. Patricia Caldwell, *The Puritan Conversion Narrative: The Beginnings of American Expression* (Cambridge: Cambridge University Press, 1983), 45, referring to Edmund S. Morgan's *Visible Saints: The History of a Puritan Idea* (New York, NY: New York University Press, 1963).

72. Caldwell, *The Puritan Conversion Narrative*, 50.

73. Procter-Smith, *In Her Own Rite*, 136-63.

The inconsistency in the practice of the Lord's Supper is very visible in tribal churches of North East India. Outside the church, women are equal participants in the production of agricultural products and the primary constituents in preparing and serving food at home. Inside the church, when food is served in the Lord's Supper, women are excluded. Men make women cook and serve food at home because they think it is beneath them to do these lowly tasks. But in worship, where the administration of the Lord's Supper is invested with implications of power and symbols of domination, men take the lead and deny those tasks to women.

Now, I have discussed the Lord's Supper in the previous chapter under "building up community through worship." However, ritual and storytelling did not figure in the discussion there. So here, I would like to revisit the Lord's Supper and discuss it from the perspective of ritual-making and storytelling.[74] The tradition of the institution of the Lord's Supper goes back to Jesus who commanded his followers to break bread together and share wine in remembrance of him. The "last" meal was a rehearsal of his death. Broken bread represented his broken body, his death on the cross. Thus for the early Christians, the common meal stood at the centre of the community. It fired Christian imagination not only of the death of Jesus but also of his life. He not only gave them bread to eat but was himself the bread that gives life. It ritualized the many meals Jesus ate with his disciples and especially with tax-collectors, prostitutes, and sinners. But Jesus did not just eat food with them. Around every meal, Jesus, the great teller of stories, listened to the stories of those sharing the table with him. He understood people. He heard and understood the story of a grieving widow (Luke 7:11-17), the ordeal of the leper (Mark 1:40-45; Matt 8:1-4; Luke 5:12-16), the pain of a father whose daughter lay dying (Mark 5:21-24, 35-36; Matt 9:18-19, 23-26; Luke 8:40-42, 49-56), the afflictions of a woman with haemorrhage (Mark 5:25-34; Matt 9:20-22; Luke 8:43-68), the hardship of a woman with many men in her life (John 4:1-42), the struggles of a tax-collector (Luke 19:1-10), and the impulse of a woman who felt driven to anoint him with costly perfume (Mark 14:3-9; Luke 7:36-50). He listened to their stories, he healed, and he forgave. Jesus also learned from their stories. Faced with

74. Diann L. Neu offers two stories of feminist Eucharist as models for communities to create and celebrate during graces and meals. Neu, "Feminist Eucharists at Wisdom's Many Tables," in *New Feminist Christianity*, ed. Hunt and Neu, 195-199.

the tenacious Syro-Phoenician woman (Mark 7:24ff), who insisted on telling her side of the story around a meal analogy, Jesus changed his attitude. This account not only testifies to the power of story but also to what happens when God's narrative and human stories are brought "into dangerous and transformative proximity to each other."[75] In a real sense, he took their stories and made them God's story. Or, to use the idiom of Anderson and Foley again, God and people become "coauthors."[76] The Lord's Supper is a dangerous ritual. It will make the community notice those who are at the margins of society. It will demand nourishment for the poor and sustenance for the weak. It will necessitate the presence of the human story within the ritual. Without a connection with real-life stories, the ritual will be a meaningless act without power to affect human life or inspire hope.

Women's cry for liturgical reform became prominent in the second half of the twentieth century. The first collection of feminist liturgies, *Sistercelebrations*, was published in 1974.[77] Over the years, prayer, ritual, and liturgies have become crucial issues in women's search for an egalitarian Church. More resources have become available.[78] But of course many ritual performances are never published as they are produced in local settings to meet specific local needs. Catherine Bell

75. Anderson and Foley, *Mighty Stories*, 154.

76. Anderson and Foley, *Mighty Stories*, 149-66.

77. Arlene Swidler, ed., *Sistercelebrations: Nine Worship Experiences* (Philadelphia, PA: Fortress Press, 1974).

78. Excluding those that have already been cited elsewhere in this work: Nancy Schreck and Maureen Leach, eds., *Psalms Anew: An Inclusive Language* (Winona, MN: Saint Mary's Press, 1986); Janet Schaffran and Pat Kozak, eds., *More Than Words: Prayer and Ritual for Inclusive Communities*, 2nd ed. (Oak Park, IL: Meyer Stone Books, 1988); Miriam Therese Winter, *Womanword: A Feminist Lectionary and Psalter: Women of the New Testament* (New York: Crossroad, 1990); Rosemary Catalano Mitchell and Gail Anderson Ricciuti, *Birthings and Blessings: Liberating Worship Services for the Inclusive Church* (New York: Crossroad, 1991); idem, *Birthings and Blessings, II: More Liberating Worship Services for the Inclusive Church* (New York: Crossroad, 1993); Hannah Ward and Jennifer Wild, comp., *Human Rites: Worship Resources for An Age of Change* (London: Mowbray, 1995); St. Hilda Community, *The New Women Included: A Book of Services and Prayers* (London: SPCK, 1996); Teresa Berger, ed., *Dissident Daughters: Feminist Liturgies in Global Context* (Louisville, KY: Westminster John Knox Press, 2001).

says, the "right to ritual" is "the symbolic equivalent of the right to vote and receive equal pay."[79]

Catherine Bell notes some of the major themes of feminist rituals:

> In general, feminist rituals focus on several major themes such as bonding among women, embodied modes of shared symbolic communication, and personal empowerment. For example, feminist ritualization "reclaims" menstruation and childbirth, areas in which religion and ritual have tended to cast women as polluted or "cursed." New rites reinterpret these fundamental female experiences in ways that contribute to positive self-images and a sense of connectedness to nature and other women. Most commonly, a "rite of passage" uses these themes to express personal transformation and communitas among cohorts. Another important mode of feminist ritual expression is to "rewrite" an older, male-focused ceremony using female language and images.[80]

Mary Collins states that there are five principles undergirding feminist liturgies:

> Five principles can be identified as basic to intentionally feminist liturgy. First, feminist liturgies ritualize relationships that emancipate and empower women. Second, feminist liturgy is the production of the community of worshippers, not of special experts or authorities. Third, feminist liturgies critique patriarchal liturgies. Fourth, feminist liturgies have begun to develop a distinctive repertoire of ritual symbols and strategies. Fifth, feminist liturgists produce liturgical events, not liturgical texts.[81]

These comments make it clear that feminist and women's ritual-making is a movement that seeks the recreation or rewriting of traditional liturgy. This is necessary because the language as well as the theologies which form their foundation is deeply flawed; it promotes the oppression of women and privileges the sacraments as normative. Another point to be noted is that feminist and women's ritualizing advocates the creation of new rituals. Here, the particular focus is on storytelling. How may rituals be revitalised with human stories? Anderson and Foley discuss how this can be done. They propose rituals of birth to welcome the beginning of birth, infused with stories of the family and the community, rituals of

79. Catherine Bell, *Ritual: Perspectives and Dimensions* (Oxford: Oxford University Press, 1997), 238, referred by Teresa Berger, "Mapping the Global Struggle for Women's Rites," in *Dissident Daughters: Feminist Liturgies in Global Context*, ed. Teresa Berger (Louisville, KY: Westminster John Knox Press, 2001), 13.

80. Bell, *Ritual: Perspectives and Dimensions*, 238.

81. Collins, "Principles of Feminist Liturgy," in *Women at Worship*, ed. Procter-Smith and Walton, 11.

baptism filled with stories that connect familial stories and God's stories, and rituals of marriage that invite stories of romance and courtship. And there can be rituals of encountering death and rituals of mourning when storytelling and remembering are important.

According to Anderson and Foley, new rituals can be formed around unexpected moments in life. There can be rituals for miscarriage and stillbirth to give expression to grief and loss, rituals of divorce to acknowledge thwarted dreams and promises, rituals in response to a diagnosis of Alzheimer's or other such debilitating disease, and rituals for the withdrawal of life support systems expressing compassion but letting go at the same time. New rituals can also be created for other life transitions such as adoption whether by a couple or a single adult, leaving home, or renewal of marriage vows.[82]

Traditionally, tribal life is ritualistic. In fact, ritual activity permeates every aspect of tribal life. There are the rituals of social niceties and good manners and those that require elaborate ceremonies. In a village setting, it is a courtesy to greet anyone we meet on the way. It does not make a difference whether the person you meet is a stranger or your close relative, you have to greet people. It does not matter how many people you meet, you have to greet everyone. Cerebrally, that is a social custom, but actually it much more. It is a ritual of respect, togetherness, and community. Tribal people know no other way of life than that of community. Without the ritual, tribal way of life will cease to be. Another example of a simple ritual is that of eating food. Eating food as a ritual performance is particularly evident among the Angami tribe. They eat their food only after offering some morsels of food and libation of drink first to the Mother God.[83] More elaborate forms of rituals take place for sickness, which might involve sacrificing a fowl or a goat or going to the outskirts of the village to call the spirit of the sick man to come back to him. Rituals abound around agricultural activities, the main

82. Anderson and Foley, *Mighty Stories*, 47-148. Not all of these rituals are relevant for the tribal context. For instance, the use of life support systems is a technology still uncommon if not non-existent in the region. A person "leaving home" when he or she reaches a certain age is also unfamiliar. In tribal societies, children stay with their parents until they get married. And at least one of the children, usually one who would inherit the parental house, continues to live with the parent after marriage so that parents are taken care of in their old age. But the notion of creating new worship rituals is not just applicable but necessary.

83. Angami, "Ukepenuopfü: An Exploration of the Goddess," in *Tribal Christian Theology*, ed. Lasetso and Vashum, 234.

occupation of tribal people. Among the Angamis, sowing and reaping commence only after the appropriate ritual is performed by *Tsakro* (the first sower) and *Liedepfü* (the first reaper). *Tsakro* and *Liedepfu* are both women assigned to perform the ceremony.[84] Then at harvest, there would be celebrations with dance and music.

In tribal worldview, rituals are not mere acts but are effective. It is one of the elements of tribal life through which the inexplicable connection between the holy and the profane, and the inseparability of body and soul, is made evident. This is why rituals are effective means of settling disputes. Among the A·chik, all forms of discord, be it a quarrel between a wife and her husband, a dispute between neighbours, or a conflict between clans, are settled by performing various rituals that culminate in sharing a drink of rice brew and eating food together.[85] Likewise, rituals accompany every aspect of life. Birth, marriage, funeral, all require rituals in response. The rituals link the phenomenological stories of the individual and the community with stories of the spirit world. Tribal worship rituals can draw from this heritage of rituals to give coherence to the present experience of life in the community.

When I got married back in 1995, there were over 3,000 guests. The number of guests is not unusual in a communitarian society. My husband is from another state so, except for a busload of family and friends, most people from his side could not attend the main reception which we arranged in my place. Clearly, there would have been many more guests if he had lived closer to my hometown. All the guests had to be served refreshment as soon as they arrived. Then everybody joined in a feast of various preparations of pork, beef, chicken, fish, and goat meat (and a few dishes for vegetarians). Actually, feeding of relatives and friends began weeks before the wedding because that is when people started coming to prepare for the wedding day. So for weeks the house was full. Some came to prepare cooking places, some came to prepare the place for the reception, some came to cut meat, some came to cook

84. Vimeno Lasetso, "A Search for Values in the Life of the Traditional Angami Naga Women," in *Doing Tribal Christian Theology with Tribal Resources: Cultural Resources from North East India*, ed. Razouselie Lasetso and Eyingbeni Humtsoe (Jorhat, Assam: ETC Programme Coordination, 2009), 219.

85. Marlene Marak, "The Understanding and Practice of Peace and Reconciliation in the A·chik Community," in *Garnering Tribal Resources for Doing Tribal Christian Theology*, Tribal Study Series 16, ed. Razouselie Lasetso (Jorhat, Assam: Eastern Theological College Programme Coordination, 2008), 99-100.

for those who were working, and some came to help those who were cooking. Fortunately, the family does not have to supply all the food, for people come with pigs, goats, chickens, or pumpkins. Some bring betel nuts and betel leaves, chewing which is customary in any community affair. Those who lived nearby went back when it got dark but those who lived further away slept on the floor of the house and in the houses of neighbours. Preparation for a wedding is not based on practicality. It is a community affair. It is a time for people, particularly for the clan, to get together and catch up on each other's lives.

Tribal background of ritualistic traditional life, particularly communal rituals can be a guide for developing new rituals for worship that are relevant for the people. The worship rituals we inherited from the West have nothing to do with our culture, our values, and the way we see the world. So they do not make much sense to us. Rituals from the West are for tribals as singing and praying in Latin was to the reformers. We have to draw their ritual prototypes from their cultural traditions. But we need to be keenly aware of the fact that even within our "communitarian" system of tribal communities, women are excluded. Within the tribal kinship system, in all the levels of relationship—family, village, clan, khel, tribe, and ethnic group—women are not given full community. Therefore, it is necessary to sift and strain through traditional practices when we look for community values. Our ritualizing must arise from, to borrow C. S. Song's terminology (from a different context), "the womb"[86] of tribal cultures. The "womb" analogy can be a constant reminder that we are looking specifically to build rituals on traditions that are inclusive and those that nurture. Our newly ritualized space will be a creative space, like the womb. In that sacred space, women can say and do what traditional culture forbade just because they were girls. The possibilities are many - music, dance, riddles, food, and stories; cooking, weaving, knitting, and fetching water; marriage, pregnancy, birth, youth, and death; remembering the past, welcoming new seasons, and honouring God; incantations, chants, invocations, purification. Whatever shape it takes, our rituals will be meaningful because then they will speak to us of our life. Such ways of ritualizing are ways of connecting our stories of the past with the present, acknowledging both continuity and discontinuity, and of connecting our human stories with God's story.

---

86. C. S. Song, *Theology from the Womb of Asia* (Maryknoll, NY: Orbis Books, 1986).

In the introductory chapter of this work, I discussed tribal storytelling through weaving. Weaving is from the "womb" of tribal culture. It is not only a metaphor for storytelling, but is itself an act of storytelling.[87] In most tribal communities, weaving is an activity that belongs exclusively to women. All tribes (and there are over 300 tribes in North East India) associate their tribal identity with the cloth they wear, particularly in the shawls (a long cloth worn by men and women over the body) and the *mekhela* (*dakmanda* in A·chik; a long piece of cloth worn by women; a wraparound worn like a long skirt). Every tribe has its own distinctive patterns and colours, which are the pride of the tribe. Misusing the traditional cloths is viewed as an insult to the entire tribe. In the traditional method of weaving, it takes several months to make a single piece of shawl or *mekhela*. Thus we can understand why in the past, the wealth of people was often measured in terms of the number of shawls (and *mekhelas* in the case of women) they owned. In fact, before weaving can begin, there has to be preparation of the cotton fields, sowing the seeds, picking cotton, spinning it into yarn, and dyeing it.

The predominant method of weaving in the region is back-strap weaving. The loom has a continuous warp one end of which is fastened to a post, wall, or any other suitable form of support, and the other end has a strap which goes around the woman's waist. The woman sits on a small low seat with her feet pushing against a firm support in order to keep the tension on the warp. Yarn is wound onto a spindle by hand and then onto a long smooth stick which is passed across the warp like the shuttle in more modern looms. A weaving sword is used to beat the weft into place. Patterns are created by using different colour threads in the warp and weft.

Now it is significant that it is women alone who have recaptured the history of their tribes and retold it in the designs and colours of the cloths they weave. Thus women have been instrumental in representing their culture. Unfortunately, this contribution is not acknowledged and women themselves are not conscious of the stories they are telling in the tapestry of the cloths they weave. Actually, cloths present stories visually. It is a different way of signifying, different from speech but no

---

87. Nancy K. Miller employs weaving as a metaphor for women's writing. Nancy K. Miller, *Subject to Change: Reading Feminist Writing* (New York: Columbia University Press, 1988), 83. Cf. idem, "Arachnologies: The Woman, the Text, and the Critic," in *The Poetics of Gender*, ed. N. K. Miller (New York: Columbia University Press, 1986), 270-96.

less potent. As we come together in worship, it is advantageous for the communities to acknowledge and recover the stories that are buried in the patterns of the traditional cloths. Some of the tribal designs in weaving are easily recognisable. There are animals, birds, flowers, and implements of hunting and war such as spears, shield, and dao (long-bladed knife). Some of these, particularly birds and animals, are totems of the tribe. Other images represent things that are important to the community. Certain tribal designs are not quickly decipherable. Strong colours, checked patterns, zigzags, and waves recur often. These have profound symbolic significance. The meanings of these designs are to be seen in the fervour with which people identify with these signs and symbols. Their full significance may be found more in inexplicable feelings rather than in conscious thought. Thus there are stories to be discovered in the weaving of women. More than that, we can weave new patterns to tell new stories as we become more aware of new ways of knowing the world and new ways of telling our narratives. The powerful medium of storytelling through weaving has to be re-enacted, ritualized in worship, to give birth to new stories.

Re-imagining Biblical Stories

The reading of the Bible, or rather its interpretation, does not take place in a vacuum. It has always been read from certain perspectives and to support certain notions. In other words, there is a play of power and politics in the reading of the Bible. Feminist biblical scholars have shown that the Bible has been written from the perspective of patriarchal cultures and as such is infused with androcentric terms, phrases, and images. Women cannot afford to be uncritical of the use of biblical texts to subjugate women. Women should not read as men. We have to read as women. Our reading of the Bible must therefore be a conscious effort to "read against the grain."

Eryl W. Davies calls the critical female reader "the dissenting reader."[88] This is an appropriate term because female readers have to resist or dissent from reading the Bible from the male viewpoint. Other terms which are applicable to explain the process are "anamnesis" or

88. Eryl W. Davies, *The Dissenting Reader: Feminist Approaches to the Hebrew Bible* (Aldershot: Ashgate, 2003), 42ff. Also relevant is Judith Fetterlet's idea of the "resisting reader." Judith Fetterley, *The Resisting Reader: A Feminist Approach to American Fiction* (Bloomington: Indiana University Press, 1978).

profound remembering and "feminist imagination."[89] Anamnesis, as used by Procter-Smith, involves the recovery of the memory of the past in order to have a future. Imagination is essential in reconstructing feminist memory. I see the work by Athalya Brenner, *I am... Biblical Women Tell Their Own Stories*[90] as an example using imagination to recover biblical stories of women. The personal voice that Brenner gives the female characters of the Bible is not only a refreshing approach to telling their stories but also unravels aspects of the stories that are hidden when read from the patriarchal perspective. A wide range of feminist literature on reclaiming of women's history through retelling of women's stories is available.[91] For my own purposes, I wish to focus on the primary women in the Bible—Eve and Mary. The story of Eve, however, is best heard within the wider context of the legends about Lilith and also of Norea. Hence, I will focus on Lilith, Eve, Norea, and Mary.

Lilith

Lilith is unknown in tribal communities. Her existence comes as something of a big surprise to tribals whose knowledge is confined to the canonical Bible. Isaiah 34:13 is the only place in the canonical Bible where Lilith is mentioned:

> Wildcats shall meet with hyenas,
> goat demons shall call to each other;
> there too Lilith shall repose,

89. These technical liturgical terminologies are used by Procter-Smith, *In Her Own Rite*, 36-58.

90. Athalya Brenner, *I Am... Biblical Women Tell Their Own Stories* (Minneapolis: Fortress Press, 2005).

91. To name a few: J. Cheryl Exum, *Fragmented Women: Feminist (Sub)versions of Biblical Narratives*, Journal for the Study of the Old Testament Supplement Series 163 (Sheffield: Sheffield Academic Press, 1993); Harold C. Washington, Susan Lochrie Graham and Pamela Thimmes, ed., *Escaping Eden: New Feminist Perspectives on the Bible* (Sheffield: Sheffield Academic Press, 1998); Katharine Doob Sakenfeld, *Just Wives? Stories of Power and Survival in the Old Testament and Today* (Louisville, KY: Westminster John Knox Press, 2003); Judith E. McKinlay, *Reframing Her: Biblical Women in Postcolonial Focus*, The Bible in the Modern World 1 (Sheffield: Sheffield Phoenix Press, 2004); Irmtraud Fischer, *Women Who Wrestled with God: Biblical Stories of Israel's Beginnings*, trans. Linda M. Maloney (Collegeville, MN: Liturgical Press,2005); Cheryl A. Kirk-Duggan and Tina Pippin, eds., *Mother Goose, Mother Jones, Mommie Dearest: Biblical Mothers and Their Children* (Atlanta, GA: Society of Biblical Literature, 2009).

and find a place to rest.

This verse provides a link for the telling of the story of Lilith. Tribal Christians of North East India will not accept a story as credible or of spiritual value unless it is found in the canonical literature. Isaiah gives reason for unearthing and telling the story of Lilith. To be sure, the myth of Lilith is not from Christian tradition but is a Jewish midrash, which emerged from biblical narrative. Judith Plaskow, a Jewish feminist theologian, explains how the story of Lilith developed from biblical narrative.

> Midrash is a form of biblical interpretation that often begins from a question, silence, gap, or contradiction in a biblical story and writes the story forward in response to the interpreter's questions. Thus the original Lilith midrash emerged from the contradiction between the creation narratives in Genesis 1 and Genesis 2. Because in Genesis 1 the man and woman are created simultaneously and apparently equally, while in Genesis 2 Eve is created from Adam's rib, the rabbis wondered whether the stories might not describe two different events in the history of creation. Their response was that, indeed, Adam did have a first wife named Lilith, who fled the garden when Adam tried to subordinate her. God sent three angels after her to bring her back, at which point in the midrash Lilith turns into a demon, killing new babies in retaliation for the deaths of her own children.[92]

Researchers think that the myth of Lilith is derived from Lilitu, a blood-sucking seductress in ancient Mesopotamian texts (2400 BCE).[93] She appears in the Sumerian epic *Gilgamesh and the Huluppu Tree* (ca. 2000 BCE) as one who built her house in the Huluppu tree. She flees into the desert when Gilgamesh slays the dragon that had its nest at the base of the tree. A Babylonian terra-cotta relief of approximately the same period depicts Lilith as a slender nude female. She has wings and owl-feet. Her appearance changed over the centuries. In a 7th century BCE tablet, she is depicted as a winged sphinx.[94]

---

92. Judith Plaskow, "Lilith Revisited," in *The Coming of Lilith: Essays on Feminism, Judaism, and Sexual Ethics, 1972-2003*, ed. Judith Plaskow with Donna Berman (Boston: Beacon Press, 2005), 85.

93. Heidi M. Szpek, "'In the Image of God He Created Them': Adam and Lilith," in *Re-Imagining Eve and Adam: And Other Brief Essays* (Lincoln, NE: iUniverse, 2002), 19.

94. Raphael Patai, *The Hebrew Goddess*, 4th enlarged ed. (Detroit, MI: Wayne State University Press, 1990), 222.

While there are several sources for the myth of Lilith, most interpreters refer to a rabbinic text of the 10th-11th CE known as *Alphabet of Ben Sira*, which gives the fullest detail. Its actual writer is anonymous, although it is attributed to Ben Sira.[95] In the *Alphabet of Ben Sira 23*, it is said that Nebuchadnezzar asked Ben Sira to heal his son with his wisdom or face the death penalty.[96] An amulet with the names of three angels inscribed on it is prepared for healing Nebuchadnezzar's son. The names of the three angels are Senoy, Sansenoy, and Semangelof. And the legend of Lilith is then narrated to explain the significance of the amulet.

According to the *Alphabet of Ben Sira 23*, when God created Adam, the first man, Adam was alone. Not wanting Adam to be alone, God created a woman from the earth, the same way he had created Adam, and God called her Lilith. Immediately, Adam and Lilith started fighting because Adam wanted to be superior which Lilith did not accept. Lilith reasoned that they were equal because they were both created from the earth. Finally, seeing there would be no end to the quarrel between them, Lilith uttered the name of God and flew off into the air. Then Adam complained to God saying that the woman God gave him had run away. So God sent three angels to bring her back. God told Adam that if she comes back, all is good. But if she refuses, she has to allow one hundred of her children to die every day. The angels pursuing Lilith caught up with her in the middle of the waters where the Egyptians were destined to drown and they delivered God's message to her. But she refused to return. They threatened to drown her in the sea but she told them to leave her, for she was created only to make infants sick. Her power over a male infant was for eight days from the day of his birth and twenty days over a female infant. When they insisted that she should return, she promised them (in exchange for her freedom) that if she saw their names or images on an amulet, she will not have power over the infant wearing it. She also agreed to let a hundred of her children die every day. Hence, one hundred demons die every day. And this was also the

95. A parallel version is found in *Gen R.* 17:4 and Babylonian Talmud *Jeb.* 63a. Kocku von Stuckrad, "Constructing Feminity – the Lilith Case," in *Gender, Tradition and Renewal*, Religions and Discourse 13, ed. Robert L. Platzner (Bern: Peter Lang, 2005), 84.

96. This is historically implausible because Nebuchadnezzar lived about four hundred years before Ben Sira. Evidently, the anonymous author is using the name of Ben Sira to give it greater credibility.

reason for writing the names of the angels on amulets for sick children so that they would recover.[97]

Aramaic incantation inscriptions on bowls from about 600 CE reveal that the Jews of this period feared Lilith.[98] In the Kabbalah, Lilith is re-imagined as one who seduces men and kills children. The Zohar states that Lilith plays with men in their sleep, causing them to have nocturnal emissions. And from this fornication with men in their sleep she produces demon children. It was believed that Lilith had power to kill children, especially those children who are conceived when a man couples with his wife in candlelight, or with his wife naked, or at a time when sex with her is forbidden.[99] In Kabbalistic texts, Lilith is married to Samael who is known as "Angel Satan" or the "Other God" but takes to fornicating with men after Samael is castrated. The 13th century Kabbalists split Lilith into Lilith the Elder and Lilith the Younger.[100]

The demonization of Lilith is evidence of the effort of patriarchal storytellers to ensure male dominance. A heroic archetypal feminist who insisted on her equality with Adam and refused to submit to male domination did not fit with the idea of women held by rabbinic authorities.

Plaskow demonstrates that the story of Lilith can be re-imagined. She depicts a new Lilith in a new midrash. In Plaskow's retelling, Lilith is not a demon but a courageous woman who, all alone, attempts to re-join the human community in the garden. She attempts to breach the wall but is not successful. Then she storms the main gate but is repulsed yet again. However, before being defeated Lilith withdraws and Eve sees her for the first time. Curiosity and doubt begins to grow in Eve's mind. Eventually, Lilith and Eve meet on the other side of the garden wall. They sit together and converse for a long time teaching each other many things and telling stories to each other. They laugh and they cry and the bond of sisterhood grows between them.[101] In another re-imagination of Lilith, Joy Kogawa recalls the legend of Lilith as a feminist Paradise Lost. Lilith as Kogawa sees her, returns to the children of Adam and Eve offering them her

97. Paraphrase mine. A translation by Szpek is found in "'In the Image of God He Created Them': Adam and Lilith," in *Re-Imagining Eve and Adam*, 23-24.

98. Patai, *Hebrew Goddess*, 224ff.

99. Patai, *Hebrew Goddess*, 233ff.

100. Patai, *Hebrew Goddess*, 244-49.

101. Judith Plaskow, "The Coming of Lilith: Towards a Feminist Theology," in *The Coming of Lilith: Essays on Feminism, Judaism, and Sexual Ethics, 1972-2003*, ed. Judith Plaskow with Donna Berman (Boston: Beacon Press, 2005), 31-32.

wisdom, her sense of autonomy, and her daring.[102] These and such other re-imaginations of Lilith illustrate how the legend of Lilith may be retold in contemporary times to give new insight to the lives of countless women in our own generation who are unconventional and rebellious and are therefore labelled as shameless, wicked, or with loose morals.

Eve

The stories of Eve and Lilith are opposites. One flees from the domineering Adam, the other stays. But they are both victims. Lilith is demonised. Eve is blamed for bringing sin into the world, expulsion from paradise, and consequently, human toil and pain. This view of Eve as the cause of "the Fall of man" finds its unfortunate expression in 1 Tim 2:9-15:

> Women should dress themselves modestly and decently in suitable clothing, not with their hair braided, or with gold, pearls, or expensive clothes, but with good works, as is proper for women who profess reverence for God. Let a woman learn in silence with full submission. I permit no woman to teach or to have authority over a man; she is to keep silent. For Adam was formed first, then Eve; and Adam was not deceived, but the woman was deceived and became a transgressor. Yet she will be saved through childbearing, provided they continue in faith and love and holiness, with modesty.

Susan T. Foh maintains that 1 Tim 2:12 is reason enough for not ordaining women: "There is only one valid argument against women's ordination to the ministry: scriptural prohibition. This prohibition is found in 1 Tim 2:12."[103]

---

102. Joy Kogawa, *A Song of Lilith* (New York: Laurel Glen, 2001).

103. Susan T. Foh, "The Head of the Woman is the Man" (1989 CE), in *Eve and Adam: Jewish, Christian, and Muslim Readings on Genesis and Gender*, ed. Kristen E. Kvam, Linda S. Schearing and Valarie H. H. Ziegler (Bloomington, IN: Indiana University Press, 1999), 398. For more on how Eve's story has been used to blame all women and perpetuate fear of women's sexuality down through the centuries from the early Church to the Victorian period and after see Karen Armstrong, *The Gospel according to Woman* (London: HarperCollins, 1986), 52-87. For similar traditional interpretations see Andreas J. Köstenberger, Thomas R. Schreiner, and H. Scott Baldwin, eds., *Women in the Church: A Fresh Analysis of 1 Timothy 2:9–15* (Grand Rapids, MI: Baker Books, 1995); William J. Webb, *Slaves, Women and Homosexuals: Exploring the Hermeneutic of Cultural Analysis* (Downers Grove, IL: InterVarsity Press, 2001), 281-86; James M. Hamilton, "What Women Can Do in Ministry: Full Participation Within Biblical Boundaries," in *Women, Ministry and the Gospel: Exploring New Paradigms*, ed. Mark Husbands and Timothy Larsen (Downers Grove, IL: InterVarsity Press, 2007), 32-52.

Christian attitudes towards women have been largely determined by the concept of women inferred, as in 1 Timothy, from the story of Eve in the book of Genesis. Eve is blamed for allowing herself to be deceived by the serpent and for deceiving Adam. Furthermore, early Jewish and Christian traditions linked her sin to sex, erotizing the biblical account as a sexual encounter between Eve and the serpent.[104] Consequently, Eve's guilt is passed on to all women and her story, as interpreted by men, engenders a fear of women's sexuality. The biblical instruction to women in 1 Tim 2:9-10 to dress modestly is really an order to hide their sexuality, to make themselves as unattractive as possible so that men may not be led astray.[105] Titus 2:1-5 is also discriminatory towards women, requiring women to teach younger women to fit in within the culture of male dominance, to take care of the home, and to be submissive to their husbands.[106] Women are regarded as teeming with lust; every movement she makes, every glance she gives is an invitation to indulge in sexual revelry.[107] This distorted image of women has been challenged in many different ways but most vociferously by feminist writers and thinkers.

Feminist interpretations rescue Eve from the bias of patriarchal readings that have consistently painted her as a weak, manipulative, sinful, and libidinous woman.

> Eve becomes our first mother, not the prototype of weak, sinful woman. As she reclaims her name, which means 'Life', her consort Adam, is reduced to

---

104. Philo, *De Opificio Mundi* 151-52, 165-66; *Yebamoth* 103b; *Apocalypse of Moses* 19.3.

105. The injunction not to wear jewellery or expensive clothes is echoed in the misogynistic admonitions found in the second century CE pseudepigraphical work, *The Testament of Reuben* 5. Cf. 1 Pet 3:3; Titus 2:3-5.

106. Baptists, in particular, have tended to interpret these passages uncritically and have used them to attack feminism as against God, against the family, and detrimental to society. Letha Dawson Scanzoni, "Why We Need Evangelical Feminists," in *New Feminist Christianity: Many Voices, Many Views*, ed. Mary E. Hunt and Diann L. Neu (Woodstock, VT: SkyLight Paths Publishing, 2010), 74. For a feminist assessment of the Household Code see Fiorenza, *In Memory of Her*, 260-66 for 1 Pet and 288-315 for the Pastoral Epistles.

107. In many cases of rape, the woman is regarded as having invited it upon herself either by dressing provocatively or by her manner. Pamela Abbott, Claire Wallace, and Melissa Tyler, *An Introduction to Sociology: Feminist Perspectives*, 3rd ed. (Abingdon, Oxon: Routledge, 2005), 292ff.

normal size. 'Adam', which means 'Earthling', is no more prototype of Man than Eve is of Woman.[108]

Feminist interpretations of Genesis 2 and 3 try to highlight aspects of the narrative that have been ignored. For instance, in Genesis 3:6 the text says:

> So when the woman saw that the tree was good for food, and that it was a delight to the eyes, and that the tree was to be desired to make one wise, she took of its fruit and ate; and she also gave some to her husband, who was with her, and he ate.

Eve shows initiative. She is the spokesperson. She is the one who takes decisions.[109] Adam was present during conversation between Eve and the serpent. The text says Eve gave some of the fruit to her husband, *who was with her*.[110] Susan Niditch finds that in Gen 3 the woman played a decisive role to bring about "a movement from a fixed and unchanging world to a new nonstatic world."[111] She looks at the narrative from the perspective that what the snake said to the woman was not a lie but the truth.

> She (the woman) is no easy prey for a seducing demon, as later tradition represents her, but a conscious actor choosing knowledge. Together with the snake, she is the bringer of culture.... It is she who first dares to eat of God's tree, to consume the fruit of the divine, thereby becoming, as the rabbis say of human beings, like the angels in having the capacity to discriminate and like the animals who eat, fornicate, defecate, and die [*b.Hag.* 16a]. The woman herself comes to have the most earthly and the most divine of roles, conceiving, containing,

108. Janet Wootton, "Women's Leadership in the Church and Feminist Theology," in *This is Our Story: Free Church Women's Ministry*, ed. Janet Wootton (Peterborough: Epworth, 2007), 84.

109. Phyllis Trible, "Depatriarchalizing in Biblical Interpretation," *Journal of the American Academy of Religion* 41 (1973): 30-48; idem, *God and the Rhetoric of Sexuality*, 110; Tikva Frymer-Kensky, "Women," in *Harper's Bible Dictionary*, ed. Paul Achtemeier (San Francisco: Harper & Row, 1985), 1138-41.

110. Thus the man and the woman share equal responsibility for what happened – both are judged by God and expelled from the God's garden. Phyllis Trible, " 'Not a Jot, Not a Tittle: Genesis 2-3 after Twenty Years' (1995 CE)," in *Eve and Adam: Jewish, Christian, and Muslim Readings on Genesis and Gender*, ed. Kristen E. Kvam, Linda S. Schearing and Valarie H. H. Ziegler (Bloomington, IN: Indiana University Press, 1999), 439-44.

111. Susan Niditch, "Genesis," in *The Women's Bible Commentary*, ed. Carol A. Newsom and Sharon H. Ringe (Louisville, KY: Westminster/John Knox Press, 1992), 14.

and nurturing new life. She is an especially appropriate link between life in God's garden and life in the thornier world to which all of us are consigned.[112]

There are other ways of reading. For instance, Carol Meyers argues that Gen 2-3 is a wisdom tale. She reads it within the context of the struggles of highland life.[113] Jon L. Berquist proposes a new interpretation of Gen 2-3. According to Berquist, "This is the story not of God's creation nor of human relationships, but of the *earth's* fall from grace." The story begins with and ends with the earth. At the beginning God makes the earth bountiful, but at the end the earthling has to toil and make things grow on the earth.[114] These and other feminist approaches to the reading of Genesis 2 and 3 are attempts to redeem the text from its misogynist and patriarchal interpretations. But this is not easy because the text is deeply interwoven with patriarchal notions. It is a tragedy at several levels. If the story is read with God as the main character (which is an aspect of traditional interpretations), we see God creating, God in relationship, God discovering a problem, and God punishing and sentencing the guilty. The serpent is defeated. God is victorious, but it is a hollow victory. God ends up all alone. Paradise is empty.

Feminist interpretations begin with Eve as the protagonist. She is God's ultimate creation. God thought it was not good for the earthling to be alone and created Eve to be his companion. Eve is not created inferior. She is intelligent and she responds to the serpent with clear knowledge of what God had said. She understands correctly that the fruit would increase her knowledge. Her eating of the fruit is not a mistake but an intelligent decision to change things from an undiscerning world to a world of discernment. Their mistake was not in eating the fruit. Actually, it is possible to read the narrative without looking for a point where the woman and man made a mistake. It is striking that before they ate the fruit, Eve and Adam were so ignorant as to be unaware that they were naked. By the same token, it is possible to assume that Adam did not realize he was doing back-breaking work and eating the plants of the fields and likewise Eve did not realize that she was experiencing pain during childbirth. The knowledge acquired from eating the fruit made them realise that they were naked. Thus, God's pronouncement of their

112. Niditch, "Genesis," in *The Women's Bible Commentary*, ed. Newsom and Ringe, 14.

113. Meyers, *Discovering Eve*.

114. Jon L. Berquist, *Reclaiming Her Story: The Witness of Women in the Old Testament* (St. Louis, MO: Chalice Press, 1992), 26-40, quote is from 38.

suffering (not curses or punishment)—that the woman will have more pain during childbirth but her desire will be for her husband, and that the man will toil to produce crops from the ground and eat bread by the sweat of his face—may simply be seen as a statement of a reality they were unaware of before they ate the fruit; not a new reality brought about by their disobedience. If Eve had not taken the decision to eat the fruit, it can be argued, theologically, that humanity would still be living naked and living ignorant.

Feminists also look at the story of Eve (and Adam) as a story of human relationship. Such a reading is particularly helpful in rescuing not only Eve but Adam. Looking at the story again, I am drawn to Heidi Szpek's retelling of the story not as a tragedy, but as a love story.[115] Szpek points to the often overlooked fact that Eve and Adam shared a relationship and re-imagines Eve and Adam as "beloved and friends."

As Szpek sees it, the relationship between Eve and Adam endures through the most overwhelming events. They made a mistake in disobeying God and suffer the consequences. Szpek considers it significant that, after their disobedience, Adam names the woman Eve, meaning "(mother of all) living" in Gen 3:20 because he would not have gifted the woman with a name if he had harboured anger against her. This shows that their relationship did not collapse in the face of grave adversity. Their relationship endures when they are expelled from the garden. They experience joy when Cain and Abel are born to them. Sorrow follows when the elder brother murders the younger brother (Gen 4). They not only lose Abel but Cain too, who becomes a fugitive. Their grief does not separate them. Instead they turn to each other for support. Soon, joy comes again with the birth of Seth. The story of Eve and Adam is not narrated in detail after this but it is possible to gather that their relationship continued in loving intimacy. The narrator tells us in Genesis 5:1 that Adam had other sons and daughters. The re-imagining of the story of Eve and Adam as a love story is poignantly expressed by playwright Elizabeth Swados, who takes the words of the Song of Songs and puts them on the lips of Eve and Adam, in the Broadway musical

115. Heidi M. Szpek, "'This is My Beloved and This is My Friend': Re-Imagining Eve and Adam," in *Re-Imagining Eve and Adam: And Other Brief Essays* (Lincoln, NE: iUniverse, 2002), 3-8.

Bible Women.[116] The closeness of Eve and Adam and their closeness with God also comes through in the Renaissance painting of the Dominican friar Fra. Bartolommeo, *The Creation of Eve.* This painting shows the moment when God created Eve. It portrays Adam resting on the grassy floor and Eve emerging naked from Adam's left side. Eve's outstretched fingertips are seen gently touching the fingertips of God. The delicacy of the scene is remarkable. In the background, there is a man and a woman with two small boys who are apparently Adam, Eve and their sons, Cain and Abel.

Norea

Eve has a daughter who is called Norea.[117] The story of Eve and Norea is found in a 3rd century CE Coptic manuscript of the Nag Hammadi called the *Hypostasis of the Archons*. It is sometimes translated as *The True Nature* (or *Reality*) *of the Rulers* and contains revisions or a retelling of Genesis 1-6.[118] The text is often referred to as "the book of Norea" because towards the end the narrator speaks through Norea, making it a direct narrative from Norea to the reader. There are other Nag Hammadi manuscripts such as the *Apocryphon of John* and *On the Origin of the World* that give further variations, but I will confine this discussion to the *Hypostasis*.[119]

The manuscript is evidence that interpreting the Genesis narrative was not unusual for the ancient Jews and early Christians. The freedom to re-imagine and retell the well-known story of the garden from an unusual and surprising perspective can be liberating. Appropriating the *Hypostasis* to tell the story of Eve and Norea is to challenge the notion that only one interpretation is authoritative. However, the story of Norea

116. Milan Entertainment, 1995. Referred to in Szpek, " 'This is My Beloved and This is My Friend': Re-Imagining Eve and Adam," in *Re-Imagining Eve and Adam* 3n6.

117. Fuller story in Appendix G: "The Story of Norea, Daughter of Eve."

118. The date of the document is debated. It is tentatively dated in the 3rd century CE and no later than the 4th century. Its provenance is also debated. It is assigned to Egypt, Syria, or Alexandria.

119. For the following discussion: Bentley Layton, trans., "The Hypostasis of the Archons (II, *4*)," in *The Nag Hammadi Library*, ed. Marvin W. Meyer and James McConkey Robinson (Leiden: E. J. Brill, 1977), 153-60; Karen L. King, "The Book of Norea, Daughter of Eve," in *Searching the Scriptures*, vol. 2: *A Feminist Commentary*, ed. Elisabeth Schüssler Fiorenza (New York, NY: Crossroad, 1994), 66-85; Rosemary Radford Ruether, *Goddesses and the Divine Feminine: A Western Religious History* (Berkeley: University of California Press, 2005), 115-18.

not only contests the traditional interpretation of Eve but shakes the very foundation of the concept of the creator God in Genesis.

Hypostasis begins with a prologue that refers to Col 1:13 and Eph 6:11-12. Perhaps this suggests that the struggle against the rulers and the authorities is a continuing reality (Eph 6:11-12). It could also point to the reality of the realized eschatology in which God has overcome the power of darkness (Col 1:13).[120] The story of Norea in the *Hypostasis* takes place in a context where the Archons, or Rulers, have already established their authority over the dark world below. Their Chief Ruler, or Archon, is the creator God who is arrogant and ignorant. He claims to be the only God without knowing that there were others above him, Entirety and Incorruptibility (a female being), and above all, the Father of Light who determines everything. So Incorruptibility calls the Chief Ruler, "Samael" (meaning the God of the blind). His ignorance is unmasked further through his mother Pistis Sophia and her daughter Zoe. Like their Chief Ruler, the Archons are also weak, lacking in spiritual powers, and controlled by their violent lusts.

The *Hypostasis* presents the story of Eve from a perspective entirely different from the story we find in the canonical Bible. Eve is created as a result of an attempt by the Archons to entrap Incorruptibility in order to satisfy their lust for her. It so happened that the Archons made a male model hoping it will attract Incorruptibility yet their plan fails to work. Unlike the biblical account, it is not the creator God but the Spirit who gives life to the man and names him Adam for she found him crawling on the ground. It is also not the creator God but the Archons who place Adam in a garden to cultivate it. And it is they who use some of their ignorance to put Adam to sleep and extracted the Spirit as a living woman from his side. On seeing the Spirit woman, the Archons' lust is aroused and they attempt to rape her. But the Archons manage only to rape her shadow, her material body, for she had transferred her

120. Anne McGuire, "Virginity and Subversion: Norea Against the Powers in the *Hypostasis of the Archons*," in *Images of the Feminine in Gnosticism*, Studies in Antiquity and Christianity, ed. Karen L. King (Harrisburg, PA: Trinity Press International, 2000), 242-43. According to Elaine Pagels, the opening lines of the Hypostasis signal "the author's intention to read Genesis through Paul's eyes." Elaine Pagels, "Pursuing the Spiritual Eve: Imagery and Hermeneutics in the *Hypostasis of the Archons* and the *Gospel of Philip*," in *Images of the Feminine in Gnosticism*, Studies in Antiquity and Christianity, ed. Karen L. King (Harrisburg, PA: Trinity Press International, 2000), 192.

true self, Spirit, to a tree before they caught her. Thus the Spirit woman is split into two – the Spiritual principal and the Carnal woman.

In the *Hypostasis* the snake in the garden is the Spiritual principal who enters the snake and instructs her counterpart, the Carnal woman to eat the fruit from the tree of the knowledge of good and evil in order to become like gods. It was part of the Father's plan all along, that they should eat and know the truth about themselves. The Spiritual woman spoke the truth. So immediately after eating the fruit, Adam and the Carnal woman became enlightened and realized that they were naked and that they possessed soul but not Spirit. In a further inversion of the Genesis story, it is the Archons who throw Adam and the yet to be named Carnal woman into a life of toil and distraction so that humanity would be occupied by worldly affairs and not pursue spiritual powers.

After the Carnal woman gives birth to Cain, Abel, and Seth she comes to be called by the name Eve.[121] Eve's story elucidates the background of gender of domination against which Norea struggles and is victorious. When Eve gives birth to Norea, she proclaims that this daughter "is a virgin begotten as an assistance for many generations of humanity."[122] And the narrator adds that "She is the virgin whom the forces did not defile." While it is possible that Norea is the female counterpart of Seth, she supersedes Seth in the narrative. According to Anne McGuire:

> Within the narrative world of the *Hypostasis of the Archons*, Norea stands as a figure of spiritual insight and power. Like the female image in the waters, Norea is a figure whose spiritual significance cannot be grasped as if she were a "counterpart" or subordinate to the Rulers, or even to her brother Seth. She stands apart, rather, as a figure who subverts such schemes of dominance and displaces the Rulers, Seth, and perhaps even our own readings from their positions of dominance in the world of the text and the world of scholarship.[123]

121. However, there is sufficient textual ambiguity for a reader of the text to infer that Cain was not from Adam but the outcome of the rape by the Archons. Unlike the birth account of other children, Cain's birth is not preceded by a statement of Adam "knowing" his wife. The text states only that she gave birth to "their" son Cain.

122. Based on the text it has been argued that Norea is not Adam's daughter but is from Eve alone, and not from the Carnal Eve but from the Spiritual Eve. Seth and Norea are both born from the Spiritual Eve. Seth's father is Adam. In the case of Norea, no father is named, possibly indicating she, among all the offspring, is the only one from a purely spiritual source. Cf. Ingvild Sælid Gilhus, *The Nature of the archons: A Study in the Soteriology of a Gnostic Treatise from Nag Hammadi (CGII, 4)*, Studies in Oriental Religions 12 (Wiesbaden: O. Harrassowitz, 1985), 79-80.

123. McGuire, "Virginity and Subversion," in *Images of the Feminine in Gnosticism*, ed. King, 247-48.

Norea is, in a sense, the rebirth of the Spiritual principle that was taken from Eve. Seeing the Spiritual principal in Norea, the Archons are aroused and they try to pursue her and defile her, as they had done to Eve. But Norea confronts them with the truth. She names them "rulers of darkness" and thereby frees herself from their domination.[124] She tells them they did not rape her mother but a false image. She informs them that she is not their descendant but she came from the world above. Then she calls the true God of the Entirety to save her and the Great Angel, Eleleth, appears to her. Eleleth assures Norea that the Archons have no power over her for she is from the abode of Incorruptibility, from the primordial Father of Light, whereas the archons are of the fallen world. He also reveals to Norea the prehistory of the cosmos. The treatise ends with a prediction of the coming of the True Man who will reveal the Spirit of truth.

The *Hypostasis* presents the Entirety as a male being, the True Man, who will end human bondage. It further imagines that the best in the future is an existence under the Father and the Son. Such elements may be taken as indications of a patriarchal system. The intention of the text is obviously not to change or redeem the gendered social roles but to expose them.[125] Looking at the text from the perspective of Pauline and Pastoral Epistles, Gillian Beattie offers this statement:

> Even if traditional constructions of gender do remain in place, it cannot be denied that the author of *Hyp. Arch.* deploys them in a particularly striking and effective fashion. What better way to demonstrate the foolishness and inadequacies of the rulers of this (patriarchal) world than to have them outwitted by a woman? To those who might seek one, *Hyp. Arch.* offers no simple corrective to the stance adopted in the Pastoral Epistles; there are no explicit directions here for women to teach, or to free themselves from familial obligations. However, by offering a very different reading of Genesis from those found in 1 Corinthians and 1 Timothy, *Hyp. Arch.* effectively undermines the scriptural justification used by Paul and by the Pastor to authorize their

124. "Norea's speech provides a model for subverting the claims of illegitimate power through the power of the Spirit." McGuire, "Virginity and Subversion," in *Images of the Feminine in Gnosticism*, ed. King, 253.

125. King, "The Book of Norea, Daughter of Eve," in *Searching the Scriptures*, ed. Schüssler Fiorenza, 76. Further on this, Karen L. King, "Ridicule and Rape, Rule and Rebellion: The Hypostasis of the Archons," in *Gnosticism and the Early Christian World*, ed. James E. Goehring et al. (Sonoma, CA: Polebridge Press, 1990), 2-24.

> instructions on women's behaviour, and in doing so leads the reader to look at those instructions in a new light.[126]

I agree wholeheartedly. However, I think the story actually challenges patriarchal ideologies much more than the above statement acknowledges. The preponderance of female deities (Incorruptibility, Pistis Sophia, Zoe, Spirit) is remarkable. So also is the presence of extraordinary females. There is the original Spirit Woman and the Spiritual principle. Eve, her Carnal component, is down but never out and the Spiritual principle is reborn through her as Norea. Norea is the indomitable woman. With her breath she blows on the ark of Noah and causes it to be consumed with fire. With her divine faculty of speech she calls God's name and resists the Archons.

Looking at the accounts of Genesis from a very unusual perspective offers challenges as well as possibilities. The most challenging aspect of the story is the presentation of the creator God of Genesis as an arrogant and ignorant ruler or Archon who does not know what is happening. Yet this should not be an insurmountable problem if we keep in mind that the text is not making God appear foolish, it is making a mockery of a false apprehension of God.

The story reverses traditional perceptions about Adam and Eve. For instance, Adam is portrayed as inferior to the woman. Adam has a soul, an element of the world below, given to him by the Archons. But he lacks Spirit, a superior element of the world above. He receives the Spirit when she (Spirit) sees him and indwells him. When she (Spirit) is removed from his side, Adam is left once again with only a soul.

The rape of the Carnal woman is disturbing. Although she is shown as laughing and mocking the stupidity of the Archons who manage only to defile her carnal body because her Spirit has become a tree (or flown into a tree), the gang rape of her body is still violent. The split of the Spirit woman's personality into two matches what is understood in modern terms as Dissociative Identity Disorder. This term is used to define multiple personality disorder, which psychiatrists say is a survival mechanism in cases of extreme trauma when the person locks up the

126. Gillian Beattie, *Women and Marriage in Paul and His Early Interpreters* (London: T & T Clark, 2005), 146.

abusive memory in order to protect the other part of the whole, resulting in split personality.[127]

The Eve of Genesis is not raped but her fate is not any better. She is blamed for all the ills of the world. In the *Hypostasis*, the woman is not the cause of the downfall of humanity but a saviour. One of the most consistent and recurring themes of the story is the ignorance of the Archons. They are depicted as blundering fools, often comically so. They neither know what is happening, nor do they have any power to determine the course of events. In contrast, Norea shows wisdom. She is not fooled or intimidated by the Archons. She knows God's name and uses her divine speech to call on the name of God. As the ancestress of all those who know the Spirit of Truth, she transmits her power to her children, enabling them to bring down illegitimate powers of domination and expose their falsity.

Mary

Retelling the story of Mary is risky. The reason is obvious: while Mary is the most outstanding woman in the Bible,[128] she is also the most controversial figure. Among the Catholics (and to some extent, the Anglican and Orthodox Christians), she occupies an exalted position. Mary is called "Our Lady" (*Notre Dame*, *Nuestra Señora*, *Nossa Senhora*, *Madonna*) and titles such as "Mother of God" (*Theotokos*), "Queen of Heaven" (*Regina Caeli*), and "Star of the Sea" (*Stella Maris*) are used to refer to her. The Marian dogmas such as the Immaculate Conception, the belief that at the moment of her conception Mary was preserved from the stain of original sin, Perpetual Virginity, the belief that Mary was not only a virgin but continued to be so after the birth of Jesus, and Mary's Assumption, the belief that after her death or dormition she was corporeally assumed into heaven, testify to her centrality in the faith of the Catholic Church. Marian feast days, prayers, devotions, and

---

127. Jo L. Ringrose, *Understanding and Treating Dissociative Identity Disorder (or Multiple Personality Disorder)* (London: Karnac Books, 2012), 1-10; Adah Sachs and Graeme Galton, eds., *Forensic Aspects of Dissociative Identity Disorder*, Forensic Psychotherapy Monograph Series (London: Karnac Books, 2008).

128. Mary is also regarded highly in the Quran. In it, she is mentioned thirty-four times as opposed to twenty-two times in the New Testament (Matthew 5 times, Mark 2 times, Luke 12 times, John 2 times, Acts 1 time). Only one of the 114 suras or chapters of the Quran is named after a woman and that name is "Maryam" (Mary).

shrines are further expressions of the veneration of Mary. The impetus for the veneration of Mary comes not only from the official dogmas of the Catholic Church but from the movement of ordinary believers. Not least is that of reported Marian apparitions, or the appearances of Mary to individuals or groups of people, such as "Our Lady of Lourdes," "Our Lady of Guadalupe," and "Our Lady of Fatima." On the other hand, most Protestants think that the Catholic veneration of Mary is wrong and regard it as Mariolatry. Mary, in a sense, is symbolic of the chasm that exists between the Catholic and the majority of the Protestant churches.

Re-readings of Mary's story from a feminist perspective are not as frequently found in feminist literature as one would have expected given the fact that she is one of the most important, if not the most important, female figure in the Bible.[129] The widely divergent views about Mary and the zeal with which those views are supported make the story of Mary particularly difficult to deal with because any retelling of her story has to intrude into theological positions and doctrinal dogmas. Jaroslav Pelikan expresses it thus:

> Although many feminist scholars have gone to great lengths to investigate and "reclaim" the lives of women whose role in Scripture is in some cases quite modest or has been suppressed altogether, they have shown comparatively limited interest in Mary, even though among biblical women she is rivaled only by Eve as a presence in the modern world (and Eve is really a distant second). Whereas some feminists celebrate images of motherhood and childbirth in the Bible, especially when that imagery seems to have been officially discouraged, in the case of Mary they have tended not to make very much of such imagery, or to treat it with suspicion, precisely because it has been officially celebrated. When the subject of Mary does come up, the focus is often less on positive features of her religious symbolism than on irritation and impatience with any negative ones.[130]

---

129. Feminist literature on Mary is comparatively lesser as compared to other female figures of the Bible. But there are a few that adopt a radical perspective in interpreting Mary: Jane Schaberg, *The Illegitimacy of Jesus: A Feminist Theological Interpretation of the Infancy Narratives*, New ed., The Biblical Seminar 28 (Sheffield: Sheffield Academic Press, 1995); Lisa Isherwood, "Our Lady of Perpetual Succour: Mother of Phallic Fetishes? [Queering the Queen of Heaven]," in *Post-Christian Feminisms: A Critical Approach*, ed. Lisa Isherwood and Kathleen McPhillips (Aldershot: Ashgate, 2008), 117-27. A significant theological work on Mary is that of Elizabeth A. Johnson, *Truly Our Sister*.

130. Murphy, *The Word according to Eve*, 167-68.

Now, it is not my intention to enter into a protestant versus Catholic/ Orthodox debate. What I am interested in, however, is to tell to story of Mary in a way which people of my denominational persuasion do not often hear. To do that, I turn to the apocryphal work known as *Protevangelium of James*.[131] In Papyrus Bodmer V, which belongs to the third century CE, its title is "Birth of Mary. Apocalypse of James."[132] *Protevangelium of James* is believed to have been written during the second half of the second century.[133] It was widely circulated in early Christian communities. It was frequently copied and translated into many languages and survives in a number of variations. Besides its original Greek, which was highly influential in the Byzantine Empire, it has also survived in Syriac, Georgian, Latin, Irish, Armenian, Arabic, Coptic (Sahidic), Ethiopic, and Slavonic.[134] It had a profound impact on Christian art and liturgy. The text of this Gospel was read liturgically during feasts honouring Mary (birth of Mary on September 8 and the presentation of Mary in the temple on November 21). Its influence is also seen in paintings of later Christians whose artistic renderings depict scenes known only from *Protevangelium of James*.[135] The *Protevangelium of James* is akin to a Midrash (Jewish rabbinical exegesis of sacred texts) of Matthew

131. Fuller story in Appendix H: "Mary in the *Protevangelium of James*."

132. Jane Schaberg, "The Infancy of Mary of Nazareth," in *Searching the Scriptures*, vol. 2, *A Feminist Commentary*, ed. Elisabeth Schüssler Fiorenza (New York, NY: Crossroad, 1994), 710.

133. J. K. Elliott, "The Protevangelium of James," in *The Apocryphal New Testament: A Collection of Apocryphal Christian Literature in an English Translation Based on M. R. James* (Oxford: Oxford University Press, 1994), 49. Some think that it might have been written during the last quarter of the second century or the first quarter of the third century. Paul Foster, "The *Protevangelium of James*," in *The Non-Canonical Gospels*, ed. Paul Foster (London: T & T Clark, 2008), 124.

134. Oscar Cullmann, "Infancy Gospels," in *New Testament Apocrypha*, vol. 1: *Gospels and Related Writings*, rev. ed., ed. Wilhelm Schneemelcher and R. McL. Wilson (Louisville, KY: Westminster John Knox Press, 2003), 421-22.

135. W. S. Vorster, "The Annunciation of the Birth of Jesus in the *Protevangelium of James*," in *A South African Perspective on the New Testament: Essays by South African New Testament Scholars Presented to Bruce Manning Metzger During His Visit to South Africa in 1985*, ed. J. H. Petzer and P. J. Hartin (Leiden: E. J. Brill, 1986), 39; Ronald F. Hock, *The Infancy Gospels of James and Thomas: With Introduction, Notes, and Original Text Featuring the New Scholars Version Translation*, The Scholars Bible 2 (Santa Rosa, CA: Polebridge Press, 1995), 27-28.

and Luke's infancy narratives.[136] Paul Foster suggests that it should be described as "sub-canonical," or even "almost canonical."[137] Latin scholars of the sixteenth century thought that the infancy narratives of Matthew and Luke were derived from this source, the proto-Gospel, and gave it the designation "Protevangelium" (i.e. "first gospel").[138] According to the *Protevangelium of James* 25.1, its author is James the step-brother of Jesus by Joseph's first marriage but this is an instance of the ancient practice of ascribing authorship of a document to a prominent figure in order to give it a stamp of authority.[139] The author is, in fact, unknown. But he (or she) may not have been a Jew as he (or she) appears to be ignorant about Palestinian geography and Jewish customs. Before proceeding, it is necessary to provide a summary of the *Protevangelium of James*.

Joachim, a wealthy man, is unhappy and ashamed before righteous Israel because he has no offspring unlike other righteous men. Anna, his wife, also laments her fate and she feels worthless because of her childlessness. Their prayers are answered when an angel appears to Anna and tells her that she will become pregnant and give birth. Joachim too receives a similar message from an angel. Accordingly, Anna conceives and gives birth to Mary.

Mary is brought up with no chance of corruption. From the time she is six months old, her mother makes a sanctuary in her bedroom and allows only undefiled (virgin) Jewish girls to serve the child. When Mary is three years old, she is taken to the temple where the priests bless and receive her. Mary is raised in the temple in complete innocence. When she is twelve, following the advice of an angel of the Lord to Zacharias,

136. Elliott, "The Protevangelium of James," in *The Apocryphal New Testament*, 48-52.

137. Foster, "The *Protevangelium of James*," in *The Non-Canonical Gospels*, ed. Foster, 124. In Orthodoxy it is regarded as an important text. Roman Catholicism rejected it because of its failure to preserve Joseph's virginity. However, its influence on the Mariology of the Catholic Church is undeniable.

138. Pheme Perkins, *Introduction to the Synoptic Gospels* (Grand Rapids, MI: William B. Eerdmans, 2007), 246.

139. The Eastern Orthodox Churches, deriving from *Protevangelium of James*, hold that "the brothers (and sisters) of Jesus" (Mark 6:3 Cf. Matt 13:56 has "sisters") are Jesus' step-brothers and step-sisters from Joseph's prior marriage. The Roman Catholic Church holds that "the brothers (and sisters) of Jesus" are his cousins based on the teaching of Jerome who insisted that both Mary but Joseph were virgins. Hence the Roman Catholic Church has tended to emphasize a later text, the *Pseudo-Gospel of Matthew*, which is a Latin compilation of the sixth century.

the high priest, Mary is given to the care of an old widower named Joseph.[140] This is a chaste relationship in which Mary is Joseph's ward and not his wife. So as soon as he brings Mary to his house, Joseph leaves her, going away to build his buildings.

One day an angel informs Mary that she will become pregnant and give birth to the Son of the Most High (echoes of Luke 2:26-38). Mary is sixteen years old at this time. When she was six months along in her pregnancy, Joseph comes home to find her pregnant. Joseph feels that he has failed in his duty to protect the virgin. But an angel comes to him in a dream and assures him that the child in Mary is from the Holy Spirit and tells him to call his name Jesus (echoes of Matt 1:18-25). Mary's pregnancy is also discovered by the priests in the temple. They make Joseph and Mary drink the water of conviction to test their innocence, which is proved when the water does no harm to either of them.

A decree of a census of Bethlehem and Judea from King Augustus compels Joseph to undertake a journey with the pregnant Mary and two of his sons. Halfway through the journey, they take shelter in a cave because the time for Mary's delivery is near. Joseph finds a midwife but as they approach the entrance of the cave they see a bright cloud covering the cave. Then the cloud disappears but it is followed by a blinding light. When they are able to see again, they see the baby appear and take the breast of its mother.[141] The midwife goes and tells Salome (introduced into the narrative without introduction) that a virgin has given birth to a child.[142] Salome is sceptical and she comes to the cave and sticks her

---

140. According to Pieter W. van der Horst, Joseph is presented as being around 50 to 55 years; deduced from Joseph calling himself old. "A *presbytês* is not yet a *gerôn*, but it often indicates a person of about 50-55 years." The author is putting a gap of about 40 years between Mary and Joseph not only to suggest the unlikelihood of a sexual relationship between Joseph and Mary but also as a means of explaining the brothers and sisters of Jesus in the canonical Gospels. Pieter W. van der Horst, "Sex, Birth, Purity and Asceticism in the *Protevangelium Jacobi*," in *A Feminist Companion to Mariology*, ed. Amy-Jill Levine and Maria Mayo Robbins (London: T & T Clark International, 2005), 62.

141. The baby simply appears. Obviously, the blinding light serves not only to suggest that a sacred event is taking place but also enables the "birth" to take place without pain, blood, and mess.

142. For a discussion of the possibility that a "Doubting Salome" story was introduced from a pre-existing account see George Themelis Zervos, "Christmas with Salome," in *A Feminist Companion to Mariology*, ed. Amy-Jill Levine and Maria Mayo Robbins (London: T & T Clark International, 2005), 77-98.

finger in to examine Mary.[143] Immediately, Salome screams out at the calamity that has befallen her, for due to her unbelief and lawlessness her hand is falling away from her and on fire. When she repents for her misdeed, an angel directs her to touch the child and she is healed. The narrative jumps to an account of a tumult in Bethlehem, wise men, Herod, and a star that leads the wise men to the cave, the return of the wise men to their country by another route, and Herod's massacre of children (echoes of Matt 2). Mary hides her baby from Herod by wrapping him in swaddling clothes and laying him in an ox-manger. Elizabeth runs with her baby, John, to the hill country and a mountain opens up and hides them in its bowels. Zacharias, the high priest, is questioned and killed in the temple. His body disappears and his blood turns into stone. The story ends with the narrator identifying himself as James and that the account is written during the disturbance during the time of the death of Herod, implying that the document comes from the time when Jesus is still an infant.

As apocryphal texts were regarded differently from canonical gospels, it was easier to add in stories to apocryphal texts. This means that some portions of the *Protevangelium of James* could be later than the second century. However, it is also very likely that the text includes material from an earlier source.[144] The *Protevangelium of James* attempts to provide the details that are missing in the gospels. The author claims that Jesus did not come from a poor family. Joseph is a building contractor. Mary is not guilty of sexual irregularity. Her conception of Jesus is a virginal conception and his birth too preserves her virginity (virginity *in partu* and *post partum*). And the brothers and sisters of Jesus who are mentioned in the gospels are actually Joseph's children from a previous marriage. Mary's lineage is traced back to David, which has apologetic significance if Joseph's Davidic ancestry was being considered irrelevant because he was not the biological father of Jesus. It is believed that the composition is a defence of Christianity from accusations levelled against it by the likes of

143. This is obviously a reference to an examination of her hymen. van der Horst, "Sex, Birth, Purity and Asceticism in the *Protevangelium Jacobi*," in *A Feminist Companion to Mariology*, ed. Levine and Robbins, 62.

144. George Themelis Zervos, "Dating the *Protevangelium of James*: The Justin Martyr Connection," in *Society of Biblical Literature Seminar Papers, 1994*, SBLSP 33, ed. Eugene H. Lovering (Atlanta: Scholars Press, 1994), 415–34; idem, "An Early Non-Canonical Annunciation Story," in *Society of Biblical Literature Seminar Papers, 1997*, SBLSP 36 (Atlanta: Scholars Press, 1997), 664–91.

the Syrian Jew in Celsus' *Logos Alethes* (*True Doctrine*, ca. 178 CE; found in Origen's *Against Celsus*) who ridiculed the idea of virginal conception and mocked the lowly origins of Jesus, that he was the illegitimate son of a soldier named Panthera.[145] But this analysis has to go beyond the apologetic function of the text.

In retelling the story of Mary using *Protevangelium of James*, what new things can we learn? Does this document render the image of Mary better or worse? Mary F. Foskett summarises the positive image of Mary portrayed in *Protevangelium of James*.

> Even a cursory reading of the *Protevangelium of James* reveals something significant about the portrayal of Mary, the mother of Jesus, in this early Christian narrative. In a word, she is different. She is different – not only from other women (*Prot. Jas.* 11.6), but different also from the Mary we discover in reading the Gospel of Luke. For example, the Lukan Mary bears little social status. The Gospel mentions only a few details concerning the circumstances in which we find her, and almost nothing is said of her family and kin. In contrast, the Jacobean Mary is born into a wealthy family, a great deal is made of her parents' standing within Israel, and the text repeatedly details the circumstances in which she lives and the characters with whom she interacts. Mary is a figure of significant standing and the central protagonist of the later narrative.[146]

Foskett sees the portrayal of Mary as a virgin (παρθένος) whose virginity (παρθενία) is intact not only before marriage (as in the Gospels) but even after childbirth, as the most striking feature of the apocryphal text. According to Foskett, Mary's virginity serves an encomiastic purpose, to express her purity par excellence. Thus she becomes "a sacred object."[147] However, she notes in the end that the *Protevangelium of James* promotes an androcentric perspective.

In contrast to Foskett's generally positive analysis of the *Protevangelium of James*, Jane Schaberg is highly critical of the obsession with Mary's virginity in the document.

145. Schaberg, "The Infancy of Mary of Nazareth," in *Searching the Scriptures*, ed. Schüssler Fiorenza, 718; Cullmann, "Infancy Gospels," in *New Testament Apocrypha*, ed. Schneemelcher and Wilson, 417.

146. Mary F. Foskett, "Virginity as Purity in the *Protevangelium of James*," in *A Feminist Companion to Mariology*, ed. Amy-Jill Levine and Maria Mayo Robbins (London: T & T Clark International, 2005), 67.

147. Foskett, "Virginity as Purity in the *Protevangelium of James*," in *A Feminist Companion to Mariology*, ed. Levine and Robbins, 76.

> Many of the themes of future Mariology are present here in embryonic form. But is the aim of the author "the glorification of Mary," as all previous commentators have argued? I think not. This reading of the texts of Matthew and Luke aims primarily to defeat and silence an alternative reading, the tradition of Jesus' illegitimacy. The notion of God's miraculous action in creating this pregnancy seems designed to overwhelm and blot out any suspicion of negative male sexual behavior involved in the appearance of the Christ, to ward off any slurs that might stain him, and to protect God's honor. What results is a deforming constriction of the Lukan character of Mary, the dehumanizing of Jesus, and the despotization of God.[148]

Jane Schaberg insists that in comparison to Mary's depiction in the Gospel of Luke, her character is reduced and deformed in the *Protevangelium of James*. In the latter work, Mary is not a woman of faith who decides to submit herself to the plan of God. She is not the woman who functions as a prophet in uttering her Magnificat. The account centres on her virginity but it is not her choice. Her mother chooses it for her before she is conceived, and then her parents, the priests, and Joseph keep her in it. About her conception she consents to the angel's words but she forgets about it so that she is perplexed when she becomes pregnant. She is passive; does not exercise judgment, makes not decision, shows no virtue, barely speaks, and never prays. The *Protevangelium of James* also depicts God as a despot. God uses Mary and her sexuality to make her the mother of the Saviour. The episode of Salome's disbelief and her punishment shows how this God punishes those who doubt Mary's virginity.

Schaberg points out that in the second and third centuries CE big numbers of Christian women chose the ascetic life and devoted themselves to a life of continence and virginity (cf. 1 Cor 7:34). This choice enabled them to live autonomous and independent lives and participate actively in public life. Thus women lived marriage-free lives in order to realise the egalitarian life of the Jesus movement. But in the *Protevangelium of James* the emphasis on virginity is not from the perspective of offering liberation, empowerment, or independence to women. Schaberg concludes:

> This story should not be ignored. It depicts restrictive aspects of the lives of millions of women on our globe even today, women whose lives are hemmed in, hounded and bullied by traditions and customs not of their making, women

148. Schaberg, "The Infancy of Mary of Nazareth," in *Searching the Scriptures*, ed. Schüssler Fiorenza, 720-21.

> glorified but denied equality. At the same time, the story of the spinster Virgin Mary has been and can be read as supporting a woman's right or calling to be consecrated, the right not to marry, not to have children, not to have male-dominated heterosexual relations, not to live a life focused on the needs of men. Never, however, the right not to mother.[149]

As well, Bettina Eltrop and Claudia Janssen highlight the negative presentation of Mary in the *Protevangelium of James*. They maintain that "the changes the Protevangelium of James undertakes involve thoroughgoing losses compared with the New Testament tradition."[150] Although they do not refer to Schaberg, they echo most of what she says. According to their analysis, despite the inclusion of traditions handed by woman and the presence of a good number of women, the *Protevangelium of James* is not favourable to women. Its interest in women is limited to their reproductive capabilities and issues about their sexuality. Women are always in the background as wives, undefiled daughters, and virgins, who have no control over their own sexuality. Mary never has a life or thought of her own. She is passed from her parents to the male priests in the temple and then to Joseph.

In my opinion the portrayal of Mary in the *Protevangelium of James* is not an acceptable example for women. Its character of Mary is an unnatural model. Whereas Jesus becomes human to save humanity, in the *Protevangelium of James* Mary becomes non-human, devoid of sexual passion and lacking personality in order to be exalted. In effect, she becomes one that no human, whether male or female, would emulate; not simply because it is impossible but more so because it is undesirable. This does not mean her story should not be told. Although her story is unacceptable as an illustration of how godly women should live, it can be powerful as an example of how patriarchal Church and society manipulate and control women's sexuality so that we, like Mary, are made to have no right over our own bodies and no voice to tell our own stories. Another way of re-reading and re-imagining Mary's story would be to start with the question, "Where is the real Mary?" as a hermeneutical

149. Schaberg, "The Infancy of Mary of Nazareth," in *Searching the Scriptures*, ed. Schüssler Fiorenza, 726.

150. Bettina Eltrop and Claudia Janssen, "Protevangelium of James: God's Story Goes On," in *Feminist Biblical Interpretation: A Compendium of Critical Commentary on the Books of the Bible and Related Literature*, ed. Luise Schottroff and Marie-Theres Wacker (Grand Rapids, MI: Wm B. Eerdmans, 2012), 995.

lens for viewing the disappearance of the human Mary and actualising the flesh-and-blood Mary in our own lives today.

Looking at the stories of Lilith, Eve, Norea, and Mary afresh can be a liberating experience for women as well as men. The problem with the Bible is not only that it has been interpreted from patriarchal perspectives but that the text itself is hostile towards women.[151] The use of extra-biblical sources enables us to think about these women beyond the confines of what we have been taught over many years. Referring to those sources does not mean questioning the authority of the Bible. Rather, they offer us new ways of looking at biblical narratives by widening our frame of reference.

Tribal Storytelling in Worship

I have just stated that women can re-imagine and re-tell the stories of the Bible creatively in order to make it a liberating experience for women as well as men. Expanding our frame of reference by taking insights from sources other than the Bible helps us to see things differently. In this section, I want to discuss how tribals can tell their stories in worship. Tribal culture has been preserved in the past through the oral transmission of the great stories of the people from generation to generation. Not all tribal stories are applicable or good. This is because tribal culture is also deeply patriarchal. So my focus will be on ways of telling stories in tribal ways that are helpful for women and consequently lead to greater equity in worship.

The poem, entitled *Anga Me·chik* (I, a Woman), written by a woman named Jonmoni in 1940 in Achikku, the language of the A·chik people tells the story of an A·chik woman who laments her fate as a woman.[152]

Anga Me·chik	I, a Woman
Atchiaba me·chik ong·e *Pilak dukko ra·na,* *Sinteoba mikkang chone* *Amjaba namatna.*	Born a female All sorrows to bear, Lament with downcast face Cannot make it better.

151. Katheryn Pfisterer Darr, *Far More Precious Than Jewels: Perspectives on Biblical Women* (Louisville, KY: Westminster John Knox, 1991), 35-37.

152. Translation is mine. The A·chik version is found in Jonmoni D. Shira, "Anga Me'chik," in *A·chik Poedorang*, 3rd ed., comp. L. D. Shira (Tura: Hawakhana Book Emporium, 1994), 37-39. Used by permission.

Hoba da·nang papko dake
Mesokjok a·sakna,
Jrimbata balrang jajrenge
Re·bajok me·chikna.

Poor Hoba [Eve] committed sin
Has shown the world,
Heavier loads and worries
Has come to the woman.

Atchianin bil kombata
Mikkang nitobata
Me·asani ning·o dongna
Skiakosa man·a.

From birth, of less power
The face is prettier,
To stay under men
Was taught, and received.

Dambemiting salrangonin
Dongna nangjok ning·o,
Jonggipani satkapanan
Grapaijok a·brobro.

From tender days
Have to stay beneath.
A slap from the younger brother
Cried and wailed loudly.

Skatang re·pana man·ja
Sukni salan dong·ja,
Songrepana ina kata
Jumanggitan nikja.

Cannot go out freely
There's not a single happy day.
"To travel," that kind of word
Did not see even in dreams.

Uipaachim gisikchide
Kattachongmotkoan,
Nama namja mai ong·gen
Katta bichongkoan.

At least I know, in my mind
The truth about the word (travel),
The good, the bad, what might happen
The root of the word.

Indioba man·pajake
Ku·sa agannaan,
Jrip dongbo Me·chik gisikgri
Ina kattanaan.

Even then, it is not possible
To speak a word
Keep quiet, you stupid woman!
Was the comment.

Atchongpana cha·chedamo,
Cha·pana gitchaako,
Mandeskaan sola man·a
Chonaatna an·tangkon.

To sit on a pile of husks
And eat the leftovers,
Ridiculed by fellow humans
To make one feel small.

Chame ane nanggipako
Anga mikchpaoba,
Angni namnikgijanasa
Ku·chakdraatjok angko.

Having a beloved
Even if I fall in love,
The one that I don't like
I am forced to give my consent.

Panterangna mikchapaoba
Duksa ong·aiake,
Angni chona gualanan
Angko wataiake!

Even if I fall in love with the bachelors
It just makes me sad,
For my small mistake
They rejected me.

O, Pante gisik rakbone
Kamrang gimaijane,
Basakoba dukni walo

O young man, know this
The deeds do not simply disappear,
Sometime into a night of sorrow

Na·a ga·akgene.	You too might fall.
Da·o anga me·amajok	Now I am a mother
Duksa baribajok,	Sorrows have increased,
Deko ba·e sitengtona	Bearing children in agonising pain
Angni kamanjok.	Has become my work.
On·timinti gualanan	For a little mistake
Angko satkapaijok,	I was just slapped,
Deni grapanan da·nang	For the child's cry
Walo mikrakaijok!	Had to wake up at night
Angni duk saknako da·nang	Poor me, my sorrows and pains
Uipaja angse,	My husband doesn't know,
Sabisirang bang·bataba	My sicknesses have increased
Da·nang angna gose.	O, poor me! Woe is me!
Walo walni chakatean	Getting up before the break of dawn
Anga miko song·jok,	I cooked rice,
Salgimiko a·baosa	Whole day in the field
Salko re·ataijok.	The day was spent.
Balko ole re·bapiljok	Returned home carrying a heavy load
Noko kamko ka·jok,	Did the works at home,
Waltingoba neng·takjajok	Did not rest till late night
Miko su·na nangjok.	For I had to pound rice.
Neng·skime be·en ram·jok	Out of exhaustion my body grew thin
Anga nitojajok,	I am not beautiful anymore,
Angse da·nang sakgipinko	Poor me, my husband
Am·na gisik najok.	Started to look for another.
Indioba angni gisik	But my mind
Rongtala chanchijok,	Has pure thoughts,
Angse onai dakengoba	Though my husband insults me
Anga chakaijok.	I just bear it.
Janggirangde jrip dongja	The souls do not keep quiet
Na·a dal·batjawa.	You (husband) will never be superior,
Nang·ni kamrangni bite	As a result of your deeds
Noroknin jokjawa.	You will not escape from hell.
Uni gimin me·asa na·a	Therefore, you man,
Gisiko mikrakbo.	Keep this in mind,
Me·chikrangni dukrangkode	The sorrows of women
Na·a nichongmotbo.	You have to look into.
Angni katta ong·jaode	If my word is not correct

Na·a jee galbo,	You can reject it,
Na·a an·tang gualode	But if you are the one who is at fault
Da·on gisik pil·bo.	Repent right now.

Jonmoni's story is representative of the stories of women in North East India. There are so many women who would identify with Jonmoni's experience.

For instance, Antyle tells the stories of Ningtingle, Rianile, and Aramle (names changed to protect persons involved). Ningtingle is forced into marriage at the age of 16. Her husband who happens to be a drunkard, abuses her. He keeps telling her that she is ugly and to go back to her house. After five years of marriage, he deserts her and their three children. To support herself and her children, she starts selling liquor. Her society regards women who sell liquor as prostitutes and so she is rejected by her family, her in-laws, her church, and her society. Rianile is married to a well-to-do medical doctor who dominates her life. She has to do all the household chores. He treats her like a servant and not like a wife or partner. She is caught in this oppressive marriage and continues to experience physical and mental abuse every day. Similarly, Aramle lives with a husband who batters her for no reason. Often, he pulls her hair and drags her from one room to another. And habitually he punches her as he would if he were fighting with other men. His argument is that women should be beaten just as drums are beaten. She cannot go to visit her parents or her neighbours because that would result in more beatings.[153]

So Jonmoni's story resonates in the lives of many women. The hearer may think that hers is a story of abuse, discrimination, and suffering of a woman. Of course, those features are part of the story but the important point is that Jonmoni made this a legitimate text for women's narrative in a society dominated by patriarchal discourse. By telling her story, Jonmoni finds a medium to communicate with others. This is significant because it breaks the silence. It is inability to tell stories, lack of discursive space to communicate their thoughts, and absence of opportunity to narrate their experiences that alienates women from community. Communication, the fundamental component of human existence, is needed by everyone in order for us to articulate a sense of our self and the community we live in.

153. Antyle, "Zeliangrong Women Experiences: Challenges and Theological Reflection in the Light of the Nazareth Manifesto," in *No More Sorrow in God's Garden of Justice: Tribal Women Doing Theology*, ed. Limatula Longkumer (Jorhat, Assam: Women Study Department, Eastern Theological College, 2007), 147-49.

An important theoretical basis of my study is that we make stories and those stories make us who we are. Our stories define who we are because others know us through our stories. In the act of telling her story, Jonmoni concretises her suffering and doing so enables her to transcend it. She is no longer storyless. And because she told her story, other women who hear her story are able to find echoes of their own experiences in it. Her story establishes commonness and solidarity between her and her listeners. By communicating and sharing a story, they become more coherent as a community. Jonmoni's story may not resonate as strongly for men and women who have grown up in more privileged societies, for narrative is always interpreted on the grid of our social, cultural, and personal experiences. But if they listen with sympathetic ears, narrative has the potential to open new worlds of experiences. Hearers who may not have suffered like Jonmoni are still able to empathise with her because stories trigger the imagination and allow those who are outside the narrative to experience it in the act of hearing. This is really why storytelling is so important—to connect people from diverse cultures who would not have a clue about the other unless there is a story to help them imagine what the other experienced. Any storytelling needs two performers—one to tell the story and another to listen. Both teller and listener relive the story. Storytelling needs reciprocal cooperation that establishes or renews the relationship between the teller of the story and its hearer. Thus the story establishes commonness and solidarity between the storyteller and the listeners and thereby initiates community. It enables the stranger, the refugee, the alien, the gay or lesbian, the other gender, or whoever is different from us to become familiar.

Community, as I see it, is not a homogenous group of people in a specified geographical location or any group unified by religion, profession, culture, or interests. Community means communication and communion across ethnic diversity, gender divide, and varieties of religious conviction. In a sense, community is people woven together by a tapestry of stories.

A new orientation about what constitutes a story, how stories are told, and how they should be heard is needed. It is important to recognize that women and men do not narrate and interpret their narratives in the same way. Women's stories are not only different, but the way they tell their stories is also different. Women's narrative counters the hegemony of patriarchal discourse that excludes and marginalizes women. In religious narrative a woman cannot celebrate her sexuality. Nor is she allowed to forget it. A woman, Eve, is the archetype of human weakness and sin.

Another woman, Mary, is epitomized as the perpetual virgin mother. Thus in the Christian world, women are placed in an untenable situation. We are loathed for being morally weak. We are seen as prone to tempt men into depravity. Our sexuality is seen to be a threat. Renouncing bodily pleasures is propounded as a virtue. Thus in religious life, women are constrained to become what they are not, to suppress their sexuality, to suspect their thoughts and emotions, and to live according to the dictates of men.

Rediscovering women's narrative is an attempt to establish the links of communication and the bond of communion and community between women and men. To do that, we have to debunk patriarchal discourses that disguise themselves as universal truths rather than discourses of power and domination. However women's narrative is not just meant to rival patriarchal narratives. Its purpose is to create inclusive community. It encourages pluralism instead of setting a standard by which everybody must abide. We expect, in community, the presence of many voices telling many stories. Not surprisingly, women's narrative text differs from traditional forms of public communication such as published treatises, formal books, academic writings, and transcripts of speeches or statements of heads of state or qualified people. We turn instead to private diaries, letters, songs, poems, paintings, and personal prayers. We also use dance, craft, drama, and signs and symbols from the activities of daily life and various creative forms to tell our stories.

These theoretical foundations for interpreting stories and storytelling are significant for the application of storytelling in worship. The basis for storytelling in worship in the tribal communities of North East India comes the notion put forward by theologians and feminist liturgists, which is that our personal stories are sacred stories. The text of our life is the script of our sacred worship. By telling our stories in worship, we will reinvent ourselves and redeem sacred space not only for women but for all.

Tribal ways of telling stories are not based on formal categories. They are spontaneous and informal. Thus tribal women's storytelling implies changing the existing model of sitting rigidly and silently in church to be preached at, as though divinity will be displeased or disappear from the place of worship if members other than the preacher make noise. Tribal women's storytelling entails changing the practice of standing and sitting only when asked to do so, as though the clergy/leader has greater authority than others and subservience to them is worship to God. Tribal women's storytelling also necessitates changing the physical arrangement of worship space, making it like a warm home where people are gathered around the fireplace to eat, drink, and share stories. Storytelling obliges us to change the way we preach, the way we read biblical narratives, and the way we pray as we interweave the stories of our life with these elements of worship. Storytelling in worship understands that oral narration is only one of the ways of communicating. It envisages new forms of storytelling such as through songs, poems, paintings, and crafts like weaving. In an inclusive tribal worship, there has to be dialogical singing that initiates conversation between women and men and also conversation between women from diverse backgrounds. There will be new rituals that blur the distinctions between the sacred and the profane. Such rituals may re-enact the act of weaving, remembering the contribution of women to tribal history and culture in the patterns that are visually presented to the worshipping community. Acknowledging the contribution of women is recognising their worth and their indispensability to the community. Furthermore, in the re-enactment is a rediscovery of the function of women as storytellers of the tribe. The task of storytelling is two-fold—telling the stories of the past and making new stories. Before stories are told, stories have to be made. A story is made when we inhabit an experience and give it meaning. Women who tell stories are story-makers first before they become storytellers. Thus in storytelling the past meets the future.

7

CONCLUSION: AS ONE

Finally, it is time sum up the research, to highlight the main points I have made along the way, and say a few words about what I consider to be prospects for the future of inclusive worship in the Baptist churches of North East India. The objective of the research was to employ an eclectic method that combines the theoretical principles of narrative theory and communication studies—"a narrative communication approach"—to look at the content and practice of worship in order to evolve a model of storytelling for inclusive worship.

I began by articulating the method of research. Although communication studies and narrative theory are two distinct disciplines, they share a close affinity. The most obvious is that narrative is a form of communication. Besides that, narrative fulfils the purpose of Christian communication, which is to establish relationship between people by referring to their shared experiences and alluding to their perceptions of the world or of religious belief. Communication is synonymous with communion and community. Communication creates community and communion. Story, as the most powerful form of communication, can be employed to create community and foster communion. The need for women to tell their stories is particularly urgent because patriarchal discourse is a barrier to true communication as it silences women's narratives. Without narratives of their own, women are compelled to communicate with language and categories that stem from men's experiences and men's ways of thinking and doing. Thus women continue to use communication systems that insult women, vilify them, and regard them as inferior to men.

Narrative communication looks to recover women's stories because community will remain imperfect unless women's stories become part of the community's stories. While recovering women's stories, it has to be understood that women tell their stories differently from men. The signifiers women use—the signs, symbols, and words—are different from the narrative system that patriarchal discourse has established as the normative paradigm.

An important aspect of the theoretical assumption of narrative communication is the construal of story and storytelling. We live in a world designed by stories. Life itself is comprehensible to us because of the stories it tells us. We also make ourselves coherent to each other by means of our stories. In other words, we make stories and our stories make us. Stories invite the hearers to experience something different, to feel the joy, angst, fear, doubt, or anything else felt by the storyteller, and to view something from a different perspective. Stories draw the hearers into the world of the story and transform them because a person cannot remain the same after experiencing a different way of looking at the world. When stories are misinterpreted or misunderstood they can create friction and fissure in the community. However, stories that are understood and appreciated by responsive hearers can bring reconciliation and healing of relationships. Stories trigger the imagination so that those who are healthy can imagine what it is like to be sick, and those who are at the centre can imagine what it is like to be at the margins. Thus stories broaden the scope of community and foster cohesion within the community.

In chapter two, I attempted to explain why the space of worship needs to be revamped because of its apartheid against women. The language of worship reflects cultures in which women are regarded as nonpersons and men rule over women. The predominance of masculine pronouns in hymns and liturgies sends the message that women are unimportant. The tribal languages of North East India do not have gender-differentiating pronouns and so there is a distinct advantage for tribal people to rely more on their tribal language in reading and interpreting the Bible. However, unfortunately, tribals have not been able to resist Western influence. Consequently, English masculine pronouns have found their way into tribal conceptualisations of biblical teachings. The androcentric language of worship is further buttressed by the literal interpretation of biblical passages that demean women. Women are told to cover their heads because of 1 Cor 11:4-6, a symbolic action that is seen as depicting their lowly status in the presence of men and of the male God. Because of some other Pauline injunctions such as 1 Cor 14:34-35 and Tim 2:11-12, women in many churches of the region are not allowed to preach or teach in church and are cut off from full participation in church ministry. These biblical passages have become interlinked with tribal patriarchal culture in such a way that speaking for women's equal participation is seen as going against both biblical teachings and tribal culture.

At the heart of the segregation of women in worship is the theological construction of God as a male being. In English language the problem is at the very roots of the word God. For "God" is a masculine noun. The use of masculine pronouns for God may be avoided by repeating the word "God" or by using gender neutral metaphors, but that does not solve the problem because the word "God" still connotes a male deity. I do not know how the English-speaking world will eventually resolve this problem. However, in the context of tribals, the use of personal names for God sidesteps the masculine word "God." Then there are the concepts about Jesus. Theologically, Jesus has been depicted as Black, Hispanic, Indic, Chinese, and other ethnic representations. These images are regarded as cultural expressions of Jesus. However, most people that I know cannot accept a female Jesus. This is because gender is considered to be the defining characteristic of Jesus. The maleness of Jesus has become a stumbling block for the equal participation of women in Church ministry for it is argued that women cannot represent the male Jesus and the male Father God. The concept of a male God and a male Saviour combines to give the impression that male language adequately defines the divine. The male becomes the norm and so to be female is to be an oddity. Of the three persons of the Trinity, the concept of the Holy Spirit is most amenable for an inclusive image of divinity. The Holy Spirit encapsulates the notion of the feminine divine. However, in the doctrinal pronouncements the Holy Spirit is made subservient to the purpose of the "Father" God and the "Son" Jesus.

In chapter three, I explored the dimensions of koinonia, particularly Trinitarian koinonia which is a great model for a community in communion that shares a common life. The raison d'être for an egalitarian community arises from the mutual indwelling of the Trinity expressed in John 14-17, which does not lead to a merging of the persons and a loss of identity. The persons of the Trinity exist in communion but continue to maintain their distinctiveness from one another. Likewise, unity in the community is to be expressed in diversity. In the second part of the chapter, I looked at the significance of the presence of the Holy Spirit in the community. In order to broach a pneumatology, I compared the experience of the Holy Spirit as described in the book of Acts and the experience of the Holy Spirit among the people of North East India. Acts describes the early days of the spirit-filled Church as a time of impartiality and egalitarianism when women received the Holy Spirit and spiritual gifts along with male believers. Women were very prominent in the early Church, holding leadership positions in house churches, in ordained ministry, and in missionary work. However, as the enthusiasm died down, women's role in ministry was curbed and replaced by a male-oriented hierarchical Church structure. A similar thing happened with the revival movement or movements that swept across North East India during the early twentieth century. The revival started in the Khasi hills and spread to the Mizo region, and from there to the Kuki tribes and the Tangkhul Nagas, and then to the Nagas of Nagaland. The filling of the Holy Spirit was characterised by the reception of ecstatic gifts such as seeing visions, prophesying, and speaking in tongues. These revival movements enabled women to break free from the constraints of a deeply patriarchal culture as they exercised their gifts of the Holy Spirit. They were not challenged because their activity was perceived as prompted or initiated by the power of God. However, as the revival fires died down and churches became organised, women were excluded from the life and ministry of the Church. The analysis of the experience of the Holy Spirit in the early Church and among the tribals of North East India indicates that the Holy Spirit breaks down barriers that separate one section of the community from another. The presence of the Holy Spirit in the community therefore implies the existence of an inclusive community in which men and women participate as equals.

Chapter four is about what worship should be especially in light of the view that the Church is an inclusive community of believers. The theological rationale for inclusive worship comes from the notion that the purpose of humanity is to enjoy God and give glory to God in worship. In further explication of community and worship, I refer to the values in tribal communitarian life. Tribal practice of sharing and helping can contribute to a deeper understanding of the Christian concept of koinonia. At the same time, tribal patriarchal culture in tandem with patriarchal Church structures inherited from the West stand in the way of the realization of Church as an egalitarian and inclusive community. Churches may speak of all being baptized into the one body of Christ but in practice there are hierarchical forms of leadership in the Church, implying that some are spiritually superior to others. The churches have to evaluate their discriminatory practices and seek equality in worship. A "roundtable" which has no sides, no head, and no preferred seating aptly captures the image of a Church that is not based on the exercise of power and domination but on fellowship. This in essence is what I construe to be the ultimate goal of the feminist enterprise. It is not to have females become the dominant force in place of males nor to have an equal number of males and female members in the committees and other bodies. It is to transform worship so that men and women see themselves as equally sinful and equally saved and none superior or inferior to the other.

I argued that Christian community can be built through a recovery of the significance of the Lord's Supper and Baptism. The recovery of their meaning takes place in conversation with the theological and doctrinal debates that have enmeshed them over the centuries. Contrary to the general tendency to interpret the Lord's Supper as a symbolic ritual, I agreed with other scholars that it was a common meal that reflected the sharing of all resources in the community founded on Jesus' proclamation of an alternative way of life. Regarding baptism, it was observed that while there is plenty of discord among various Christian denominations, there is room for greater understanding and acceptance of each other's practices. Baptism, as I see it, is not dependent on the manner in which a person is baptised. It is not primarily an initiation into denominational church. Baptism is initiation into a new humanity and a new value system. Thus in its fullest sense, baptism is new creation. By means of baptism the barrier between Jews and Gentiles, male and female, slave and free is broken and all share a new identity as a new community.

In chapter five, I tried to delineate models of worship that follow storytelling principles or have story as a central component of worship. A women's worship initiative to tell women's stories in worship is an attempt to legitimate women's narrative as inseparable from sacred narrative. However, women's stories cannot be told unless they are first recovered. Women have been rendered storyless by traditional ways of worship (liturgy). Because we are storyless, we continue to have to derive our identity from the dominant male in our family whether it is a father, a brother, or a husband. Storytelling in worship aims to turn women's silence into speech, to ritualize and make sacred women's experiences, and to tell of our storylessness and make it a story too. It asserts that women are no longer willing to live as stereotypes within the stories of men but that women wish to make themselves known in and by their own story.

Storytelling in worship may be thought of as a project aimed at finding sacred space for women. An explication of sacred space includes a new arrangement of physical space that represents the equality of the gathered. It also involves the liberation of liturgy from androcentric language and patriarchal concepts. Using non-sexist language in hymns, prayers, and other aspects of the liturgy is a primary step but not the central factor. Transforming the liturgy requires much more intrusive surgery than changing words, although it is understood that without changing the sexist language there is no possibility of moving forward. Beyond the use of gender neutral language, liturgical transformation requires new ways of reading the Bible, new songs to sing, new symbols to represent, and new ways of narrating our lives. For the Christians of North East India, I proposed new ways of imagining and naming God derived from our stories. Likewise, our ways of praying arise from our contextual locations so that we are able to pray with our stories embedded in poetry, dance, or music and in non-hierarchical space. Sermons are a particular worship activity that can be transformed by storytelling (to be distinguished from narrative preaching). Telling stories in sermons need not necessarily be oral narration; it can be enacted in drama, play, skit, dance, or some other style of performance. Rituals too can be transformed by our stories. Rituals such as the Lord's Supper can be revitalised by interweaving it with personal, community, and family stories. At the same time, we can also develop new rituals around important events of our lives (such as welcoming a birth, facing death, young people courting, and celebrating marriage) as well as unexpected moments in life (such as miscarriage and stillbirth, divorce, adoption, and the like). Ritualizing the act of weaving is seen as a pertinent medium for telling the stories of women, acknowledging women as makers of tribal culture and pointing towards the creation of new stories.

Transforming worship involves re-imagining biblical stories. Tribal women need to understand that biblical interpretation is a place of ideological struggles. Women have to resist traditional forms of interpreting the Bible from patriarchal perspectives. We have to read as women, using creative imagination to reconstruct and recover biblical stories of women. In my search to discover how the two primary women in the Bible, Eve and Mary, can be re-imagined I turned to extra-biblical sources. So I retold the story of Lilith and Norea to complement Eve's story and offer a perspective that had been lost. Lilith is the opposite of Eve. Her story is found in the *Alphabet of Ben Sira 23*. She is Adam's first wife who insists on her equality with Adam and flees from the garden to escape his dominance. Traditional interpretations of Eve's story blame her for bringing sin to the world. However, there are other ways of looking at Eve. One of those is to see the story of Adam and Eve as a story about love and romance. Norea is the daughter of Eve. Her story is found in the *Hypostasis of the Archons*, which also describes Eve as the spirit who gives life to Adam. Norea is a woman of wisdom who resists the attempts of the rulers to dominate her. For retelling Mary's story, I turned to the apocryphal *Protevangelium of James*. According to this second century work which probably incorporates tradition from earlier sources, Mary is born miraculously to a rich couple. She is raised in the temple as a virgin who is served by pure virgins. When she is twelve years old, she is given to Joseph as his ward. She remains a pure virgin but conceives by the word of God and she continues to be a virgin even after giving birth to Jesus. The story of Mary in the P*rotevangelium of James* betrays an unhealthy obsession with Mary's virginity. The question, "Where is the real Mary?" can be used as an interpretive key to rediscover a Mary whose sexuality has not been hijacked by a despotic God and a patriarchal culture. Re-imagining the stories of biblical women and recovering their stories from traditions that have been ignored challenges the traditional notion that only one interpretation is authoritative. Rethinking biblical women and telling their stories from a fresh perspective can be a liberating experience for women as well as men.

Within the discussion, various ways of how tribal women can tell stories in worship is presented. Some of the outstanding ones are telling stories through tribal paintings that connect stories of women of the past with the stories of contemporary women. Another way is telling stories through tribal songs. A prominent pattern found in tribal songs is a dialogical form of singing. Tribal love songs are especially relevant as they refer to women with love and honour. Yet another is weaving, an activity performed solely by women. Tribal women's weavings tell of the great stories of their tribes in the patterns and colours of the cloths. Re-enacting the act of weaving in worship is to acknowledge the role of women in preserving the history of the tribe and to recover their function as storytellers.

The personal journey that this research prompted me to undertake has been exhausting and exhilarating. Throughout the research, I have tried to lend my personal voice to the discussion so that any pretext of an objective approach may not cloud the passion of this enterprise (although I do try to be objective). Anyway, stories are best told in the first person. Every chapter has been directed towards the heart of the thesis—how can tribals evolve ways of worship that encompass the marginalized in the community, and that which looks beyond gender distinctions. I hope I have managed to establish a few theological bases by which inclusive community may be built through worship. Building inclusive community requires having a new understanding of community not as a group of people bound together by similar backgrounds and common interests but as a communion of strangers. Strangers make community by overcoming their strangeness to one another by sharing their stories. Once stories are shared, people can no longer be indifferent towards each other because when they enter into the stories they are transformed. Therefore, stories are able to elicit the full potential of rituals such as the Lord's Supper and baptism.

Most of the time, stories happen to us. The tragedies and misfortunes as well as the loves and achievements of life happen to us; we have no control over them. Those are our stories. But our stories are also those that we make. Resisting patriarchal interpretations of the Bible and refusing to conform to sexist views are new stories we can make. Whether our stories happened to us or we made them, tribal women must insist that they be heard.

APPENDICES

Appendix A – CBCNEI at a Glance

Conventions	Associations	Churches	Members
Assam Baptist Convention Golaghat, Assam	6	746	35,169
Arunachal Baptist Church Council Naharlagun, Arunachal Pradesh	19	1,027	92,284
Garo Baptist Convention Tura, Meghalaya	12	2,750	2,83,923
Karbi Anglong Baptist Convention Diphu, Assam	13	315	31,746
Manipur Baptist Convention Imphal, Manipur	29	1,303	1,96,217
Nagaland Baptist Church Council Kohima, Nagaland	20	1,585	5,86,593
Total	*99*	*7,726*	*1,225,932*
Associate Members			
Evangelical Church of Maraland	1	91	42,588
Mising Baptist Kebang Dhemaji, Assam	7	115	4,300
Shillong Baptist Church Shillong, Meghalaya		1	184
Zomi Baptist Church Champhai, Mizoram	1		
Total	9	207	47,072[1]

1. *CBCNEI Diary, 2017*; with additional input from various sources.

Appendix B – Women in Ministry under CBCNEI

ASSAM BAPTIST CONVENTION

Ordained Woman:

Frolina D. Shira	Assam Baptist Convention

MANIPUR BAPTIST CONVENTION

Ordained Women:[1]

Bongshot Dulburg	Lamkang Baptist Association
R. T. Margaret	Anal Naga Baptist Association
Apila Thangal	Thangal Naga Baptist Association

Woman in Executive Position:

Apila Thangal	Thangal Naga Baptist Association

NAGALAND BAPTIST CHURCH COUNCIL

Women Pastors:[2]

S. Anungla	Chang Baptist Church, Kohima Chang Baptist Lashoung Thangyen
Neino Zhotso	Minister's Hill Baptist Church, Kohima Angami Baptist Church Council
Neitsukhaü Akami	Chizami Baptist Church, Phek Dist. Chakhesang Baptist Church Council
Bano Sapu	Sekrezu Baptist Church, Pheck Dist. Chakhesang Baptist Church Council

Woman Associate Pastor:

Juliet Shikhu	Sumi Baptist Church, Dimapur Sumi Baptist Convention

1. Tingneilhing Kipgen, Women Secretary, MBC, message to the author on October 15, 2012.

2. With input from Rukuzo Ruho who is currently pursuing his DTh in Christian Theology at Eastern Theological College, Jorhat, and Zoche-ü Khutso who is doing my MTh in Christian Ministry at Eastern Theological College, Jorhat.

Ordained Women:

Noksangchila	Ao Baptist Arogo Mungdang
Senangshila Benjamin	Ao Baptist Arogo Mungdang
Narola Imchen	Ao Baptist Arogo Mungdang
T. Narola	Ao Baptist Arogo Mungdang
Yashila Jamir	Ao Baptist Arogo Mungdang
I. Amenla	Ao Baptist Arogo Mungdang
Limatula Longkumer	Ao Baptist Arogo Mungdang
Kezütshüloü Kapfo	Chakhesang Baptist Church Council

A·CHIK BAPTIST DAL·GIPA KRIMA/GARO BAPTIST CONVENTION

Women Pastors:[3]

Christie Ch. Marak	Bajengdoba Baptist Church, Krima I[4]
Chonmerina G. Momin	Berubari Baptist Church, Krima I
Walme Ch. Marak	Chisim A·pal Baptist Church, Krima I
Balinda D. Sangma	Sambrak Baptist Church, Krima I
Biolish Ch. Marak	Nekora Baptist Church, Krima III
Sweety Ch. Marak	Goanang Baptist Church, Krima IV
Breneditha R. Marak	Da·kopgre Baptist Church, Krima IV
Monjilla G. Momin	Jengitchakgre Baptist Church, Krima IV
Chaitian B. Sangma	Rongram Allagre Baptist Church, Krima IV
Rositha A. Sangma	Tebronggre Baptist Church, Krima IV
Silse Ch. Marak	Kongbe Alotgre Baptist (Branch) Church, Krima IV
Simmera N. Sangma	Do·bu Rim·ding Baptist Church, Krima V
Niksilchi Ch. Marak	Asinagre Baptist Church, Krima VI
Grellina D. Sangma	Santipur Baptist Church, Krima VII
Priscalitha D. Sangma	Williamnagar Town Baptist Church, Krima XI
Walme Marak	Nongchram Baptist Church, Krima V

3. With input from Rettiar G. Momin, former General Secretary, GBC, Tura, email message to author October 11, 2012.

4. The associations under GBC are not named after their geographical location but are numbered. The associations are called krimas.

Women Associate Pastors:[5]

Neharika Marak	Nisangram Baptist Church, Krima I
Jessi G. Momin	Pedaldoba Baptist Church, Krima I
Gloria S. Marak	Baghmara Baptist Church, Krima III
Jaksil A. Sangma	Hawakhana Baptist Church, Krima IV
Selisha R. Marak	Tura Baptist Church, Krima IV
Tracy Ch. Marak	Modynagar Baptist Church, Krima IV
Maylitha N. Sangma	Wa·danang Baptist Church, Krima IV
Balme Ch. Momin	A·konggre Baptist Church, Krima IV
Winnie G. Momin	Dalu Baptist Church, Krima IV
Jessica A. Sangma	Dalu Baptist Church, Krima IV
Shikali P. Marak	Hawakhana Baptist Church, Krima IV
Evie Pamade R. Marak	Hawakhana Baptist Church, Krima IV
Timse Sangma	Babelapara Baptist Church, Krima IV
Morjina R. Marak	Rongjeng Baptist Church, Krima V
Lovely Sangma	Simsanggre Baptist Church, Krima V
Kokkila R. Marak	Williamnagar Baptist Church, Krima V
Elhana R. Marak	Ku·simkol Baptist Church, Krima V
Brejitha A. Sangma	Nogorpara Baptist Church, Krima VI
Prenitha Sangma	Immanuel Baptist Church, Krima VIII
Sangeetha Arengh	Chigitchakgre Baptist Church, Krima VIII

Among the pastors, one is a BTh graduate and the other four are BD degree holders. Among the associate pastors, two have Certificate in Theology, six have BTh degree, and the rest fourteen are BD graduates.

Ordained Women:

There are 57 ordained ministers under GBC of which 8 are women.

Wirollinda Ch. Marak	Tura Baptist Church, Krima IV
Marlene Ch. Marak	Tura Baptist Church, Krima IV

5. Interestingly, in GBC, the designation given to the church ministers immediately under the pastors is "assistant pastor." However, it is clear from their status and role that they are actually associate pastors.

Fraidabell Marak	Bangsi Apal Baptist Church, Krima I
Lalhmingthangi Ch. Marak	Shyamnagar Baptist Church, Krima X
Selisha R. Marak	Tura Baptist Church, Krima IV
Rinje N. Sangma	Tura Baptist Church, Krima IV
Chakme Ch. Marak	Tura Baptist Church, Krima IV
Sweety Ch. Marak	Goanang Baptist Church, Krima IV[6]

One of the women ordained by GBC, Selitha N. Sangma, of Tura Baptist Church, Krima IV, who served at Women Secretary of GBC passed away in 2013.

Woman in Executive Position:

Sangeeta Arengh	Puksora Centre

Placement of Ordained Women Under CBCNEI

1. Frolina D. Shira: She is a member of Ranibari Baptist Church, Kamrup District, and she is serving as the Women Secretary of Assam Baptist Convention.

2. Bongshot Dulburg: She is working as a translator of the Old Testament in the Lamkang Baptist Association in Chandel District, Manipur.

3. R. T. Margaret: She is running Emmanuel Children's Home, which is an orphanage as well as a residential school. She often assists in the ministry of the Modi Baptist Church in Chandel District, Manipur.

4. Apila Thangal: She is serving as the Executive Secretary of the Thangal Naga Baptist Association.

5. Senangshila Benjamin: She served as the pastor of Süngratsü Baptist Church, Mokokchung, for a few years. She is the only one among the ordained women under CBCNEI who served as pastor of a local church. After retiring from active service, Senangshila is residing at Dimapur, Nagaland.

6. Noksangchila: She served as the chaplain of Christian Medical College, Vellore, for many years and at present she is serving as a warden at Referral Hospital, Dimapur, Nagaland.

7. Awala Longkumer: She worked in ABAM as its youth director, in the Women's Desk of the National Council of Churches in India, and in Nagaland

6. Of the 57 ordained ministers, three are serving as officers of the Convention, eighteen are Krima officers, seven are serving at Harding Theological College, twenty-three are serving as pastors, three are engaged in own ministry after retirement, and three are retired. Janang R. Sangma, Genereal Secretary, GBC, electronic message to author, July 24, 2018. Data updated by me from other personal sources.

Baptist Church Council as its women's secretary. At present, she is living in Dimapur, Nagaland. She is not serving under any specific office but is often engaged as resource person by churches and organizations.

8. Narola Imchen: She is a professor in the Department of History of Christianity and the Vice-Principal of Eastern Theological College, Jorhat, Assam.

9. T. Narola: She is serving as the women secretary under Nagaland Baptist Church Council, Kohima, Nagaland.

10. Yashila Jamir: She is working as associate pastor of the women's department at Kohima Ao Baptist Church, Kohima, Nagaland.

11. I. Amenla: She is the associate pastor of Mokokchung Town Baptist Church, Mokokchung, Nagaland.

12. Limatula Longkumer: She is a professor it the department of Christian Education at Eastern Theological College, Jorhat, Assam, and was its Vice-Principal for a tenure.

13. Kezütshüloü Kapfo: She served as women secretary of NBCC and after finishing her tenure, she is taking care of a hostel run by Council of Naga Baptist Churches in Dimapur, Nagaland.

14. Wirollinda Ch. Marak: She worked under various departments of the GBC and has retired from active office work but she continues to do ministerial work at Tura Baptist Church, Tura, and its sister churches.

15. Marlene Ch. Marak: She is an Associate Professor in the department of Communication at Eastern Theological College, Jorhat, Assam.

16. Lalhmingthangi Ch. Marak: She is an Assistant Professor of Old Testament at Harding Theological College, Tura, Meghalaya.

17. Selisha R. Marak: She is an Associate Pastor at Tura Baptist Church.

18. Rinje N. Sangma: She is an Assistant Professor of New Testament at Harding Theological College.

19. Chakme Ch. Marak: She is an Assistant Professor of History of Christianity at Harding Theological College.

Appendix C – Woven Creations of North East India

ARUNACHAL PRADESH[1]

Sherudukpen tribe	*bogre, muhkak*
Pailibos tribe	*kedu, sisak kedu, sab-ki, nara, namu, jepu-sube, jepo, jeli-jebor, eje-serak, tayen-soba, tari-lisup, jeli-sube, jemu-sube, tayen-seak, sopin-dumlop, sotum-dumlop, dumlop, atak, lakbu, lub-bin, tal-gor*
Singpho tribe	*patep, bamo, pachang, mikheng pukang, mathat pukang, mukiya pukang, turban*

ASSAM[2]

Bodo tribe	*mekhela, chaddar, riha, dhoti*
Dimasa Kachari tribe	*rishi, rimsao, turban, rigu, rijamphai, rikhaosa*
Mech Kachari tribe	*dhoti, turban, shawl, chaddar, mekhela chaddar*
Thai Phake tribe	*fatong, sho, fa ho ho, fafek mai, chin, fa nangwait, chairchin, fafek, chaddar, chekhamchum*

1. Indira Gandhi National Centre for the Arts (IGNCA), "Textiles of Arunachal Pradesh," http://ignca.gov.in/divisionss/janapada-sampada/northeastern-regional-centre/textiles-of-arunachal-pradesh/ (accessed June 20, 2019). See further, Chander Sheikhar Panchani, *Arunachal Pradesh: Religion, Culture, and Society* (New Delhi: Konark Publishers, 1989); Tai Nyori, *History and Culture of the Adis* (New Delhi: Omsons Publications, 1993). For North East Textiles in general, see: Indira Gandhi National Centre for the Arts (IGNCA), "Arts and Crafts of Northeast India," http://ignca.gov.in/divisionss/janapada-sampada/northeastern-regional-centre/arts-and-crafts-of-northeast-india/ (accessed June 20, 2019); Elwin, *The Art of Northeast Frontier of India*; G. K. Ghosh and Shukla Ghosh, *Indian Textiles: Past and Present* (New Delhi: APH Publishing Corporation, 1995).

2. Indira Gandhi National Centre for the Arts (IGNCA), "Textiles of Assam," http://ignca.gov.in/divisionss/janapada-sampada/northeastern-regional-centre/textiles-of-assam/ (accessed June 20, 2019). See further, Enakshi Bhavnani, *Folk and Tribal Designs of India: Hundreds of Designs and Motifs from the Folk and Tribal Craft of India, Drawn from Original Sources by Kiran Malhotra, Devi Thapa, Roshan Ali and Percy Bhathenna* (Bombay: Taraporevala, 1974); Philippa Scott, *The Book of Silk* (London: Thames and Hudson, 2001); V. V. Giri National Labour Institute, *Women Weavers of Sualkuchi: The Silk Town of Assam*, NIL Research Studies Series 2001/030 (Noida: V. V. Giri National Labour Institute, 2002).

MANIPUR[3]

Meitei Community	*lamphie, ningthouphee, saijounba, phirananba, namthang-khut-hut, khamenchatpa, phiranji*
Kabui tribe	*pheishoi, lejing phel shoi, langu pheihoi, nai, ranglan, song nai, phaingao, philak, thiam phai, kharam phai*
Hmar tribe	*thangsuo puon, puon laisen, hmarm, zakuolaisen*
Kuki tribe	*khamtang, thang nang, saipikhup, maijapem, puonpaul, deitang*
Paitei tribe	*thangou puon, puon dum, jawl puon, puon pie, nikkiat*
Tangkhul tribe	*phangvai kashan, changkham, seiyang kashan, khankhan, kongla kashan, kashang kashan, khoram phi, thang-gang, phalengchi*

MEGHALAYA[4]

Khasi tribe	*dhoti, turban, jainsem, tapmoh, jainkup*
Khynrium tribe	*jainsem, tapmoh khlieh, jain-tapmoh, jainkirshah, pla-kieng, jynphong, turban*
War Khasi tribe	*jymphong, turban, ka jyaanpien, jainsem*
Bhoi Khasi	*kajampein, ka jainsem, jymphong, turban*
Garo tribe	*eking, dakmanda, turban*
Hajong tribe	*pathani, gamocha/vija kapod*
Koch tribe	*tintikiya, lufan, kambang, paga, dhoti, sari*
Mikir/Karbi tribe	*rikong, choi, poho, pini, pekok, wam kok*
Boro tribe	*gamsa, dakhan, phasra; dakmanda, dhara, jainsem, dakhana, endi silk*

3. Indira Gandhi National Centre for the Arts (IGNCA), "Textiles of Manipur," http://ignca.gov.in/divisionss/janapada-sampada/northeastern-regional-centre/textiles-of-manipur/ (acccessed June 19, 2019). See further, Nilima Roy, *Art of Manipur* (Delhi: Agam Kala Prakashan, 1979); Chander Sheikhar Panchani, *Manipur: Religion, Culture, and Society* (New Delhi: Konark Publishers, 1987).

4. Indira Gandhi National Centre for the Arts (IGNCA), "Textiles of Meghalaya" http://ignca.gov.in/divisionss/janapada-sampada/northeastern-regional-centre/textiles-of-meghalaya/ (accessed June 20, 2019).

MIZORAM[5]

Hmar tribe	*thangsuo puon, puon laisen, hmarm, zakuolaisen*
Paitei tribe	*thangou puon, puon dum, jawl puon, puon pie*
Riang tribe	*khutai, arnai, marki*

NAGALAND[6]

Ao tribe	*tsungkotep su, aomelep su, rongsu, tiongkong su, tabensa su, lungkhum subang, keyi su, bangmeren su, azu jangnup, ngami su, yongzujangau*
Angami tribe	*loramhoushü, lohe, phichu-pfe, rata-pfe, pfemhou*
Sangtam tribe	*rongsu, supong, tsingrang su*
Sema tribe	*akhum, avi-kiyi-phi, lototsu*
Yimchunger tribe	*kechinger ronfkhim, tsungrem khim, sangkonglim khim, amerthre khim, rehuke khim, mokhok khim, amurk khim, kechingperu khim, alongza khim, langa imjung*
Phom tribe	*vihe-ashak, nempong-ashak, fanet, henyu, shungnang, shaka*
Rengma tribe	*rhikho, moyet tsu, alungtsu, teri phiketsu*
Lotha tribe	*sutam, phangrhup, eshamsu, loroesu, lungpensu*
Konyak tribe	*nye-myon, nikola, shatni, meyni, hompani, nyauni*

5. Indira Gandhi National Centre for the Arts (IGNCA), "Textiles of Mizoram," http://ignca.gov.in/divisionss/janapada-sampada/northeastern-regional-centre/textiles-of-mizoram/ (accessed June 20, 2019). See further, N. Chatterji, *Puan – the Pride of Mizoram* (Aizawl: Tribal Research Institute, 1978).

6. Indira Gandhi National Centre for the Arts (IGNCA), "Textiles of Nagaland," http://ignca.gov.in/divisionss/janapada-sampada/northeastern-regional-centre/textiles-of-nagaland/ (accessed June 19, 2019). See further, Milada Ganguli, *Naga Art* (New Delhi: Oxford & IBH Pub. Co., 1993); Naga Institute of Culture, *The Arts and Crafts of Nagaland* (Kohima: Naga Institute of Culture, Government of Nagaland, 1968).

SIKKIM[7]

	carpet, blanket, coat

TRIPURA[8]

Halam tribe	*pachchra, risha*
Khakloo tribe	*rikutu gamcha, kubai, pagri, rinai, risa*
Kuki-Chin tribe	*thangang, saipi-khup, ponmongvom, khamtang, chaga*

7. Tika Prasad Sharma and S. K. Borthakur, "Traditional Handloom and Handicrafts of Sikkim," *Indian Journal of Traditional Knowledge* 9/2 (April 2010): 375-77, http://nopr.niscair.res.in/bitstream/123456789/8188/1/IJTK%20 9%282%29%20375-377.pdf (accessed June 20, 2019); All India Artisans and Craftworkers Association (AIACA), *Artistic Textiles of Sikkim - Diagnostic Study and Business Development Plan*, prepared by AIACA and presented to Development Commissioner, Handicraft, Government of Sikkim, 2009.

8. Indira Gandhi National Centre for the Arts (IGNCA), "Textiles of Tripura," http://ignca.gov.in/divisionss/janapada-sampada/northeastern-regional-centre/ textiles-of-tripura/ (accessed June 19, 2019). See further, Nasreen Askari, Liz Arthur, *Uncut Cloth: Saris, Shawls and Sashes* (London: Merrell Holberton Publishers, 1999).

Appendix D – The *Mendu* Plant as a Boundary Marker

Long ago, there lived a man named Bonepa Janepa.[1] The season for *jhum*[2] cultivation had come round so he paid his respects to the gods by performing the necessary religious ceremonies. After that, he began to clear the jungle at a place called Denggadare Silkongkhante Misi Kokdok Arapetchok. When he had finished cutting the trees, he went to visit his niece Mejini Me·chik Bangsni Bi·sa. In the land where she lived, Mejini Me·chik had befriended a fountain of living water, which had portentous powers. She kept some of the water from the fountain in an earthen pitcher. Whenever it was about to rain, the water in the vessel would overflow and whenever it got sunny, the water would dry up.

Mejini Me·chik prepared the choicest food and drinks for her maternal uncle and served them to him. While having food, they talked about his *jhum* cultivation and Bonepa expressed that he had not fully prepared the clearing as he was uncertain when rain would come. Mejini Me·chik went and looked into the earthen pitcher where she kept the living water.

She saw that the water was about to overflow and said to him, "My pitcher with the living water has come up to the brim, it is close to overflowing. It will not be long before it rains. Do not delay by going back to the village, or by going back to your house. Instead, you must rush back straight to your *jhum* field and burn the trees you have felled before it starts to rain."

Hearing these words, Bonepa rushed back to complete his work in the *jhum* field. Now Bonepa's field lay adjacent to the field of a man called Misipa. Bonepa informed Misipa that it was going to rain very soon and that he should complete his *jhum* clearing at the earliest.

It happened that Misipa also had an earthen pitcher of the living water. He replied, "My friend, the living water in my pitcher has not come up to the brim, it is not stirring, and it is not close to overflowing. The pitcher is yet to fill; there is still plenty of time."

1. Rongmuthu, comp., *Folktales of the Garos*, 255-58.

2. *Jhum* is a traditional form of slash-and-burn shifting cultivation. It involves clearing a patch of forest land and burning the vegetation and tree branches that had been cut down. The clearing is cultivated for 2-3 years and then left fallow for 10-20 years while the cultivation is shifted to another site. Rotating the cultivation enables the soil to regain its fertility.

Thus Misipa did not believe Bonepa because his earthen pitcher of living water did not indicate approaching rain. On the contrary, Bonepa had no doubt that it would rain soon and so he set fire to his *jhum* field.

Unknown to him, Nambok Me·a Namsang Pante, the favourite son of Misipa, was sitting on the leafless limb of a tree that had been pruned. He was sitting there and singing about a monster moving towards him. And indeed a monster was approaching, drawing nearer and nearer to him, flicking its tongue and devouring everything in its path—it was the inferno from Bonepa's field. Before long, the fire spread into Misipa's field. The boy was caught in the fire and he fell down from the branch and died.

Enraged by the killing of his son, Misipa took an oath of vengeance against Bonepa.

He railed against Bonepa, "Because of your carelessness my son is dead. I declare a war on you."

Bonepa snapped back in reply, "I told you that it was time to burn the *jhum* clearing. Why did you disregard my words? You have slighted me and shown your contempt for me by not believing me."

Just as Mejini Mechik had said, the rain really came the very next day. Misipa did not even notice it because he was preoccupied with plans to avenge the death of his son.

When Misipa and Bonepa were about to meet head-on in a fight, there appeared three honourable celestial beings before them: Misi Susime, Katchi Beari, and Aijangga Redingbanda.

They told the two men who were about to slay each other: "You Misipa, stay, and you, Bonepa also, let it be. Fighting and locking horns against each other is futile. Pick up the bones of Nambok Me·a Namsang Pante, the bones of his limbs and his body, and mark the boundary of your field with them by placing them as posts, as you would with logs of wood. From his bones a new plant known as *mendu* or *landu* (*cystisus cajan*) will sprout and a beanstalk creeper will grow. The *mendu* will produce seeds and multiply, and be the indicators of the boundary of your respective fields for generations. Do as you have been told, and let there be peace between you. Fighting brings you nothing but misery and loss."

Heeding these words, Bonepa and Misipa immediately reconciled with each other. They picked up the charred bones of Nambok Me·a Namsang Pante and used them as pickets fencing their respective fields. In due course, just as it had been said, the bones sprouted into golden beanstalks and silvery *mendu* plants. Since then, the A·chiks have been using the *mendu* plants for setting the boundaries of their fields.

Appendix E – The Story of the Sun and the Cock

A long time ago, in the age of peace and tranquillity, when all the creatures of the world spoke only one language, a particular day was appointed for a big festival to be celebrated with dancing.[1] All the living creatures were invited and they came to the festival dressed in all their finest attires. They danced throughout the whole day until late afternoon, when they began to tire and began to disperse. At that time the Sun and the Moon, a sister and a brother, arrived and began to dance. There was nothing wrong with the way they danced; they did not miss the dance steps or anything like that. Yet the creatures jeered and laughed scornfully at them, saying that it was wrong for a sister and a brother to dance together.[2] This happened because sin had seeped in the heart of people that an innocent dance could not take place.[3] People saw evil where there was none. In shame (or indignant anger at the hurtful insinuations about the nature of her relationship with her brother), the Sun ran away and hid herself in *Ka Krem Lamet Ka Krem Latang*.[4] Immediately, the world was plunged in darkness. Why was there darkness? Was it because the Sun had hidden herself in *Ka Krem Lamet Ka Krem Latang*? No. It was because humans had been blinded by their sin and that brought an end to the golden age of peace and tranquillity.

1. Mawrie, *The Khasi Milieu*, 34-35; B. Sohkhlet, "A Phenomenological Study of the Understanding of God as Emerging from Selected Myths and Rituals in the Traditional Religion of the Khasi Pnars" (DTh Thesis, Senate of Serampore College, 2008), 145ff. For parallels of this story other cultures see Rudolf Rahmann, "Quarrels and Enmity between the Sun and the Moon: A Contribution to the Mythologies of the Philippines, India, and the Malay Peninsula," *Folklore Studies* 14 (1955): 202-14.

2. Other accounts say that the Moon desired to marry his own sister and in anger she threw hot ash on his face and ran away. Verrier Elwin, *Myths of Middle India* (Bombay: Oxford University Press, 1949), 53, 55f.

3. The shift of the narrative from "all creatures" to "human beings" is not explained. It is that "human beings" is a way of making the behaviour of the creatures understandable to the human hearers—by speaking of the creatures as though they were human beings. The Sun and the Moon and other characters of the story all behave like human characters.

4. Some say she went and hid in a cave but *Ka Krem Lamet Ka Krem Latang* appears to refer to an obscure place beyond the hills.

The world had never been as dark or as terrible as those days of *Ka Krem Lamet Ka Krem Latang*. Humans could only stumble and grope in the darkness. There was utter chaos. Caught in this helpless situation, humans tried to reason why this had happened. They tried to find someone who could go to the sun and plead for her forgiveness. But no one dared to do it for they all felt guilty. Finally, a bird came up and expressed his willingness to approach the Sun. So they assigned this bird to entreat the Sun for her forgiveness. However, when the bird came close to the Sun his arrogance was revealed. So the Sun got angry and chased him away. Then other creatures also tried to approach the Sun but they were all unsuccessful. Finally, only one creature was left. He was a cock. He lived in the bushes of a sacred grove and never ventured out because he was very poor, not having even a simple wrap over his body. He had always been humble and obedient to God. When he came to know about the trouble facing the creatures, he decided to come out and do his bit. Coming to the humans, he offered his assistance with a request to provide him with a cover for his body. The humans agreed to do that and so the cock went to the Sun. Approaching the Sun, he prayed with all humility and meekness for forgiveness. Because of such respectful request, the Sun finally relented and forgave humans and the other creatures. Then with the crowing of the cock, the Sun came out of hiding and the world was lighted up once again.

When the humans went to God and the Sun to thank them, God explained to them their weakness of their nature and the problems they will continuously face because of that. Humans prayed to God for mercy and in response God instituted religion. God made it so that humans can seek and receive God's approval with a cock (or hen or other animals) sacrifice. In this way, religion was established as a covenant between God and humans.

Appendix F – The Navel of Heaven

About thirteen miles or so North of Shillong, there is a peak towering above a sacred forest. This peak is called *U Lum Sohpetbneng*, which means "the navel peak of heaven." The Khasi-Pnar tribes of Meghalaya tell this story about it.[1]

During a time when righteousness prevailed among humanity and *U Blei* (God) walked with humans, a tree known as *jingkieng ksiar*, meaning "golden ladder," stood at the centre of the world, on top of *U Lum Sohpetbneng*. It was the umbilical cord connecting the sky with the earth below. Humanity was known as *Ki Khathynriew Trep ki Khathynriew Skum*, which means "sixteen huts," or "sixteen families." They all lived with God in heaven but every morning they descended by the tree-ladder to cultivate the earth and returned to heaven in the evening.

It so happened that a man became dissatisfied with life in heaven. He desired to have a kingdom of his own. For many months he plotted and planned. Secretly, he whittled away at the tree-ladder. Then one day, when seven of the families had come down to earth this man swiftly felled the tree-ladder and severed the link between heaven and earth. The seven families were stranded on earth. Thus the Khasis-Pnar tribes are known as *U Hynniew Trep Hynniew Skum*, which means "seven huts, seven nests." Today, whenever they pray to *U Blei*, they still remember their kin in heaven, the nine families above called *Ki Khayndai Hajrong*, and seek their forgiveness from them for their sins and wrongdoings.

1. Bijoya Sawian, *Khasi Myths, Legends and Folk Tales* (New Delhi: Sanbun Publishers, 2010), 35-36; Mawrie, *The Khasi Milieu*, 33-34. A different version of this story is found in S. T. Das, *Life Style: Indian Tribes – Locational Practice*, vol. 2 (New Delhi: Gyan Publishing House, 2000), 179 ff.

Appendix G – The Story of Norea, Daughter of Eve

The ignorant and arrogant creator God, the Chief Ruler or Archon named Samael (god of the blind), claims "blindly" that he is the only God. This was blasphemy because in the true spiritual world that transcends him there was Entirety, Incorruptibility (a female figure), and above all, the Father of Light who determines everything that happens. Samael's speech reaches Incorruptibility and a voice from her replies, "You are mistaken." As Incorruptibility rebukes Samael and looks down into the waters, her image is reflected on it. The Archons of this world of darkness see it and they become impassioned by lust. But they are unable to lay hold of her because they are inferior beings of the world below whereas she is from above. The Archons then devise a plan to entrap her by making a model of a man with soil from the earth, after their body and in the likeness of the form that had appeared on the waters. They thought she might be attracted by their model of a male counterpart and they may then be able to seize her. They are able to give their male model a soul but he remains inert on the ground for they are powerless to make him rise. They keep blowing on the man like storm winds but they are unable to enliven him.

Afterwards, the Spirit sees the man with a soul on the ground. Coming forth from the Adamantine land, the Spirit descends on him and the man becomes a living soul. The Spirit names the man Adam because he was found moving on the ground. Then the voice of Incorruptibility summons the Archons to assist Adam. The Archons bring to Adam all the animals and birds and Adam gives a name to each of them. The Archons then put Adam in the garden to tend it. They tell him to eat from every tree in the garden, but from the tree of the knowledge of good and evil he is not to eat or touch for he would die the day he ate from it. They do not know it, but this was according to the Father's will whose plan is for Adam to eat from the tree so that his nature would no longer be exclusively material.

Next, the Archons, using some of their ignorance, bring a deep sleep upon Adam, and they open his side to remove the living woman (Spirit). Then they fill the gap on his side with some flesh. Adam is left with only soul. The Spirit woman awakens Adam. When he sees her, he knows instantly that it is she who gave him life. He calls her "Mother of the living" for she is his mother. The authorities (other name for Archons) see the Spirit woman talking with Adam and they become agitated by their lust. They crave to sow their seed in her and pursue her. But she merely laughs at their foolishness and their blindness. Just as they catch her, she becomes a tree (or transfers her Spirit to a tree), leaving her shadowy reflection behind.[1] It is this shadowy body they rape and defile, bringing condemnation upon themselves because she stamped the form with her likeness and they had modelled it after their own image. From here on, the personality of the Spirit woman is split into two: the Spiritual principle (the one who escaped from the clutches of her would-be rapists), and the Carnal woman (the one who was raped).

In the next scene, the Spiritual principle enters the snake, the Instructor, and speaks to the Carnal woman. The snake tells the Carnal woman that eating from the tree of knowledge of evil and good will not make them die. Rather, their eyes will be opened and they will become like gods, recognising evil and good. After this dialogue the Spiritual principle leaves the snake and only a mere thing of the earth is left. Then the Carnal woman eats from the tree and gives to her husband as well. As soon as they eat from the tree, they understand that they are naked of the Spiritual element. They possessed only soul and no Spirit.

The Chief Ruler arrives in the garden seeking Adam for he did not know what happened. Adam tells him that he was hiding because he heard the Ruler's voice and he was afraid because he was naked. The Ruler realises that they have eaten from the tree. Like the Genesis account, the man blames the woman and the woman blames the snake. The snake is cursed, for they did not know that it was a form they had modelled themselves. The snake was to come under the curse until the coming of the All-powerful Man. Adam and his wife are also cursed and expelled from the garden. The human beings are thrown into a life of toil so that the hardship might keep them distracted and prevent them from getting an opportunity to pursue the Spirit.

The story continues with the birth of Cain and Abel. Abel is murdered by Cain. Then Adam "knew" his wife again and she gives birth to Seth. Here, for the first time, the woman's name is given, Eve. Again she

1. Karen King offers this analysis: "The psychic dissociation depicted here is a common, although painful survival response by victims of rape and incest. While psychic dissociation can be effective at maintaining some personal integrity in the face of attempts to destroy one's self, ultimately it is an extremely painful solution to violence, insofar as it abandons the body as one's self." King, "The Book of Norea, Daughter of Eve," in *Searching the Scriptures*, ed. Schüssler Fiorenza, 70.

becomes pregnant and gives birth to Norea, who, the narrator inserts, is "the virgin whom the forces did not defile." The Archons decide to cause a flood to obliterate humans and beasts from the face of the earth. Noah is instructed by the Ruler of the forces (either Samael or his son Sabaoth) to build an ark and set it upon Mount Sir. Orea (another name for Norea) comes to Noah wanting to board the ark. When he refuses to let her, she blows on the ark and causes it to burn up.[2] So Noah has to build it all over again. Next, the Archons come to Norea. Their intention is to sexually possess Norea. First, they lie to her: "Your mother Eve came to us." But Norea is not taken in by their lie. She calls them Rulers of the Darkness. She tells them they did not violate her mother but a false image. She asserts that she is not their descendant because she is from the world above. At this, the Ruler is enraged and commands Norea to render service to them as her mother did. But Norea shouts to the Holy One, the God of the Entirety, to save her. At this, the Great Angel comes down from the heavens and the Archons withdraw from her. When Norea asks who he is, he replies that he is Eleleth who stands in the presence of the Holy Spirit. He adds that he has been sent to save her from the clutches of the lawless and teach her about her roots.

After Eleleth has introduced himself, the account is narrated in the first person. It is Norea who is speaking directly to the reader. She reports what Eleleth tells her. The Archons do not have power to defile her for she comes from the abode of Incorruptibility. Norea asks to know about the Archons and how they have come into being. Eleleth then instructs her about the prehistory of the cosmos.

Pistis Sophia, dwelling in the realm of Incorruptibility, decides to procreate alone without the consent of her consort. What she produces is a celestial being but it is like an aborted foetus, an arrogant beast resembling a lion, and it is androgynous. He becomes arrogant and declares that he is the only God. A voice comes forth from the realm above calling him Samael, which means "god of the blind," and tells him that he is mistaken. He is later called Yaltabaoth. He demands to be shown if anything existed before him. At this, Sophia stretches her finger and introduces light into matter, into the region of chaos (the world below). Samael then creates a realm for himself and produces seven androgynous beings for himself. He tells his offspring that he is the god of the Entirety. Zoe, the daughter of Pistis Sophia rebukes him

2. It is not clear why Noah did not want Norea to board the ark. Some Gnostic sources refer to Norea as the wife of Noah.

and breathes into his face. Her breath becomes an angel and this angel casts him into Tartaros below the Abyss. When his offspring Sabaoth sees the power of the angel he repents and repudiates his parents and sings songs of praise to Sophia and her daughter Zoe. Because of this, Sophia and Zoe put him in charge of the seventh heaven and he is called "God of the forces, Sabaoth."

Next Norea asks about her relation to the Archons. Eleleth reaffirms that she is from above, from the primeval Father, out of the imperishable light. The Archons are powerless to approach those who have the Spirit of truth within them. And they are not subject to death. However truth will not become known yet. It will be known after three generations when the children of light will be freed from the bondage of the Archons. Now Norea asks how much longer it will be. He tells her that this will come about when the True Man appears and reveals the Spirit of truth. Then there is a triumphant declaration of what the True Man will achieve when he comes to acquaint the children of light with the truth, with their roots, and with the Father of the Entirety and the Holy Spirit. The text ends with praises for the Father and Son.

Appendix H – Mary in the *Protevangelium of James*

The *Protevangelium of James* takes the reader back to the events surrounding the birth of Mary.[1] Joachim is a very rich man who wishes to bring his gifts to God, twofold, but Reuben[2] reproaches him because he is childless. Joachim checks the record book of the twelve tribes and finds out all the righteous had indeed raised up offspring. He remembers Abraham who was granted a son in his old age. Becoming very sad, he does not show himself to his wife Anna and withdraws into the wilderness in order to fast for forty days and forty nights. Anna sings a dirge to bewail her widowhood (because she had become like a widow) and grieves her childlessness. Even her maid Judith[3] rebukes her because of her childlessness. Anna goes out into her garden and sits beneath a laurel tree. And she prays to God to bless her like Sarah was blessed. She sings another dirge lamenting the womb that gave birth to her. She is sorrowful that the birds, the beasts, the waters, and the earth are all fruitful but she was born a curse. Then an angel appears to her and informs her that the Lord has heard her prayer. She would conceive and bear an offspring who would be spoken of throughout the world. Anna promises that she will dedicate the child, whether male or female, to serve God in the temple. Then two angels come to Anna and inform her that Joachim is coming with his flocks. Joachim had also been informed by an angel that God has heard his prayer and that his wife would conceive and bear a child. As Joachim comes with his flock, Anna runs out and throws her arms around his neck and tells him that God has greatly blessed her. She, the widow, is no longer a widow, and she, the childless, will conceive. Thus

---

1. In retelling the story, I am freely paraphrasing from Elliott, "The Protevangelium of James," in *The Apocryphal New Testament*, 57-67. Elliot's translation is based on the Tischendorf version, the composite text created by Tischendorf from eighteen manuscripts (another important version is Papyrus Bodmer V from the third century CE). Wherever the narrative parallels the canonical gospels, I narrate in greater detail so that the reader or hearer can make his or her own conclusions about the relation of this tract to the canonical material.

2. A peculiar trait of the narrative is to introduce characters suddenly and without any indication of who they are. Sometimes a character's name is not given when the person first makes an appearance but the name is mentioned later in the narrative.

3. Euthine in variant.

Anna conceives and, in the ninth month,[4] she gives birth to a child, a girl, and she names her Mary.

As days go by, the child grows in strength. When she is six months old,[5] she walks seven steps. Then her mother takes her up saying she would walk no more until she is brought to the temple of the Lord. Her mother turns her bedroom into a sanctuary and chooses undefiled Jewish girls to serve her. On her first birthday, the chief priests, the priests, the scribes, the elders, and the people of Israel are invited to a great feast and she is blessed by the priests and the chief priests. Anna takes the child into the bedroom sanctuary and suckles her and sings a song of praise to God. When the child is two years old, Joachim proposes that they should take her to the temple, but Anna pleads to wait one more year so that the child will not long for her parents. Joachim concurs. When the child is three years old, they take her to the temple led by Hebrew virgins bearing burning torches. Here, the priest kisses and blesses the child. Then he places her on the third step of the altar, and the child dances with her feet and all the people who are present love her. Her parents return home marvelling and praising God because the child did not turn back.

Mary is raised in the temple, nurtured like a dove and fed food from the hand of an angel. When she attains the age of twelve,[6] the priests call a council to decide what to do with her because she might defile the temple.[7] They request the high priest to enter the sanctuary and seek God's counsel. Accordingly, Zacharias, the high priest, enters the Holy of Holies and prays concerning her. An angel of the Lord appears to him and tells him to assemble all the widowers in Israel, and the Lord will give a sign to let him know whose wife she should become. Heralds are sent out throughout the country and people come running.

Joseph hears the message and throws down his adze (axe) to go and attend the meeting. Each widower brings a rod and gives it to the high priest. The high priest takes their rods, enters the temple and prays.

4. Variants have "sixth," "seventh," or "eighth."

5. Variant has "nine."

6. Some variants say "fourteen" while others say "ten." Twelve appears to be the correct reading. van der Horst, "Sex, Birth, Purity and Asceticism in the *Protevangelium Jacobi*," in *A Feminist Companion to Mariology*, ed. Levine and Robbins, 61.

7. The text is silent about the reason why she might defile the temple. But it is easily understood from the cultural perspective of the time that the reason is her menstruation.

Coming out, he gives them the rods, but receives no sign on them. Joseph receives the last rod, and as he receives it a dove comes out of the rod and flies on to his head. The priest tells Joseph that he has been chosen to receive the virgin as his ward. Initially, Joseph protests. He tells the priest that he is old with sons of his own while she is just a girl. Joseph feels that he will become a laughing-stock of the people if he received the girl as his ward. However, the high priest points out to him that Dathan, Abiram, and Korah received judgment from God because of their rebellion. With these examples he persuades Joseph to change his mind and Joseph takes Mary home as his ward. Then leaving her in his house he goes away to build his buildings.

The priests have a council and determine to have a veil made for the temple. They summon the pure virgins of the tribe of David to weave the veil. The officers search and bring seven virgins. Then the priest remembers the child Mary who is also of the tribe of David and is pure before God. And she is brought to the temple. Lots are cast to see who will weave the gold, the amiantus, the linen, the silk, the hyacinth-blue, the scarlet, and the pure purple. The lot falls on Mary for weaving the pure purple and scarlet. And she takes them and goes home. Then Zacharias becomes mute.[8] Samuel takes his place until he is able to speak again.

Taking the scarlet, Mary spins it. And she goes out with a pitcher to draw water. She hears a voice saying, "Hail, highly favoured one, the Lord is with you, you are blessed among women." But when she looks around she sees no one. Trembling, she goes home and puts down the pitcher. She takes the purple and sits down to spin. And she sees an angel of the Lord standing before here. The angel tells her, "Do not fear, Mary; for you have found grace before the Lord of all things and shall conceive by his Word." Contemplating what she had heard, she asks the angel whether she would become pregnant by God as happens to every woman who becomes pregnant. The angel replies, "Not so, Mary; for the power of the Lord shall overshadow you; wherefore the holy one who is born of you shall be called the Son of the Most High. And you shall call his name Jesus; for he shall save his people from their sins." Mary responds, "Behold, I am the handmaid of the Lord before him: be it to me according to your word."[9]

8. In Luke 1:20-23, Zechariah becomes mute because he did not believe Gabriel when he brought the news that his wife Elizabeth would bear a son.

9. The close parallel to Luke 1:26-28 is evident.

After spinning the purple and the scarlet, Mary takes them to the priest. The priest blesses her and declares that the Lord God has magnified her name and that she would be blessed among all generations of the earth. Rejoicing, Mary goes to visit Elizabeth her kinswoman.[10] When Elizabeth sees her, she exclaims, "How is it that the mother of my Lord should come to me? For behold, that which is in me leaped and blessed you." Forgetting what the archangel Gabriel had told her, Mary raises a sigh towards heaven, "Who am I, Lord, that all generations of the earth count me blessed?" She stays with Elizabeth for three months. As her womb grows day by day Mary is afraid and goes to her house and hides herself from the people. At this time Mary is sixteen years old.[11]

In the sixth month of Mary's pregnancy, Joseph comes from his buildings to find her pregnant. He is greatly distressed. He strikes his face, throws himself down on the ground on sackcloth, and weeps bitterly. He thinks he has failed to protect the virgin he received from the temple. He fears that the story of Adam has been repeated in him. For when Adam was absent the serpent had found Eve alone and deceived her. Then he chastises Mary for humiliating her soul, for forgetting God although she was brought up in the Holy of Holies and received food from the hand of an angel. Mary weeps bitterly and insists that she is pure and that she has not known a man.[12] Joseph tells her that he does not know why such a thing has happened to him.

In great fear Joseph departs from Mary and ponders what he should do with her. He finds himself in a quandary. If he concealed her sin, he would be in contravention of the law. If he exposed her, and if the child in her happened to be from the angels, he would be guilty of delivering innocent blood. Finally, he decides to put her away secretly. And in the night an angel appears to him in a dream saying, "Do not fear this child. For that which is in her is of the Holy Spirit. She shall bear a son, and you shall call his name Jesus; for he shall save his people from their sins."[13] Arising from sleep, Joseph glorifies God. And he guards Mary.

10. This section appears to be a version of Luke 1:39-56.

11. Variants say "fourteen" and "fifteen." Note that Mary's pregnancy occurs two to four years after she is placed in the care of Joseph (at the age of twelve).

12. Mary's silence about the revelation she received from the angel is strange. In the account of her visitation to Elizabeth it is mentioned that she had forgotten what the archangel Gabriel said to her. Perhaps the narrator means to imply that it was not a momentary forgetfulness.

13. The material here is parallel to Matt 1:18-25.

Annas the scribe comes to visit Joseph and discovers that Mary is pregnant. He runs to the priest and informs him that Joseph has defiled the virgin he received from the temple, that he has secretly consummated his marriage with her. Officers go and find that indeed Mary is pregnant. They bring her and Joseph to the court. The priest questions Mary, asking her why she has humiliated her soul and forgotten God although she was brought up in the Holy of Holies and received food from the hand of an angel, and heard hymns, and danced before God. Mary weeps bitterly and says that she is pure and that she has not known a man. The priest also questions Joseph. And Joseph claims he has not been with Mary. When the priest tells Joseph to return the virgin he received from the temple, Joseph bursts into tears.

Then the priest gives them both to drink the water of the conviction of the Lord (Cf. Num 5:11-31), which would make their sins manifest. First, the priest gives Joseph the drink and sends him to the hill-country. Joseph returns unharmed. Next, the priest gives Mary to drink and sends her to the hill-country. Mary, too, returns whole. All the people marvel because sin did not appear in them, proof of their innocence. The priest releases them and Joseph takes Mary to his house, rejoicing and glorifying God.

A decree goes out from King Augustus that all the people in Bethlehem and Judea should be registered. Joseph decides to enrol his sons, but he wonders what he should do with the child. He deliberates enrolling her as his wife, but is ashamed to do that. His other option is to enrol her as his daughter, but he does not find it appealing either because people of Israel know that she is not his daughter. He decides to let God do as he wills.

Saddling his she-ass, Joseph sits Mary on it. His son takes the lead and he follows behind. Two of Joseph's sons accompany them; one son is named Samuel while the other is not named. During the course of their journey, Joseph turns round and sees Mary sad and tells himself that perhaps the child within her is causing her pain. Another time, Joseph turns around and sees her laughing. He asks her why her face is filled with laughter one moment and at another sad. She replies that she has seen two people – one weeping and the other rejoicing. Halfway through the journey, Mary tells Joseph to take her down because she is about to give birth. Joseph takes her down from the she-ass saying to her, "Where shall I take you and hide your shame? For the place is a desert." However, Joseph is able to find a cave and brings her into it. Leaving her in the care of his sons he goes out to look for a Hebrew midwife in the region of Bethlehem. A shift in the narrative takes place at this point. Joseph becomes the narrator and he speaks in the first person singular. He narrates the next segment of the story.

As Joseph goes to search for a Hebrew midwife, he has a sort of ecstatic experience. He observes things happening rather strangely. In a monologue, he narrates what he sees as though he were describing a world that has suddenly come to a standstill.[14] He sees the birds of the heaven motionless. People are chewing and yet not chewing, people are lifting up and yet not lifting, and people are putting something to their mouth yet putting nothing to their mouth. He sees everybody looking upwards. Sheep are being driven but they stand still. The shepherd has his hand raised up to strike them with his staff but his hand remained there. He sees the mouths of the children over the river and they do not drink. And then suddenly everything is normal again.[15]

Joseph meets a woman who came down from the hill-country and tells her that he is looking for a midwife. The midwife enquires who it is that is about to give birth in the cave. Joseph replies that it is his betrothed. The midwife is curious that it is not his wife. So Joseph explains to her that Mary was brought up in the temple and he received her by lot as his wife. And she is not his wife, but she conceived by the Holy Spirit. When they reach the entrance of the cave, they see a bright cloud overshadowing the cave. The midwife says, "My soul is magnified today, for my eyes have seen wonderful things; for salvation is born to Israel." Immediately, the cloud disappears and a bright light appears and their eyes were unable to bear it. A short time later the light withdraws and the baby appears and takes the breast of its mother Mary.[16] The midwife exclaims, "This day is great for me, because I have seen this new sight." When the midwife comes out of the cave, she meets Salome and tells her that a virgin has given birth to a child. Salome is sceptical and says that she will not believe unless she inserts her finger and test her condition.

---

14. A "hushed expectancy" as nature holds its breath for the great event that is about to take place. Hans-Josef Klauck, *Apocryphal Gospels: An Introduction*, trans. Brian McNeil (London: T & T Clark, 2003), 70.

15. This monologue is not found in Papyrus Bodmer.

16. It is noteworthy that the birth itself occurs mysteriously in the glow of the bright light that made it impossible for human eyes to see what is happening. The midwife does not assist in birthing the child. Her role is to be an eyewitness to the miraculous birth.

The midwife goes back into the cave to tell Mary to prepare herself because there is some disagreement about her. Then Salome inserts her finger to test her condition. Immediately, she cries out for her wickedness and unbelief. For she has tested the living God, and she finds her hand falling away from her, consumed by fire.[17] And she bows her knees to God praying to the Lord to restore her. An angel appears to her and tells her that God has heard her prayer and that she should bring her hand to the child and touch him. She is healed when she does so. As she goes out of the cave, an angel cries out to her, "Salome, Salome, do not report what marvels you have seen, until the child has come to Jerusalem."

A tumult occurs in Bethlehem. Wise men had come there asking, "Where is the new-born king of the Jews? For we have seen his star in the east and have come to worship him."[18] Herod hears this and he sends officers to the wise men. He also calls the high priests and asks them, "How is it written concerning the Messiah? Where is he born?" They reply, "In Bethlehem of Judaea; for thus it is written." Then Herod questions the wise men, "What sign did you see concerning the new-born king?" And they reply, "We saw how an indescribably greater star shone among these stars and dimmed them, so that the stars no longer shone; and so we knew that a king was born for Israel. And we have come to worship him." Herod tells them, "Go and seek, and when you have found him, tell me, that I also may come to worship him." Then the wise men go out and the star, which they had seen in the east, leads them until they come to the cave. And the star stands over the cave. The wise men see the child with Mary his mother, and they take out their gift pouches: gold, frankincense, and myrrh. They are warned in a dream not to go into Judaea, and they return to their country by another route.

When Herod hears that he has been deceived he gets very angry and sends his murderers to kill all the children who are two years and under. Mary hears that babies are to be killed and she takes the baby, wraps him in swaddling clothes, and lays him in an ox-manger (cf. Luke 2:7). Elizabeth hears that John is being sought and takes him up to

---

17. This became a basis for the notion that Mary remained a virgin while giving birth (*in partu*) and after giving birth (*post partum*).

18. This section resonates with the narrative of Matthew 2 with some notable differences. The flight to Egypt is omitted. Rather, Mary wraps her child in swaddling clothes and places him in an ox-manger to conceal him from the murderers of Herod.

the hill-country.[19] She is unable to find a hiding place or climb the mountain so she prays, "O mountain of God, receive a mother with a child." Immediately, the mountain opens up and receives her. But they are not kept in darkness in the bowels of the mountain—a light shines for them because an angel of God is with them, protecting them.

Herod now sends his officers to Zacharias to question him about the whereabouts of his son. Zacharias denies any knowledge for he is a minister of God and serves in the temple. Zacharias is questioned and then killed in the temple, but the people of Israel did not know about it.[20]

When the hour of salutation arrives, the priests wait for the customary blessing of Zacharias but he does not appear. They are all fearful, but one of them takes courage and goes inside to find congealed blood beside the altar. A voice is heard saying, "Zacharias has been slain, and his blood shall not be wiped away until his avenger comes." When the man hears this he is afraid and goes out and tells the priests what he has seen. When the priests enter, they hear the ceiling panels of the temple wailing and they tear their clothes from top to bottom. They do not find his body, but they find that his blood has turned into stone. Coming out, they tell the people that Zacharias has been slain and all the tribes mourn his death for three days and three nights. After that Symeon (or Simeon) is appointed by lot to take the place of Zacharias (Luke 2:25-35). Symeon is the one about whom the Holy Spirit revealed that he would not see death until he has seen the risen Christ in the flesh.

In the conclusion, the narrator speaks in the first person singular, stating that this history was written by James in Jerusalem during the time of the disturbance that arose during the time of the death of Herod.[21]

---

19. The text does not say anything about the circumstances of the birth of John except that the baby in Elizabeth leaped and blessed Mary when she came to visit Elizabeth.

20. The martyrdom of Zacharias resonates with 2 Chr 24:20-22 (cf. Matt 23:35).

21. The narrator may have wished to identify the author as one of the sons of Joseph in which case he would have been an eyewitness to most of what has been narrated in the tract. The reference to the time of the death of Herod suggests that he is writing at a time when Jesus is still a child.

BIBLIOGRAPHY

Abbott, H. Porter. *The Cambridge Introduction to Narrative*. Cambridge: Cambridge University Press, 2002.

Abbott, Pamela, Claire Wallace, and Melissa Tyler. *An Introduction to Sociology: Feminist Perspectives*. 3rd ed. Abingdon, Oxon: Routledge, 2005.

Ackerman, Susan. "Isaiah." In *The Women's Bible Commentary*, edited by Carol A. Newsom and Sharon H. Ringe, 161-68. Louisville, KY: Westminster/John Knox Press, 1992.

Adams, Susan. "Towards Partnership: Race, Gender, and the Church in Aotearoa/ New Zealand." In *No Easy Peace: Liberating Anglicanism: A Collection of Essays in Memory of William John Wolf*, edited by Carter Heyward and Sue Phillips, 91-102. Lanham, MD: University Press of America, 1992.

Aldredge-Clanton, Jann. *In Search of the Christ-Sophia: An Inclusive Christology for Liberating Christians*. Mystic, CT: Twenty-Third Publications, 1995.

______. *In Whose Image? God and Gender*. Rev. and expanded ed. New York: Crossroad, 2001.

All India Artisans and Craftworkers Association (AIACA). *Artistic Textiles of Sikkim - Diagnostic Study and Business Development Plan*. Prepared by AIACA and presented to Development Commissioner, Handicraft, Government of Sikkim, 2009.

Allen, John. *Apartheid South Africa: An Insider's Overview of the Origin and Effects of Separate Development*. Lincoln, NE: iUniverse, 2005.

Allison, Dale C. *Jesus of Nazareth: Millenarian Prophet*. Minneapolis, MN: Fortress Press, 1998.

Allison, Robert W. "Let Women be Silent in the Churches (1 Cor. 14.33b-36): What Did Paul Really Say, and What Did it Mean?" *Journal for the Study of the New Testament* 32 (1988): 44-53.

Althaus, Paul. *The Theology of Martin Luther*. Philadelphia, PA: Fortress Press, 1966.

Althaus-Reid, Marcella. *Indecent Theology: Theological Perversions in* Sex, *Gender and Politics*. London: Routledge, 2000.

Altman, Rick. *A Theory of Narrative*. New York: Columbia University Press, 2008.

Amadi-Azuogu, Adolphus Chinedu. *The Politics of Power and the Ordination of Women*. Gender and Power in the New Testament and the Church Today. Fairfax: Xulon Press, 2007.

Anderson, Herbert, and Edward Foley. *Mighty Stories, Dangerous Rituals: Weaving Together the Human and the Divine*. San Francisco, CA: Jossey-Bass, 1998.

Andolsen, Barbara Hilkert, Christine E. Gudorf, and Mary D. Pellauer, eds. *Women's Consciousness, Women's Conscience: A Reader in Feminist Ethics*. Minneapolis, MN: Winston Press, 1985.

Andrews, David. "The Lord's Table, the World's Hunger: Liturgy, Justice, and Rural Life." In *Liturgy and Justice: To Worship God in Spirit and Truth*, edited by Anne Y. Koester, 63-73. Collegeville, MN: Liturgical Press, 2002.

Angami, Zhodi. "Ukepenuopfü: An Exploration of the Goddess." In *Tribal Christian Theology: Methods and Sources for Constructing a Relevant Theology for the Indigenous People of North East India*, edited by Razouselie Lasetso and Yangkahao Vashum, 231-41. Jorhat, Assam: ETC Programme Coordination, 2007.

Antyle. "Zeliangrong Women Experiences: Challenges and Theological Reflection in the Light of the Nazareth Manifesto." In *No More Sorrow in God's Garden of Justice: Tribal Women Doing Theology*, edited by Limatula Longkumer, 146-61. Jorhat, Assam: Women Study Department, Eastern Theological College, 2007.

Ao, O. Alem. *Tsüngremology: Ao Naga Christian Theology*. Aolijen, Mokokchung: Clark Theological College, 1994.

Armour, Ellen T. *Deconstruction, Feminist Theology, and the Problem of Difference: Subverting the Race/Gender Divide*. Chicago: University of Chicago Press, 1999.

Armstrong, Karen. *The Gospel according to Woman*. London: HarperCollins, 1986.

Ashley, Benedict M. *Justice in the Church: Gender and Participation*. Washington, DC: The Catholic University of America Press, 1996.

Askari, Nasreen, Liz Arthur. *Uncut Cloth: Saris, Shawls and Sashes*. London: Merrell Holberton Publishers, 1999.

Avis, Paul, ed. *Paths to Unity: Explorations in Ecumenical Method*. London: Church House Publishing, 2004.

______. "Rethinking Ecumenical Theology." In *Paths to Unity: Explorations in Ecumenical Method*, edited by Paul Avis, 91-106. London: Church House Publishing, 2004.

Ayto, John. "Apartheid." In *Dictionary of Word Origins*. New York: Arcade, 1990.

Baker, Robert A. *The Baptist March in History*. Nashville, TN: Convention Press, 1958.

Baker, Robert Andrew, Edward Anderson Freeman, Watson Kirkconnell, Martin Luther Leuschner, Albert Nash Rogers, Edward Caryl Starr, and Davis Collier Wooley, eds. *Baptist Advance: The Achievements of the Baptists of North America for a Century and a Half*. Nashville, TN: Broadman Press, 1964.

Baker, Robert. "Pricks and Chicks: A Plea for Persons." In *Feminist Philosophies: Problems, Theories, and Applications*, edited by Janet A. Kourany, James P. Sterba, and Rosemarie Tong, 49-59. Englewood Cliffs, NJ: Prentice Hall, 1992.

Baker-Fletcher, Karen. *Dancing* with *God: The Trinity* from a *Womanist Perspective*. St. Louis, MO: Chalice Press, 2006.

Bal, Mieke. *Lethal Love: Feminist Literary Readings of Biblical Love Stories*. Bloomington: Indiana University Press, 1987.

______. *Narratology: Introduction to the Theory of Narratives*. Translated by C. van Boheemen. Toronto: University of Toronto Press, 1985.

______. "Sexuality, Sin, and Sorrow: The Emergence of the Female Character." In *Women, Gender, Religion: A Reader*, edited by Elizabeth A. Castelli and Rosamond C. Rodman, 149-73. New York, NY: PALGRAVE, 2001. Originally published as idem, "Sexuality, Sin and Sorrow: The Emergence of the Female Character (A Reading of Genesis 1-3)." *Poetics Today* 6 (1985): 21-42. Found also in idem, "Sexuality, Sin, and Sorrow: The Emergence of the Female Character." In *Lethal Love: Feminist Literary Interpretations of Biblical Love Stories*, 104-30. Bloomington: Indiana University Press, 1987.

Balz, Horst, and Gerhard Schneider, eds. *Exegetical Dictionary of the New Testament*. Vol. 2. Grand Rapids, MI: Wm B. Eerdmans, 1991.

Bandyopadhyay, P. K. "The Coming of the Alphabet: A Study on the Scripts of Some North-Eastern Languages." In *Linguistic Situation in North-East India*, edited by Mrinal Miri, 69-75. Shillong: North-East India Council for Social Science Research, 1982.

Baptist Church of Mizoram. "Outreach Missions." https://www.mizobaptist.org/outreach-missions/ (accessed Aug 28, 2018).

Barber, E. J. W. [Elizabeth Wayland]. *Prehistoric Textiles: The Development of Cloth in the Neolithic and Bronze Ages with Special Reference to the Aegean*. Princeton, NJ: Princeton University Press, 1991.

______. *Women's Work: The First 20,000 Years – Women, Cloth, and Society in Early Times*. New York: W. W. Norton, 1994.

Bareh, Hamlet. *The History and Culture of the Khasi People*. Calcutta: n.p.

Barlow, Tani E. *The Question of Women in Chinese Feminism*. Durham: Duke University Press, 2004.

Barr, James. "Abba isn't 'Daddy'." *Journal of Theological Studies* 39 (1988): 28-47.

Barreto, Manuela, Michelle K. Ryan, and Michael T. Schmitt, eds. *The Glass Ceiling in the 21st Century: Understanding Barriers to Gender Equality, Psychology of Women*. Washington, DC: American Psychological Association, 2009.

Barstow, Anne L. "The Prehistoric Goddess." In *The Book of the Goddess, Past and Present: An Introduction to Her Religion*, edited by Carl Olson, 7-15. New York: Crossroad, 1983.

Barthes, Roland. "Introduction to the Structural Analysis of Narratives." In *A Barthes Reader*, edited by Susan Sontag, 251-96. New York: Hill and Wang, 1982.

Bates, Albert. *The Singer of Tales*. 2nd ed. Harvard Studies in Comparative Literature 24. Cambridge, MA: Harvard University Press, 2003.

Bauer, Walter, W. F. Arndt, F. W. Gingrich, and F. W. Danker, eds. *A Greek-English Lexicon of the New Testament and Other Early Christian Literature*. 3rd ed., edited and rev. by Frederick William Danker. Chicago: University of Chicago Press, 2000.

Bausch, William J. *Storytelling: Imagination and Faith.* Mystic, CT: Twenty-Third Publications, 1984.

Baylor, Michael G., ed. *The Radical Reformation*, Cambridge Texts in the History of Political Thought. Cambridge: Cambridge University Press, 1991.

Beattie, Gillian. *Women and Marriage in Paul and His Early Interpreters.* London: T & T Clark, 2005.

Beckman, Ninna Edgardh. "Sophia: Symbol of Christian and Feminist Wisdom?" *Feminist Theology* 16 (1997): 32-54.

Beinart, William, and Saul Dubow, eds. *Segregation and Apartheid in Twentieth-Century South Africa.* London: Routledge, 1995.

Bell, Catherine. *Ritual: Perspectives and Dimensions.* Oxford: Oxford University Press, 1997.

Bellis, Alice Ogden. *Helpmates, Harlots, and Heroes: Women's Stories in the Hebrew Bible.* 2nd ed. Louisville, KY: Westminster John Knox Press, 2007.

Benson, Mary. *South Africa: The Struggle for a Birthright.* Harmondsworth: Penguin Books, 1966.

Berger, Arthur Asa. *Narratives: in Popular Culture, Media and Everyday Life.* London: Sage Publications, 1997.

Berger, Teresa, ed. *Dissident Daughters: Feminist Liturgies in Global Context.* Louisville, KY: Westminster John Knox Press, 2001.

______. "Mapping the Global Struggle for Women's Rites." In *Dissident Daughters: Feminist Liturgies in Global Context*, edited by Teresa Berger, 1-26. Louisville, KY: Westminster John Knox Press, 2001.

______. "Women in Worship." In *The Oxford History of Christian Worship*, edited by Geoffrey Wainwright and Karen B. Westerfield Tucker, 755-68. New York, NY: Oxford University Press, 2006.

______. *Women's Ways of Worship: Gender Analysis and Liturgical History.* Collegeville, MN: Liturgical Press, 1999.

Berger, Teresa, and Bryan D. Spinks, eds. *The Spirit in Worship – Worship in the Spirit.* Collegeville, MN: Liturgical Press, 2009.

Berquist, Jon L. *Reclaiming Her Story: The Witness of Women in the Old Testament.* St. Louis, MO: Chalice Press, 1992.

Bertrand, Gabrielle. *Secret Lands Where Women Reign.* London: Robert Hale Limited, 1958.

Best, Thomas F. ed. *Baptism Today: Understanding, Practice, Ecumenical Implications.* Faith and Order Paper No. 207. Collegeville, MN: Liturgical Press, 2008.

Best, Thomas F., and Günther Gassmann, eds. *On the Way to Fuller Koinonia: Official Report of the Fifth World Conference on Faith and Order.* Faith and Order Paper 166. Geneva: WCC Publications, 1994.

Betteridge, Alan. *Deep Roots, Living Branches: A History of Baptists in the English Western Midlands.* Leicester: Matador, 2010.

Bhandari, Vandana. *Costume, Textiles and Jewellery of India: Traditions in Rajasthan.* Mercury Books, 2005.

Bhavnani, Enakshi. *Folk and Tribal Designs of India: Hundreds of Designs and Motifs from the Folk and Tribal Craft of India, Drawn from Original Sources by Kiran Malhotra, Devi Thapa, Roshan Ali and Percy Bhathenna.* Bombay: Taraporevala, 1974.

Bird, Darlene, and Yvonne Sherwood, eds. *Bodies in Question: Gender, Religion, Text.* Aldershot: Ashgate Publishing House, 2005.

Black, Kathy. *A Healing Homiletic: Preaching and Disability.* Nashville, TN: Abingdon Press, 1996.

Bloch, Abraham P. *The Biblical and Historical Background of Jewish Customs and Ceremonies.* New York: KTAV Pub. House, 1980.

Blohm, Uta. *Religious Traditions and Personal Stories: Women Working as Priests, Ministers and Rabbis.* Studies in the Intercultural History of Christianity 137. Frankfurt am Main: Peter Lang, 2005.

Blomberg, Craig. *1 Corinthians.* NIV Application Commentary. Grand Rapids, MI: Zondervan Publishing House, 1995.

Boff, Leonardo. *Holy Trinity, Perfect Community.* Translated by Phillip Berryman. Maryknoll, NY: Orbis Books, 2000.

______. *The Maternal Face of God: The Feminine and Its Religious Expressions.* Maryknoll, NY: Orbis Press, 1987.

Bond, L. Susan. *Trouble With Jesus: Women, Christology, and Preaching.* St. Louis, MO: Chalice Press, 1999.

Bonhoeffer, Dietrich. *Act and Being: Transcendental Philosophy and Ontology in Systematic Theology.* Deitrich Bonhoeffer Works 2. Trans. H. Martin Rumscheidt. Minneapolis, MN: Fortress Press, 2009.

Borg, Marcus J. *Jesus, A New Vision: Spirit, Culture, and the Life of Discipleship.* San Francisco: Harper & Row, 1987.

______. *Jesus in Contemporary Scholarship.* Valley Forge, PA: Trinity Press International, 1994.

______. *Meeting Jesus Again for the First Time.* San Francisco: HarperSanFrancisco, 1994.

Boritt, Gabor S., ed. *Why the Civil War Came.* Oxford: Oxford University Press, 1996.

Bower, Bruce. "Stone Age Art Gets Animated: Ancient Cave Paintings Depict Moving Animals." *Science News* 181/13 (June 30, 2012), 12. http://www.sciencenews.org/view/generic/id/341206/description/Stone_Age_art_gets_animated (accessed July 22, 2018).

Bradley, C. Randall. *From Memory to Imagination: Reforming the Church's Music.* Grand Rapids, MI: Wm B. Eerdmans Publishing, 2012.

Bramly, Serge and Bettina Rheims. *I.N.R.I.* New York: Monacelli Press, 1999.

Brand, Eugene L. "Vocation and Ministry." In *In Search of a Round Table: Gender, Theology & Church Leadership*, edited by Musimbi R. A. Kanyoro, 12-27. Geneva: WCC Publications, 1997.

Brenner, Athalya, ed. *A Feminist Companion to Exodus and Deuteronomy*. Sheffield: Sheffield Academic Press, 1994.

______, ed. *A Feminist Companion to Genesis*. Sheffield: Sheffield Academic Press, 1997.

______, ed. *A Feminist Companion to the Later Prophets*. Sheffield: Sheffield Academic Press, 1995.

______, ed. *Genesis: A Feminist Companion to the Bible (Second Series)*. Sheffield: Sheffield Academic Press, 1998.

______. *I Am... Biblical Women Tell Their Own Stories*. Minneapolis: Fortress Press, 2005.

Britt, Mary E. *In Search of New Wine-Skins: An Exploration of Models of Christian Community*. Pastoral Investigation of Contemporary Trends, National Catholic Research Council. Melbourne: Collins Dove, 1988.

Brock, Rita Nakashima. *Journeys by Heart: A Christology of Erotic Power*. New York: Crossroad, 1988.

Bronner, Leila Leah. *From Eve to Esther: Rabbinic Reconstructions of Biblical Women*. Gender and the Biblical Tradition. Louisville, KY: Westminster John Knox Press, 1994.

______. "From Veil to Wig: Jewish Women's Hair Covering." *Judaism* 42 (Fall 1993): 465-77.

Brown, Mary Ellen. "Soap Opera and Women's Culture: Politics and the Popular." In *Doing Research on Women's Communication: Perspectives on Theory and Method*, edited by Kathryn Carter and Carole Spitzack, 161-90. Norwood, NJ: Ablex Publishing Corporation, 1989.

Bruce, Elizabeth McIsaac. "Narrative Inquiry: A Spiritual and Liberating Approach to Research." *Religious Education* 103/3 (May-June 2008): 323-38.

Bruner, Jerome. *Actual Minds: Possible Worlds*. Cambridge, MA: Harvard University Press, 1986.

Bruzelius, Caroline A. "Hearing Is Believing: Clarissan Architecture, ca. 1213-1340." *Gesta* 31 (1992): 83-91.

Buber, Martin. *Between Man and Man*. Translated by Ronald Gregor Smith. London: Fontana Library, 1961.

______. *I and Thou*. Translated by Ronald G. Smith. New York: Scribner's, 1968.

Buckley, Belinda. *Children's Communication Skills: From Birth to Five Years*. London: Routledge, 2003.

Buechner, Frederick. *Telling the Truth: The Gospel as Tragedy, Comedy, and Fairy Tale*. San Francisco: Harper & Row, 1977.

Bullock, Katherine. *Rethinking Muslim Women and the Veil: Challenging Historical and Modern Stereotypes*. Herndon, VA: The International Institute of Islamic Thought, 2002.

Burkitt, F. Crawford. *Early Eastern Christianity: St. Margaret's Lectures 1904 on the Syriac-Speaking Church*. London: John Murray, 1904.

Burns, Stephen, Nicola Slee, and Michael N. Jagessar, eds. *The Edge of God: New Liturgical Texts and Contexts in Conversation*. London: Epworth, 2008.

Burton H. Throckmorton, ed., trans. *The Gospels and the Letters of Paul: An Inclusive Language Edition*. Cleveland, OH: Pilgrim Press, 1992.

Buttrick, David "Story and Symbol, the Stuff of Preaching." In *What's the Shape of Narrative Preaching?* edited by Mike Graves and David J. Schlafer, 99-113. St. Louis, MO: Chalice Press, 2008.

Bynum, Carolyn Walker. *Jesus as Mother: Studies in the Spirituality of the High Middle Ages*. Berkeley: University of California Press, 1982.

Cadbury, Henry J. "Note XXX. Names for Christians and Christianity in Acts." In *The Beginnings of Christianity*, Part 1: *The Acts of the Apostles*, vol. 5: *Additional Notes to the Commentary*, edited by Kirsopp Lake and Henry J. Cadbury, 375-92. London: Macmillan and Co., 1993.

Caird, G. B. *New Testament Theology*. Completed and edited by L. D. Hurst. Oxford: Clarendon, 1994.

Caldwell, Patricia. *The Puritan Conversion Narrative: The Beginnings of American Expression*. Cambridge: Cambridge University Press, 1983.

Cameron, Deborah, ed. *The Feminist Critique of Language: A Reader*. 2nd ed. London: Routledge, 1998.

______. "Lost in Translation: Non-Sexist Language." In *The Feminist Critique of Language: A Reader*, 2nd ed., edited by Deborah Cameron, 155-63. London: Routldege, 1998.

Campbell, Joseph, and Charles Musès, eds. *In All Her Names: Explorations of the Feminine in Divinity*. San Francisco: HarperSanFrancisco, 1991.

Cannon, Katie G. "Womanist Interpretation and Preaching in the Black Church." In *Searching the Scriptures*, vol. 1, *A Feminist Introduction*, edited by Elisabeth Schüssler Fiorenza, 326-37. New York: Crossroad, 1993.

Carson, Claire, and Nicola Slee. "Brokenness, Love and Embrace: Eating Disorders and the Eucharist." In *The Edge of God: New Liturgical Texts and Contexts in Conversation*, edited by Stephen Burns, Nicola Slee, and Michael N. Jagessar, 134-50. London: Epworth, 2008.

Carter, Kathryn, and Carole Spitzack, eds. *Doing Research on Women's Communication: Perspectives on Theory and Method*. Norwood, NJ: Ablex Publishing Corporation, 1989.

Castelli, Elizabeth A., and Rosamond C. Rodman, eds. *Women, Gender, Religion: A Reader*. New York, NY: PALGRAVE, 2001.

Census Population 2015 Data. "Christian Religion Census 2011." https://www.census2011.co.in/data/religion/3-christianity.html (accessed Aug 28, 2018).

Center for Reformed Theology and Apologetics. "Westminster Shorter Catechism: With Proof Texts." www.reformed.org/documents/wsc/ index.html (accessed 27 July 2010).

Chapman, Audrey R., and Hugo van der Merwe, eds. *Truth and Reconciliation in South Africa: Did the TRC Deliver?* Philadelphia, PA: University of Pennsylvania Press, 2008.

Chatman, Seymour. *Story and Discourse: Narrative Structure in Fiction and Film.* Ithaca, NY: Cornell University Press, 1978.

Chatterji, N. *Puan – the Pride of Mizoram.* Aizawl: Tribal Research Institute, 1978.

Chauhan, Gian Chand. *Origin and Growth of Feudalism in Early India: From the Mauryas to AD 650.* New Delhi: Munshiram Manoharlal Publishers, 2004.

Chong, Denise. *The Girl in the Picture: The Story of Kim Phuc, the Photograph, and the Vietnam War.* New York: Viking, 2000.

Chongloi, Satkhokai. "The Unseen Christ among the Kuki People." In *Garnering Tribal Resources for Doing Tribal Christian Theology*, Tribal Study Series 16, edited by Razouselie Lasetso, 175-95. Jorhat, Assam: Eastern Theological College Programme Coordination, 2008.

Christ, Carol P. *Laughter of Aphrodite: Reflections on a Journey to the Goddess.* San Francisco: Harper & Row, 1987.

Christians, Clifford G., et al. *Media Ethics: Cases and Moral Reasoning.* 7th ed. New York: Allyn & Bacon, 2004.

Church of the Province of New Zealand. *A New Zealand Prayer Book – He Karakia Mihinare o Aotearoa.* Auckland: Collins, 1989.

Cirksena, Kathryn and Lisa Cuklanz. "Male is to Female As ___ Is to ___: A Guided Tour of Five Feminist Frameworks for Communication Studies." In *Women Making Meaning: New Feminist Directions in Communication*, edited by Lana F. Rakow, 18-44. New York & London: Routledge, 1992.

Clague, Julie. "The Christa: Symbolizing My Humanity and My Pain." *Feminist Theology* 14/1 (September 2005): 83-108.

______. "Divine Transgressions: The Female Christ-Form in Art." *Critical Quarterly* 47/3 (Autumn 2005): 47-63.

______. "Symbolism and the Power of Art: Female Representations of Christ Crucified." In *Bodies in Question: Gender, Religion, Text*, edited by Darlene Bird and Yvonne Sherwood, 29-55. Aldershot: Ashgate Publishing House, 2005.

Clark, Elizabeth. *Women in the Early Church.* Wilmington: Michael Glazier, 1983.

Clark, Nancy L., and William H. Worger. *South Africa: The Rise and Fall of Apartheid.* Harlow: Longman, 2004.

Clark, Vivian. "Was Jesus Christ a Man's Man?" *Christianity Today* 18 (February 1983): 16-18.

Colledge, E., and J. Walsh, eds. *Julian of Norwich: Showings, Classics of Western Spirituality.* London: SPCK, 1978.

Collins, John J. *The Bible after Babel: Historical Criticism in a Postmodern Age.* Grand Rapids, MI: Wm B. Eerdmans, 2005.

Collins, Mary. "Principles of Feminist Liturgy." *Women at Worship: Interpretations of North American Diversity*, edited by Marjorie Procter-Smith and Janet Walton, 17-24. Louisville: Westminster John Knox Press, 1993.

Collins, Raymond F. *First Corinthians*. Sacra Pagina 7. Edited by Daniel J. Harrington. Collegeville, MN: The Liturgical Press, 1999.

Cone, James, and Gayraud S. Wilmore, eds. *Black Theology: A Documentary History*. Vol. 2. *1980-1992*. Maryknoll, NY: Orbis, 1993.

Congar, Yves. *Dialogue between Christians: Catholic Contributions to Ecumenism*. Translated by Philip Loretz. London: G. Chapman, 1966.

______. *I Believe in the Holy Spirit*. Vol. 3. New York: Seabury Press, 1983.

Connolly, Sean. *Apartheid in South Africa*. Oxford: Heinemann, 2001.

Conzelmann, Hans. *1 Corinthians: A Commentary on the First Epistle to the Corinthians*. Hermeneia Commentaries. Translated by James W. Leitch, edited by George W. MacRae. Philadelphia: Fortress Press, 1975.

Cooke, Bernard J. "Body and Mystical Body: The Church as *Communio*." In *Bodies of Worship: Explorations in Theory and Practice*, edited by Bruce T. Morrill. Collegeville, MN: The Liturgical Press, 1999.

Cooper, Joanne E. "Telling Our Own Stories: The Reading and Writing of Journals or Diaries." In *Stories Lives Tell: Narrative and Dialogue in Education*, edited by Carol Witherell and Nel Noddings, 96-112. New York: Teachers College, Columbia University, 1991.

Cooper, John W. *Our Father in Heaven: Christian Faith and Inclusive Language for God*. Grand Rapids, MI: Baker Books, 1998.

Cooper, Patricia J. and Norma Bradley Allen. *The Quilters: Women and Domestic Art – An Oral History*. New York: Doubleday, 1989.

Coste, Didier. *Narrative as Communication*. Theory and History of Literature 64. Minneapolis, MN: University of Minnesota Press, 1989.

Cox, Harvey. *Fire from Heaven: The Rise of Pentecostal Spirituality and the Reshaping of Religion in the Twenty-first Century*. Reading, MA: Addison-Wesley Publishing, 1995.

Craddock, Fred B. *As One Without Authority*. 3rd ed. Nashville, TN: Abingdon Press, 1979.

______. "Story, Narrative, and Metanarrative." In *What's the Shape of Narrative Preaching?* edited by Mike Graves and David J. Schlafer, 87-98. St. Louis, MO: Chalice Press, 2008.

Cramer, Robert F. "Foreign Mission Society." In *Baptist Advance: The Achievements of the Baptists of North America for a Century and a Half*, edited by Robert Andrew Baker, Edward Anderson Freeman, Watson Kirkconnell, Martin Luther Leuschner, Albert Nash Rogers, Edward Caryl Starr, and Davis Collier Wooley, 73-89. Nashville, TN: Broadman Press, 1964.

Crane, Carol. *The Handkerchief Quilt*. Ann Arbor, MI: Sleeping Bear Press, 2010.

Crawford, Matthew R. "On Faith, Signs, and Fruits: Martin Luther's Theology of the Lord's Supper." In *The Lord's Supper: Remembering and Proclaiming Christ*

Until He Comes, NAC Studies in Bible and Theology 10, edited by Thomas R. Schreiner and Matthew R. Crawford, 193-228. Nashville, TN: B & H Publishing Group, 2010.

Cross Cultural Publications. *The New Testament of the Inclusive Language Bible*. Notre Dame, IN: Crossroads Books, 1994.

Cross, Frank Moore, and David Noel Freedman. "The Song of Miriam: Exodus 15." In *Studies in Ancient Yahwistic Poetry*, Society of Biblical Literature Dissertation Series, 31-45. Grand Rapids, MI: Wm B. Eerdmans, 1975.

______. *Studies in Ancient Yahwistic Poetry*. Society of Biblical Literature Dissertation Series. Grand Rapids, MI: Wm B. Eerdmans, 1975.

Crossan, John Dominic. *The Dark Interval: Towards a Theology of Story*. Sonoma, CA: Polridge Press, 1988.

______. *The Historical Jesus: The Life of a Mediterranean Peasant*. San Francisco: HarperSanFrancisco, 1991.

______. *Jesus: A Revolutionary Biography*. San Francisco: HarperSanFrancisco, 1994.

Crotwell, Helen Gray, ed. *Women and the Word: Sermons*. Philadelphia: Fortress Press, 1978.

Cullmann, Oscar. "Infancy Gospels." In *New Testament Apocrypha*, vol. 1: *Gospels and Related Writings*, rev. ed., edited by Wilhelm Schneemelcher and R. McL. Wilson, 414-69. Louisville, KY: Westminster John Knox Press, 2003.

Cummins, Joseph. *The World's Bloodiest History: Massacre, Genocide, and the Scars they Left on Civilization*. Beverly, MA: Fair Winds Press, 2010.

Curzan, Anne. *Gender Shifts in the History of English*. Cambridge: Cambridge University Press, 2003.

D'Angelo, Mary Rose. "*Abba* and 'Father': Imperial Theology and the Jesus Traditions." *Journal of Biblical Literature* 111 (1992): 611-30.

D'Antonio, William V., James D. Davidson, Dean R. Hoge, and Ruth A. Wallace. *American Catholic Laity in a Changing Church*. Kansas City, MO: Sheed and Ward, 1989.

Daly, Mary. *Beyond God the Father: Towards a Philosophy of Women's Liberation*. Boston: Beacon Press, 1973.

______. *The Church and the Second Sex*. New York: Harper & Row, 1968.

______. *Gyn/Ecology: The Metaethics of Radical Feminism*. Boston: Beacon Press, 1978.

______. *Pure Lust: Elemental Feminist Philosophy*. Boston: Beacon Press, 1984.

Darr, Katheryn Pfisterer. *Far More Precious Than Jewels: Perspectives on Biblical Women*. Louisville, KY: Westminster John Knox, 1991.

Das, S. T. *Life Style: Indian Tribes – Locational Practice*. Vol. 2. New Delhi: Gyan Publishing House, 2000.

Daube, David. "Societas as Consensual Contract." *Cambridge Law Journal* 6 (1938): 381-403.

Davidson, Hilda Ellis. *Roles of the Northern Goddess*. London: Routledge, 1998.

Davies, Eryl W. *The Dissenting Reader: Feminist Approaches to the Hebrew Bible.* Aldershot: Ashgate, 2003.

Davies, Sioned. "Storytelling in Medieval Wales," *Oral Tradition* 7/2 (1992):231-57. http://journal.oraltradition.org/files/articles/7ii/4_davies.pdf (accessed July 22, 2018).

de Beauvoir, Simone. *The Second Sex.* New York: Vintage Books, 1953.

De Geer, Ingrid. "Music." In *The Cambridge History of Scandinavia.* Vol. 1. *Prehistory to 1520.* Cambridge History of Scandinavia 1, edited by Knut Helle, 550-56. Cambridge: Cambridge University Press, 2003.

de Gruchy, John W. and Charles Villa-Vicencio, eds. *Apartheid is a Heresy.* Grand Rapids, Michigan: Wm. B. Eerdmans, 1983.

Dempster, Murray W., Byron D. Klaus, Douglas Petersen, eds. *The Globalization of Pentecostalism: A Religion Made to Travel.* Oxford: Regnum Books Intl., 1999.

Depew, David, and John Durham Peters. "Community and Communication: The Conceptual Background." In *Communication and Community,* edited by Gregory J. Shepherd and Eric W. Rothenbuhler, 3-21. Mahwah, NJ: Lawrence Erlbaum, 2001.

Devi, Ch. Victoria. "Exploring the Lives of Manipur's Women Weavers." *Indian Journal of Gender Studies* 19/1 (February 2012): 31-55.

Devine, Elizabeth and Nancy L. Braganti. *The Traveller's Guide to Asian Customs and Manners.* New York: St. Martin's Griffin, 1998.

DNA: Daily News and Analysis. "Woman to be Ordained, but Not Made Priest in Patriarchal Mizoram." *DNA: Daily News and Analysis,* Feb. 20, 2012. http://www.dnaindia.com/india/report_woman-to-be-ordained-but-not-made-priest-in-patriarchal-mizoram_1652578 (accessed September 3, 2018).

Dokumen.com. "Arts and Crafts of North-East - Textiles of Manipur." https://dokumen.tips/download/link/manipur-enjoys-a-distinct-place-amongst-the-handloom-zones-in-india (acccessed June 19, 2019).

Douglas A. Campbell, ed. *Gospel and Gender: A Trinitarian Engagement with Being Male and Female in Christ.* Studies in Theology and Sexuality. London: T & T Clark, 2003.

Downing, Christine. *The Goddess.* New York: Crossroad, 1984.

Downs, Frederick S. *History of Christianity in India.* Vol. 5. Pt. 5: *North East India in the Nineteenth and Twentieth Centuries.* CHAI History of Christianity in India. Bangalore: The Church History Association of India, 1992.

______. *Manual of Worship.* Gauhati: Christian Literature Centre, 1975.

______. *The Mighty Works of God: A Brief History of the Council of Baptist Churches in North East India: The Mission Period 1836-1950.* Guwahati: Christian Literature Centre, 1969.

Dozo, Phuveyi. *The Cross over Nagaland.* Guwahati: Christian Literature Centre, 1983.

Dube, Musa W. *Postcolonial Feminist Interpretation of the Bible.* St. Louis, MO: Chalice Press, 2000.

Duck, Ruth C. *Circles of Care: Hymns and Songs*. Cleveland: The Pilgrim Press, 1998.

______. *Dancing in the Universe: Hymns and Songs*. Chicago: GIA Publications, 1992.

______. "Expansive Language in the Baptized Community." In *Primary Sources in Liturgical Theology: A Reader*, edited by Dwight W. Vogel, 286-94. Collegeville, MN: The Liturgical Press, 2000.

______. *Gender and the Name of God: The Trinitarian Baptismal Formula*. Cleveland, OH: The Pilgrim Press, 1991.

Dunn, James D. G. "Living Tradition." In *What is it that the Scripture Says? Essays in Biblical Interpretation, Translation and Reception in Honour of Henry Wansbrough OSB*, edited by Philip McCosker, 275-89. London: T & T Clark, 2006.

______. "Prayer." In *Dictionary of Jesus and the Gospels*, edited by Joel B. Green, Scot McKnight, and I. Howard Marshall, 617-25. Leicester: InterVarsity Press, 1992.

DuPlessis, Rachel Blau. *Writing beyond the Ending: Narrative Strategies of Twentieth-Century Women Writers*. Bloomington: Indiana University Press, 1985.

Durso, Keith E. *No Armor for the Back: Baptist Prison Writings, 1600s–1700s*. Macon, GA: Mercer University Press, 2007.

Dutta, Paritosh Chandra and Ram Krishna Mandal. *Globalisation, Growth and Inequality in North East India: Economic Disparity*. Delhi: Kalpaz Publications, 2011.

Eastwood, Cyril. *The Priesthood of All Believers: An Examination of the Doctrine from the Reformation to the Present Day*. 1960; repr., Eugene, OR: Wipf & Stock, 2009.

Ehrman, B. D. *Jesus: Apocalyptic Prophet of the New Millennium*. Oxford: Oxford University Press, 1999.

Eilberg-Schwartz, Howard, and Wendy Doniger, eds. *Off with Her Head! The Denial of Women's Identity in Myth, Religion, and Culture*. Berkeley: University of California Press, 1995.

Eisenberg, Ronald L. *The JPS Guide to Jewish Traditions*. A JPS Desk Reference. Philadelphia, PA: Jewish Publication Society, 2004.

Elkins, Heather Murray. *Worshipping Women: Reforming God's People for Praise*. Nashville: Abingdon Press, 1994.

Elliott, J. K. *The Apocryphal New Testament: A Collection of Apocryphal Christian Literature in an English Translation Based on M. R. James*. Oxford: Oxford University Press, 1994.

______. "The Protevangelium of James." In *The Apocryphal New Testament: A Collection of Apocryphal Christian Literature in an English Translation Based on M. R. James*, 48-67. Oxford: Oxford University Press, 1994.

Ellis, Christopher. "Baptists in Britain." In *The Oxford History of Christian Worship*, edited by Geoffrey Wainwright and Karen B. Westerfield Tucker, 560-73. New York, NY: Oxford University Press, 2006.

Ellis, E. Earle. *The Gospel of Luke*. NCB. London: Oliphants, 1974.

Ellis, Marc H. and Otto Maduro, eds. *The Future of Liberation Theology: Essays in Honor of Gustavo Gutiérrez*. Maryknoll, NY: Orbis Books, 1989.

Elsley, Judy. *Quilts as Text(iles): The Semiotics of Quilting*. Berkeley Insights in Linguistics and Semiotics 16. New York: Peter Lang, 1996.

Eltrop, Bettina and Claudia Janssen. "Protevangelium of James: God's Story Goes On." In *Feminist Biblical Interpretation: A Compendium of Critical Commentary on the Books of the Bible and Related Literature*, edited by Luise Schottroff and Marie-Theres Wacker, 990-96. Grand Rapids, MI: Wm B. Eerdmans, 2012.

Elwin, Verrier. *Myths of Middle India*. Bombay: Oxford University Press, 1949.

Elwin, Verrier. *The Art of Northeast Frontier of India*. Shillong: Northeast Frontier Agency, 1959.

Emswiler, Sharon Neufer, and Thomas Neufer Emswiler. *Women & Worship: A Guide to Nonsexist Hymns, Prayers, and Liturgies*. Rev. and expanded ed. San Francisco: Harper & Row, 1984.

Engelsman, Joan Chamberlain. *The Feminine Dimension of the Divine*. Philadelphia: The Westminster Press, 1979.

Erdener, Yildiray. *The Song Contest of Turkish Minstrels: Improvised Poetry Sung to Traditional Music*. Milman Parry Studies in Oral Tradition. New York: Garland Publishing, 1995.

Eschle, Catherine, and Bice Maiguashca, *Making Feminist Sense of the Global Justice Movement*. Lanham, MD: Rowman & Littlefield Publishers, 2010.

Eslinger, Richard L. *A New Hearing: Living Options in Homiletical Methods*. Nashville: Abingdon Press, 1987.

Esposito, Roberto. *Communitas: The Origin and Destiny of Community*. Cultural Memory in the Present. Translated by Timothy Campbell. Stanford, CA: Stanford University Press, 2010.

Eunice, S. "The Status of Konyak Women Under Ang System." In *No More Sorrow in God's Garden of Justice: Tribal Women Doing Theology*, Women Study Series 4, edited by Limatula Longkumer, 75-80. Jorhat, Assam: Women Study Department, Eastern Theological College, 2007.

Exum, J. Cheryl. *Fragmented Women: Feminist (Sub)versions of Biblical Narratives*. Journal for the Study of the Old Testament Supplement Series 163. Sheffield: Sheffield Academic Press, 1993.

FAO, IFAD, UNICEF, WFP and WHO. *2017: The State of Food Security and Nutrition in the World 2017-Building Resilience for Peace and Food Security*. https://docs.wfp.org/api/documents/WFP-0000022419/download/?_ga=2.268521401.974489353.1506032202-1929593996.1506032202 (accessed September 10, 2018).

Farmer, David, and Edwina Hunter, eds. *And Blessed Is She: Sermons by Women*. San Francisco: Harper & Row, 1990.

Fee, Gordon D. *The First Epistle to the Corinthians*. Grand Rapids, MI: Wm B. Eerdmans, 1987.

Ferguson, Everett. *The Church of Christ: A Biblical Ecclesiology for Today*. Grand Rapids, MI: Wm B. Eerdmans, 1996.

Ferrero, Pat, Elaine Hedges, and Julie Silber. *Hearts and Hands: The Influence of Women and Quilts on American Society*. San Francisco: Quilt Digest Press, 1987.

Fetterley, Judith. *The Resisting Reader: A Feminist Approach to American Fiction*. Bloomington: Indiana University Press, 1978.

Fiddes, Paul. "The Baptism of Believers." In *Baptism Today: Understanding, Practice, Ecumenical Implications*, Faith and Order Paper No. 207, edited by Thomas F. Best, 73-80. Collegeville, MN: Liturgical Press, 2008.

Fiensy, David A. *Jesus the Galilean: Soundings in a First Century Life*. Piscataway, NJ: Gorgias Press, 2007.

Fillon, Mike. "Real Face of Jesus: December 2002 Cover Story – Advances in Forensic Science Reveal the Most Famous Face in History," *Popular Mechanics* 179/12 (2002): 68-71. https://www.popularmechanics.com/science/health/a234/1282186/ (accessed July 26, 2018).

Finger, Reta Halteman, and Kari Sandhaas, eds. *The Wisdom of Daughters: Two Decades of the Voice of Christian Feminism*. Philadelphia, PA: Innisfree Press, 2001.

Fischer, Irmtraud. "Isaiah: The Book of Female Metaphors." In *Feminist Biblical Interpretation: A Compendium of Critical Commentary on the Books of the Bible and Related Literature*, edited by Luise Schottroff and Marie-Theres Wacker, 303-18. Grand Rapids, MI: William B. Eerdmans, 2012.

______. *Women Who Wrestled with God: Biblical Stories of Israel's Beginnings*. Translated by Linda M. Maloney. Collegeville, MN: Liturgical Press,2005.

Fisher, Peter. "Symphonic Discord: The Place of Diversity in Unity Statements." In *Paths to Unity: Explorations in Ecumenical Method*, edited by Paul Avis, 13-28. London: Church House Publishing, 2004.

Fisher, Walter R. *Human Communication as a Narration: Toward a Philosophy of Reason, Value, and Action*. Columbia, SC: University of South Carolina Press, 1987.

Fitzmyer, Joseph A. *To Advance the Gospel: New Testament Studies*. 2nd ed. Grand Rapids, MI: Wm B. Eerdmans, 1998.

______. "κύριος." In *Exegetical Dictionary of the New Testament*, vol. 2, edited by Horst Balz and Gerhard Schneider, 328-31. Grand Rapids, MI: Wm B. Eerdmans, 1991.

______. "New Testament *Kyrios* and *Maranatha* and Their Aramaic Background." In *To Advance the Gospel: New Testament Studies*, 2nd ed., 218-35. Grand Rapids, MI: Wm B. Eerdmans, 1998.

Fleetwood, Nicole R. *Troubling Vision: Performance, Visuality, and Blackness*. Chicago: The University of Chicago Press, 2011.

Foh, Susan T. "The Head of the Woman is the Man" (1989 CE). In *Eve and Adam: Jewish, Christian, and Muslim Readings on Genesis and Gender*, edited by Kristen E. Kvam, Linda S. Schearing and Valarie H. H. Ziegler, 391-401. Bloomington, IN: Indiana University Press, 1999.

Ford, Frances, et al., eds. *Out of the Darkness: Paths to Inclusive Worship*. Sydney: Australian Council of Churches, 1986.

Fortner, Robert S. *Communication, Media, and Identity*. Lanham: Rowman and Littlefield Publishers, 2007.

Foskett, Mary F. "Virginity as Purity in the *Protevangelium of James*." In *A Feminist Companion to Mariology*, edited by Amy-Jill Levine and Maria Mayo Robbins, 67-76. London: T & T Clark International, 2005.

Foster, Paul, ed. *The Non-Canonical Gospels*. London: T & T Clark, 2008.

______. "The *Protevangelium of James*." In *The Non-Canonical Gospels*, edited by Paul Foster, 110-124. London: T & T Clark, 2008.

Freedman, Maurice. *The Confirmation of Otherness: In Family, Community, and Society*. New York: Pilgrim Press, 1983.

Fry, Gladys-Marie. *Stitched from the Soul: Slave Quilts from the Ante-Bellum South*. New York: Dutton, 1990.

Frymer-Kensky, Tikva. "Women." In *Harper's Bible Dictionary*, edited by Paul Achtemeier, 1138-41. San Francisco: Harper & Row, 1985.

Fuchs, Lorelei Francis. *Koinonia and the Quest for an Ecumenical Ecclesiology: From Foundations through Dialogue to Symbolic Competence for Communionality*. Grand Rapids, MI: Wm B. Eerdmans, 2008.

Funk, F. X., ed. *Didascalia et Constitutiones Apostolorum*. Paderborn, 1905.

Gallagher, Susan VanZanten. "Reconciliation and Hope: Confessional Narratives in South Africa." In *The Gift of Story: Narrating Hope in a Postmodern World*, edited by Emily Griesinger & Mark Eaton, 207-21. Waco, TX: Baylor University Press, 2006.

Ganguli, Milada. *Naga Art*. New Delhi: Oxford & IBH Pub. Co., 1993.

Geffré, Claude. "'Father' as a Proper Name for God." *Concilium* 163 (1981): 67-77.

Gelpi, Donald. *The Divine Mother: A Trinitarian Theology of the Holy Spirit*. Lanham, MD: University Press of America, 1984.

Ghosh, G. K., and Shukla Ghosh. *Indian Textiles: Past and Present*. New Delhi: APH Publishing Corporation, 1995.

Gibson, Joan. "Could Christ Have Been Born a Woman? A Medieval Debate." *Journal of Feminist Studies in Religion* 8/1 (1992): 65-82.

Gilchrist, Roberta. *Gender and Material Culture: The Archaeology of Religious Women*. New York: Routledge, 1994.

Gilhus, Ingvild Sælid. *The Nature of the archons: A Study in the Soteriology of a Gnostic Treatise from Nag Hammadi (CGII, 4)*. Studies in Oriental Religions 12. Wiesbaden: O. Harrassowitz, 1985.

Gillespie, Spike. *Quilts around the World: The Story of Quilting from Alabama to Zimbabwe*. Minneapolis: Voyageur Press, 2010.

Gilligan, Carol, Janie Victoria Ward, Jill McLean Taylor, with Betty Bardige, eds. *Mapping the Moral Domain: A Contribution of Women's Thinking to Psychological Theory and Education*. Cambridge, MA: Harvard University Press, 1988.

Girshick, Lori B. *Woman –To-Woman Sexual Violence: Does She Call It Rape?* Northeastern Series on Gender, Crime, and Law. Boston: Northeastern University Press, 2002.

Gizelis, Gregory. *Narrative Rhetorical Devices of Persuasion: Folklore Communication in a Greek-American Community*. Athens: National Centre of Social Research, 1974.

Goehring, James E., Charles W. Hedrick, Jack T. Sanders, and Hans Dieter Betz, eds. *Gnosticism and the Early Christian World*. Sonoma, CA: Polebridge Press, 1990.

Gold, Victor Roland, et al. *The New Testament and Psalms: An Inclusive Version*. New York: Oxford University Press, 1995.

Goldenberg, Naomi. *Changing of the Gods: Feminism and the End of Traditional Religions*. Boston: Beacon Press, 1979.

González, Justo L. *The Story of Christianity*. Vol. 2. *The Reformation to the Present Day*. San Francisco: Harper & Row, 1985.

Graves, Mike, and David J. Schlafer, eds. *What's the Shape of Narrative Preaching?* St. Louis, MO: Chalice Press, 2008.

Gray, John. *Men are from Mars, Women are from Venus: A Practical Guide for Improving Communication and Getting What You Want in Your Relationships*. New York, NY: HarperCollins, 1992.

Grenz, Stanley J. *The Social Goal and the Relational Self: A Trinitarian Theology of the Imago Dei*. Louisville, KY: Westminster John Knox Press, 2001.

Grey, Mary. *Introducing Feminist Images of God*. Introductions in Feminist Theology 7. Sheffield: Sheffield Academic Press, 2001.

Griesinger, Emily, and Mark Eaton, eds. *The Gift of Story: Narrating Hope in a Postmodern World*. Waco, TX: Baylor University Press, 2006.

Grimshaw, Patricia and Andrew May, eds. *Missionaries, Indigenous Peoples and Cultural Exchange*. Eastbourne: Sussex Academic Press, 2010.

Gros, Jeffrey, Harding Meyer, and William G. Rusch, eds. *Growth in Agreement II: Reports and Agreed Statements of Ecumenical Conversations on a World Level, 1982-1998*. Faith and Order Paper 187. Geneva: WCC, 2000.

Gross, Rita M. *A Garland of Feminist Reflections: Forty Years of Religious Exploration*. Berkeley, CA: University of California Press, 2009.

______. "Steps toward Feminine Imagery in Jewish Theology." In *A Garland of Feminist Reflections: Forty Years of Religious Exploration*, 177-88. Berkeley, CA: University of California Press, 2009.

Grudem, Wayne A. *The Gift of Prophecy in 1 Corinthians*. Eugene, OR: Wipf and Stock Publishers, 1999.

Grumm, Christine. "In Search of a Round Table." In *In Search of a Round Table: Gender, Theology & Church Leadership*, edited by Musimbi R. A. Kanyoro, 28-39. Geneva: WCC Publications, 1997.

Gubrium, Jaber F., and James A. Holstein. *Analyzing Narrative Reality*. Los Angeles: Sage Publications, 2009.

Gudorf, Christine E. "The Power to Create: Sacraments and Men's Need to Birth." *Horizons* 14/2 (1987): 296-309.

Gupta, Abhik, comp. "Mizo (Hmar), Ao-Naga, Zo, Khasi and Darlong Folk-Songs." *Indian Literature* 30/4 (1987): 17-34.

Habib, Irfan. *The Agrarian System of Mughal India (1526-1707)*. Delhi: Oxford University Press, 2000.

Habib, M. A. R. *Modern Literary Criticism and Theory: A History*. Malden, MA; Oxford, 2008.

Halbertal, Moshe. *People of the Book: Canon, Meaning, and Authority*. Cambridge, MA: Harvard University Press, 1997.

Hale, Thomas A. *Griots and Griottes: Masters of Words and Music*. Bloomington, IN: Indiana University Press, 1998.

Hall, Basil. "Hoc est Corpus Meum: The Centrality of the Real Presence for Luther." In *Luther: Theologian for Catholics and Protestants*, edited by Gregory Yule, 112-44. Edinburgh: T & T Clark, 1985.

Hall, David. *Worlds of Wonder, Days of Judgement: Religious Belief in Early New England*. Cambridge, MA: Harvard University Press, 1989.

Hamilton, James M. "What Women Can Do in Ministry: Full Participation Within Biblical Boundaries." In *Women, Ministry and the Gospel: Exploring New Paradigms*, edited by Mark Husbands and Timothy Larsen, 32-52. Downers Grove, IL: InterVarsity Press, 2007.

Hampson, Daphne. *Theology and Feminism*. Oxford: Basil Blackwell, 1990.

Hardesty, Nancy A. *Inclusive Language in the Church*. Atlanta, GA: John Knox Press, 1987.

Hariman, Robert, and John Louis Lucaites. *No Caption Needed: Iconic Photographs, Public Culture, and Liberal Democracy*. Chicago: The University of Chicago Press, 2007.

Harvey, Susan Ashbrook. "The Odes of Solomon." In *Searching the Scriptures*, vol. 2, *A Feminist Commentary*, edited by Elisabeth Schüssler Fiorenza, 86-98. New York, NY: Crossroad, 1994.

Hasselgrave, David J. *Communicating Christ Cross-Culturally: An Introduction to Missionary Communication*. Grand Rapids, MI: Zondervan Publishing House, 1978.

Hayes, Diana L. *Hagar's Daughter: Womanist Ways of Being in the World*. New York: Paulist Press, 1995.

Hays, Richard B. *First Corinthians*. Interpretation. Louisville, KY: John Knox Press, 1997.

Hazarika, Eva. " 'ধৰ্ম পুস্তক'ৰ অনুসন্ধান প্ৰকাশ [Inquiry of Publication of Religious Book]." *The Dainik Janambhumi*, Jorhat, September 29, 2012.

Healey, Joseph, and Donald Sybertz. *Towards an African Narrative Theology*. Faith and Culture Series. Maryknoll, NY: Orbis Books, 1996.

Hedges, Elaine, and Ingrid Wendt, eds. *In Her Own Image: Women Working in the Arts*. New York, NY: The Feminist Press, 1980.

Hedges, Elaine. "Quilts and Women's Culture." In *In Her Own Image: Women Working in the Arts*, edited by Elaine Hedges and Ingrid Wendt, 13-19. New York, NY: The Feminist Press, 1980.

Heilbrun, Carolyn G. *Writing a Woman's Life*. New York: Ballantine Books, 2002.

Helle, Knut, ed. *The Cambridge History of Scandinavia*. Vol. 1. *Prehistory to 1520*. Cambridge History of Scandinavia 1. Cambridge: Cambridge University Press, 2003.

Heyward, Carter, and Sue Phillips, eds. *No Easy Peace: Liberating Anglicanism: A Collection of Essays in Memory of William John Wolf*. Lanham, MD: University Press of America, 1992.

Heyward, Carter. *Speaking of Christ: A Lesbian Feminist Voice*. Edited by Ellen C. Davis. New York, NY: Pilgrim Press, 1989.

Hezser, Catherine, ed. *The Oxford Handbook of Jewish Daily Life in Roman Palestine*. Oxford: Oxford University Press, 2010.

Higgins, Jean M. "The Myth of Eve: The Temptress." *Journal of the American Academy of Religion* 44 (1976): 639-47.

Hilkert, Mary Catherine. *Naming Grace: Preaching and the Sacramental Imagination*. New York, NY: The Continuum International Publishing Group, 2006.

Hindmarsh, D. Bruce. *The Evangelical Conversion Narrative: Spiritual Autobiography in Early Modern England*. Oxford: Oxford University Press, 2005.

Hiscox, Edward T. *Principles and Practices for Baptist Churches: A Guide to the Administration of Baptist Churches*. 1894; repr., Grand Rapids, MI: Kregel Publications, 1980.

Hock, Ronald F. *The Infancy Gospels of James and Thomas: With Introduction, Notes, and Original Text Featuring the New Scholars Version Translation*. The Scholars Bible 2. Santa Rosa, CA: Polebridge Press, 1995.

Hoffman, Barbara G. *Griots at War: Conflict, Conciliation, and Caster in Mande*. Bloomington, IN: Indiana University Press, 2000.

Hoffman, John C. *Faith-Full Stories: The Narrative Road to Religion*. Toronto: The United Church Publishing House, 1994.

Hofstadter, Douglas R. *Metamagical Themas: Questing for Essence of Mind and Pattern*. London: Penguin Books, 1987.

______. "A Person Paper on Purity in Language." In *Metamagical Themas: Questing for Essence of Mind and Pattern*, 159-67. London: Penguin Books, 1987. Also published as idem, "A Person Paper on Purity in Language." In *The Feminist Critique of Language: A Reader*, 2nd ed., edited by Deborah Cameron, 141-48. London: Routledge, 1998.

Holdsworth, John. *Communication and the Gospel.* London: Darton, Longman and Todd, 2003.

Hopkinson, Deborah. *Sweet Clara and the Freedom Quilt.* New York: Knopf, 1993.

Horsley, Richard A. *Jesus and the Spiral of Violence: Popular Jewish Resistance in Roman Palestine.* San Francisco: Harper & Row, 1987.

Howard, Julie. *We are the Circle: Celebrating the Feminine in Song and Ritual.* Collegeville, MN: Liturgical Press, 1993.

Huels, John M. *The Catechumenate and the Law: A Pastoral and Canonical Commentary for the Church in the United States.* Chicago, IL: Liturgy Training Publications, 2003.

Hull, John M. "'Lord, I was Deaf': Images of Disability in the Hymn Books." In *The Edge of God: New Liturgical Texts and Contexts in Conversation*, edited by Stephen Burns, Nicola Slee, and Michael N. Jagessar, 117-33. London: Epworth, 2008.

Hümtsoe, Eyingbeni. "Women's Experience of 'Sorrow' as a Source for Doing Theology from Naga Perspective." In *No More Sorrow in God's Garden of Justice: Tribal Women Doing Theology*, edited by Limatula Longkumer, 1-14. Jorhat, Assam: Women Study Department, Eastern Theological College, 2007.

Hunt, Mary E., and Diann L. Neu, eds. *New Feminist Christianity: Many Voices, Many Views.* Woodstock, VT: SkyLight Paths Publishing, 2010.

Husbands, Mark, and Timothy Larsen, eds. *Women, Ministry and the Gospel: Exploring New Paradigms.* Downers Grove, IL: InterVarsity Press, 2007.

Hymn Society in the United States and Canada. *Holding in Trust.* Carol Stream, IL: Hope Publishing, 1992.

Imchen, Narola, ed. *Women in Ministry: Practical Issues and Challenges.* Jorhat, Assam: Women Study Centre, 2012.

______. "Women's Issues in the Ministry." In *Women in Ministry: Practical Issues and Challenges*, edited by Narola Imchen, 31-44. Jorhat, Assam: Women Study Centre, 2012.

Indira Gandhi National Centre for the Arts (IGNCA). "Arts and Crafts of Northeast India." http://ignca.gov.in/divisionss/janapada-sampada/northeastern-regional-centre/arts-and-crafts-of-northeast-india/ (accessed June 20, 2019).

______. "Textiles of Arunachal Pradesh." http://ignca.gov.in/divisionss/janapada-sampada/northeastern-regional-centre/textiles-of-arunachal-pradesh/ (accessed June 20, 2019).

______. "Textiles of Assam." http://ignca.gov.in/divisionss/janapada-sampada/northeastern-regional-centre/textiles-of-assam/ (accessed June 20, 2019).

______. "Textiles of Manipur." http://ignca.gov.in/divisionss/janapada-sampada/northeastern-regional-centre/textiles-of-manipur/ (acccessed June 19, 2019).

______. "Textiles of Meghalaya." http://ignca.gov.in/divisionss/janapada-sampada/northeastern-regional-centre/textiles-of-meghalaya/ (accessed June 20, 2019).

______. "Textiles of Mizoram." http://ignca.gov.in/divisionss/janapada-sampada/northeastern-regional-centre/textiles-of-mizoram/ (accessed June 20, 2019).

______. "Textiles of Nagaland." http://ignca.gov.in/divisionss/janapada-sampada/northeastern-regional-centre/textiles-of-nagaland/ (accessed June 19, 2019).

______. "Textiles of Tripura." http://ignca.gov.in/divisionss/janapada-sampada/northeastern-regional-centre/textiles-of-tripura/ (accessed June 19, 2019).

Ingram, Kristin Johnson. "Shekinah – The Glory of God." In *The Wisdom of Daughters: Two Decades of the Voice of Christian Feminism*, edited by Reta Halteman Finger, Kari Sandhaas, 46-48. Philadelphia, PA: Innisfree Press, 2001.

International Society for Human Rights. *Apartheid – How Much Longer? Report about the Journey of an ISHR Delegation to South Africa*. London: ISHR, 1986.

Isasi-Díaz, Ada María. "*Mujeristas*: A Name of Our Own." In *The Future of Liberation Theology: Essays in Honor of Gustavo Gutiérrez*, edited by Marc H. Ellis and Otto Maduro, 410-19. Maryknoll, NY: Orbis Books, 1989.

______. "Toward an Understanding of *Feminismo Hispano* in the U.S.A." In *Women's Consciousness, Women's Conscience: A Reader in Feminist Ethics*, edited by Barbara Hilkert Andolsen, Christine E. Gudorf and Mary D. Pellauer. Minneapolis, MN: Winston Press, 1985.

Isherwood, Lisa, and Dorothea McEwan, eds. *An A to Z of Feminist Theology*. Sheffield: Sheffield Academic Press, 1996.

Isherwood, Lisa, and Kathleen McPhillips, eds. *Post-Christian Feminisms: A Critical Approach*. Aldershot: Ashgate, 2008.

Isherwood, Lisa, and Mark D. Jordan, eds. *Dancing Theology in Fetish Boots: Essays in Honour of Marcella Althaus-Reid*. London: SCM Press, 2010.

Isherwood, Lisa. "Our Lady of Perpetual Succour: Mother of Phallic Fetishes? [Queering the Queen of Heaven]." In *Post-Christian Feminisms: A Critical Approach*, edited by Lisa Isherwood and Kathleen McPhillips, 117-27. Aldershot: Ashgate, 2008.

Jansen, Jan. *The Griot's Craft: An Essay on Oral Tradition and Diplomacy*. Forschungen zu Sprachen und Kulturen Afrikas 8. Münster: Lit, 2000.

Janzen, J. Gerald. "Prayer and/as Self-Address: The Case of Hannah." In *A God So Near: Essays on Old Testament theology in Honor of Patrick D. Miller*, edited by Brent A. Strawn and Nancy R. Bowen, 113-27. Winona Lake, IN: Eisenbrauns, 2003.

Jeffrey Gros, ed. *The Search for Visible Unity*. New York: Pilgrim Press, 1984.

Jensen, Richard A. *Telling the Story: Variety and Imagination in Preaching*. Minneapolis: Augsburg, 1980.

______. *Thinking in Story: Preaching in a Post-Literate Age*. Lima, OH: CSS Publishing, 1993.

Jeremias, Joachim. *New Testament Theology: The Proclamation of Jesus*. New York: Charles Scribner's Sons, 1971.

______. *The Prayers of Jesus*. London: SCM Press, 1967.

Jervis, L. Ann. "1 Corinthians 14.34-35: A Reconsideration of Paul's Limitation of the Free Speech of Some Corinthian Women." *Journal for the Study of the New Testament* 58 (1995): 51-74.

Joel B. Green, Scot McKnight, and I. Howard Marshall, eds. *Dictionary of Jesus and the Gospels*. Leicester: InterVarsity Press, 1992.

Johnson, Elizabeth A. "The Incomprehensibility of God and the Image of God as Male and Female." *Theological Studies* 45 (1994): 331-65.

______. *She Who Is: The Mystery of God in Feminist Theological Discourse*. 10th Anniversary ed. New York, NY: Crossroad, 2005.

______. *Truly Our Sister: A Theology of Mary in the Communion of Saints*. New York: Continuum, 2006.

Johnson, Maxwell E. *The Rites of Christian Initiation: Their Evolution and Interpretation*. Rev. and expanded ed. Collegeville, MN: Liturgical Press, 2007.

Johnson, Robert E. *A Global Introduction to Baptist Churches*. Cambridge: Cambridge University Press, 2010.

Jones, Ian, Kirsty Thorpe, and Janet Wootton, eds. *Women and Ordination in the Christian Churches: International Perspectives*. London: T & T Clark, 2008.

Jones, Noragh. "Motherhood of God." In *An A to Z of Feminist Theology*, edited by Lisa Isherwood and Dorothea McEwan, 149-52. Sheffield: Sheffield Academic Press, 1996.

Juster, Susan. *Disorderly Women: Sexual Politics and Evangelicalism in Revolutionary New England*. Ithaca, NY: Cornell University Press, 1994.

Kanyoro, Musimbi R. A., ed. *In Search of a Round Table: Gender, Theology and Church Leadership*. Geneva: WCC Publications, 1997.

Kärkkäinen, Veli-Matti. *Pneumatology: The Holy Spirit in Ecumenical, International, and Contextual Perspective*. Grand Rapids, MI: Baker Academic, 2002.

Karlstadt, Andreas. "Whether One Should Proceed Slowly" [1524]. In *The Radical Reformation*, Cambridge Texts in the History of Political Thought, edited by Michael G. Baylor, 49-73. Cambridge: Cambridge University Press, 1991.

Kaufmann, Helen L. *The Little History of Music*. New York: Grosset & Dunlap, 1949.

Keener, Craig S. *Paul, Women and Wives: Marriage and Women's Ministry in the Letters of Paul*. Peabody, MA: Hendrickson Publishers, 1992.

Kemp, Wolfgang. *The Narratives of Gothic Stained Glass*. Translated by Caroline Dobson Saltzwedel. Cambridge: Cambridge University Press, 1997. Originally published in German as *Sermo Corporeus*. Munich: Schirmer/Mosel Verlag, 1987.

Kent, George. *Ending Hunger Worldwide*. London: Routledge, 2016.

Kharkongor, Felix H. *The Revealed Christ of the Khasi Religion*. Worthing: Loxwood, 1994.

Kharlukhi, Wandahilin. "The Significance of the Feminist Interpretation of the 'Image of God' for Women's Liberation in the Khasi Society." MTh Thesis, United Theological College, Bangalore, 1999.

King, Karen L. "The Book of Norea, Daughter of Eve." In *Searching the Scriptures*, vol. 2: *A Feminist Commentary*, edited by Elisabeth Schüssler Fiorenza, 66-85. New York, NY: Crossroad, 1994.

______, ed. *Images of the Feminine in Gnosticism*. Studies in Antiquity and Christianity. Harrisburg, PA: Trinity Press International, 2000.

______. "Ridicule and Rape, Rule and Rebellion: The Hypostasis of the Archons." In *Gnosticism and the Early Christian World*, edited by James E. Goehring, Charles W. Hedrick, Jack T. Sanders, and Hans Dieter Betz, 2-24. Sonoma, CA: Polebridge Press, 1990.

Kinnamon, Michael, ed. *Signs of the Spirit: Official Report, Seventh Assembly*. Geneva: World Council of Churches, 1991.

Kipgen, Tingneichong G. *Women's Role in the 20th Century Manipur: A Historical Study*. Delhi: Kalpaz Publications, 2010.

Kipgen, Tingneilhing, Women Secretary, MBC, message to the author on October 15, 2012.

Kirk-Duggan, Cheryl A., and Karen Jo Torjesen, eds. *Women and Christianity*. Women and Religion in the World. Santa Barbara, CA: ABC-CLIO, 2010.

Kirk-Duggan, Cheryl A., and Tina Pippin, eds. *Mother Goose, Mother Jones, Mommie Dearest: Biblical Mothers and Their Children*. Atlanta, GA: Society of Biblical Literature, 2009.

Klauck, Hans-Josef. *Apocryphal Gospels: An Introduction*. Translated by Brian McNeil. London: T & T Clark, 2003.

Klinck, Anne L. ed. *An Anthology of Ancient and Medieval Women's Song*. New York: Palgrave Macmillan, 2004.

Klinck, Anne L., and Ann Marie Rasmussen, eds. *Medieval Woman's Song: Cross-Cultural Approaches*. Philadelphia, PA: University of Pennsylvania Press, 2002.

Koester, Anne Y., ed. *Liturgy and Justice: To Worship God in Spirit and Truth*. Collegeville, MN: Liturgical Press, 2002.

Kogawa, Joy. *A Song of Lilith*. New York: Laurel Glen, 2001.

Korsak, Mary Phil. *At The Start... Genesis Made New: A Translation of the Hebrew Text*. Louvain: Leuvense Schrijversaktie, 1992.

______. "...et GENETRIX." In *Genesis: A Feminist Companion to the Bible (Second Series)*, edited by Athalya Brenner, 22-31. Sheffield: Sheffield Academic Press, 1998.

______. "Genesis: A New Look." In *A Feminist Companion to Genesis*, edited by Athalya Brenner, 39-52. Sheffield: Sheffield Academic Press, 1997.

Köstenberger, Andreas J., Thomas R. Schreiner, and H. Scott Baldwin, eds. *Women in the Church: A Fresh Analysis of 1 Timothy 2:9-15*. Grand Rapids, MI: Baker Books, 1995.

Kourany, Janet A., James P. Sterba, and Rosemarie Tong, eds. *Feminist Philosophies: Problems, Theories, and Applications*. Englewood Cliffs, NJ: Prentice Hall, 1992.

Kroeger, Catherine. "The Apostle Paul and the Greco-Roman Cults of Women." *Journal of the Evangelical Theological Society* 30 (1987): 25-38.

Kroløkke, Charlotte, and Anne Scott Sørensen. *Gender Communication Theories & Analysis: From Silence to Performance*. Thousand Oaks: Sage Publications, 2006.

Kröner, Daniela. *The Truth and reconciliation Commission in South Africa – A Learner's Diary, Seminar Paper*. Norderstedt: GRIN, 2006.

Kruger, Kathryn Sullivan. *Weaving the Word: The Metaphorics of Weaving and Female Textual Production*. Selinsgrove, PA: Susquehanna University Press, 2001.

Kvam, Kristen E., Linda S. Schearing and Valarie H. H. Ziegler, eds. *Eve and Adam: Jewish, Christian, and Muslim Readings on Genesis and Gender*. Bloomington, IN: Indiana University Press, 1999.

Kyung, Chung Hyun. "Come, Holy Spirit – Renew the Whole Creation." In *Signs of the Spirit: Official Report, Seventh Assembly*, edited by Michael Kinnamon, 37-47. Geneva: World Council of Churches, 1991.

LaCelle-Paterson, Kristina. *Liberating Tradition: Women's Identity and Vocation in Christian Perspective*. Grand Rapids, MI: Baker Academic, 2008.

LaCugna, Catherine Mowry. "The Baptismal Formula, Feminist Objections and Trinitarian Theology." *Journal of Ecumenical Studies* 26/2 (Spring 1989): 235-50.

______. *God For Us: The Trinity and Christian Life*. San Francisco: Harper & Row, 1991.

Lake, Kirsopp, and Henry J. Cadbury, eds. *The Beginnings of Christianity*. Part 1: *The Acts of the Apostles*, vol. 5: *Additional Notes to the Commentary*. London: Macmillan and Co., 1993.

Lalneihzovi, ed. *Changing Status of Women in North-Eastern States*. New Delhi: Mittal Publications, 2009.

Lama, A. K. General Secretary, CBCNEI, email to the author through his PA, Meera Areng, September 27, 2012.

Lamare, Gertrude. "Presbyterian Church Patriarchy." Raiot, September 22, 2015. http://raiot.in/presbyterian-church-patriarchy/ (accessed September 14, 2018).

Lang, Bernhard. *Sacred Games: A History of Christian Worship*. New Haven: Yale University Press, 1997.

Lanser, Susan S. "(Feminist) Criticism in the Garden: Inferring Genesis 2-3." *Semeia* 41 (1988): 67-84.

Larere, Philippe. *Baptism in Water and Baptism in the Spirit: A Biblical, Liturgical, and Theological Exposition*. Translated Patrick Madigan. Collegeville, MN: Liturgical Press, 1993.

Lasetso, Razouselie, and Eyingbeni Humtsoe, eds. *Doing Tribal Christian Theology with Tribal Resources: Cultural Resources from North East India*. Jorhat, Assam: ETC Programme Coordination, 2009.

Lasetso, Razouselie, and Yangkahao Vashum, eds. *Tribal Christian Theology: Methods and Sources for Constructing a Relevant Theology for the Indigenous People of North East India*. Jorhat, Assam: Programme Coordination, 2007.

Lasetso, Razouselie, ed. *Garnering Tribal Resources for Doing Tribal Christian Theology*. Tribal Study Series 16. Jorhat, Assam: Eastern Theological College Programme Coordination, 2008.

Lasetso, Vimeno. "A Search for Values in the Life of the Traditional Angami Naga Women." In *Doing Tribal Christian Theology with Tribal Resources: Cultural Resources from North East India*, edited by Razouselie Lasetso and Eyingbeni Humtsoe, 216-24. Jorhat, Assam: ETC Programme Coordination, 2009.

Lawless, Elaine J. *Women Preaching Revolution: Challenge for Connection in a Disconnected Time*. Philadelphia, PA: University of Pennsylvania Press, 1996.

Layton, Bentley, trans. "The Hypostasis of the Archons (II, *4*)." In *The Nag Hammadi Library*, edited by Marvin W. Meyer and James McConkey Robinson, 153-60. Leiden: E. J. Brill, 1977.

Lehmann, Martin E., trans. "The Marburg Colloquy and the Marburg Articles." In *Luther's Works*. Vol. 38, 3-89. Philadelphia: Fortress Press, 1971.

Lerner, Gerda. *The Creation of Patriarchy*. Oxford: Oxford University Press, 1986.

Levine, Amy-Jill, and Maria Mayo Robbins, eds. *A Feminist Companion to Mariology*. London: T & T Clark International, 2005.

Levine, Molly Myerowitz. "The Gendered Grammar of Ancient Mediterranean Hair." In *Off with Her Head! The Denial of Women's Identity in Myth, Religion, and Culture*, edited by Howard Eilberg-Schwartz and Wendy Doniger, 76-130. Berkeley: University of California Press, 1995.

Lewis, Donald M., ed. *Christianity Reborn: The Global Expansion of Evangelicalism in the Twentieth Century*. Studies in the History of Christian Missions. Grand Rapids, MI: Wm B. Eerdmans, 2004.

Linde, Charlotte. *Life Stories: The Creation of Coherence*. New York, NY: Oxford University Press, 1993.

Lindsay, Jack. *The Troubadours and their World of the Twelfth and Thirteenth Centuries*. London: Frederick Müller, 1976.

Lipsett, Linda Otto. *Remember Me: Women and Their Friendship Quilts*. San Francisco: Quilt Digest Press, 1985.

Lloyd, J. Meirion. *History of the Church in Mizoram: Harvest in the Hills*. Gospel Centenary Series, 1. Aizawl, Mizoram: Synod Publication Board, 1991.

Llyod, Genevieve. "Augustine and Aquinas." In *Feminist Theology: A Reader*, edited by Ann Loades, 90-98. Louisville, KY: Westminster John Knox Press, 1990.

Longchar, A. Wati, and Yangkahao Vashum, eds. *Tribal Worldview and Ecology*. Tribal Study Series 2. Jorhat, Assam: Tribal Study Centre, 1998.

Longchar, A. Wati. "Dancing with the Land: Significance of Land for Doing Tribal Theology." *Indian Journal of Theology* 38/2 (1996): 16-28.

Longkumer, Limatula. "Contextual Reading of the Bible: A Tribal Women's Perspective." In *No More Sorrow in God's Garden of Justice: Tribal Women Doing Theology*, Women Study Series 4, edited by Limatula Longkumer, 129-45. Jorhat, Assam: Women Study Department, Eastern Theological College, 2007.

______, ed. *No More Sorrow in God's Garden of Justice: Tribal Women Doing Theology*. Women Study Series 4. Jorhat, Assam: Women Study Department, Eastern Theological College, 2007.

______. "Response to Ecological Problem by Women of North East India." In *No More Sorrow in God's Garden of Justice: Tribal Women Doing Theology*, edited by Limatula Longkumer, 129-45. Jorhat, Assam: Women Study Department, Eastern Theological College, 2007.

Lovering, Eugene H., ed. *Society of Biblical Literature Seminar Papers, 1994*. SBLSP 33. Atlanta: Scholars Press, 1994.

Lowry, Eugene L. *Doing Time in the Pulpit: The Relationship between Narrative and Preaching*. Nashville: Abingdon Press, 1985.

______. *The Homiletical Plot: The Sermon as Narrative Art Form*. Expanded ed. Louisville, KY: Westminster John Knox Press, 2001.

______. *How to Preach a Parable: Designs for Narrative Sermons*. Abingdon Preacher's Library. Nashville: Abingdon, 1989.

______. *The Sermon: Dancing the Edge of Mystery*. Nashville: Abingdon Press, 1997.

Lundblad, Barbara K. "Gasping for Breath: Women Listening, Women Telling Stories." In *What's the Shape of Narrative Preaching?* edited by Mike Graves and David J. Schlafer, 159-74. St. Louis, MO: Chalice Press, 2008.

Luther, Martin. "The Babylonian Captivity of the Church" [1520]. In *Martin Luther: Three Treatises - From the American Edition of Luther's Works*, 2nd ed., translated by A. T. W. Steinhäuser and revised by Frederick C. Ahrens and Abdel Ross Wentz, 113-260. Philadelphia: Fortress Press, 1970.

______. *Luther's Works*. Vol. 38. Philadelphia: Fortress Press, 1971.

______. *Martin Luther: Three Treatises - From the American Edition of Luther's Works*. 2nd ed. Translated by A. T. W. Steinhäuser and revised by Frederick C. Ahrens and Abdel Ross Wentz. Philadelphia: Fortress Press, 1970.

Lynch, Kathleen. *Protestant Autobiography in the Seventeenth-Century Anglophone World*. Oxford: Oxford University Press, 2012.

Lynton, Linda, and Sanjay K. Singh. *The Sari: Styles, Patterns, History, Techniques*. New York: H. N. Abrams, 1995.

Lyons, Mary E. *Stitching Stars: The Story Quilts of Harriet Powers*. New York: Scribner's, 1993.

Ma, Wonsuk, and Robert P. Menzies, eds. *The Spirit and Spirituality: Essays in Honour of Russell P. Spittler*. Journal of Pentecostal Theology, Supplement Series 24. London: T & T Clark, 2004.

MacKinnon, Catherine A. *Toward a Feminist Theory of the State*. Cambridge, MA: Harvard University Press, 1989.

MacNichol, Sally Noland, and Mary Elizabeth Walsh. "Feminist Theology and Spirituality: An Annotated Bibliography." *Women Studies Quarterly* 21 (1993): 177-96.

Macy, Gary. *Treasures from the Storeroom: Medieval Religion and the Eucharist*. Collegeville, MN: The Liturgical Press, 1999.

Mahanta, Pona. *Western Influence on Modern Assamese Drama: From 1857 to the Present Time*. Delhi: K. M. Mittal, 1985.

Malsawma, Zari. "The Mizos of Northeast India: Proclaiming the Gospel to their Neighbors Near and Far." *Mission Frontiers* (Nov-Dec 1994). http://www.missionfrontiers.org/issue/article/the-mizos-of-northeast-india (accessed Aug 28, 2018).

Mannion, Gerard, and Lewis Mudge, eds. *The Routledge Companion to the Christian Church*. New York, NY: Routledge, 2008.

Marak, Marlene. "Matriliny and the Status of Women in the A·chik Society." In *No More Sorrow in God's Garden of Justice: Tribal Women Doing Theology*, Women Study Series 4, edited by Limatula Longkumer, 81-92. Jorhat, Assam: Women Study Department, Eastern Theological College, 2007.

______. "Tatara Rabuga: The Supreme Being of the A·chik People." In *Tribal Christian Theology: Methods and Sources for Constructing a Relevant Theology for the Indigenous People of North East India*, edited by Razouselie Lasetso and Yangkahao Vashum, 210-19. Jorhat, Assam: Programme Coordination, 2007.

______. "The Understanding and Practice of Peace and Reconciliation in the A·chik Community." In *Garnering Tribal Resources for Doing Tribal Christian Theology*, Tribal Study Series 16, edited by Razouselie Lasetso, 92-106. Jorhat, Assam: Eastern Theological College Programme Coordination, 2008.

Marak, Paulinus R. *The Garo Tribal Religion*. Delhi: Anshah Publishing House, 2005.

Mark G. Brett, ed. *Ethnicity and the Bible*. BIS 19. London: E. J. Brill, 1996.

Marriage, Alwyn. *Life-Giving Spirit: Responding to the Feminine in God.* London: SPCK, 1989.

Martos, Joseph. *Doors to the Sacred: A Historical Introduction to Sacraments in the Catholic Church*. Expanded ed. Liguori, MO: Liguori Publications, 1991.

Mathers, S. L. MacGregor. *The Kabbalah Unveiled*. 1887; repr., London: Arkana, 1991.

Matthews, Glenna. " 'Little Women' Who Helped Make This Great War." In *Why the Civil War Came*, edited by Gabor S. Boritt, 31-49. Oxford: Oxford University Press, 1996.

Mawrie, H. O. *The Khasi Milieu*. New Delhi: Concept Publishing, 1981.

May, Andrew. "The Promise of a Book: Missionaries and Native Evangelists in North-East India." In *Missionaries, Indigenous Peoples and Cultural Exchange*, edited by Patricia Grimshaw and Andrew May, 81-95. Eastbourne: Sussex Academic Press, 2010.

McBeth, H. Leon. *The Baptist Heritage*. Nashville: Broadman Press, 1987.

McClintock, Anne. *Imperial Leather: Race, Gender, and Sexuality in the Colonial Contest*. New York: Routledge, 1995.

McClure, John S. *Other-wise Preaching: A Postmodern Ethic for Homiletics*. St. Louis: Chalice Press, 2001.

McCosker, Philip, ed. *What is it that the Scripture Says? Essays in Biblical Interpretation, Translation and Reception in Honour of Henry Wansbrough OSB*. London: T & T Clark, 2006.

McFague, Sallie. "Holy Spirit." In *Dictionary of Feminist Theologies*, edited by Letty M. Russell and J. Shannon Clarkson, 146-47. Louisville, KY: Westminster John Knox Press, 1996,

______. *Metaphorical Theology: Models of God in Religious Language*. Philadelphia: Fortress press, 1982.

______. *Models of God: Theology for an Ecological, Nuclear Age* (Philadelphia: Fortress Press, 1987.

McGuire, Anne. "Virginity and Subversion: Norea Against the Powers in the *Hypostasis of the Archons*." In *Images of the Feminine in Gnosticism*, Studies in Antiquity and Christianity, edited by Karen L. King, 239-58. Harrisburg, PA: Trinity Press International, 2000.

McKean, Thomas. "A Gaelic Songmaker's Response to an English-speaking Nation," *Oral Tradition* 7/1 (1992): 3-27. http://journal.oraltradition.org/files/articles /7i/4_mckean.pdf (accessed July 22, 2018).

McKinlay, Judith E. *Reframing Her: Biblical Women in Postcolonial Focus*. The Bible in the Modern World 1. Sheffield: Sheffield Phoenix Press, 2004.

McLaughlin, Eleanor. "'Christ My Mother': Feminine Naming and Metaphor in Medieval Spirituality." *St. Luke's Journal of Theology* 18 (1975): 367-86.

______. "Feminist Christologies: Re-Dressing the Tradition." In *Reconstructing the Christ Symbol: Essays in Feminist Christology*, edited by Maryanne Stevens, 118-49. New York: Paulist Press, 1993.

McQuail, Denis. *Communication*, Aspects of Modern Sociology. Social Processes. 2nd ed. London and New York: Longman, 1984.

Meeske, Susan. "Quilt Me a Story." In *Ways of Knowing: Literature and the Intellectual Life of Children*, edited by Kay E. Vandergrift, 31-50. Lanham, MD: Scarecrow Press, 1996. https://1yearofquilts.weebly.com/uploads/3/6/0/0/3600737/quilt_me_a_story_by_susan_meeke.pdf (accessed July 22, 2018).

Mendible, Myra. "Imagining Cuba: Storytelling and the Politics of Exile." In *Telling Stories to Change the World: Global Voices on the Power of Narrative to Build Community and Make Social Justice Claims*, edited by Rickie Solinger, Madeline Fox, and Kayhan Irani, 239-48. New York: Routledge, 2008.

Metzger, Bruce M. "To the Reader." In *Holy Bible: New Revised Standard Version with the Apocrypha*, vii-ix. Peabody, MA: Hendrickson Publishers, 2004.

Meyendorff, Paul. "Toward Mutual Recognition of Baptism." In *Baptism Today: Understanding, Practice, Ecumenical Implications*, Faith and Order Paper No. 207, edited by Thomas F. Best, 195-206. Collegeville, MN: Liturgical Press, 2008.

Meyer, Harding, and Lukas Vischer, eds. *Growth in Agreement: Reports and Agreed Statements of Ecumenical Conversations on a World Level*. Faith and Order Paper 108. Geneva: WCC, 1984.

Meyer, Marvin W., and James McConkey Robinson, eds. *The Nag Hammadi Library*. Leiden: E. J. Brill, 1977.

Meyers, Carol. *Discovering Eve: Ancient Israelite Women in Context*. New York: Oxford University Press, 1988.

Middleton, J. Richard. *The Liberating Image: The* Imago Dei *in Genesis 1*. Grand Rapids, MI: Brazos Press, 2005.

Miller, Casey, and Kate Swift. *Words and Women: New Language in New Times*. Rev. ed. San Francisco: HarperCollins, 1991.

Miller, Katherine. *Communication Theories: Perspectives, Processes, and Contexts*. New York: McGraw Hill, 2005.

Miller, Marla R. *The Needle's Eye: Women and Work in the Age of Revolution*. Amherst, MA: University of Massachusetts Press, 2006.

Miller, Nancy K. "Arachnologies: The Woman, the Text, and the Critic." In *The Poetics of Gender*, edited by N. K. Miller, 270-96. New York: Columbia University Press, 1986.

______, ed. *The Poetics of Gender*. New York: Columbia University Press, 1986.

______. *Subject to Change: Reading Feminist Writing*. New York: Columbia University Press, 1988.

Mills, J. P. *The Rengma Nagas*. London: Macmillan, 1937.

Miri, Mrinal, ed. *Linguistic Situation in North-East India*. Shillong: North-East India Council for Social Science Research, 1982.

Miri, Sujata. *A Book of Paintings – On Themes from the Hills of Northeast India*. New Delhi: Mittal Publications, 2005.

Mitchell, Rosemary Catalano, and Gail Anderson Ricciuti. *Birthings and Blessings: Liberating Worship Services for the Inclusive Church*. New York: Crossroad, 1991.

______. *Birthings and Blessings, II: More Liberating Worship Services for the Inclusive Church*. New York: Crossroad, 1993.

Mombo, Esther. "The Ordination of Women in Africa: An Historical Perspective." In *Women and Ordination in the Christian Churches: International Perspectives*, edited by Ian Jones, Kirsty Thorpe, and Janet Wootton, 123-43. London: T & T Clark, 2008.

Momin, Rettiar G., General Secretary, GBC, Tura, email message to author October 11, 2012.

Montefiore, Simon Sebag. *One Hundred and One World Heroes: Great Men and Women for an Unheroic Age*. London: Quercus, 2007.

Montgomery, Michael H. "Non-Conformist Ecclesiologies." In *The Routledge Companion to the Christian Church*, edited by Gerard Mannion and Lewis Mudge, 217-33. New York, NY: Routledge, 2008.

Moore-Keish, Martha. "Baptism in the Presbyterian and Reformed Tradition," In *Baptism Today: Understanding, Practice, Ecumenical Implications*, Faith and Order Paper No. 207, edited by Thomas F. Best, 63-71. Collegeville, MN: Liturgical Press, 2008.

Moreland, J. P. *The Recalcitrant* Imago Dei: *Human Persons and the Failure of Naturalism*. London: SCM Press, 2009.

Morgan, Edmund S. *Visible Saints: The History of a Puritan Idea*. New York, NY: New York University Press, 1963.

Morrill, Bruce T., ed. *Bodies of Worship: Explorations in Theory and Practice*. Collegeville, MN: The Liturgical Press, 1999.

Mosahary, R. N. "Boro Folk-Songs: A Few Examples with their Contents." In *Essays on North-East India*, edited by Milton S. Sangma, 124-46. Shillong: Deptt. of History, North-Eastern Hill University, 1994.

Motlhabi, Mokgethi. *Challenge to Apartheid: Toward a Moral National Resistance*. Grand Rapids, MI: Wm B. Eerdmans Publishing Company, 1988.

Mumby, Dennis K., ed. *Narrative and Social Control: Critical Perspectives*. Sage Annual Reviews of Communication Research 21. London: Sage Publications, 1993.

Murphy, Cullen. *The Word According to Eve: Women and the Bible in Ancient Times and Our Own*. Boston, MA: Houghton Mifflin, 1998.

Murry, Ezamo. "Bible and Culture: A Model of Christian Acculturation of Tribal Culture." In *Doing Tribal Christian Theology with Tribal Resources: Cultural Resources from North East India*, Tribal Study Series 18, edited by Razouselie Lasetso and Eyingbeni Hümtsoe, 7-22. Jorhat, Assam: ETC Programme Coordination, 2009.

Nag, Sajal. *Contesting Marginality: Ethnicity, Insurgency and Subnationalism in North-East India*. New Delhi: Manohar, 2002.

Naga Institute of Culture. *The Arts and Crafts of Nagaland*. Kohima: Naga Institute of Culture, Government of Nagaland, 1968.

Nambiar, A. K. Krishna. *Namaste: Its Philosophy and Significance in Indian Culture*. Delhi: Spiritual India Publishing House, 1979.

Nathan, Clemens N. *The Changing Face of Religion and Human Rights: A Personal Reflection*. Leiden: Brill, 2009.

______. "The Impact of Religious Symbolism in Europe: Wearing the Hijab and Burqha." In *The Changing Face of Religion and Human Rights: A Personal Reflection*, 93-120. Leiden: Brill, 2009.

National Council of the Churches of Christ in the USA, Inclusive Language Lectionary Committee. *An Inclusive Language Lectionary*. Atlanta, GA: John Knox Press, 1983-1988.

Navone, John, and Thomas Cooper. *Tellers of the Word*. New York: Le Jacq Publishing, 1981.

Neog, Maheswar. *Asamiyā Sāhityar Ruparekhā*. [Gauhati, 1962?]

Neu, Diann L. "Feminist Eucharists at Wisdom's Many Tables." In *New Feminist Christianity: Many Voices, Many Views*, edited by Mary E. Hunt and Diann L. Neu, 190-205. Woodstock, VT: SkyLight Paths Publishing, 2010.

New World Encyclopedia. "Nagaland." http://www.newworldencyclopedia.org/entry/ Nagaland (accessed July 30, 2018).

Newsom, Carol A., and Sharon H. Ringe, eds. *The Women's Bible Commentary.* Louisville, KY: Westminster/John Knox Press, 1992.

Niccum, Curt. "The Voice of the Manuscripts on the Silence of Women: The External Evidence for 1 Cor 14.34-5." *New Testament Studies* 43 (1994): 242-55.

Nicholls, K. W. *Gaelic and Gaelicized Ireland in the Middle Ages.* 2nd ed. Dublin: Lilliput Press, 2003.

Niditch, Susan. "Genesis." In *The Women's Bible Commentary*, edited by Carol A. Newsom and Sharon H. Ringe, 10-25. Louisville, KY: Westminster/John Knox Press, 1992.

Nongbri, B. L. "Christianity, Khasi Language and Literature: An Historical Analysis of the Interaction of Christianity with Traditional Culture." In *Christianity and Change in Northeast India*, edited by T. B. Subba, Joseph Puthenpurakal, and Shaji Joseph Puykunnel, 177-93. New Delhi: Concept Publishing, 2009.

Norén, Carol M. *The Woman in the Pulpit.* Nashville, TN: Abingdon, 1991.

Northup, Lesley A. "Claiming Horizontal Space: Women's Religious Rituals." *Studia Liturgica: An Ecumenical Review for Liturgical Research and Renewal* 25/1 (Spring 1995): 86-102.

Nyori, Tai. *History and Culture of the Adis.* New Delhi: Omsons Publications, 1993.

Obelkevich, Jim, Lyndal Roper, and Raphael Samuel, eds. *Disciplines of Faith: Studies in Religion, Politics and Patriarchy.* London: Routledge and Kegan Paul, 1987.

Obelkevich, Jim. "Music and Religion in the Nineteenth Century." In *Disciplines of Faith: Studies in Religion, Politics and Patriarchy*, edited by Jim Obelkevich, Lyndal Roper, and Raphael Samuel, 550-65. London: Routledge and Kegan Paul, 1987.

Olson, Carl, ed. *The Book of the Goddess, Past and Present: An Introduction to Her Religion.* New York: Crossroad, 1983.

Ornatowski, Cezar M. "Rhetoric and the (Re)Constitution of Collective Identity: The Example of Poland." In *Bending Opinion: Essays on Persuasion in the Public Domain, Rhetoric in Society*, edited by Ton Van Haaften, Henrike Jansen, Jaap De Jong, and Willem Koetsenruijter, 291-306. Leiden: Leiden University Press, 2011.

Osmer, Richard Robert. *Confirmation: Presbyterian Practices in Ecumenical Perspective.* Louisville, KY: Geneva Press, 1996.

Ozick, Cynthia. "The Moral Necessity of Metaphor: Rooting History in a Figure of Speech." *Harper's* 272 (May 1986): 62-68.

Pachuau, Lalsangkima. "Church-Mission Dynamics in Northeast India." *International Bulletin of Missionary Research* 27/4 (October 2003): 154-61.

Pagels, Elaine. "Pursuing the Spiritual Eve: Imagery and Hermeneutics in the *Hypostasis of the Archons* and the *Gospel of Philip.*" In *Images of the Feminine in Gnosticism*, Studies in Antiquity and Christianity, edited by Karen L. King, 187-206. Harrisburg, PA: Trinity Press International, 2000.

Pakyntein, Valentina. "Gender Preference in Khasi Society: An Evaluation of Tradition, Change and Continuity." *Indian Anthropologist* 30/1-2 (June-December 2000): 27-35.

Palestinian Grassroots Anti-apartheid Wall Campaign. "Stop the Wall." http://stopthewall.org/(accessed July 25, 2018).

Panchani, Chander Sheikhar. *Arunachal Pradesh: Religion, Culture, and Society.* New Delhi: Konark Publishers, 1989.

______. *Manipur: Religion, Culture, and Society.* New Delhi: Konark Publishers, 1987.

Pandya, Amita and Joymati Thoudam. "Handloom Weaving, the Traditional Craft of Manipur," *Indian Journal of Traditional Knowledge* 9/4 (October 2010): 651-55.

Panikulam, George. *Koinōnia in the New Testament: A Dynamic Expression of Christian Life.* Analecta Biblica 85. Rome: Biblical Institute Press, 1979.

Pardes, Ilana. *Countertraditions in the Bible: A Feminist Approach.* Cambridge, MA: Harvard University Press, 1992.

Parker, Rozsika. *The Subversive Stitch: Embroidery and the Making of the Feminine.* London: Women's Press, 1984.

Parker, Russ. *Healing Wounded History: Reconciling Peoples and Healing Places.* London: Darton, Longman and Todd Ltd, 2001.

Parkinson, Rob. "Talking to the Rawi: An Encounter with a Traditional Teller of Tales in a Moroccan Market Place," (1999). http://www.imaginaryjourneys.co.uk/word_files/talkingtothe rawi.pdf (accessed July 22, 2018).

______. *Transforming Tales: How Stories Can Change People.* London: Jessica Kingsley Publishers, 2009.

Parratt, John, and Saroj N. Arambam Parratt. " 'Kabui Messiah': The Jadonong Movement in Manipur." http://thohepou.wordpress.com/2007/08/22/kabui-messiah-the-jadonong-movement-in-manipur/ (accessed Aug 28, 2018).

Parsons, Susan Frank, ed. *The Cambridge Companion to Feminist Theology*, Cambridge Companions to Religion. Cambridge: Cambridge University Press, 2002.

Patai, Raphael. *The Hebrew Goddess.* 4th enlarged ed. Detroit, MI: Wayne State University Press, 1990.

Pater, Calvin Augustine. *Karlstadt as the Father of the Baptist Movements: The Emergence of Lay Protestantism.* Toronto: University of Toronto Press, 1984.

Paul Achtemeier, ed. *Harper's Bible Dictionary.* San Francisco: Harper & Row, 1985.

Payne, Roger M. *The Self and the Sacred: Conversion and Autobiography in Early American Protestantism.* Knoxville: The University of Tennessee Press, 1998.

Pellowski, Anne. *The World of Storytelling: A Practical Guide to the Origins, Development, and Applications of Storytelling.* Expanded and rev. ed. New York: H. W. Wilson, 1990.

Penelope, Julia. *Speaking Freely: Unlearning the Lies of Fathers' Tongues.* Athene Series. New York: Pergamon Press, 1990.

Perkins, Pheme. *Introduction to the Synoptic Gospels.* Grand Rapids, MI: William B. Eerdmans, 2007.

Peterson, Brent D. *Created to Worship: God's Invitation to Become Fully Human.* Kansas City, MO: Beacon Hill Press of Kansas City, 2012.

Peterson, Eric E., and Kristin M. Langellier. "Communication as Storytelling." In *Communication as ... : Perspectives on Theory*, edited by Gregory J. Shepherd, Jeffrey St. John, and Ted Striphas, 123-31. Thousand Oaks, CA: Sage Publications, 2006.

Petzer, J. H., and P. J. Hartin, eds. *A South African Perspective on the New Testament: Essays by South African New Testament Scholars Presented to Bruce Manning Metzger During His Visit to South Africa in 1985.* Leiden: E. J. Brill, 1986.

Pinto, Ambrose. "Exodus of the North-East People: Do Our Cities Alienate Them?" *Mainstream* L/38 (September 8, 2012). http://www.mainstreamweekly.net/article3679.html (accessed October 18, 2012).

Plaskow, Judith. "The Coming of Lilith: Towards a Feminist Theology." In *The Coming of Lilith: Essays on Feminism, Judaism, and Sexual Ethics, 1972-2003*, edited by Judith Plaskow with Donna Berman, 23-34. Boston: Beacon Press, 2005.

______. "Lilith Revisited." In *The Coming of Lilith: Essays on Feminism, Judaism, and Sexual Ethics, 1972-2003*, edited Judith Plaskow with Donna Berman, 81-86. Boston: Beacon Press, 2005.

Plaskow, Judith, Donna Berman, eds. *The Coming of Lilith: Essays on Feminism, Judaism, and Sexual Ethics, 1972-2003.* Boston: Beacon Press, 2005.

Platzner, Robert L., ed. *Gender, Tradition and Renewal*, Religions and Discourse 13. Bern: Peter Lang, 2005.

Podmore, Will. *British Foreign Policy since 1870.* Philadelphia: Xlibris, 2008.

Polacco, Patricia. *The Keeping Quilt.* New York: Simon, 1988.

Polkinghorne, Donald E. *Narrative Knowing and the Human Sciences.* Albany, NY: State University of New York, 1988.

Pomeroy, Sarah B. *Goddesses, Whores, Wives, and Slaves.* New York: Schocken Books, 1975.

Porter, W. Marc, and Isaac E. Catt. "The Narcissistic Reflection of Communicative Power: Delusions of Progress against Organizational Discrimination." In *Narrative and Social Control: Critical Perspectives*, Sage Annual Reviews of Communication Research 21, edited by Dennis K. Mumby, 164-85. London: Sage Publications, 1993.

Prakash, Ved. *Encyclopaedia of North-East India.* Vol. 5. New Delhi: Atlantic Publishers and Distributors, 2007.

Presnell, Michael. "Narrative Gender Differences: Orality and Literacy." In *Doing Research on Women's Communication: Perspectives on Theory and Method*, edited by Kathryn Carter and Carole Spitzack, 118-36. Norwood, NJ: Ablex Publishing Corporation, 1989.

Prichard, Rebecca Button. *Sensing the Spirit: The Holy Spirit in Feminist Perspective.* St. Louis, MO: Chalice Press, 1999.

Priests for Equality. *The Inclusive Bible: The First Egalitarian Translation.* Lanham, MD: Rowman & Littlefield Publishers, 2007.

______. *The Inclusive New Testament.* Lanham, MD: Rowman AltaMira, 1996.

______. *The Inclusive Psalms.* Brentwoord, MD: Priests for Equality, 1997.

Procter-Smith, Majorie. "Feminist Interpretation and Liturgical Preaching." In *Searching the Scriptures*, vol. 1, *A Feminist Introduction*, edited by Elisabeth Schüssler Fiorenza, 313-25. New York: Crossroad, 1993.

______. *In Her Own Rite: Constructing Feminist Liturgical Tradition.* Nashville, TN: Abingdon Press, 1990.

______. *Praying with our Eyes Open: Engendering Feminist Liturgical Prayer.* Nashville, TN: Abingdon Press, 1995.

Procter-Smith, Marjorie, and Janet Walton, eds. *Women at Worship: Interpretations of North American Diversity.* Louisville: Westminster John Knox Press, 1993.

Propp, Vladimir. *Morphology of the Folktale.* 2nd ed. Translated by Laurence Scott. Austin, TX: University of Texas Press, 1968.

Puglisi, James F. "Rite[s] of Baptism in the Catholic Church: A Theological-Pastoral Community." In *Baptism Today: Understanding, Practice, Ecumenical Implications*, Faith and Order Paper No. 207, edited by Thomas F. Best, 29-43. Collegeville, MN: Liturgical Press, 2008.

Pui-lan, Kwok. *Discovering the Bible in the Non Biblical World.* Maryknoll: Orbis Books, 1995.

Puthenpurakal, Joseph. *Impact of Christianity on North East India.* Shillong: Vendrame Institute Publications, 1996.

Quarles, Charles L. "Ordinance or Sacrament: Is the Baptist View of the Ordinances Truly Biblical?" *Journal for Baptist Theology and Ministry* 1/1 (Spring 2003): 47-57. http://www.baptistcenter.net/journals/JBTM_1-1_Spring_2003_04_Ordinance_or_Sacrament.pdf (accessed September 3, 2018).

Rae, Eleanor, and Bernice Marie-Daly. *Created in Her Image: Models of the Feminine Divine.* New York: Crossroad, 1990.

Rahmann, Rudolf. "Quarrels and Enmity between the Sun and the Moon: A Contribution to the Mythologies of the Philippines, India, and the Malay Peninsula." *Folklore Studies* 14 (1955): 202-14.

Rakow, Lana F., ed. *Women Making Meaning: New Feminist Directions in Communication.* New York & London: Routledge, 1992.

Ramshaw, Gail. *Liturgical Language: Keeping it Metaphoric, Making it Inclusive.* Collegeville, MN: Liturgical Press, 1996.

______. *Worship: Searching for Language.* Washington, DC: The Pastoral Press, 1988.

Rao, O. M. *Baptist Distinctives: With Special Reference to the Churches of the CBCNEI.* Gauhati: Christian Literature Centre, 1980.

______. *Focus on North East Indian Christianity*. Delhi: ISPCK, 1994.

Rayan, Samuel. "Give Us this Day Our Daily Bread." In *The Challenge of Basic Christian Communities*, edited by Sergio Torres and John Eagleson, translated by John Drury, 220-27. Maryknoll, NY: Orbis Books, 1981.

Razak, Iskhandar. " 'Welfarism, Apartheid' Hurting Aborigines: CLP." http://www.abc.net.au/news/stories/2009/10/20/2718930.htm (accessed July 25, 20018).

Rees, D. Ben. "Jones, Thomas (1810-1849)." In *Vehicles of Grace and Hope: Welsh Missionaries in India 1800-1970*, edited by D. Ben Rees, 100-03. [Pasadena, CA?]: William Carey Library, 2002.

______. *Vehicles of Grace and Hope: Welsh Missionaries in India 1800-1970*. [Pasadena, CA?]: William Carey Library, 2002.

Rice, Claire Michèle, and Deryl G. Hunt. "The Ellison Unitary Model in Conflict Resolution Training." *Peace and Conflict Studies* 11/2 (Fall 2004): 35-54.

Richardson, Brian. *Narrative Dynamics: Essays on Time, Plot, Closure, and Frames*. Columbus: Ohio State University, 2002.

Riessman, Catherine Kohler. *Narrative Analysis*. Quantitative Research Methods 30. Newbury Park, CA: Sage Publications, 1993.

Riggs, John W. *Baptism in the Reformed Tradition: An Historical and Practical Theology*. Columbia Series in Reformed Theology. Louisville, KY: Westminster John Knox, 2002.

Ringrose, Jo L. *Understanding and Treating Dissociative Identity Disorder (or Multiple Personality Disorder)*. London: Karnac Books, 2012.

Robinson, Dominic. *Understanding the* "Imago Dei": *The Thought of Barth, von Balthasar and Moltmann*. Surrey: Ashgate, 2011.

Robinson, Earl. "A Salvation Army Perspective on Baptism: Theological Understanding and Liturgical Practice." In *Baptism Today: Understanding, Practice, Ecumenical Implications*, Faith and Order Paper 207, edited by Thomas F. Best, 173-80. Collegeville, MN: Liturgical Press, 2008.

Rongmuthu, Dewansing, comp. *The Folktales of the Garos*. Gauhati: Department of Publications, University of Gauhati, 1960), 255-58.

Root, Michael, and Risto Saarinen, eds. *Baptism and the Unity of the Church*. Grand Rapids, MI: Wm B. Eerdmans, 1998.

Rose, Lucy Atkinson. *Sharing the Word: Preaching in the Roundtable Church*. Louisville, KY: Westminster John Knox Press, 1997.

Rosner, Brian S. *Paul, Scripture and Ethics: A Study of 1 Corinthians 5-7*. Leiden: E. J. Brill, 1994.

Ross, Susan A. *Extravagant Affections: A Feminist Sacramental Theology*. New York, NY: The Continuum International Publishing Group, 2001.

Roy, J. L. "Primal Vision and Hermeneutics in North-East India – A Protestant Tribal View." *Indian Journal of Theology* 31/3-4 (July-Dec 1982): 314-22.

Roy, Nilima. *Art of Manipur*. Delhi: Agam Kala Prakashan, 1979.

Rubin-Dorsky, Jeffrey, and Shelley Fisher Fishkin. *People of the Book: Thirty Scholars Reflect on their Jewish Identity*. Madison, WI: The University of Wisconsin Press, 1996.

Ruether, Rosemary Radford. *To Change the World: Christology and Cultural Criticism*. New York: Crossroad, 1988.

______. *Goddesses and the Divine Feminine: A Western Religious History*. Berkeley: University of California Press, 2005.

______. *Sexism and God-Talk: Toward a Feminist Theology*. Boston, MA: Beacon Press, 1983

______. *Women-Church: Theology and Practice of Feminist Liturgical Communities*. New York: Harper & Row, 1985.

Rusch, William G. " 'Baptism, Eucharist and Ministry' – and Reception." In *The Search for Visible Unity*, edited by Jeffrey Gros, 129-42. New York: Pilgrim Press, 1984.

Russell, Letty M., and J. Shannon Clarkson, eds. *Dictionary of Feminist Theologies*. Louisville, KY: Westminster John Knox Press, 1996.

Sachs, Adah, and Graeme Galton, eds. *Forensic Aspects of Dissociative Identity Disorder*. Forensic Psychotherapy Monograph Series. London: Karnac Books, 2008.

Sakenfeld, Katharine Doob. *Just Wives? Stories of Power and Survival in the Old Testament and Today*. Louisville, KY: Westminster John Knox Press, 2003.

Sampley, J. Paul. *Pauline Partnership in Christ: Christian Community and Commitment in Light of Roman Law*. Philadelphia: Fortress Press, 1980.

Sandel, Michael J. *Democracy's Discontent: America in Search of a Public Philosophy*. Cambridge, MA: Belknap Press of Harvard University Press, 1998.

Sangma, Mihir N. *Some Important Festivals and Ceremonies of the Garos: Hundred Drums Wangala Festival*. Tura: Narayan Group, 2001.

Sangma, Milton S., ed. *Essays on North-East India*. Shillong: Deptt. of History, North-Eastern Hill University, 1994.

Savi, Akhrieno. "Through the Eyes of a Painter: A Naga Woman's Perspective." In *No More Sorrow in God's Garden of Justice: Tribal Women Doing Theology*, edited by Limatula Longkumer, 48-62. Jorhat, Assam: Women Study Department, Eastern Theological College, 2007.

Saward, John. *Christ and His Bride*. London: Church Literature Association, 1977.

Sawian, Bijoya. *Khasi Myths, Legends and Folk Tales*. New Delhi: Sanbun Publishers, 2010.

Sawyer, Birgit and P. H. Sawyer. *Medieval Scandinavia: From Conversion to Reformation, Circa 800-1500*. Nordic Series 17. Minneapolis, MN: University of Minnesota Press, 1993.

Scanzoni, Letha Dawson. "Why We Need Evangelical Feminists." *New Feminist Christianity: Many Voices, Many Views*, edited by Mary E. Hunt and Diann L. Neu, 64-76. Woodstock, VT: SkyLight Paths Publishing, 2010.

Schaberg, Jane. *The Illegitimacy of Jesus: A Feminist Theological Interpretation of the Infancy Narratives*. New ed. The Biblical Seminar 28. Sheffield: Sheffield Academic Press, 1995.

______. "The Infancy of Mary of Nazareth." In *Searching the Scriptures*, vol. 2, *A Feminist Commentary*, edited by Elisabeth Schüssler Fiorenza, 708-27. New York, NY: Crossroad, 1994.

Schaffran, Janet, and Pat Kozak, eds. *More Than Words: Prayer and Ritual for Inclusive Communities*. 2nd ed. Oak Park, IL: Meyer Stone Books, 1988.

Scharer, Matthias and Bernd Jochen Hilberath. *The Practice of Communicative Theology: An Introduction to a New Theological Culture*. New York, NY: Crossroad Publishing, 2008.

Schmidt, Alvin J. *Veiled and Silenced: How Culture Shaped Sexist Theology*. Macon, GA: Mercer University Press, 1989.

Schmitt, Mary Kathleen Speegle. *Seasons of the Feminine Divine: Christian Feminist Prayers for the Liturgical Year, Cycles A-C*. New York: Crossroad, 1993-1995.

Schneemelcher, Wilhelm, and R. McL. Wilson, eds. *New Testament Apocrypha*, vol. 1: *Gospels and Related Writings*. Rev. ed. Louisville, KY: Westminster John Knox Press, 2003.

Schottroff, Luise. "The Creation Narrative: Genesis 1:1-2.4a." In *A Feminist Companion to Genesis*, edited by Athalya Brenner, 24-38. Sheffield: Sheffield Academic Press, 1997.

______. *Lydia's Impatient Sisters: A Feminist Social History of Early Christianity*. Translated by Barbara and Martin Rumscheidt. Louisville, KY: Westminster John Knox Press, 1995.

Schottroff, Luise, and Marie-Theres Wacker, eds. *Feminist Biblical Interpretation: A Compendium of Critical Commentary on the Books of the Bible and Related Literature*. Grand Rapids, MI: Wm B. Eerdmans, 2012.

Schreck, Nancy, and Maureen Leach, eds. *Psalms Anew: An Inclusive Language*. Winona, MN: Saint Mary's Press, 1986.

Schreiner, Thomas R., and Matthew R. Crawford, eds. *The Lord's Supper: Remembering and Proclaiming Christ Until He Comes*. NAC Studies in Bible and Theology 10. Nashville, TN: B & H Publishing Group, 2010.

Schüngel-Straumann, Helen. "Genesis 1-11: The Primordial History." In *Feminist Biblical Interpretation: A Compendium of Critical Commentary on the Books of the Bible and Related Literature*, edited by Luise Schottroff and Marie-Theres Wacker, 1-14. Grand Rapids, MI: Wm B. Eerdmans, 2012.

______. "God as Mother in Hosea 11." In *A Feminist Companion to the Later Prophets*, edited by Athalya Brenner, 194-218. Sheffield: Sheffield Academic Press, 1995.

______. "On the Creation of Man and Woman in Genesis 1-3: The History and Reception of the Texts Reconsidered." In *A Feminist Companion to Genesis*, edited by Athalya Brenner, 53-76. Sheffield: Sheffield Academic Press, 1997.

Schüssler Fiorenza, Elisabeth. *But She Said: Feminist Practices of Biblical Interpretation*. Boston: Beacon Press, 1992.

______. *Discipleship of Equals: A Critical Feminist Ekklēsia-logy of Liberation*. New York: Crossroad, 1993.

______. "Feminist Studies in Religion and The*logy In-Between Nationalism and Globalism." *Journal of Feminist Studies in Religion* 21/1 (2005): 111-19. https://muse.jhu.edu/article/183428/pdf (accessed July 26, 2018).

______. *Jesus: Miriam's Child, Sophia's Prophet: Critical Issues in Feminist Christology* (New York: Continuum, 1994.

______. *In Memory of Her: A Feminist Theological Reconstruction of Christian Origins*. London: SCM Press, 1983.

______, ed. *Searching the Scriptures*. Vol. 1. *A Feminist Introduction*. New York: Crossroad, 1993.

______, ed. *Searching the Scriptures*. Vol. 2. *A Feminist Commentary*. New York, NY: Crossroad, 1994.

______. *Wisdom Ways: Introducing Feminist Biblical Interpretation*. Maryknoll, NY: Orbis Books, 2001.

Scott, Jacqueline, Rosemary Crompton, and Clare Lyonette, eds. *Gender Inequalities in the 21st Century: New Barriers and Continuing Constraints*. Cheltenham: Edward Elgar Publishing, 2010.

Scott, Janet. "Baptism and the Quaker Tradition." In *Baptism Today: Understanding, Practice, Ecumenical Implications*, Faith and Order Paper 207, edited by Thomas F. Best, 81-88. Collegeville, MN: Liturgical Press, 2008.

Scott, Philippa. *The Book of Silk*. London: Thames and Hudson, 2001.

Segal, Alan. *Paul the Convert: The Apostate and Apostasy of Saul the Pharisee*. New Haven: Yale University Press, 1990.

Segovia, Fernando F. *Toward a New Heaven and a New Earth: Essays in Honor of Elisabeth Schüssler Fiorenza*. Maryknoll, NY: Orbis Books, 2003.

Sehgal, Sunil. *Encyclopaedia of Hinduism (H-Q)*. Vol. 3. New Delhi: Sarup & Sons, 1999.

Sen, Soumen. "Folk-Songs of the North-Eastern Hills: An Introduction." *Indian Literature* 30/4 (1987): 11-16.

Shabatay, Virginia. "The Stranger's Story: Who Calls and Who Answers?" In *Stories Lives Tell: Narrative and Dialogue in Education*, edited by Carol Witherell and Nel Noddings, 136-52. New York: Columbia University, 1991.

Shakabpa, Tsepon Wangchuk Deden. *One Hundred Thousand Moons: An Advanced Political History of Tibet*. Vol. 1. Translated by Derek F. Maher. Leiden: Brill, 2010.

Shangpliang, Rekha M. "Ecological Basis of Khasi Ethno-Cultural Traits." In *Christianity and Change in Northeast India*, edited by T. B. Subba, Joseph Puthenpurakal, and Shaji Joseph Puykunnel, 219-31. New Delhi: Concept Publishing, 2009.

Sharma, R. S. *Indian Feudalism, c. AD 300-1200*. 3rd ed. New Delhi: Macmillan India, 2006.

Sharma, Suresh K. *Documents of North-East India: An Exhaustive Survey*. Vol. 3. *Assam* [1664-1935]. New Delhi: Mittal Publications, 2006.

Sharma, Tika Prasad, and S. K. Borthakur. "Traditional Handloom and Handicrafts of Sikkim." *Indian Journal of Traditional Knowledge* 9/2 (April 2010): 375-77. http://nopr.niscair.res.in/bitstream/123456789/8188/1/IJTK%209%282%29%20375-377.pdf (accessed June 20, 2019)

Shepherd, Gregory J. "Communication as Transcendence." In *Communication as ... : Perspectives on Theory*, edited by Gregory J. Shepherd, Jeffrey St. John, and Ted Striphas, 22-30. Thousand Oaks, CA: Sage Publications, 2006.

______. "Community as the Interpersonal Accomplishment of Communication." In *Communication and Community*, edited by Gregory J. Shepherd and Eric W. Rothenbuhler, 25-35. Mahwah, NJ: Lawrence Erlbaum, 2001.

Shepherd, Gregory J., and Eric W. Rothenbuhler, eds. *Communication and Community*. Mahwah, NJ: Lawrence Erlbaum, 2001.

Shepherd, Gregory J., Jeffrey St. John, and Ted Striphas, eds. *Communication as ... : Perspectives on Theory*. Thousand Oaks, CA: Sage Publications, 2006.

Shira, Jonmoni D. "Anga Me'chik," in *A·chik Poedorang*, 3rd ed., comp. L. D. Shira, 37-39. Tura: Hawakhana Book Emporium, 1994.

Shira, L. D., comp. *A·chik Poedorang*. 3rd ed. Tura: Hawakhana Book Emporium, 1994.

Shiva, Vandana. *Stolen Harvest: The Hijacking of the Global Food Supply*. Culture of the Land. Lexington, KY: University Press of Kentucky, 2016.

______. *The Violence of the Green Revolution: Third World Agriculture, Ecology, and Politics*. Culture of the Land. Lexington, KY: University Press of Kentucky, 2016.

Shlezinger-Katsman, Dafna. "Clothing." In *The Oxford Handbook of Jewish Daily Life in Roman Palestine*, edited by Catherine Hezser, 362-81. Oxford: Oxford University Press, 2010.

Shore, Megan. *Religion and Conflict Resolution: Christianity and South Africa's Truth and Reconciliation Commission*. Surrey: Ashgate, 2009.

Singh, Manpreet. "The Soul Hunters of Central Asia." *Christianity Today* (Feb 1, 2006). http://www.christianitytoday.com/ct/2006/february/38.51.html (accessed Aug 28, 2018).

Slee, Nicola. "The Holy Spirit and Spirituality." In *The Cambridge Companion to Feminist Theology*, Cambridge Companions to Religion, edited by Susan Frank Parsons, 171-89. Cambridge: Cambridge University Press, 2002.

______. *Praying Like a Woman*. London: SPCK, 2004.

Smith, Christine M. *Preaching as Weeping, Confession, and Resistance: Radical Responses to Radical Evil*. Louisville, KY: Westminster John Knox Press, 1992.

______. *Weaving the Sermon: Preaching in a Feminist Perspective*. Louisville, KY: Westminster John Knox Press, 1989.

Smith, Elizabeth J. *Bearing Fruit in Due Season: Feminist Hermeneutics and the Bible in Worship*. Collegeville, MN: Liturgical Press, 1999.

Smith, Gordon T. *Transforming Conversion: Rethinking the Language and Contours of Christian Initiation.* Grand Rapids, MI: Baker Academic, 2010.

Snyder, Susanna. "'Strangers' in the Sanctuary: Asylum Seekers, Faith and the Church." In *The Edge of God: New Liturgical Texts and Contexts in Conversation*, edited by Stephen Burns, Nicola Slee, and Michael N. Jagessar, 73-87. London: Epworth, 2008.

Soares, Theodore Gerald. *A Baptist Manual: The Polity of the Baptist Churches and of the Denominational Organizations.* Philadelphia: American Baptist Publication Society, 1911.

Society of Biblical Literature. *Society of Biblical Literature Seminar Papers, 1997.* SBLSP 36. Atlanta: Scholars Press, 1997.

Soffer, O., J. M. Adovasio, and D. C. Hyland. "The 'Venus' Figurines: Textiles, Basketry, Gender, and Status in the Upper Paleolithic." *Current Anthropology* 41/4 (August-October 2000), 511-37. https://www.researchgate.net/publication/235979951_The_Venus_Figurines_Textiles_Basketry_Gender_and_Status_in_the_Upper_Paleolithic (accessed July 23, 2018).

Sohkhlet, B. "A Phenomenological Study of the Understanding of God as Emerging from Selected Myths and Rituals in the Traditional Religion of the Khasi Pnars." DTh Thesis, Senate of Serampore College, 2008.

Solinger, Rickie, Madeline Fox, and Kayhan Irani, eds. *Telling Stories to Change the World: Global Voices on the Power of Narrative to Build Community and Make Social Justice Claims.* New York: Routledge, 2008.

Song, C. S. *The Believing Heart: An Invitation to Story Theology.* Minneapolis, MN: Fortress Press, 1999.

______. *Theology from the Womb of Asia.* Maryknoll, NY: Orbis Books, 1986.

Sonneborn, Liz. *The End of Apartheid in South Africa.* Milestones in Modern World History. New York, NY: Chelsea House, 2010.

Sontag, Susan, ed. *A Barthes Reader.* New York: Hill and Wang, 1982.

South African Democracy Education Trust. *The Road to Democracy in South Africa.* Vol. 2. *[1970-1980].* Pretoria: University of South Africa, 2006.

Speiser, E. A. *Genesis.* The Anchor Bible. Garden City, NY: Doubleday, 1964.

Spender, Dale. *Man Made Language.* London: Routledge & Kegan Paul, 1980.

Spinks, Bryan D. *Reformation and Modern Rituals and Theologies of Baptism: From Luther to Contemporary Practices.* Aldershot: Ashgate Publishing, 2006.

Spinning a Sacred Yarn: Women Speak from the Pulpit. New York: Pilgrim Press, 1982.

St. Hilda Community. *The New Women Included: A Book of Services and Prayers.* London: SPCK, 1996.

Starhawk, Miriam. *The Spiral Dance: A Rebirth of the Ancient Religion of the Great Goddess.* San Francisco: Harper & Row, 1979.

Steimle, Edmund A., Morris J. Niedenthal, and Charles L. Rice. *Preaching the Story.* Philadelphia: Fortress Press, 1980.

Steinberg, Leo. *The Sexuality of Christ in Renaissance Art and in Modern Oblivion.* Chicago: University of Chicago Press, 1983.

Stevens, Maryanne, ed. *Reconstructing the Christ Symbol: Essays in Feminist Christology.* New York: Paulist Press, 1993.

Stirn, Aglaja and Peter Van Ham. *The Seven Sisters of India: Tribal Worlds between Tibet and Burma.* Munich: Prestel, 2001.

Stone, Merlin. *When God was a Woman.* New York: Dial Press, 1976.

Strawn, Brent A., and Nancy R. Bowen, eds. *A God So Near: Essays on Old Testament theology in Honor of Patrick D. Miller.* Winona Lake, IN: Eisenbrauns, 2003.

Subba, T. B., Joseph Puthenpurakal, and Shaji Joseph Puykunnel, eds. *Christianity and Change in Northeast India.* New Delhi: Concept Publishing, 2009.

Sweetman, Caroline, ed. *Gender in the 21st Century.* Oxfam Focus on Gender. Oxford: Oxfam, 2000.

Swidler, Arlene, ed. *Sistercelebrations: Nine Worship Experiences.* Philadelphia, PA: Fortress Press, 1974.

Swidler, Leonard J. *Biblical Affirmations of Woman.* Philadelphia, PA: The Westminster Press, 1979.

Sword, Victor Hugo. *Baptists in Assam: A Century of Missionary Service 1836-1936.* Guwahati: Spectrum Publications, 1992.

Syiem, Darilyn. "Women and Sacred Medicines among the Khasis in the Highlands of Northeast India." In *Women and Indigenous Religions*, Women and Religion in the World, edited by Sylvia Marcos, 115-25. Santa Barbara, CA: Praeger, 2010.

Szpek, Heidi M. " 'In the Image of God He Created Them': Adam and Lilith." In *Re-Imagining Eve and Adam: And Other Brief Essays*, 19-26. Lincoln, NE: iUniverse, 2002.

______. *Re-Imagining Eve and Adam: And Other Brief Essays.* Lincoln, NE: iUniverse, 2002.

______. " 'This is My Beloved and This is My Friend': Re-Imagining Eve and Adam." In *Re-Imagining Eve and Adam: And Other Brief Essays*, 3-8. Lincoln, NE: iUniverse, 2002.

Tamez, Elsa. *Against Machismo.* Oak Park, IL: Meyer Stone Books, 1987.

Taylor, Joan E. *What Did Jesus Look Like?* London: Bloomsbury T&T Clark, 2018.

______. " 'The Woman Ought to Have Control over her Head because of the Angels' (1 Corinthians 11.10)." In *Gospel and Gender: A Trinitarian Engagement with Being Male and Female in Christ*, Studies in Theology and Sexuality, edited by Douglas A. Campbell, 35-57. London: T & T Clark, 2003.

Taylor, John. *Body Horror: Photojournalism, Catastrophe and War.* Manchester: Manchester University Press, 1998.

Thanzauva and R. L. Hnuni. "Ethnicity, Identity and Hermeneutics: An Indian Tribal Perspective." In *Ethnicity and the Bible*, BIS 19, edited by Mark G. Brett, 343-57. London: E. J. Brill, 1996.

Thanzauva, K. *Theology of Community: Tribal Theology in the Making*. Aizawl, Mizoram: Mizo Theological Conference, 1997.

The Clothesline Project. http://www.theclotheslineproject.org/.

The Times of India. "First Woman Priest for Mizoram." *The Times of India*, March 11, 2012. https://timesofindia.indiatimes.com/city/guwahati/First-woman-priest-for-Mizoram/articleshow/12224006.cms (accessed July 23, 2018).

Thompson, Marianne Meye. *The Promise of the Father: Jesus and God in the New Testament*. Louisville, KY: Westminster John Knox Press, 2000.

Thorpe, Kirsty. "Women's Ministry – a Developing Story." In *This is Our Story: Free Church Women's Ministry*, edited by Janet Wootton, 30-49. Peterborough: Epworth, 2007.

Tilley, Terrence W. *Story Theology*. Wilmington, DE: Michael Glazier, 1985.

Tirkey, C. A. B. *Religion, Primal Religions*. Delhi: ISPCK, 1998.

Titunik, I. R., trans., and ed. with Neal H. Bruss. *Freudianism: A Critical Sketch*. Bloomington and Indianapolis: Indiana University Press, 1987.

Torres, Sergio, and John Eagleson, eds. *The Challenge of Basic Christian Communities*. Translated by John Drury. Maryknoll, NY: Orbis Books, 1981.

Townes, Emilie M. *Womanist Justice, Womanist Hope*. Atlanta, GA: Scholars Press, 1993.

Trebilco, Paul. "The Significance of the Distribution of Self-Designations in Acts." *Novum Testamentum* 54 (2012): 30-49.

Trepp, Leo. *A History of the Jewish Experience*. Rev. and updated ed. Springfield, NJ: Behrman House, 2001.

Trible, Phyllis. "Depatriarchalizing in Biblical Interpretation." *Journal of the American Academy of Religion* 41 (March 1973): 30-48.

______. *God and the Rhetoric of Sexuality*. Overtures to Biblical Theology. Philadelphia: Fortress Press, 1978.

______. "Journey of a Metaphor." In *God and the Rhetoric of Sexuality*, Overtures to Biblical Theology, 31-59. Philadelphia: Fortress Press, 1978.

______. " 'Not a Jot, Not a Tittle: Genesis 2-3 after Twenty Years' (1995 CE)." In *Eve and Adam: Jewish, Christian, and Muslim Readings on Genesis and Gender*, edited by Kristen E. Kvam, Linda S. Schearing and Valarie H. H. Ziegler, 439-44. Bloomington, IN: Indiana University Press, 1999.

______. Review of Hamerton-Kelly's *God the Father: Theology and Patriarchy in the Teaching of Jesus*, Overture to Biblical Theology 4. Philadelphia: Fortress, 1979, in *Theology Today* 37 (1980): 116-19.

Turle, Gillies. *The Art of the Maasai: 300 Newly Discovered Objects and Works of Art*. New York: Knopf, 1992.

Turner, Mary Donovan, and Mary Lin Hudson. *Saved from Silence: Finding Women's Voices in Preaching*. St. Louis, MO: Chalice Press, 1999.

Turner, Max. "The Churches of the Johannine Letters as Communities of 'Trinitarian' Koinōnia." In *The Spirit and Spirituality: Essays in Honour of Russell*

P. Spittler, Journal of Pentecostal Theology, Supplement Series 24, edited by Wonsuk Ma and Robert P. Menzies, 53-61. London: T & T Clark, 2004.

Turner, Paul. *When Other Christians become Catholic*. Collegeville, MN: The Liturgical Press, 2007.

Twelftree, Graham H. *People of the Spirit: Exploring Luke's View of the Church* Grand Rapids, MI: Baker Academic, 2009.

underwood, erin daina and Lawrence R. Frey. "Communication and Community: Clarifying the Connection Across the Communication Community." In *Communication Yearbook 31*, 370-419. New York, NY: International Communication Association/Lawrence Erlbaum, 2008. eBook Taylor & Francis e-Library, 2009; New York, NY: International Communication Association/Lawrence Erlbaum, 2008, 377-80.

underwood, erin daina and Lawrence R. Frey. *Communication Yearbook 31*. New York, NY: International Communication Association/Lawrence Erlbaum, 2008.

United Church of Christ. *The New Century Hymnal*. Cleveland, OH: Pilgrim Press, 1995.

V. V. Giri National Labour Institute. *Women Weavers of Sualkuchi: The Silk Town of Assam*. NIL Research Studies Series 2001/030. Noida: V. V. Giri National Labour Institute, 2002.

van der Horst, Pieter W. "Sex, Birth, Purity and Asceticism in the *Protevangelium Jacobi*." In *A Feminist Companion to Mariology*, edited by Amy-Jill Levine and Maria Mayo Robbins, 56-66. London: T & T Clark International, 2005.

Van Haaften, Ton, Henrike Jansen, Jaap De Jong, and Willem Koetsenruijter, eds. *Bending Opinion: Essays on Persuasion in the Public Domain, Rhetoric in Society*. Leiden: Leiden University Press, 2011.

Van Leeuwen, Mary Stewart, Annelies Knoppers, Margaret L. Koch, Douglas J. Schurman, and Helen M. Sterk, eds. *After Eden: Facing the Challenge of Gender Reconciliation*. Grand Rapids, MI: William B. Eerdmans, 1993.

van Wijk-Bos, Johanna W. H. *Reimagining God: The Case for Scriptural Diversity*. Louisville, KY: Westminster John Knox Press, 1995.

Vandergrift, Kay E., ed. *Ways of Knowing: Literature and the Intellectual Life of Children*. Lanham, MD: Scarecrow Press, 1996.

VanderWilt, Jeffrey T. *A Church Without Borders: The Eucharist and the Church in Ecumenical Perspective*. Collegeville, MN: The Liturgical Press, 1998.

______. *Communion with Non-Catholic Christians: Risks, Challenges, and Opportunities*. Collegeville, MN: The Liturgical Press, 2003.

Vanlalthanpuii, Mary. "The Changing Roles of Churchwomen in Mizoram (1904-1994): A Study of Mizoram Presbyterian Church Synod." *IOSR Journal of Humanities and Social Science (IOSR-JHSS)*, 19/10, Ver. VII (October 2014): 1-8.

Vanlaltlani, T. "History of Mizo Women and Future Hope." In *No More Sorrow in God's Garden of Justice: Tribal Women Doing Theology*, Women Study Series

4, edited by Limatula Longkumer, 93-110. Jorhat, Assam: Women Study Department, Eastern Theological College, 2007.

______. *Mizo Hmeichhiate Kawngzawh*. Aizawl: Mizoram Publication Board, 2005.

______. "Participation of Women in the Church – With Reference to North East India." In *Changing Status of Women in North-Eastern States*, edited by Lalneihzovi, 129-52. New Delhi: Mittal Publications, 2009.

Verdoolaege, Annelies. *Reconciliation Discourse: The Case of the Truth and Reconciliation Commission*. Discourse Approaches to Politics, Society and Culture 27. Amsterdam: John Benjamins, 2008.

Vogel, Dwight W. ed. *Primary Sources in Liturgical Theology: A Reader*. Collegeville, MN: The Liturgical Press, 2000.

Vološinov, V. N. "Discourse in Life and Discourse in Art (Concerning Sociological Poetics)." In *Freudianism: A Critical Sketch*, translated by I. R. Titunik and edited in collaboration with Neal H. Bruss, 93-116. Bloomington and Indianapolis: Indiana University Press, 1987.

von Stuckrad, Kocku. "Constructing Feminity – the Lilith Case." In *Gender, Tradition and Renewal*, Religions and Discourse 13, edited by Robert L. Platzner, 67-92. Bern: Peter Lang, 2005.

Vorster, W. S. "The Annunciation of the Birth of Jesus in the *Protevangelium of James*." In *A South African Perspective on the New Testament: Essays by South African New Testament Scholars Presented to Bruce Manning Metzger During His Visit to South Africa in 1985*, edited by J. H. Petzer and P. J. Hartin, 33-53. Leiden: E. J. Brill, 1986.

Wainwright, Geoffrey, and Karen B. Westerfield Tucker, eds. *The Oxford History of Christian Worship*. New York, NY: Oxford University Press, 2006.

Wallace, Robin Knowles. *Moving Toward Emancipatory Language: A Study of Recent Hymns*. Lanham, MD: Scarecrow Press, 1999.

Wallman-Girdlestone, Jane E. "Blurring the Edges: Finding Commonality by Smudging our Differences." In *The Edge of God: New Liturgical Texts and Contexts in Conversation*, edited by Stephen Burns, Nicola Slee, and Michael N. Jagessar, 104-16. London: Epworth, 2008.

Walton, Janet R. *Feminist Liturgy: A Matter of Justice*. American Essays in Liturgy. Collegeville, MN: Liturgical Press, 2000.

Ward, Hannah, and Jennifer Wild, comp. *Human Rites: Worship Resources for An Age of Change*. London: Mowbray, 1995.

Ware, Bruce. "The Meaning of the Lord's Supper in the Theology of Ulrich Zwingli (1484-1531)." In *The Lord's Supper: Remembering and Proclaiming Christ Until He Comes*, NAC Studies in Bible and Theology 10, edited by Thomas R. Schreiner and Matthew R. Crawford, 229-47. Nashville, TN: B & H Publishing Group, 2010.

Washington, Harold C., Susan Lochrie Graham and Pamela Thimmes, ed. *Escaping Eden: New Feminist Perspectives on the Bible*. Sheffield: Sheffield Academic Press, 1998.

Watson, Natalie K. *Introducing Feminist Ecclesiology*. Introductions in Feminist Theology. London: Sheffield Academic Press, 2002.

Webb, Val. *Why We're Equal: Introducing Feminist Theology*. St Louis, MO: Chalice Press, 1999.

Webb, William J. *Slaves, Women and Homosexuals: Exploring the Hermeneutic of Cultural Analysis*. Downers Grove, IL: InterVarsity Press, 2001.

Wenger, Etienne. *Communities of Practice: Learning, Meaning and Identity*. Cambridge: Cambridge University of Press, 1998.

Wessinger, Catherine, ed. *Religious Institutions and Women's Leadership: New Roles Inside the Mainstream*. Columbia, SC: University of South Carolina, 1996.

Westerhoff, John H. *Living the Faith Community*. New York: Seabury Classics, 2004.

White, Susan J. *Foundations of Christian Worship*. Louisville, KY: Westminster John Knox Press, 2006.

Wijngaards, John. *No Women in Holy Orders? The Women Deacons of the Early Church*. Norwich: Canterbury Press, 2002.

Wild Goose Publications. http://www.ionabooks.com/.

Wilson, Richard A. *The Politics of Truth and Reconciliation in South Africa: Legitimizing the Post-Apartheid State*. Cambridge: Cambridge University Press, 2001.

Windley-Daoust, Susan. *The Redeemed Image of God: Embodied Relations to the Unknown Divine*. Lanham, MD: University Press of America, 2002.

Winkler, Gabriele. "The Original Meaning of the Prebaptismal Anointing and Its Implications." *Worship* 52 (1978): 24-45.

Winter, Bronwyn. *Hijab and the Republic: Uncovering the French Headscarf Debate*. Syracuse, NY: Syracuse University Press, 2008.

Winter, Miriam Therese. *Woman Prayer, WomanSong: Resources for Ritual*. Oak Park, IL: Meyer-Stone Books, 1987.

______. *Womanword: A Feminist Lectionary and Psalter: Women of the New Testament*. New York: Crossroad, 1990.

Wire, Antoinette Clark. *The Corinthian Women Prophets: A Reconstruction through Paul's Rhetoric*. Minneapolis: Fortress Press, 1990.

Witherell, Carol, and Nel Noddings. "Prologue: An Invitation to our Readers." In *Stories Lives Tell: Narrative and Dialogue in Education*, edited by Carol Witherell and Nel Noddings, 1-12. New York: Columbia University, 1991.

______, eds. *Stories Lives Tell: Narrative and Dialogue in Education*. New York: Columbia University, 1991.

Witherington, Ben. *The Acts of the Apostles: A Socio-Rhetorical Commentary*. Grand Rapids, MI: William B. Eerdmans, 1998.

______. *Women in the Earliest Churches*. SNTSMS. Cambridge: Cambridge University Press, 1988.

Women's Co-ordinating Group, Churches Together in England. *What is This Place?* 55. https://www.cte.org.uk/Publisher/File.aspx?ID=138037 (accessed July 23, 2018).

Wood, Susan K. *One Baptism: Ecumenical Dimensions of the Doctrine of Baptism*. Collegeville, MN: The Liturgical Press, 2009.

Wootton, Janet, ed. *This is Our Story: Free Church Women's Ministry*. Peterborough: Epworth, 2007.

______, ed. *This is Our Song: Women's Hymn Writing*. London: Epworth Press, 2010.

______. "Women's Leadership in the Church and Feminist Theology." In *This is Our Story: Free Church Women's Ministry*, edited by Janet Wootton, 82-104. Peterborough: Epworth, 2007.

World Association for Christian Communication. *Statements on Communication by World Association for Christian Communication*. Rev. ed. London: WACC, 1995.

World Council of Churches. *Baptism, Eucharist, and Ministry*. Faith and Order Paper No. 111. Geneva: World Council of Churches, 1982.

______. "Called to be the One Church." The Porto Alegre Ecclesiology Text. Geneva: World Council of Churches, 2006.

______. *The Nature and Mission of the Church: A Stage on the Way to Common Statement*. Faith and Order Paper No. 198. Geneva: World Council of Churches, 2005.

Wren, Brian. *What Language Shall I Borrow? God-Talk in Worship: A Male Response to Feminist Theology*. London: SCM Press, 1989.

Wright, N. T. "Worship and the Spirit in the New Testament." In *The Spirit in Worship – Worship in the Spirit*, edited by Teresa Berger and Bryan D. Spinks, 3-24. Collegeville, MN: Liturgical Press, 2009.

Yamaguchi, Satoko. "Father Image of G*d and Inclusive Language: A Reflection in Japan." In *Toward a New Heaven and a New Earth: Essays in Honor of Elisabeth Schüssler Fiorenza*, edited by Fernando F. Segovia, 199-224. Maryknoll, NY: Orbis Books, 2003.

Yoder, John Howard. *Body Politics: Five Practices of the Christian Community before the Watching World*. Nashville, TN: Discipleship Resources, 1992.

Young, Frances. "Songs without Words: Incorporating the Linguistically Marginalized." In *The Edge of God: New Liturgical Texts and Contexts in Conversation*, edited by Stephen Burns, Nicola Slee, and Michael N. Jagessar, 91-103. London: Epworth, 2008.

Yule, Gregory, ed. *Luther: Theologian for Catholics and Protestants*. Edinburgh: T & T Clark, 1985.

Zagano, Phyllis, and Terrence W. Tilley, eds. *Things New and Old: Essays on the Theology of Elizabeth A. Johnson*. New York, NY: Crossroad, 1999.

Zairema Memorial Society. "Bible Translation in North East India: With Special Reference to Cultural Background." http://www.revzairema.com/?p=729 (accessed on Nov 29, 2011). The same article is posted in http://nghakmawia.

blogspot.com/2013/08/bible-translation-in-north-east-india.html (accessed July 26, 2018).

Zelizer, Barbie. *About to Die: How News Images Move the Public*. Oxford: Oxford University Press, 2010.

Zervos, George Themelis. "Christmas with Salome." In *A Feminist Companion to Mariology*, edited by Amy-Jill Levine with Maria Mayo Robbins, 77-98. London: T & T Clark International, 2005.

______. "Dating the *Protevangelium of James*: The Justin Martyr Connection." In *Society of Biblical Literature Seminar Papers, 1994*, SBLSP 33, edited by Eugene H. Lovering, 415-34. Atlanta: Scholars Press, 1994.

______. "An Early Non-Canonical Annunciation Story." In *Society of Biblical Literature Seminar Papers, 1997*, SBLSP 36, 664-91. Atlanta: Scholars Press, 1997.

Zimmermann, Reinhard. *The Law of Obligations: Roman Foundations of the Civilian Tradition*. Oxford: Oxford University Press, 1996.

Zodin Sanga, "Mizos' Migration to Myanmar, Israel – All for Faith," Heritage Explorer, July 2012, 11, http://www.heritagefoundation.org.in/Download/heritage_explorer/2012/heritage_july_2012.pdf (accessed on July 30, 2018).

Zwingli, Ulrich. *Commentary on True and False Religion*. Edited by Samuel Macauley Jackson and Clarence Nevin Heller. 1929; repr., Durham, NC: The Labyrinth Press, 1981.

______. "On the Lord's Supper." In *Zwingli and Bullinger*, Library of Christian Classics 24, edited by G. W. Bromiley, 176-238. London: SCM Press, 1953.

______. *Zwingli and Bullinger*. Library of Christian Classics 24. Edited by G. W. Bromiley. London: SCM Press, 1953.